WASHINGTON, D.C.

THE COMPLETE GUIDE
1989–90 EDITION

WASHINGTON, D.C.

THE COMPLETE GUIDE
1989–90 EDITION

JUDY DUFFIELD

WILLIAM KRAMER

CYNTHIA SHEPPARD

VINTAGE BOOKS

A Division of Random House

NEW YORK

Second Vintage Books Edition, December 1988

Text copyright © 1982, 1987, 1988 by Judy Duffield, William Kramer,
Cynthia Sheppard

Maps copyright © 1987 by Dyno Lowenstein

All rights reserved under International and Pan-American Copyright
Conventions. Published in the United States by Random House, Inc.,
New York, and simultaneously in Canada by Random House of Canada
Limited, Toronto. A first edition was published by Random House, Inc.,
in 1982 and a first revised edition was published by Vintage Books, a
division of Random House, Inc., in 1987.

Library of Congress Cataloging in Publication Data
Duffield, Judy, 1946–
Washington, D.C., the complete guide.
Includes index.
1. Washington (D.C.)—Description—1981– —
Guide-books. I. Kramer, William, 1946–
II. Sheppard, Cynthia, 1955–. III. Title.
Fl92.3.D8 1987   917.53′044   88-40339
ISBN 0-679-72167-3

Map courtesy of Washington Metropolitan Area Transit Authority

Designed by Robert Bull

Manufactured in the United States of America

10 9 8 7 6 5 4 3 2 1

CONTENTS

8

NORTHWEST · 144

9

OTHER D.C. AREAS · 173

10

SUBURBAN VIRGINIA · 182

11

NEARBY MARYLAND · 220

12

A SHORT HISTORY OF WASHINGTON · 242

13

ENTERTAINMENT · 252

Let Us Introduce You . . . Live Music . . . Comedy Clubs . . . Classical Music,
Ballet and Opera . . . Theaters . . . Local Theaters . . . Children's Theaters
and Attractions . . . Dinner Theaters . . . Outdoor Music and Pavilions
. . . Free Music and Theater . . . The Bar Scene . . . Movie Theaters . . . Boat
Rides . . . Amusement Parks

14

SHOPPING · 275

Federal Finds . . . Department Stores . . . Art Galleries . . . Street Vendors
. . . Main Shopping Areas

15

OUTDOOR WASHINGTON/SPORTS · 285

Picnicking . . . Gardens . . . Hiking—Woodland Trails . . . Jogging . . .
Bicycling . . . Boating . . . Tennis . . . Golf . . . Ice Skating . . . Horseback
Riding . . . Playing Fields . . . Swimming . . . Spectator Sports

16

ADVICE TO GROUPS · 303

Transportation . . . Lodging . . . Sightseeing . . . Eating . . . Entertainment
. . . Useful Phone Numbers

17

TIPS FOR VISITORS WITH DISABILITIES · 312

Washington's Access Rating . . . Metrobus and Metrorail . . . Theater Tickets
. . . For Those with Limited Mobility . . . For Those with Visual Impairments
. . . For Those with Hearing Impairments . . . Hearing-Impaired Person's
Quick Guide to Washington . . . National Organizations

18

A WELCOME TO INTERNATIONAL VISITORS · 328

Planning the Trip . . . Arrival . . . When in Town

19

WASHINGTON ON THE RUN:
ONE-, TWO- AND THREE-DAY TOURS AND SPECIALIZED TOURS · 333

Day One . . . Day Two . . . Day Three . . . Major Attractions Arranged by
Interest Area

HOTELS · 338

CALENDAR OF ANNUAL EVENTS · 352

INDEX · 357

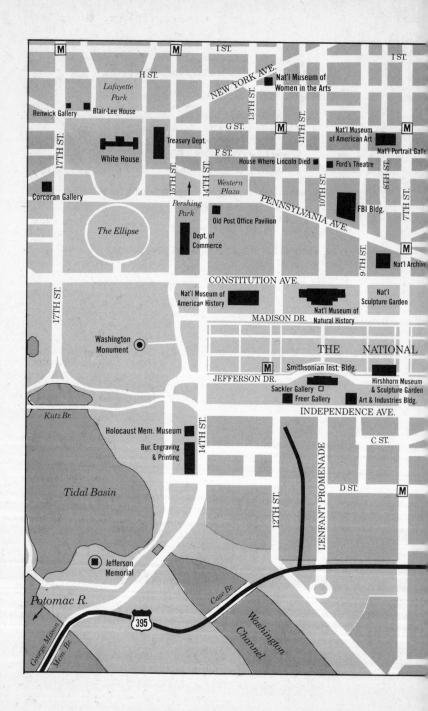

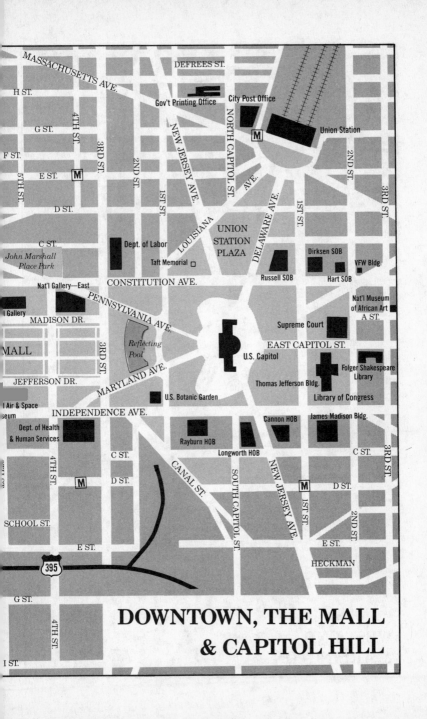

MASSACHUSETTS AVE.

DEFREES ST.

H ST.

G ST.

4TH ST

F ST.

3RD ST.

5TH ST.

E ST.

2ND ST.

D ST.

NEW JERSEY AVE.

NORTH CAPITOL ST.

Gov't Printing Office

City Post Office

M

Union Station

2ND ST.

3RD ST.

1ST ST.

LOUISIANA

DELAWARE AVE.

1ST ST.

C ST.

John Marshall
Place Park

Dept. of Labor

Taft Memorial

UNION
STATION
PLAZA

Dirksen SOB

VFW Bldg.

Russell SOB

Hart SOB

Nat'l Gallery—East

CONSTITUTION AVE.

Nat'l Museum
of African Art

A ST.

Gallery

PENNSYLVANIA AVE.

MADISON DR.

3RD ST.

Reflecting
Pool

MARYLAND AVE.

Supreme Court

EAST CAPITOL ST.

U.S. Capitol

MALL

Folger Shakespeare
Library

JEFFERSON DR.

U.S. Botanic Garden

Thomas Jefferson Bldg.

Library of Congress

Air & Space
seum

INDEPENDENCE AVE.

Cannon HOB

James Madison Bldg.

Dept. of Health
& Human Services

Rayburn HOB

Longworth HOB

C ST.

4TH ST.

C ST.

3RD ST.

CANAL ST.

M

D ST.

M

D ST.

2ND ST.

SCHOOL ST.

SOUTH CAPITOL ST.

NEW JERSEY AVE.

1ST ST.

E ST.

E ST.

HECKMAN

395

G ST.

4TH ST

I ST.

DOWNTOWN, THE MALL
& CAPITOL HILL

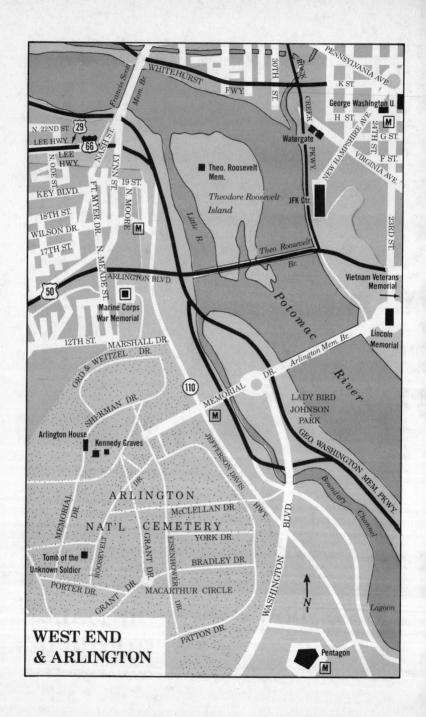

WEST END
& ARLINGTON

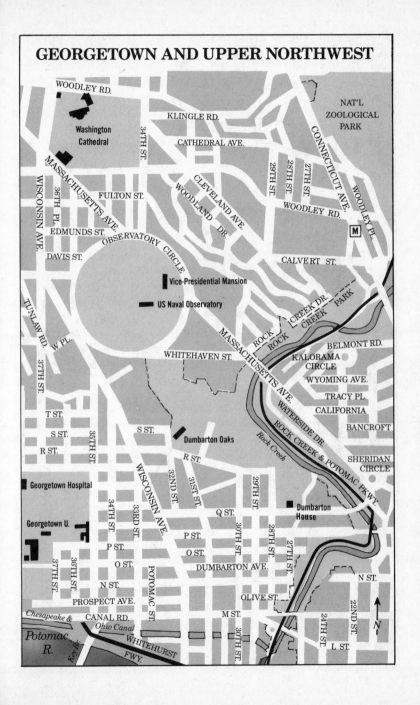

GEORGETOWN AND UPPER NORTHWEST

WOODLEY RD.

Washington Cathedral

KLINGLE RD.

CATHEDRAL AVE.

NAT'L ZOOLOGICAL PARK

34TH ST.

MASSACHUSETTS AVE.

36TH PL.

WISCONSIN AVE.

FULTON ST.

CLEVELAND AVE.

WOODLAND DR.

29TH ST.

28TH ST.

27TH ST.

CONNECTICUT AVE.

WOODLEY PL.

WOODLEY RD.

M

EDMUNDS ST.

DAVIS ST.

OBSERVATORY CIRCLE

CALVERT ST.

TUNLAW RD.

W PL.

Vice-Presidential Mansion

US Naval Observatory

ROCK CREEK DR.

CREEK PARK

37TH ST.

WHITEHAVEN ST.

ROCK

ROCK

BELMONT RD.

KALORAMA CIRCLE

WYOMING AVE.

TRACY PL.

CALIFORNIA

MASSACHUSETTS AVE.

WATERSIDE DR.

BANCROFT

35TH ST.

T ST.

S ST.

R ST.

S ST.

Dumbarton Oaks

R ST.

Rock Creek

ROCK CREEK & POTOMAC PKWY.

SHERIDAN CIRCLE

Georgetown Hospital

WISCONSIN AVE.

32ND ST.

31ST ST.

29TH ST.

Q ST.

Dumbarton House

Georgetown U.

34TH ST.

33RD ST.

P ST.

O ST.

POTOMAC ST.

30TH ST.

28TH ST.

27TH ST.

37TH ST.

36TH ST.

N ST.

DUMBARTON AVE.

N ST.

PROSPECT AVE.

OLIVE ST.

22ND ST.

24TH ST.

Chesapeake & Ohio Canal

CANAL RD.

M ST.

30TH ST.

Potomac R.

Key Br.

WHITEHURST FWY.

L ST.

N

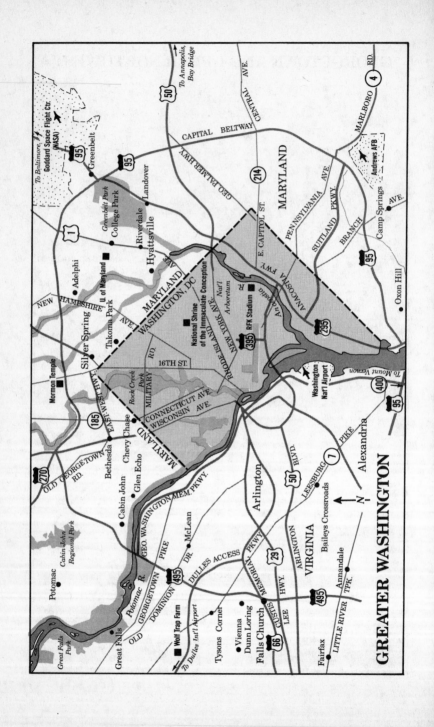

GREATER WASHINGTON

INTRODUCTION

Washington, D.C.: The Complete Guide has one simple purpose: to be the visitor's most useful and usable guidebook to the nation's capital. As we wrote this book, we assumed that almost every sightseeing venture is dominated by one factor: time—or, rather, less than enough of it to see and enjoy all the places you may have traveled miles to visit. Our purpose is to help you make the best use of your time, and so make your Washington experience as trouble-free, relaxed and rewarding as possible.

The authors, all natives or long-time residents and fans of the District, have concentrated on the basic questions facing all tourists: what to see; when to see it; and how to get there and back. Beyond these, we also responded to concerns that other guidebooks tend to overlook: is there a place to eat? are there special accommodations for groups? is the site accessible to people with disabilities? and, if you plan ahead, can extra features and services be made available? We have employed a simple but extensive set of graphic symbols for ready reference. An explanation of these symbols follows in the next chapter.

While the *Guide* may be most useful to visitors to Washington, the information it contains will also introduce new residents to the delights (and pitfalls) of the area. And we trust that with our help even old Washington hands will be able to discover new aspects of their city.

The book is organized in straightforward fashion: we have divided the city into distinct geographical sections, starting where *you* are most likely to start—at the Mall, that grassy expanse stretching between the U.S. Capitol and the Lincoln Memorial, around whose borders are many of the principal attractions of "Federal Washington." After the Mall, we present the other parts of the city: Capitol Hill, Downtown, Georgetown/Foggy Bottom/The West End, Upper

Northwest, other areas of interest in the city, suburban Virginia and nearby Maryland. Each area is briefly introduced; the site reports for the area are then presented alphabetically. For each site you will find our set of symbols for quick reference, a short description of particular points of interest and other useful information. Each section concludes with a brief review of several area restaurants. (Telephone numbers are provided; reservations are advisable.)

The remainder of the *Guide* consists of short chapters designed to make your visit more rewarding. We have included suggestions for one-, two- and three-day tours; a directory of local hotels and motels in an easy-to-read listing indicating price ranges and services; a description of recreation and sports opportunities in the area; an introduction to unusual or unique shopping opportunities; a chapter on entertainment—for those who still have the strength; and an overview of Washington's history and people.

To the out-of-town driver, Washington streets and traffic circles are a life-size version of bumper cars gone haywire. It's easy to lose your way or your good humor as you try to navigate around the District. Public transportation in Washington is the best alternative to the private automobile, and may even be preferable. Each site description in the *Guide* keys you to public transportation possibilities and advises you on the parking situation in the site's vicinity. We also devote a chapter to "Getting to and Around Town," which details Washington's excellent public-transport systems, cracks the code on the myriad street signs you'll encounter and tells you what to do if your car gets towed (the District police's ticketing and towing divisions are the nation's most efficient).

For people with limited mobility, touring many places is virtually impossible. Our nation's capital, however, responded with unusual speed and thoroughness to the laws of the early 1970s that directed public facilities to provide access for those who have handicaps or other problems of mobility. Every major tourist attraction is accessible; in addition, special services are available in many places. We make clear, in the site reports and in a separate chapter near the end of the book, how people with disabilities can take full advantage of the treasures of the city with the least trouble and unnecessary expenditure of energy and time. We tell you, for example, which entrances to use and how to arrange for special tours.

Many of you will be introduced to Washington in a group. Logistics for a large group are complex and subject to breakdown—and the consequences can be dismaying. One bad hotel, one inedible meal, one wrong turn and the entire trip can turn sour. Again in a separate chapter near the end of the book, we examine the problems of traveling and sightseeing as a group, and recommend how to make it through your trip without losing your patience—or a member of your ensemble.

International visitors can be beset with the same problems as well as the unique difficulties of currency exchange, language, etc.; we offer advice and resources in a chapter aimed at their needs.

Our own touring, both here and elsewhere, has made it clear that too much information can often be worse than not enough. We have tried to strike a balance: we include the information that is practical to have in advance, and we direct those who want to read more to worthwhile printed material. We have also included a chapter of planning tips for before you hit town and for each day you're here.

A caveat: nothing stands still. While we have made every effort to provide accurate information, the hours, prices, services and events described in the following pages are current as of publication. We suggest checking essential facts before setting off into the wilds of Washington to make sure the day's schedule will turn out as planned.

If you discover anything has changed or anything new that we've missed, please let us know. We'd appreciate your contributions for the next edition; send them to us at Vintage Books.

Washington is a city of almost limitless resources. We have lived here for many years, yet the experience of writing this book has uncovered many new features of the city for us. We hope the *Guide* will serve to open doors for you and give you pleasure for the moment, memories to take away and the desire to come back again and again. We love Washington—for its people, its energy and its elegant beauty. We think you will, too. If this *Guide* makes it easier for you to draw from the well of over 200 years of our country's rich history and to navigate through the modern reality of a busy urban area, we will have done our job. Happy touring!

WASHINGTON, D.C.

THE COMPLETE GUIDE
1989–90 EDITION

1

THE KEY

TO THE CITY

The essence of this *Guide* is the geographical presentation of the special attractions Washington has to offer. Each city section is introduced briefly to give you a sense of its flavor, tone and history. Each section concludes with a listing of typical and available restaurants. The core of each section, and of the entire *Guide,* is the site reports. To help you make best use of your time, we have devised the following format for the site descriptions to give you basic information in a bold, easy-to-read manner.

SITE'S NAME   **Phone Number**
(An official name, if different, may appear in parentheses)
Street Address
A mailing address, if different, will appear beneath.
Hours: For some Washington sites, these differ from summer to winter.
   Unless otherwise specified, summer hours are in effect from
   Memorial Day until Labor Day.
Price of Admission   (Most are free)

 Metro. Washington's subway system. The nearest subway stop to the site is noted (the subway line is given in parentheses). If the route from the subway to the site isn't obvious, brief walking instructions are provided.

 Bus system. The buses that pass the site are listed; stops are also listed for the Tourmobiles that circulate along the Mall to the

Capitol, museums, monuments, White House, Kennedy Center, Arlington National Cemetery and Custis-Lee Mansion. Since we don't know your point of origin on Metrobus routes, you should call Metrobus at 637-7000 to find out which bus or buses can take you from your starting point to the site. The Metrobus TDD Number for those who are hearing-impaired is 638-3780.

 Taxis. We note the street or streets nearest the site where you can hail a taxi most easily. In some cases a building entrance is listed if it is a place where cabs congregate to wait for fares.

 Parking. The parking situation in the neighborhood of the site is described.

 Food. We note if food is available on the premises of the site, and the hours of availability if they differ radically from those of the site. Most places will close their eating establishments at least a half hour before general closing time. We also let you know if picnicking is possible.

 Kids. We point out a site's particular appeal to children and list any exhibits or services that are especially for kids.

 Groups. Included here are special arrangements that can or should be made when you're taking a group to the site.

 Impaired Mobility. We note if a site is *fully accessible*—that is, if it can be entered and toured, without assistance, by a person in a wheelchair. "Fully accessible" also means that there are phones and bathrooms designed for use by people in wheelchairs. The most accessible entrance to the site will be noted, if other than the main entrance. If the site has *limited access* we detail the limitations. If the site is *inaccessible* to a person in a wheelchair without assistance, but on-site assistance is available, we provide a phone number to request this service.

 Impaired Vision. Any special provisions that are made for blind or visually impaired people are indicated here.

 Impaired Hearing. Special provisions made for visitors who are hearing-impaired or deaf are noted, as well as material that can help the nonhearing person enjoy a site more fully. A TDD phone number is usually provided in each site report.

 Advance Planning. Here we let you know about any special benefits available if you make arrangements in advance of your visit to the site. We note if you need to write far in advance, or whether a call to the site a day or two before your visit will suffice. If your visit is in the busy summer months or Easter week, you will always do well to write ahead. We'd like to mention here that very often your representatives in Congress can arrange special tours for you if you advise them of your visit far enough in advance. We note in the site reports if special tours for constituents are provided on a regular basis. In addition, members of Congress often have printed information they can send to help you plan your trip.

A note to those who have flexibility in timing their visit: consider Washington's weather. Summer can be beastly with high temperatures, high humidity and pollution inversions. Spring and fall are sublime; be advised, though, that the city is clogged with tourists during Easter week and at the end of the school year when kids are on class trips. Winter is not without its cold and rainy periods, but since it's the quietest tourist season, Washington's points of interest are more accessible at this time of year. See the "Outdoor Washington/Sports" chapter for a month-by-month temperature guide.

T *Tours.* We conclude by noting the times when scheduled tours of the site are conducted.

2

GETTING TO

AND AROUND TOWN

YOUR ARRIVAL IN WASHINGTON

Getting to Washington and getting around once you're here can be much easier if you take a little time to familiarize yourself with the city and its various means of transport.

By Air

If you're flying to Washington, you'll land in one of the three area airports: Washington National, Baltimore-Washington International or Dulles International.

National Airport is the most convenient to the city, since it's just three miles from the White House, across the Potomac River in Virginia. A Depression-era facility, National is undergoing massive renovation and expansion. From National, you can take Metrorail, Washington's subway system, and you'll be downtown in just a few minutes. Taxis are plentiful; expect to pay about $8 (not including tip) to get downtown. Major hotels, including the Capital and Washington Hiltons and the Sheraton Washington run limousine services every half hour for about $5. There is also limousine service between National and the other airports.

Baltimore-Washington International Airport (BWI) is about 40 minutes from downtown Washington. There is hourly limousine service between BWI and the Capital Hilton in downtown Washington for $17. Amtrak trains run between Union Station and BWI about every two hours, six times daily. The one-way fare is approximately $6. While the airport is about two miles from the BWI train station, there are free shuttle buses operating according to the train's schedule. In addition, there are buses every hour between BWI and National at 15 minutes past the hour. One-way fare is $12. Call Airport Connection at 441-2345 for information.

Dulles International Airport is located 26 miles from the White House in Virginia. Frequent limousines and buses run to Dulles from the Capital Hilton, Washington Hilton and hotels in Gaithersburg and Rockville, Maryland (Washington Flyer, 685-1400), and cost $12 each way. Taxi rides to town are expensive—about $30.

By Train

Amtrak serves the Washington area at two stations:

Capital Beltway—Lanham, Maryland (Route 95 Beltway, Exit 19B West, and then follow signs)

Union Station—at 1st Street and Massachusetts Avenue, NE, near the Capitol

By Bus

Washington is well served by bus routes, although the station is not located in the best of neighborhoods. Greyhound-Trailways (565-2662) is at 1105 1st Street, NE.

By Car

There are as many routes into D.C. as there are roads. The *Guide* provides a map of major routes from all directions, but come prepared with a good, up-to-date road map of your own.

GETTING AROUND TOWN

Washington has the reputation of being a difficult city to get around in. That reputation is largely undeserved—the city does have a rational plan to it.

The basic layout is simple. The city is divided into four sections—Northeast, Northwest, Southeast and Southwest, usually denoted by initials—NE, NW, SE and SW. The dividing lines are North Capitol Street, South Capitol Street, East Capitol Street and the Mall, radiating like the spokes of a wheel from the Capitol. North-south streets are numbers; east-west streets are letters in alphabetical order (there are no J, X, Y or Z streets). When the city planners ran out of letters, they gave the streets two-syllable names, e.g., Calvert Street, in alphabetical order, and followed them with three-syllable names, e.g., Cathedral Street, reaching out to the Washington-Maryland border in upper Northwest and Northeast. Diagonal thoroughfares, designated "Avenues," are named for various states. Circles and squares occur at the intersection of diagonal avenues and numbered and lettered streets.

Be careful to check the quadrant indicators—500 C Street can be found in four different locations as 5th and C Streets intersect in NW, NE, SE and SW. A Washington trick is that the street number will help you figure out what the crossroad is. For example, the White House, at 1600 Pennsylvania Avenue, NW, is at 16th and Pennsylvania; 1990 K Street, NW, is between 19th and 20th Streets; and 510 7th Street, NW, is found between E and F Streets—that is, between the fifth and sixth letters of the alphabet.

Driving here is not for the faint of heart or for a navigator who wants to observe the passing street scene. Fortunately, the area is served by quite reliable mass transit—a fleet of Metrobuses and a sleek, new Metrorail system. Taxis are inexpensive and plentiful in most parts of the city. The District's small scale makes this a good walking city, and we recommend as much touring on foot as your legs will take.

Metrorail

A ride on Washington's modern, five-line subway system is almost always a delight. The trains are speedy, quiet and well designed. Perhaps an adventure in twenty-first-century mass transit, riding "the Metro," as it's called, deserves to rank high on any visitor's list of "must do" activities. Thus, we sing Metro's praises throughout the *Guide:* we strongly endorse this as the most efficient, pleasant and inexpensive way to get about town. In fact, even if you drive to Washington, you may want to leave your car at a special Metro station and then do your touring.

The *Guide's* maps indicate stations with a big "M," and there's a handy system map in this book. Best of all, each of our site reports includes directions on just how to get there by Metrorail. The stations are safe and well located, and Metro is easy to use once you learn how.

You'll recognize Metro stations around town by the bronze pillar with an illuminated "M" at the top; the station name is posted at the entrance. Nearly all of the tracks are underground, and the stations have both the escalators and elevators (see the "Tips for Visitors with Disabilities" chapter for station entrances with elevators).

Each station displays a stylized map of the various train lines, which are identified by five different colors, plus you'll find an overview of the system with the area streets and landmarks above it. If your destination is on another train line, the map shows where to transfer from one line to another.

Metrorail currently runs Monday to Friday from 6 A.M. to midnight, Saturday from 8 A.M. to midnight and Sunday from 10 A.M. to midnight. On major holidays, the system runs on a weekend schedule. During rush hour, trains are spaced five minutes apart, and they run every 10 minutes other times.

Fares, which are posted in each station, vary according to the length of your trip, as well as time of day. On weekends and holidays, you can buy a $5 Family Packet for four people, good for a day's worth of unlimited travel. You can ask for help or get various brochures from the information booth in any station.

Metrobus

While speeding along underground on Metrorail is almost sure to get you there faster, riding a bus allows you to see the streetscape and how portions of the city interrelate. Red, white and blue Metrobuses plod along metropolitan area streets, following nearly 400 basic routes. You can ride for a basic fare of 80¢ within the District, and more for trips into the suburbs or during rush hour. Metrobus stops, usually located before street intersections, display red, white and blue striped signs and indicate the routes served.

Fares are exact change only, or you can buy bus tokens at 1422 New York Avenue, NW; 600 5th Street, NW; 10th and Pennsylvania Avenue, NW; the Pentagon Concourse; or at any of the eight Metrobus garages.

If your trip requires changing to another route, you should tell the driver your destination when you board, pay your whole fare on the first bus, and ask for a transfer. Each transfer is punched to indicate the zone and time; transfers are free and good for up to two hours. Should your trip require using both Metrobus and Metrorail, you can get a free transfer from rail to bus; oddly enough, there is a charge for transfers in the other direction.

If you'll be here for a considerable time, and expect to use Metrobus often, call a Metro sales outlet (962-2329) for information on special fares and the Metro Flash Pass.

You can call 637-7000 for route information over the phone, 6 A.M. to 11:30 P.M., every day. Metrobus will mail you information on specific routes if you call 637-7000, or write to Washington Metropolitan Transit Authority, 600 5th Street, NW, Washington, D.C. 20001. Hearing-impaired people should call the Metro TDD at 638-3780.

Tourmobile, Old Town Trolley Tours and Other Tours

Tourmobile, a National Park Service concessionaire, provides an opportunity to see the major sites easily, inexpensively and at your own pace. The Tourmobile offers a respite to the footweary visitor. The basic, narrated tour, which costs about $7 for adults and $3.50 for children (ages 3–11), will take you around all the Mall sites, Kennedy Center, Arlington Cemetery Visitors' Center, the White House and the Capitol. The service runs from 9 A.M. to 6:30 P.M., June 15 through Labor Day, and 9:30 A.M. to 4:30 P.M. during the rest of the year.

You can get off at any site, look around as you like, and reboard another bus later in the day for no extra charge. Tickets purchased after 2 P.M. are good for the next day, at a price of $9 for adults and $4.50 for children. Or, if you prefer a quick and restful tour, stay on the Tourmobile you first board, listen to the narration and watch the sights, and land back at your starting point 90 minutes later. While the route officially begins at the East Front of the Capitol, you can simply look for the Tourmobile Shuttle Bus sign at any of the sites included, buy a ticket from the driver and start your excursion, or purchase tickets at ticket booths along the Mall.

Tourmobile also offers a complete Arlington Cemetery tour, which includes stops at the President John F. Kennedy and Senator Robert F. Kennedy gravesites, the Tomb of the Unknown Soldier (Changing of the Guard) and Arlington House. This leg of the journey costs an additional $2.25 for adults and $1 for children and operates from 8:30 A.M. until 6:30 P.M. An excursion to Mount Vernon includes a trip through historic Old Town, Alexandria, and this costs about $13.50 for adults and $6.25 for children, which includes the admission fee to the plantation. Call Tourmobile for this tour's schedule since it varies throughout the year. A two-day ticket, good for all three of the tours, costs around $21 for adults and $10 for children. Watch for promotional discount coupons at various tourism outlets. Groups of 20 or more are eligible for a discount, too. To listen to a tape recording about the Tourmobile, call 554-7020.

Old Town Trolley Tours offers a narrated two-hour tour aboard old-fashioned, all-weather trolleylike buses. The 16-stop tour includes Capitol Hill, the Smithsonian, Dupont Circle, Embassy Row, Georgetown and the Cathedral; it stops at some major hotels as well as tourist sites. You can stay aboard the trolley for the full tour, or you may get off to sightsee and reboard another trolley later for no extra charge. Trolleys run every 30 minutes from 9 A.M. to the last full tour at 4 P.M. Adults $11; seniors, military and students $9; children 12 and under free with adult. Call 269-3020 for details.

A variety of other tour services are listed in the District of Columbia yellow pages. (If you're coming as a group, many other tour services are available if you plan in advance. See Chapter 16.) Here are a few you may want to call for further information and comparative shopping:

Grayline Tours offers a variety of different tours. On the all-day deluxe tour you'll see all the major Washington and Arlington sites, and it costs about $34 for adults and $17 for children. "Washington After Dark" is a three-hour tour of the major sites, available late-March through October; it costs about $15 for adults and $7 for children. There are also excursions to outlying sites, such as Mount Vernon, Annapolis, Maryland, or the Shenandoah Valley, as well as other tailored tours in town. Grayline is located at 4th and E Streets, NW, and the phone number is 479-5900.

American Sightseeing International, a family-owned business, has been showing off Washington for 30 years. Tours are given by experienced guides. The one-day tour covers all the major Washington sites in seven hours and costs about $21 for adults and $11 for children. The deluxe one-day tour, including a boat trip to Mount Vernon, takes about eight hours and costs around $30 for adults and $15 for children. The company is located at 519 6th Street, NW, and the phone number is 393-1616.

Spirit of '76 is another unusual way to tour Washington. Groups can rent this double-decker, London-style bus for about $50 an hour, with a four-hour minimum. Call (301) 731-4050 for information.

City Sights Tours offers some nice specialized tours of black, Hispanic and Jewish interest, as well as a full line of general tours. City

Sights can be reached at 2025 I Street, NW, Suite 721, Washington, D.C. 20006, 785-4700.

City Sights also offers a variety of deluxe tours for individuals or groups; reservations are a must.

Taxicabs

Taxis in Washington are relatively inexpensive and easy to hail. The fare is based on a zone system, with a basic charge of $2.10 for travel within a single zone. To give you some idea, a single zone charge buys you a ride between the Capitol and Downtown (a system rumored to exist in order to allow congresspeople a Downtown lunch at minimal transportation cost). The zone system can be tricky for the consumer, though; before paying, even veteran travelers often ask the driver exactly what zones they traversed. To cloud the picture more, there's an additional $1 charge for travel companions, as well as a $1 rush-hour surcharge. Taxis licensed only in Maryland or Virginia cannot transport passengers between points within the District. Taxis are permitted to pick up additional passengers headed for different destinations, but the driver must first obtain the original passenger's permission, and it cannot result in more than a five-block diversion.

Driving in the District

Best of luck to the visitor who expects to drive and enjoy sightseeing, too. While many come to Washington by car, smart visitors use their wits, and now this *Guide,* to plan convenient and inexpensive excursions around town. In general, the traffic, poorly marked routes and scarce parking combine to make driving here a frustrating experience. Also, if you use a map, make sure it's up-to-date. Route numbers and even Beltway exit numbers have been known to change. If you want to brave it, please read through the rest of this section to familiarize yourself with the common practices as well as the idiosyncrasies here.

For starters, rush hour brings more chaos than just impatient drivers caught in snarled traffic. Many one-way streets, and some lanes of others, change direction during rush hour, weekdays 6:30 to 9 A.M. and 4 to 6:30 P.M.

Many Metrorail stations offer inexpensive parking, for $1 to $1.25, on a first-come, first-served basis. We strongly recommend that visitors, especially those staying outside the city, leave their cars behind at one of the many suburban stations with parking lots.

Metered parking spaces have a two-hour maximum, although

many Downtown are limited to one hour or even a half hour. Along Independence Avenue by the Mall you can park for three hours. If you're even luckier, you might find free, all-day parking in West Potomac Park along Ohio Drive, south of the Lincoln Memorial.

If you opt for the convenience of commercial parking lots, you are warned: they are expensive—generally up to $13.50 per day in prime Downtown and other Northwest areas. In the evening many lots are discounted to just a few dollars.

Police and other officials do indeed ticket cars, so this is no town for carelessness (D.C. has the most efficient parking-control system in the country). Fines start at $15 for an expired meter. The Bureau of Traffic Adjudication, Cashiers Office, is located at 165 K Street, NW, and the telephone number is 727-5000. You can settle fines by paying cash or with a personal check, money order, VISA or MasterCard. The office is open Monday to Friday, 8:30 A.M. to 7 P.M. and 8:30 A.M. to noon on Saturday.

If your car is towed, call 727-5000 for information on its retrieval.

Car Rentals

Various car-rental companies are located at the airports, in town and throughout the suburbs. Many of them offer courtesy transportation to and from nearby airports and Metro stations. You may also want to compare any special discounts such as three-day, holiday or weekend rates when you call these or other companies.

Ajax Rent-A-Car: 979-3700; (800) 421-0896
All-State Car Rental: 638-6533
Avis: 467-6585; (800) 331-1212
Budget Rent-A-Car: 628-2750; (800) 527-0700
Hertz: (800) 654-3131; 659-8702
National Car Rental: (800) 328-4567; 783-1590 (National Airport)
Nationwide Rent-A-Car: 863-2600
Sears: 638-0277; (800) 527-0770
Thrifty Rent-A-Car: 548-1600; (800) 367-2277
USA-MPG: 289-0283

Transportation Numbers

Metrobus and Metrorail:

Bus and Metrorail information	637-7000
Complaints and suggestions	637-1328

Charter information	637-1315
Bulk purchase of farecards	962-1590
Information on Flash Passes, Senior Citizen Discounts, Sales Outlet locations	637-7000
Lost and found	962-1195
Traffic and parking information	727-5000
TDD	638-3780
Police emergency	962-1289
Police general	962-2121
Railroads	
Amtrak	1-800-USA-RAIL
Commuter (Baltimore, WV)	1-800-585-RAIL

3

PLANNING

AHEAD

Advance planning can help ensure that your visit to Washington will be especially rewarding. Try to plan your activities several weeks before your trip; if you are traveling in a group, are requesting special tours or are visiting from abroad, it is essential to make arrangements even further in advance (see the "Advice to Groups," "Tips for Visitors with Disabilities" and "A Welcome to International Visitors" chapters for specific tips). Once you're in Washington, make daily plans, remembering to call ahead to double-check special events before you schedule your activities around them. This chapter presents some additional planning hints that we hope will make your visit run smoothly and with a great measure of enjoyment.

BEFORE YOU ARRIVE

A variety of organizations will mail you information to help you plan activities in advance. When time allows, it's best to write to them well ahead of your trip, particularly between Easter and Labor Day or if you need special arrangements. Individual site reports also contain advice on advance planning, so it's a good idea to study them before you get to town. If you want to go to the theater, you should write ahead for tickets, since many Washington runs are short.

Many museums, galleries and other locations will send you free calendars of events (see individual site reports for addresses). To obtain information on all the Smithsonian museums or to make spe-

cial arrangements contact the Visitor Information Center, Smithsonian Institution, Washington, D.C. 20560, (202) 357-2700.

There are a number of useful resource centers from which you can
obtain information. They are:

- The Washington Area Convention and Visitors Association, 1575
  I Street, NW, Washington, D.C. 20005, (202) 789-7000.
- Visitor Information Center, 1400 Pennsylvania Avenue, NW,
  (202) 789-7000; maps and attraction brochures are available on
  arrival, not over the phone.
- Alexandria Tourist Council, 221 King Street, Alexandria, VA
  22314, (703) 838-4200; maps, brochures, calendar of events, din-
  ing/shopping guide.
- Baltimore Office of Promotion and Tourism, 34 Market Place,
  Baltimore, MD 21202, (301) 837-4636; the office publishes *Baltimore! Good Times,* a terrific free handout listing everything to do
  and see, places to stay and eat, complete with maps.
- Virginia Division of Tourism, 202 N. 9th Street, Suite 500, Richmond, VA 23219, (804) 786-4484.
- Maryland Office of Tourist Development, 45 Calvart Street, Annapolis, MD 21401 (801) 269-3517.

Capital Reservations (1-800-VISIT-DC) books hotels for families
primarily, but groups, too. See "Hotels" for details.

Your representative or senator may be able to reserve a place for
you on various special tours of the Capitol, White House, FBI Building and government agencies (see site reports). You should call his or
her local office well in advance of your visit and see if the staff can
arrange tours for you. Your members of Congress can also provide
bounteous brochures on particular sites that may be of interest to you.

FIRST MOVES

When you arrive in the nation's capital, you'll find your bearings a lot
more quickly if you become familiar with Washington's staple sources
of information. Complement this *Guide* with the vast amount of free
literature widely available. *Where* and *This Week in the Nation's
Capital* are free, widely distributed publications full of listings and
tourist-related advertisements. Reading *The Washington Post* any day

can provide great orientation. Every Friday, the *Post* contains a wonderful supplement, called "Weekend," which highlights special events. On Thursday, the *Post* lists notable community events in "This Week." Also, take note of the *Post*'s official listings on weekdays, generally at the bottom of a page in Section A. Here you'll find the day's Supreme Court schedule and what the House, the Senate and their committees have on the agenda. *Washingtonian,* an excellent local monthly magazine, contains a thorough listing of events in "Where and When," including a section for kids.

If you find a live event—theater, music or dance—that interests you, you will want to check with Ticketplace, 842-5387, a service offering half-price tickets to most live attractions in town. Half-price tickets are for that day's performances only, and must be paid for in cash. Full-price tickets are also available for future performances with credit cards.

As mentioned previously, a good first stop is the Washington Area Convention and Visitors Association, where you can collect a variety of brochures. To listen to their tape recording of things to do, call 737-8866 anytime.

Once in town, almost all the telephone calls you'll make to sites for information will be local, so there's no need to dial an area code. The *Guide* often provides the area code in case you're calling from out of town; where not given, note that the Washington area code is 202, suburban Maryland is 301 and suburban Virginia is 703.

We want to stress the importance of calling ahead for all your stops to double-check hours, exhibits and, for restaurants and shops, their very existence.

NUMBERS TO HELP YOU PLAN
YOUR ACTIVITIES—OR JUST FOR FUN

*Sampler of Week's Events	737-8866
*Dial-A-Museum (Smithsonian Information)	357-2020
*Smithsonian Earth and Space Report	357-2000
*Dial-A-Park	485-PARK
*Dial-A-Story	638-5717
D.C. Department of Recreation	673-7671
*Audubon Voice of Naturalist	652-1088
*National Archives Smithsonian	523-3000
*Congressional Proceedings	
House, Democratic	225-7400
House, Republican	225-7430
Senate, Democratic	224-8541
Senate, Republican	224-8601
Congressional Switchboard	224-3121
National Park Service, Office of Public Affairs	485-9666
White House Switchboard	456-1414
*Tourmobile	554-7950
*Time	844-1111
*Weather	936-1212

* Tape recordings

4

THE MALL

The Mall is the heart of our nation's capital and, with good cause, the focus of every tourist's visit to Washington. An elegant stretch of open space extending for two miles from the U.S. Capitol to the Lincoln Memorial, the Mall is flanked by the White House, the Jefferson Memorial, the myriad of museums that comprise the Smithsonian Institution and numerous government agencies. Its focal point—indeed, the pinnacle of the city—is the Washington Monument. As the tallest edifice in the city, the monument provides a spectacular view of Washington and its surrounding communities.

The Mall reflects the basic plan drawn up by Pierre L'Enfant for the new city of Washington in 1791. L'Enfant viewed the Mall as a dramatic span of land that would visually join the "Congress House" on Jenkins Hill to the parklike banks of the Potomac River. The central avenue would be flanked by trees, academies and other sites of learning and entertainment, as well as by a grand canal to supply merchants' needs.

Unfortunately, after only one year, L'Enfant was fired from his post as city planner. While Pennsylvania Avenue flourished and became a bustling commercial strip during the years that followed, the Mall lay bare except for the financially unsuccessful Washington Canal and a scattering of shacks and shanties. At the outset of the Civil War in 1860, the Mall was still a rough-hewn place: lumber and coal yards dotted its northern border and the Washington Monument sat, stalled by the war, at only one fourth its final height.

At last, in 1900, Senator James McMillan of Michigan, chairman of the Senate District Committee, appointed a panel of leading architects and planners to study the park needs of the District of Columbia. The McMillan Plan of 1902 made sweeping proposals that called for the implementation of many of L'Enfant's original ideas. A railroad was removed from the Mall to a new terminal, Union Station; the Botanic Garden's conservatory was moved from the Mall's center to its southeastern edge. In the 1920s, the Lincoln Memorial and its reflecting pool were added to become the westernmost structure on the Mall. The Jefferson Memorial, south of the Tidal Basin, was dedicated in 1943. In the 1970s, the Mall's interior streets were transformed into grass and pathways, and the Constitution Gardens were created between the Washington Monument and Lincoln Memorial. The Vietnam Veterans Memorial was dedicated in 1982. Far from a static row of memorials and museums, the Mall is alive and lively, a microcosm of the nation's past and present.

Today, the Mall serves not only tourists, but entices lunchtime joggers from surrounding offices. On weekends, it attracts recreation seekers from throughout the region who come to bike, picnic, fly kites and play baseball, rugby, volleyball, cricket and polo on its many fields. In the summer, rides on an antique carousel can be enjoyed in front of the Arts and Industries Building. At night, a drive around the Mall can be quite spectacular, since the museums and monuments are flooded with light.

The Cherry Blossom Festival, complete with parade, is held annually, sometimes from mid-March to mid-April, depending on the trees' "schedule." The festival celebrates the blooming of the breathtaking Yoshino and Akebono Japanese cherry trees that surround the Tidal Basin. Since 1967, the Festival of American Folklife has drawn working people, craftspeople, dancers and musicians from across the country to exhibit and share their traditional ways. During the festival, usually held around the Fourth of July, the Mall comes alive with the smells of regional cooking and the sounds of traditional music, be it Cajun, Gospel, Chicago blues or Native American. Also on July 4, a truly wonderful fireworks display takes place on the Mall; it's certainly among the finest pyrotechnical performances in the country.

In recent times the Mall has functioned as the meeting ground for Americans expressing concern about issues of national interest. In the 1960s and 1970s, many civil rights, antipoverty and antiwar rallies were held along the Mall; later, thousands of farmers organized to drive their tractors along its bordering streets to the Capitol.

The Mall is dominated by the Smithsonian Institution; it is comprised of the following components:

- Arts and Industries Building
- Freer Gallery of Art (closed until 1992)
- Hirshhorn Museum and Sculpture Garden
- National Air and Space Museum
- National Gallery of Art and its spectacular East Wing (while under the Smithsonian umbrella, the gallery has its own administration)
- National Museum of African Art
- National Museum of American History
- National Museum of Natural History
- Arthur M. Sackler Gallery
- Smithsonian Institution Building (The Castle)

In other parts of the city the Smithsonian encompasses:

- Anacostia Neighborhood Museum
- Barney Studio House
- John F. Kennedy Center for the Performing Arts
- National Museum of American Art
- National Portrait Gallery
- National Zoo
- Renwick Gallery

Under this vast umbrella, the Smithsonian carries out its goal: "the increase and diffusion of knowledge among men." The Institution preserves and displays the nation's treasures, sponsors research, publishes a vast array of periodicals and tackles countless other tasks. One treasure is the *Official Guide to the Smithsonian,* on sale in all the museums and galleries for $2.95, which we recommend highly if you'd like more in-depth information on this grand complex. The guide is also available in Braille, on cassette tape and as a talking-book tape (this version must be played on special equipment that is furnished free by the Library of Congress). Call 357-2020 for "Dial-A-Museum," a daily announcement of new exhibits and special events, and 357-2000 for the Smithsonian Earth and Space Report, an announcement recorded weekly on stars, planets and worldwide occurrences of short-lived phenomena.

The Smithsonian Museum shops are treasure troves of gifts and memorabilia, including minerals, rocket models, antique dolls and countless books and art reproductions. Of special note is the Smithsonian Collection of Recordings, which includes reissues of classics in American jazz, musicals and country recordings. These records are available only through Smithsonian catalogs and these shops.

The Smithsonian also sponsors a concert series of musical theater, dance, black gospel, jazz, country and chamber music. Call 357-3030 for ticket and schedule information or see the "Entertainment" chapter.

Where you begin your tour of the Mall depends on your own interests. The site descriptions that follow will give you a good idea of what each site offers, including such planning essentials as tour times, ticket requirements and eating facilities. A familiarity with the site reports should eliminate some of the running back and forth that can take the enjoyment out of sightseeing.

Numerous ways exist to get you to and around the Mall. The Metro subway system and the Metrobus system have plentiful stops in the area. In addition, the Mall is served extensively by Tourmobiles (discussed more thoroughly in the chapter "Getting to and Around Town"). If you aren't among the hale and hearty or wish to save your energy for walking through, rather than to, the museums, the Tourmobile is your best bet for Mall locomotion; you can get off and on at almost every point of interest.

Street parking on the Mall is difficult. The Smithsonian has now closed all of its parking lots—the sad impact of fear of terrorism. Use public transportation or Tourmobile if possible.

The absolute best bet for eating on the Mall is the cafeteria at the National Gallery of Art. The food is fresh, reasonable, attractive and varied (*every* member of the family can find something here), and the setting, for a cafeteria, is quite elegant—you can watch water cascade from the Mall down the sculptured waterfall as you eat amidst a contemporary chrome decor. Fruit and salad to roast beef and chicken—and everything in between—are offered, complete with wine, beer and a multitude of other beverages. Several other museums also have cafeterias, but only the new eateries at Air and Space rival the National Gallery of Art.

The Mall is the perfect place for picnics—if you aren't seeking solitude, that is—so if you can, bring your own food. In addition, street vendors selling a variety of foods cluster in front of the National

Air and Space Museum on Independence Avenue, along the sides of the Ellipse across from the Washington Monument and in front of the Natural History and American History museums on Constitution Avenue. Refreshment kiosks are scattered along the Mall itself in warm weather.

If you are on the south side of the Mall, consider the L'Enfant Plaza complex, two blocks south of the Mall between 7th and 9th Streets, SW. On the hotel's main floor are several rather expensive restaurants; the shopping mall below offers deli and snacks during business hours. If you are on the north side of the Mall, you are not far from The Pavilion at the Old Post Office and The Shops at National Place.

Check restaurant recommendations for nearby Capitol Hill if none of the Mall ideas inspires your palate.

ARTS AND INDUSTRIES BUILDING · 357-1300
900 Jefferson Drive, SW 20560
Hours: Summer—extended hours determined annually; usually
10 A.M.–9 P.M. daily
Winter—10 A.M.–5:30 P.M. daily
Closed Christmas
Free Admission

M Smithsonian stop (orange and blue lines); use Mall exit.

🚌 13's, 30, 32, 34, 36, 52, 60, 70; Tourmobile.

🚗 Jefferson Drive or Independence Avenue.

P Competitive parking on the Mall.

🍽 None on premises. The building is convenient to cafeterias in other museums on the Mall, to street vendors on Independence Avenue and to restaurants at L'Enfant Plaza.

👥 Recommended. The Discovery Theater is a great resource for children (adults will enjoy the presentations, too!). The theater presents month-long residences from October to May by troupes ranging from puppetry to pantomime. Performances are Tuesday to Friday at 10 and 11:30 A.M., and Saturday and Sunday at 1 and 2 P.M. Tickets are $3 for adults, $2.50 for children under 12, and are also available from the Smithsonian Box Office at 357-1500. Group rates are available for 20 or more. In addition, sign language and/or oral interpretation of performances are available upon request. To schedule an interpretation, call 357-2700 or TDD 357-1929.

 No special arrangements necessary.

 Fully accessible. People with wheelchairs should use the Victorian Garden entrance on the building's west side.

 Special tours can be arranged by calling 357-1502.

 Tours in sign language can be arranged in advance by calling 357-2700 or TDD 357-1729; give at least 48 hours' notice.

A As noted above.

T Docents (occasionally garbed in Victorian costume) conduct tours on an irregular schedule.

The Arts and Industries Building will whisk you back over 100 years to the Philadelphia Centennial of 1876. The four exhibit halls of the museum display steam motors and Victorian whimsy; a highlight is a 42-foot model of the naval cruiser *Antietam,* which was a steam-powered sloop of war.

Construction of the building, which was designed by Adolph Cluss, commenced in 1879, making this the second oldest of the Smithsonian Mall museums. In 1881, President Garfield's inaugural ball was held here. The body of the Smithsonian's technological and aeronautic displays was exhibited in this building until the 1960s and 1970s, when other museums absorbed them. Closed in 1975, the Arts and Industries Building was totally renovated; it reopened with the continuing Centennial exhibit in 1976. A Victorian Horticultural Extravaganza is on the second floor; a formal Victorian "embroidery garden" graces the outside of the building. A lovely fountain flows beneath the main rotunda.

The museum gift shop (357-2700) is a delight, offering books, records, stationery, jewelry, soaps, old-fashioned dolls and glass jars and special toys for kids. The museum puts out a mail-order catalog three times a year and displays all of the mail-order items in the shop. For a copy of the catalog write: Smithsonian Mail Order, P.O.B. 199, Washington, D.C. 20560.

BUREAU OF ENGRAVING AND PRINTING   447-1391
14th and C Streets, SW 20228
Hours: 7:30 A.M.–3:30 P.M. weekdays
        Closed legal holidays
Free Admission

 Smithsonian stop (orange and blue lines); use Independence Avenue exit.

 13's, 50, V4, V6; Tourmobile.

 Independence Avenue.

 Very difficult street parking.

 None on premises. The bureau is convenient to Mall museum cafeterias and L'Enfant Plaza restaurants.

 Recommended.

 No special arrangements necessary.

 Limited accessibility. The tour is wheelchair-accessible and a wheelchair will be supplied if requested. The bathroom is accessible, but the phone is not. Call ahead for arrangements, 449-9435.

 No special services available.

 No special services available.

A None necessary.

T Self-guided tours are given from 9 A.M. to 2 P.M. Monday to Friday.

Since August 1872, every piece of paper money issued by the United States government has been printed here, at the Bureau of Engraving and Printing. The bureau is also responsible for printing postage stamps, food stamps and any other official paper that carries monetary value.

Tours are self-guided. During the peak tourist season, waiting time will average one hour. The self-guided tour winds through the building, explaining the work of the various machines and describing the complicated and delicate process of printing currency as you observe the task being done.

FREER GALLERY OF ART (Closed until 1992)　　357-2104
1200 Jefferson Drive, SW 20560
Hours: 10 A.M.–5:30 P.M. daily
　　　Closed Christmas
Free Admission

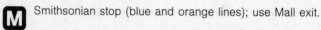

M Smithsonian stop (blue and orange lines); use Mall exit.

9, 13's, 30, 32, 34, 36, 50, 52, V4, V6; Tourmobile.

Independence Avenue or Jefferson Drive.

P Competitive parking on the Mall and Independence Avenue.

None on premises. The gallery is convenient to cafeterias in museums on the Mall, street vendors on Independence Avenue and restaurants at L'Enfant Plaza.

Call or write two weeks in advance to arrange tours for grades 5 and up.

Write or call 357-4886 at least two weeks in advance to arrange for a group tour.

Limited accessibility. There is a ground-level entrance with a ramp on the Independence Avenue side of the building; on weekdays a staff member will escort wheelchairs in the service elevator to the gallery level; on weekends the guard must be contacted at 357-2101. The bathroom is accessible; the museum shop is not.

Tours can be arranged by calling 357-4886 at least 48 hours in advance.

Tours can be arranged by calling 357-4886 or TDD 357-1696 at least 48 hours in advance.

A As noted above.

T Several guided tours are offered daily: on weekdays at 10:15 A.M. and 1 P.M., and Saturday and Sunday at 1 P.M.

Unfortunately, the Freer Gallery of Art is one of the most frequently overlooked members of the Smithsonian Institution. A small, intimate museum, the Freer houses one of the world's leading collections of art from the Near and Far East. It also has one of the finest collections of work of the expatriate American painter, James McNeill Whistler, who was a friend of the museum's founder, Charles Lang Freer. The

Freer's collection also includes works by other American painters who were contemporaries of Whistler, including Albert Pinkham Ryder, Winslow Homer and John Singer Sargent. Because of the large size of the Freer's collection and the limited amount of gallery space, exhibits change often.

Opened in 1923, the Freer was designed to resemble a Florentine palace; it has a lovely open courtyard in the center of the galleries. Works exhibited include paintings, sculpture, pottery, lacquerware, metalwork and manuscripts from China, Japan, Korea, India, Iran, Egypt and Syria. One of the gallery's prizes is the Peacock Room; Whistler designed the entire room—walls, fixtures and paintings—for the home of an English merchant.

You can request an appointment to see anything not on display, including collections of Chinese calligraphy, James McNeill Whistler prints, Japanese ceramics and others.

The Freer has a library of works dealing with Oriental art open to the public 10 A.M. to 5 P.M. on weekdays; call 357-2091 to arrange to use this facility. The Freer's small gift shop (357-1432) sells some attractive and unusual gift items as well as postcards, reproductions and posters of very fine quality.

The Freer is closed for renovations until 1992.

HIRSHHORN MUSEUM AND SCULPTURE GARDEN 357-1300
Independence Avenue at 8th Street, SW 20560

Hours: 10 A.M.–5:30 P.M. daily
Sculpture Garden
7:30 A.M.–dusk daily
Closed Christmas

Free Admission

M Smithsonian or L'Enfant Plaza stop (blue and orange lines).

🚌 9, 13's, 30, 32, 34, 36, 70; Tourmobile.

🚗 Independence Avenue.

P Competitive parking on Mall.

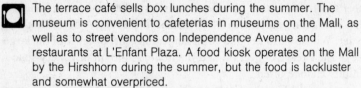
The terrace café sells box lunches during the summer. The museum is convenient to cafeterias in museums on the Mall, as well as to street vendors on Independence Avenue and restaurants at L'Enfant Plaza. A food kiosk operates on the Mall by the Hirshhorn during the summer, but the food is lackluster and somewhat overpriced.

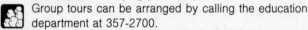
Recommended. On Saturdays—except in the summer—at 11 A.M., special lectures with animated films are presented for kids; special tours for groups of children can be arranged by writing or calling 357-3235. No strollers are permitted in the museum; they can be checked, and the museum will issue you a backpack for carrying your baby.

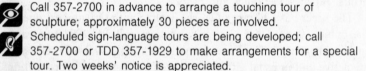
Group tours can be arranged by calling the education department at 357-2700.

Fully accessible; Sculpture Garden is accessible from the Mall.

Call 357-2700 in advance to arrange a touching tour of sculpture; approximately 30 pieces are involved.

Scheduled sign-language tours are being developed; call 357-2700 or TDD 357-1929 to make arrangements for a special tour. Two weeks' notice is appreciated.

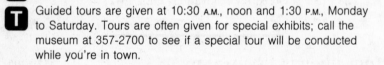
As noted above.

Guided tours are given at 10:30 A.M., noon and 1:30 P.M., Monday to Saturday. Tours are often given for special exhibits; call the museum at 357-2700 to see if a special tour will be conducted while you're in town.

The Hirshhorn Museum and Sculpture Garden originally was built for the collection of approximately 6,000 pieces of twentieth-century and late-nineteenth-century paintings and sculpture donated to the Smithsonian by Joseph Hirshhorn. Since its opening in 1974, the museum's collection has expanded to over 6,500 works.

Designed by Gordon Bunshaft, the four-story cylindrical building surrounds an inner courtyard. The inner galleries of the museum, which look out on the courtyard, display the museum's indoor sculptures. Sculpture is also displayed outdoors on the plaza around the building and in the sunken sculpture garden across Jefferson Drive. Though the sculpture collection has many works by European artists, the paintings and drawings exhibited in the windowless outer galleries are primarily the work of Americans. Exhibits change often because space limitations allow only a small part of the collection to be shown at one time.

Among the sculptors represented in the Hirshhorn are Auguste Rodin, Henry Moore, David Smith, Louise Nevelson, Claes Oldenburg, Joseph Cornell and Mark di Suvero. The painting collection includes pieces from most of the major movements in modern American art: representatives of the early twentieth-century Ash Can School's seamy realism; works of the photo-secessionists, including Georgia O'Keeffe and John Marin; a large collection of the work of the abstract expressionists who dominated the 1940s and 1950s, such as Pollack, Rothko and de Kooning; and more recent pieces by artists who are working in genres that are still being defined.

The Hirshhorn has a museum shop (357-1429) on the entrance level that sells books, posters and cards related to the collection, as well as some gift items.

From time to time the museum sponsors special lectures and shows films; for information, call 357-3280. In addition, occasional concerts of the Smithsonian Museum Masterpiece series are given in the Hirshhorn auditorium. Tickets range from $5 to $8, with discounts available to students, senior citizens and groups. Call 357-1618 for information.

JEFFERSON MEMORIAL   426-6841
Tidal Basin, West Potomac Park
Mailing Address: National Park Service, Mall Operations,
                    900 Ohio Drive, SW 20042
Hours: Always open; park ranger available from 8 A.M. to midnight,
       except Christmas
Free Admission

 Smithsonian or L'Enfant Plaza stops (orange and blue lines). This entails a *long* walk along the Mall and around the Tidal Basin.

 13's, 50, V4, V6 (get off at Bureau of Engraving and walk around Tidal Basin); Tourmobile.

 Independence Avenue.

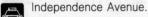 Parking is available at the memorial; it's difficult during the Cherry Blossom Festival and on summer weekends.

None on premises. Take a picnic to eat on the edge of the Tidal Basin, or return to the Mall's museum cafeterias.

 Recommended.

 There are no regular tours, but to inquire about arranging special tours, call 426-6841. Be sure to call well in advance.

 Accessible. The site, bathroom and phone are accessible to those in wheelchairs.

 Special "touch" tours can be arranged in advance by calling 426-6841.

 Sign-language tours can be arranged in advance by calling 426-6841.

 As noted above.

 Interpretations are given as needed when staffers are available in spring and fall.

Dedicated in 1943, 200 years after Jefferson's birth, this is one of the loveliest memorials in Washington—or beyond, for that matter. The 19-foot bronze statue of our third President stands beneath a simple rotunda inscribed with some of his most compelling words from the Declaration of Independence, the Virginia Statute of Religious Freedom and other works. The site looks out over the Tidal Basin and is imposing (especially at night) in both sentiment and physical appeal. Its beauty is particularly striking when you realize that this site was formerly the Potomac River!

Jefferson was not only a President; he served as George Washington's secretary of state, drafted the Declaration of Independence, founded the University of Virginia and was an inventor, botanist and architect. The memorial design by John Russell Pope incorporates several favorite architectural motifs used by Jefferson in his own designs—rotunda and columns.

In early April, the monument is enveloped in the soft pink and white of Japanese cherry blossoms—and the cars of the many trying to glimpse them.

A small shop in the lower level of the memorial sells postcards, film and related memorabilia. There is also a bookshop in the lower lobby.

LINCOLN MEMORIAL   426-6841
West end of Mall
Mailing Address: National Park Service, Mall Operations,
                    900 Ohio Drive, SW 20242
Hours: Always open; park ranger available from 8 A.M. to midnight,
          except Christmas
Free Admission

M Smithsonian or Foggy Bottom stops (orange and blue lines). A
long walk from either. From Foggy Bottom stop, walk down 23rd
Street.

13's, 80; Tourmobile.

Constitution Avenue or Independence Avenue.

P Competitive parking in West Potomac Park; follow signs for Ohio
Drive. Don't try to drive here during rush hour; you'll most
assuredly wind up in Virginia since the roadway design is
demonic.

None on premises. Snacks are available at a nearby kiosk. Since
the museum cafeterias are on the other end of the Mall, we
suggest you take a picnic if you intend to eat around the time
you plan to see this memorial.

Recommended; although there are lots of stairs, an elevator is
available.

Special tours can be arranged in advance by calling 426-6841.
Resources are limited, so call well in advance.

Accessible. The memorial (via elevator) and bathroom are
accessible to those in wheelchairs; special parking has been set
aside for handicapped people. There is no telephone.

Special ''touch'' tours can be arranged in advance by calling
426-6841.

Signing tours can be arranged in advance by calling 426-6841.

A As noted above.

T Interpretive talks are given as needed when staff are available.

Many find this the most human and inspiring of memorials. A weary,
pensive Lincoln sits, his large hands resting on his chair arms as he
gazes down the Mall toward the Washington Monument. The 19-foot

marble statue is flanked by the moving Gettysburg Address on the south wall and the Second Inaugural Address on the north wall.

The memorial, designed by Daniel Chester French in the classic Greek manner, was completed in 1922 on reclaimed swampland. The view from the back of the memorial—across the Potomac River along the majestic Memorial Bridge to Arlington National Cemetery—is almost as lovely as the Mall panorama afforded by the front view. On clear days, Lincoln's statue is, indeed, reflected in the pool below.

Short interpretive talks are given by park rangers throughout the year. On weekdays at 7 P.M. and Saturday and Sunday at 2 P.M., tours are also given of the caves *below* the statue, resplendent with dripping stalactites and stalagmites formed by water seeping from the memorial's steps. Reservations should be made for this tour by calling 426-6841 several months in advance.

A free, informative pamphlet is available at the site. There is also a bookshop on the lower level.

NATIONAL AIR AND SPACE MUSEUM   357-2700
6th Street and Independence Avenue, SW 20560   **TDD 357-1729**
Hours: Summer—extended hours determined annually; usually
       10 A.M.–9 P.M. daily
       Winter—10 A.M.–5:30 P.M. daily
       Closed Christmas
Free Admission

 L'Enfant Plaza stop (blue and orange lines). Walk north on 7th Street to Independence Avenue.

 13's, 30, 32, 34, 36, 70's; Tourmobile.

 Independence Avenue.

 Competitive street and Mall parking.

 Cafeteria and restaurant. At press time, two new eating facilities opened at this museum. Flightline is billed as a first-rate cafeteria offering a wide range of fresh foods, from subs and pizza to hot entrees. The Wright Place is a restaurant with a more ambitious menu, a solace for the foot-weary tourist. Both are enclosed in an enormous glass addition to the museum, which offers a grand view of the Capitol.

Highly recommended. This is heaven for most kids; there's lots to play with and crawl on. A baby service station next to Gallery 107 offers a comfortable place to change or nurse babies.

Tours available. Special group tours can be arranged; appointments should be made two to six weeks in advance. Group reservations for films can be made, with a minimum of two weeks' advance notice, by calling 357-1400.

Fully accessible. The General Aviation gallery offers a flight simulation with cockpit controls especially for people in wheelchairs. Wheelchairs are available on request. Space has been set aside in the theater and planetarium for wheelchairs.

Tours for visually impaired people can be arranged by writing the education office of the museum or by calling 357-1400. Guide materials are available in Braille and recorded form. Museum brochures are available in Braille, large-print and tape-recorded editions at the information desk, as are recorded tours of some of the galleries. Braille and cassette editions of the booklet *Celebrating the National Air and Space Museum* may be purchased in the museum shop.

Write the education office or call 357-1400 or TDD 357-1729 to arrange for a tour in sign language at least two weeks in advance.

As noted above.

Guided tours leave from the tour desk in Gallery 100 on the first floor at 10:15 A.M. and 1 P.M. daily. The tour guides are well versed in their subject—a few are pilots (2 hours).

The National Air and Space Museum, which opened in 1976, is the most popular museum in the world, drawing over 10 million visitors annually. The huge building, covering several blocks of the Mall, houses 23 galleries dealing with different aspects of air and space travel. While the museum displays 240 aircraft and 50 missiles and rockets, it is not just a repository for historically significant artifacts. Air and Space houses a multimedia extravaganza with slide shows, do-it-yourself consoles, a how-to-fly training school and many other devices visitors of all ages can play with and feel a part of the show.

In the Milestones of Flight gallery, such prizes as the Wright brothers' *Kitty Hawk Flyer,* Lindbergh's *Spirit of St. Louis* and the *Gossamer Albatross,* the first man-powered plane to cross the English

Channel, are suspended from the ceiling; the Apollo 11 and Viking Lander are also displayed. Voyager, the first airplane to circumnavigate the earth without stopping to refuel, was placed on display at the Independence Avenue entrance in the spring of 1988. Don't miss the re-creation of a World War I forward airfield in Gallery 209 or Sea-Air Operations in Gallery 203. Model builders will be awed by the phenomenal model of the carrier U.S.S. *Enterprise* outside. No question, Air and Space is worth a long visit.

The two newest galleries are Looking at Earth, a survey of aerial photography from the age of balloons to satellite imagery, and Space Science Satellites, a European show that embodies the new international bent intended by the museum's new director, Martin Harwit. Mr. Harwit plans exhibits that examine current issues in space and flight, as well as an examination of past accomplishments.

The museum also houses the Langley Theater, which projects films onto a five-story-high screen with exhilarating results. Five wonderful films are shown: *To Fly, Living Planet, Flyers, On the Wing* and *The Dream Is Alive.* Films and the planetarium cost the same—$2 for adults and $1 for children, students and seniors. The Albert Einstein Planetarium is on the museum's second floor. Find out the schedule for these movies and shows when you enter the museum; it's smart to buy your tickets early to be sure you can get into a show when you'd like.

The Air and Space Museum gift shop (357-1387) sells a large variety of items, including kites, model airplanes, posters, T-shirts and books. The museum also has a large library and research facility for historical aerospace work, open 10 A.M. to 4 P.M. weekdays. Call 357-3133 for information on its use.

Suitland, Maryland, about a half-hour's drive away, is the site of the museum's restoration and repair facility. You can reserve a space on the daily tour by calling 357-1300.

NATIONAL ARCHIVES AND   **523-3000**
RECORDS SERVICE   **(Recorded information)**
Constitution Avenue at 8th Street, NW 20480
  (visitors)
8th Street and Pennsylvania Avenue, NW 20480
  (research and special tours)

Hours: Exhibition Hall: April 1–Labor Day—10 A.M.–9 P.M. daily
September–March—10 A.M.–5:30 P.M. daily
Closed Christmas
Research Room: 8:45 A.M.–10 P.M. weekdays
9 A.M.–5 P.M. Saturdays
Closed holidays
Free Admission

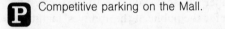 Federal Triangle stop (red line); walk east on Constitution Avenue.

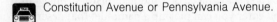 30, 32, 34, 36, 54, 60, 70, A6; Tourmobile.

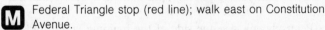 Constitution Avenue or Pennsylvania Avenue.

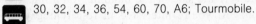 Competitive parking on the Mall.

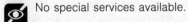 Snack bar on premises. Convenient to cafeterias on the Mall.

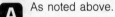 Recommended. School tours and workshops can be arranged by calling 523-3183 or writing the Tour Office, National Archives, NEE, Room G-9, Washington, D.C. 20480.

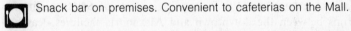 A 90-minute Behind the Scenes tour through the working areas of the archives can be arranged by writing or calling 523-3216.

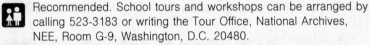 Fully accessible. Use the special entrance on Pennsylvania Avenue.
No special services available.

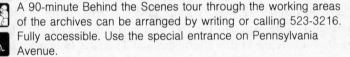 With advance notice, the staff will try to arrange for a signer to accompany the Behind the Scenes tour.
As noted above.

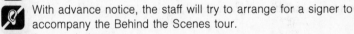 A short tour of the Exhibition Hall is given daily at 12:15 P.M.

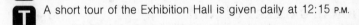

The National Archives are responsible for preserving, and making available for reference, all those records of the United States government that are considered permanently valuable. Within the building are 21 floors of storerooms, library stacks and offices, most of which are never open to the public. The files are available to researchers, however, and contain such historic items as all the treaties the government has signed with American Indian tribes over the years, every law enacted by Congress since the nation began and Gerald Ford's pardon of Richard Nixon.

The Archives' Exhibition Hall, on the Constitution Avenue side of the building, has a permanent display of the Declaration of Independence, the Constitution and the Bill of Rights. Great efforts have been made to preserve these documents; at night or in emergencies their helium-filled cases are automatically lowered into a vault. A gallery behind the Exhibition Hall has changing exhibits from the archives' massive collection, including photographs and other nonwritten materials.

On the Pennsylvania Avenue side of the building you'll find the archives' research rooms. If you're interested in researching your family background or a specific piece of American history, this is the place to go. When you enter you can pick up a pamphlet that describes available records; a staff member will show you how to use them. The Watergate tapes are available for the public at the archives' facility in Alexandria, located at 841 S. Pickett Street (703-756-6498). A shuttle bus runs between the downtown and Alexandria facilities, leaving from the 7th Street side of the building five times daily, starting at 8:30 A.M.

The archives has a gift shop that sells reproductions of the documents on display as well as some posters, cards, mugs, T-shirts, sweatshirts, tote bags and the like. In the spring and fall, free films are shown here on Friday afternoons and Thursday evenings; check to see what's on at 523-3000, or get a copy of the archives' calendar of events in the gift shop. In recent years the archives has developed an extensive public program series, so it pays to check.

NATIONAL GALLERY OF ART   737-4215
Constitution Avenue, between 4th and 6th Streets, NW 20565
Hours: Summer—10 A.M.–5 P.M. Monday to Saturday
　　　　　Winter—10 A.M.–5:30 P.M. Monday to Saturday
　　　　　Noon–9 P.M. on Sundays
　　　　　Closed Christmas and New Year's
Free Admission

Federal Center SW or Federal Triangle stops (blue and orange lines); Judiciary Square stop (red line); use 4th Street exit.
A2, A4, 13D, 30, 32, 34, 36, 60, 62, 70; Tourmobile.

Constitution Avenue, or east wing entrance where cabs often park to pick up fares.

 Competitive parking on the Mall.

 On premises. A cafeteria (10 A.M. to 3:30 P.M. Monday to Saturday, noon to 6 P.M. Sunday) and the Cascade Café (11 A.M. to 2:30 P.M. for lunch; 2:30 to 4 P.M. for tea and ice cream) are on the concourse level, where the food is tasty and reasonably priced. Through a glass wall you can watch a waterfall cascade down from the Mall. This is one of the best eating bets in town. The Terrace Café (11 A.M. to 4:30 P.M. Monday to Saturday, noon to 6 P.M. Sunday in summer) on the second floor of the east wing has more expensive meals, but a lovely view of the Mall; it's the perfect place for coffee and a pastry. A café in the garden court of the west wing serves light fare from 11 A.M. to 4:30 P.M.

 East wing recommended. This would be a good museum in which to introduce a child to artworks. It's an interesting space, complete with escalators, people to watch and good food. Many of the exhibits are small enough to be managed by a child. One permanent exhibit of metal sculpture is particularly appealing. Strollers are available at the main entrance. West Building not recommended for young children unless they have a particular interest in art, but fine for ages 10 and up.

 Tours for both the permanent collection and some (not all) special exhibits are available for 15 or more. Arrangements can be made for special tours by contacting the education office at least two weeks in advance by calling 737-4215 and asking for the office of Special Tour Arrangements.

 Fully accessible. Wheelchairs are available at the entrance. Use Constitution Avenue entrance to West Building.

 Special tours of sculpture can be arranged by writing or calling the tour office at 842-6246, at least two weeks in advance.

 Call 842-6246 to arrange for special tours. You must bring your own interpreter; the gallery does not have any on call.

 For foreign-language tours, contact the education department at 842-6246, at least two weeks in advance. Regularly scheduled foreign-language tours in French, Spanish, and German are offered Tuesdays at noon in the rotunda in the West Building. Check to see which language will be offered.

 A one-hour introductory tour to the National Gallery is given at 11 A.M. and at 3 P.M. Monday to Saturday, and at 1 and 5 P.M. on Sunday. During the winter a 50-minute Tour of the Week, focusing on a specific style of painting on exhibition, is offered at 1 P.M. Tuesday to Saturday, and at 2:30 P.M. on Sunday. The Gallery also offers a tour at 11 A.M. Monday to Friday of either a special exhibit or a period of art history. Check the calendar of events at the information desk. A 15-minute Collection Highlight talk is given at noon and 2 P.M. Monday to Saturday, and at 2 P.M. on Sunday. Check at the information desk to find out what the weekly specials are; you can also rent a recorded tour of the gallery at this location.

East Building

The soaring east wing of the National Gallery of Art, opened in 1978, is a work of art in its own right. Designed by I. M. Pei and Partners, the two triangular buildings make spectacular use of the trapezoidal plot of land on which the gallery sits. The quarry from which the marble was taken in the 1930s for the original National Gallery (West Building) was reopened to supply the same stone for this new East Building. The smaller triangle contains gallery offices and the Center for Advanced Study in the Visual Arts; the larger building encompasses the galleries where works of the old masters and the twentieth century are displayed.

As its designer had hoped, this museum is "a place to be." Many of the craftspeople who worked on the building received awards for their fine contributions. While every detail was tended to, the building is not prissy—it's inviting and exciting, offering bold internal vistas and intimate galleries.

Many works of art were commissioned especially for the east wing. A Henry Moore sculpture greets you at the entrance; just inside you encounter two enormous pieces—a tapestry by Joan Miró and a mobile by Alexander Calder. Sculptures by Noguchi, Caro, Rosati and Smith can be found throughout the building.

The museum shop sells reproductions, postcards and books; postcards and catalogs are also available on the mezzanine. Special exhibits often have special shops. Recorded tours are often available for special exhibits.

Weekends—particularly Sundays—lure large crowds to the East Building, so try to plan your visit during the week.

West Building

The West Building of the National Gallery of Art, one of the world's finest art museums, is a wonderful place to visit. The art is excellent, the guards are friendly and informative, two lovely garden courts offer respite among beautiful plants and superior free literature on the gallery and its exhibits abounds.

The West Building was constructed with funds provided by Andrew Mellon, a philanthropist who served as secretary of the treasury under Presidents Harding, Coolidge and Hoover. Mellon's personal collection of art from the thirteenth to the nineteenth century forms the nucleus of the West Gallery's present distinguished collection.

Andrew Mellon's original bequest has been augmented by gifts from other benefactors. The Chester Dale collection of nineteenth- and twentieth-century French painting that includes works by all the major Impressionist painters—Degas, Renoir and Monet among others—is one of the most popular sections of the gallery. The museum has one of the best collections of Italian art outside of Europe, including works by Leonardo da Vinci, Raphael, Titian and Bernini, to name just a few of the most famous. There are also galleries of Flemish, German, Dutch, Spanish and British art, as well as an extensive collection of American art. Major special exhibitions are an important part of the gallery's program these days. In 1989 and 1990, these will include "Treasures from the Museum, Cambridge," "History of Photography," "Matisse in Morocco," and an exhibit of ancient Egyptian art of the pharaohs.

The National Gallery has three major collections that are rarely shown publicly but are accessible by making an appointment. The Prints and Drawings assemblage has about 5,000 pieces dating from the fifteenth century to the present. Watercolors and photographs depicting objects of popular American art dating from the seventeenth century to 1900 form the Index of American Design collection. The third rarely shown collection is Decorative Arts, an extensive group of European furniture, tapestries, ceramics, jewelry and church vessels, as well as Chinese porcelains.

The building was designed by John Russell Pope, who also planned the Jefferson Memorial; it opened to the public in 1941. A massive marble structure, the museum has an interior that is both rich and majestic. Somehow, though the spaces are quite grand, the gallery manages to have a very comfortable quality.

On Sundays in the spring, art history lectures are given at 4 P.M. in the auditorium by visiting experts or by staff members. On Sunday evenings at 7 P.M. (except from late June to September) free classical music concerts are given in the gallery's East Garden Court; seats to the popular concerts become available at 6 P.M. Both of these ongoing events are open to the public on a first-come, first-served basis. A monthly calendar of events can be picked up at the information desk, which details the special events at the gallery.

The gallery has several large publications sales areas—one on the concourse level of the East Building and one on the ground floor of the West Building. Postcards, variously priced reproductions, catalogs of the collections, slides, recordings and more are available.

NATIONAL MUSEUM OF AFRICAN ART   **357-4000**
950 Independence Avenue, SW 20560
Hours: 10 A.M.–5:30 P.M. daily
          Closed Christmas
Free Admission

M Smithsonian stop (blue and orange lines); use Mall exit.

🚌 13's, 30, 32, 34, 36, 50, 52, V4, V6; Tourmobile.

🚗 Independence Avenue or Jefferson Drive.

P Competitive parking on the Mall and Independence Avenue.

🍽 None on premises. Cafeterias are in nearby Smithsonian museums; street vendors on Independence Avenue.

👫 Recommended. Special tours can be arranged. Call 357-4860, ask for tour scheduler, at least one month in advance.

👨‍👩‍👧 Group tours can be arranged. Call 357-4860, or write, at least one month in advance.

♿ Fully accessible.

👁 Special programs under development. Call Education Office (357-4860) for information.

👂 Special programs under development. Call Education Office (357-4860) for information.

A As above.

T Regular guided tours are offered. Monday to Friday 10:30 A.M. and 1 P.M., Saturday and Sunday 11 A.M., 1 P.M. and 3 P.M.

Founded in 1964 as a private educational institution, the museum became part of the Smithsonian Institution in 1979. Until its move to the Mall late in 1986, it occupied the house of Frederick Douglass (316-318 A Street, NE), the famous abolitionist and writer, and former slave.

In its sumptuous new quarters beneath the Mall, the museum displays many more of its 6,000-object collection of African art, one of the finest collections in the world. In addition, it will host a number of international exhibitions.

Exhibits planned for 1989 and 1990 include "Gold of Africa," "Sounding Forms: African Musical Instruments," and "Archetypes: Five Themes in the Visual Arts of Africa."

In addition to exhibition facilities, the new museum is equipped with public education rooms for classes, workshops and presentations; offices for visiting scholars; an art research library; an art conservation laboratory; and a photographic archive, The Eliot Elisofon Archive, with more than 150,000 color slides, 70,000 black-and-white photographs and 50 feature films. The library and archive are open to interested students and scholars by appointment.

The museum shop stocks museum-quality reproductions of African jewelry, sculpture, textiles and games for adults and children, art reproductions and books of interest to the general public and scholars.

NATIONAL MUSEUM OF AMERICAN HISTORY   357-2700
Constitution Avenue at 13th Street, NW 20565
Hours: 10 A.M.–5:30 P.M. daily
        Closed Christmas
Free Admission

 Federal Triangle stop (blue and orange lines).

 13's, 30, 32, 34, 36, 52, 54; Tourmobile.

 Constitution Avenue.

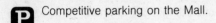

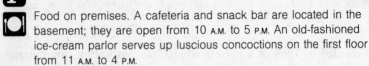

P Competitive parking on the Mall.

|O| Food on premises. A cafeteria and snack bar are located in the basement; they are open from 10 A.M. to 5 P.M. An old-fashioned ice-cream parlor serves up luscious concoctions on the first floor from 11 A.M. to 4 P.M.

👥 Recommended. During school months, Discovery Corners invite participation in the Spirit of '76 and Electricity. Children can handle the clothes and equipment of a Revolutionary War soldier, experiment with electrical paraphernalia and examine prosthetics and other aids for handicapped people. Discovery Corners are open daily except Monday from 11:30 A.M. to 3 P.M.

👪 To arrange a group tour, call 357-1481. School tours must obtain and fill out a form.

♿ Fully accessible.

👁 Tours for the blind and vision-impaired can be arranged in advance by calling 357-1481. A large-print edition of the museum brochure with floor plans is available at the information desks.

🤟 Tours are conducted in sign language on Sundays at 11 A.M. Other tours can be arranged in advance by calling TDD 357-1729. Auditorium is equipped with loop-amplification system.

A As mentioned above.

T A variety of walk-in tours are given from October to May; call 357-2700 to find out tour schedules, which are determined anew each year.

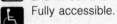

The original Star-Spangled Banner that inspired Francis Scott Key to pen our national anthem, the very desk on which Jefferson wrote the Declaration of Independence, Alexander Graham Bell's telephone, Eli Whitney's cotton gin, the gowns of the First Ladies of our nation—these and other less stirring but essential items of our heritage are displayed in the National Museum of American History. Formerly the National Museum of History and Technology, this is a true repository of the American people and their accomplishments in science, technology, politics, home life, armed forces and communications.

The ground floor houses machinery from railroad locomotives to atom smashers, computers to tunnel-digging machinery. The exhibits on the second floor focus on the people of our nation, our lives in our homes, our communities and the world beyond. One of the most popular displays is of gowns worn by the First Ladies, from Martha Washington to Nancy Reagan.

The third-floor exhibits run the gamut from musical instruments to instruments of war. Printing, photography and news reporting are all examined here. In addition, pieces of one of the world's most extensive collections of ceramics and glass are on display.

The museum offers a variety of tours starting from both the Mall and Constitution Avenue entrances. Highlights is offered Monday to Saturday, 10 and 11 A.M. and 1 P.M.; Sunday at 11 A.M. and 1 P.M. The First Ladies Gowns Tour is given Monday to Saturday at 10:30 and 11:30 A.M. and 1:30 P.M.; Sunday at 11:30 A.M. and 1:30 P.M. Needlework is offered Tuesdays and Thursdays at 1:30 P.M. (Mall entrance only). A special quilt tour (limit of 10 people per tour) is given by appointment, Tuesdays at 11 A.M. Every person who wishes to go on the tour must call 357-1889 at least two weeks in advance; a single call does not suffice for a group. Demonstrations are given in the 1776 Gallery, Monday, Wednesday and Friday from noon to 3 P.M.; in the Electricity Gallery, Tuesday to Friday noon to 3 P.M.; and in the Pain Gallery (first-floor Medical Gallery), Monday to Friday noon to 3 P.M.

The Dibner Library of the History of Science and Technology and other facilities are available for research; call 357-2414 to make arrangements.

The museum has a gift shop (357-1527), with postcards, slides and memorabilia, but it also operates a transplanted nineteenth-century country store and post office that can postmark your letters with a unique Smithsonian seal. The Smithsonian Bookstore (357-1784) is in this museum, offering an extensive range of books on American history and other subjects.

NATIONAL MUSEUM OF NATURAL HISTORY　　357-2700
Constitution Avenue at 10th Street, NW 20565
Hours: Summer—extended hours determined annually; usually
　　　10 A.M.–9 P.M. daily
　　　Winter—10 A.M.–5:30 P.M. daily
　　　Closed Christmas
Free Admission

M Federal Triangle stop (blue and orange lines).

🚌 13's, 30, 32, 34, 36, 52, 54; Tourmobile.

🚗 Constitution Avenue.

P Competitive parking on the Mall.

🍽 On premises. Cafeteria open 10:30 A.M. to 5:30 P.M.

👫 Highly recommended. School groups can arrange for lesson tours and access to the Discovery Room from late September to mid-May by calling 357-2747 or writing at least one month in advance to: Scheduler, Office of Education, Room 212, Stop 158, National Museum of Natural History, Washington, D.C. 20560.

👥 Adult group tours can be arranged in most cases for permanent and temporary exhibits. Call 357-1756 one month ahead.

♿ Fully accessible. Use Constitution Avenue entrance.

👁 Call 357-1756 to arrange special tour. The "By-word" desk in the rotunda has "touch and feel" guides and audio wands for self-guided tours (adults $2, children $1). The Discovery Room and Naturalist Center have Braille labels.

👂 Special tours can be arranged. Call two weeks in advance, 357-1756, TDD 357-1729.

A As above.

T Tours of the museum's highlights are given daily at 10:30 A.M. and 1:30 P.M. from mid-September to June. Audio wands for self-guided tours are available in English, French, Spanish, German and Japanese.

The Museum of Natural History is a wonderfully complex institution; the building is also the home of the National Museum of Man, so exhibits are as diverse as a Neanderthal burial ceremony and a working beehive. The preindustrial life of many cultures is shown through objects and dioramas. Follow the colorful banners from the rotunda to Fossils, Mammals, Birds, Bones, Geology of the Earth, and you discover fantastic worlds. The staff and volunteers here are extremely helpful. Stop by the information desk in the rotunda if you have questions or need help.

The ground floor, accessed from Constitution Avenue or the elevator or escalator from the rotunda, is usually devoted to special exhibits. Always interesting, and sometimes spectacular, the special exhibits are worth seeing.

On the first floor, from the rotunda you can head toward the paleontology exhibit, Fossils: The History of Life, which includes recently remodeled and expanded exhibits of early life, dinosaurs and the chain of life forms spanning millions of years. The newest exhibit is The Earliest Traces of Life, which features a film on the origin of the first living cells, the oldest fossil evidence of life and a spectacular mural of a 3.5-billion-year-old shoreline.

Opposite the dinosaurs is the Life in the Sea exhibit, which contains a living coral reef and many inhabitants. A 92-foot model of a blue whale dominates the exhibit hall. At the far end, you can see a short film on pinnipeds—seals and walruses. Beyond the marine exhibits are thousands of specimens of birds, sea life, reptiles, amphibians and mammals.

The first floor houses one of our favorite rooms, Splendors of Nature, displaying some of the most beautiful and fantastic of nature's creations: shells, butterflies, minerals, insects, feathers and objects man has wrought from these naturally occurring phenomena. On this floor will also be found exhibits of African, Asian, Pacific, Eskimo and Indian cultures, as well as a dramatic room on the dynamics of evolution.

The second floor houses the minerals and gems, the most famous of which is the Hope Diamond, once owned by Mrs. Evalyn Walsh McLean, a Washington socialite. Don't be too dazzled by the Hope; there are many more beautiful and fabulous gems in the collection. Other exhibits on this floor include Earth, Moon and Meteorites, Prehistoric North American Cultures, South America: Continent and Culture, Human Origin and Variation, Western Civilization: Origins and Traditions, Bones, and Reptiles.

Two rooms of special note: the Discovery Room and the Insect Zoo. The Discovery Room (first floor) is designed for children of all ages. It is stocked with a wealth of items, such as elephant tusks, arrowheads, petrified wood and coral, all of which are available for hands-on study. It also has a dress-up corner where kids can try on costumes from all over the world. The Discovery Room is open from noon to 2:30 P.M. Monday to Thursday, and 10:30 A.M. to 3:30 P.M. Friday to Sunday. Weekends, holidays and other busy days, free tickets must be picked up at the information desk in the rotunda so that the room does not become overcrowded. Check first.

The Insect Zoo (second floor) is another treat for everyone, but especially kids. It combines traditional exhibits of live insects, dioramas of prehistoric insects, a working beehive and talks and demonstrations by museum staff. When you arrive, the Zoo's giant cockroaches might be out for discussion and handling, or the tarantula might be getting his monthly meal.

Finally, we want to mention the Naturalist Center. Each department of the museum has contributed some part of its collection to be used by the serious amateur naturalist or collector. Six major areas are represented: rocks and minerals, invertebrate zoology, insects, plants, vertebrate zoology and anthropology. You may bring in specimens in any of these areas for identification. The center is open to adults and children 12 and over, Monday to Saturday, 10:30 A.M. to 4 P.M., and Sunday, noon to 5 P.M.. You must call 357-2804 or 257-1503, or write ahead, for admission. Groups are limited to six. A library, audio-visual room and laboratory are part of the Center.

The museum's gift shops are excellent. The main shop (357-1535) is on the first floor, by the cafeteria. Books, projects, toys, minerals and gems as well as many other items are available. A small annex has opened on the third floor. Fridays at noon, the museum offers a one-hour film/lecture series in Baird Auditorium (loop-amplification system for hearing-impaired). Check at the information desk for seasonal schedule.

ARTHUR M. SACKLER GALLERY   357-2700
1050 Independence Avenue, SW 20560
Hours: 10 A.M.–5:30 P.M. daily
            Closed Christmas
Free Admission

 Smithsonian stop (blue and orange lines); use Mall exit.

 9, 13's, 30, 32, 34, 36, 50, 52, V4, V6; Tourmobile.

Independence Avenue or Jefferson Drive.

 Competitive parking on the Mall and Independence Avenue.

 None on premises. Cafeterias are in nearby museums on the Mall, and street vendors gather on Independence Avenue.

 Not recommended for young children. Call or write two weeks in advance to arrange tours for grades 5 and up.

 Write or call 357-4886 at least two weeks in advance to arrange for a group tour.

 Fully accessible.

 Tours can be arranged by calling 357-1696 at least 48 hours in advance.

 Tours can be arranged by calling 357-1696 or TDD 357-1729 at least 48 hours in advance.

 As noted above.

 Guided tours are held Monday to Saturday at 10:30 A.M. and 1:30 P.M., Sunday at 1:30 P.M.

The Sackler Gallery is a new Smithsonian museum specializing in the arts of Asia—a stunning addition to the museum scene. The gallery consists of an aboveground entrance pavilion and two floors belowground for exhibitions, offices and support activities.

Dr. Arthur M. Sackler, a New York research psychiatrist and medical publisher, pledged nearly 1,000 masterworks of Asian and Near Eastern art and donated $4 million toward museum construction; he began collecting art as a medical student and became intrigued by the ancient cultures of Asia. The Sackler Collection includes many important twentieth-century Chinese paintings, representing a major new area for Smithsonian scholarship and exhibitions. It also includes many Chinese bronzes, jades and paintings, as well as excellent examples of Chinese lacquerware and metalwork. Some 475 Chinese jades span the millennia from 3000 B.C. into the twentieth century.

Programs include loan exhibitions and major international shows and will often be enhanced by public programs and scholarly presentations.

Research is the fundamental focus of the Sackler Gallery, and plans are underway for programs involving fellowship awards and

scholarly publications. The new research library, serving both the
Sackler and Freer Galleries, is housed here. A museum shop offers
reproductions and gifts related to the collection.

SMITHSONIAN INSTITUTION BUILDING   357-2700
(The Castle)
1000 Jefferson Drive, SW 20560
Hours: 10 A.M.–5:30 P.M. daily
        Closed Christmas
Free Admission

Smithsonian stop (orange and blue lines); use Mall exit.

13's, 30, 32, 34, 36 (get off at Independence Avenue), 52, 60,
70; Tourmobile.

Independence Avenue or Jefferson Drive.

Competitive parking on the Mall.

None on premises. The museum is convenient to cafeterias in
other Smithsonian buildings or restaurants in L'Enfant Plaza.

Not recommended. If your visit is brief enough, however, kids
should be fine.

No tours available.

Limited access. Bathroom, phone and water fountain accessible.
Electric lift at entrance requires some guard assistance.

No special services available. Mary Livingstone Ripley Garden
outside allows hands-on enjoyment of textures, scents, and
sounds.

A captioned, multilingual slide show is shown continuously to
explain the Smithsonian's many offerings. Visitor information TDD
is 357-1729.

None necessary.

No tours are given.

The Smithsonian Institution Building, more commonly known as the
Castle, is worth a quick look if only because it is the Smithsonian's
original building. Designed by architect James Renwick, the Castle

opened to the public in 1855. Today, this whimsical structure houses the administrative offices of the Smithsonian as well as a visitor information center. The information center offers a slide show (in four languages) of the Smithsonian's highlights. The Castle also harbors the crypt of the Smithsonian's English benefactor, James Smithson. In his will, Smithson provided for the establishment of an institution bearing his name "for the increase and diffusion of knowledge among men" in the United States, a country he had never even visited. Though Smithson's money arrived in 1838, Congress did not agree to accept it until eight years later when they finally set Renwick to work designing this building.

TIDAL BASIN
West Potomac Park in front of the Jefferson Memorial
Free Admission

 Smithsonian stop (orange and blue lines); use Independence Avenue exit. It's a quarter-mile walk.

 13's, 50, V4, V6; Tourmobile.

 Independence Avenue or 14th Street.

 A small parking lot at the paddle-boat concession, the lot at the Jefferson Memorial and competitive parking in West Potomac Park.

 Paddle-boat concession sells hot dogs, burgers, etc. You might like to take a picnic to eat on the edge of the Tidal Basin.

 Recommended. Children under 16 cannot go on paddle boats without adults.

 No special services available.

 Walkway around basin is wheelchair-accessible.

 No special services available.

 No special services available.

 None necessary.

 No tours are given.

When the Jefferson Memorial was built, its site was reclaimed from the Potomac River; what remains of the river's presence is the Tidal Basin. Connected by a small channel, the river and basin are, indeed, tidal in nature.

The Tidal Basin is a lovely place; on hot days, the trees can offer shade, and the paddle boats provide a leisurely way to catch the water's breezes. On the basin's southern shore is the Jefferson Memorial (see site report). The western edge is bordered by over 600 Yoshino and Akebono cherry trees, a gift from Japan in 1912. The U.S. was able to return the favor by sending cuttings back to Japan after its native trees in Tokyo had suffered irreparable damage from pollution. A Cherry Blossom Festival is held annually around bloom time, which lasts for one week anytime from mid-March to mid-April. The festival, which is scheduled each year to try to coordinate with the trees, includes a parade and other festivities. When in full bloom, the trees are breathtaking—but so is the bumper-to-bumper traffic. Walk around the basin, or avoid the crush by driving out to Kenwood, Maryland, northwest of the District line, for a less crowded yet dazzling display of cherry trees decked out in their best blossoms (see the "Outdoor Washington/Sports" chapter).

West Potomac Park, replete with playing fields, stands just west of the basin. Polo is played at 3 P.M. on Sunday afternoons from April to November; permanent seats border the field for spectators, and there's ample space for picnics.

To the east of the Tidal Basin are the "floral libraries" of tulips and annual flowers. These small planted areas add a gay spot to the area in spring, summer and fall. A paddle-boat concession is also on the east side of the Tidal Basin, renting boats from 11 A.M. to 6 P.M. daily. The concession is generally open from April to October, closing earlier than 6 P.M. in spring and fall. Call 484-0845 to check the hours while you're in town. The boat rental charge is $5.50 per hour; you must leave an ID with the concessionaire when you rent a boat.

━━━━━━━━━━━━━━━

U.S. HOLOCAUST MEMORIAL MUSEUM
(Scheduled to open 1991)
Constitution Avenue between 14th and 15th Streets, NW

Mailing Address: U.S. Holocaust Memorial Council
2000 L Street, NW, Suite 588, 20036
Free Admission

In 1980, Congress established the U.S. Holocaust Memorial Council and made a commitment to establish an official remembrance of one of the darkest chapters in modern history—the Holocaust. (The museum is scheduled to open in late 1991. The cornerstone-laying ceremony was held October 5, 1988, with President Reagan and many other public officials in attendance.)

The museum will tell the story of the Holocaust in all its dimensions and will memorialize the six million Jews, including more than one million Jewish children, who were systematically annihilated. It will also memorialize the millions of others who suffered torment and death throughout the countries occupied by Germany during World War II.

The museum will integrate the crucial roles of remembrance, teaching and documenting both history and human response. It will support academic research, curriculum development and teacher training.

VIETNAM VETERANS MEMORIAL   426-6841

21st Street and Constitution Avenue, NW (south side)
Mailing Address: National Park Service, Mall Operations,
900 Ohio Drive, SW 20242
Hours: Always open; park ranger available from 8 A.M. to midnight, except Christmas
Free Admission

 Foggy Bottom stop (orange and blue lines); walk seven blocks down 23rd Street.

 13's, 80, 81, A2, A4; Tourmobile.

 Constitution Avenue or Independence Avenue.

 Competitive parking in West Potomac Park; follow signs for Ohio Drive.

None on premises. Snacks are available at a nearby kiosk. Since the museum cafeterias are at the other end of the Mall, we suggest you take a picnic if you intend to eat around the time you plan to see this memorial.

Recommended; a visit to the memorial is a good way to inform children about the war.

National Park Service staff will gladly talk with visitors on an impromptu basis.

Accessible. Special parking off Constitution Avenue at 21st and 22nd Streets. Accessible restroom at Constitution Gardens (1,000 feet away).

Visitors can feel the names inscribed in the granite; a park ranger or volunteer will help locate a particular name (arranged by date of casualty).

No special services.

Visitors may want to bring mementos and tokens of remembrance to leave at the memorial; rubbings may be made of the names of loved ones. Veterans' groups wishing to hold a wreath-laying ceremony should call ahead for a permit. Write or call several days in advance to arrange for a special tour of the Vietnam Veterans Memorial and the Lincoln Memorial.

Staff will talk with visitors upon request. An informative brochure is available. When trying to locate a name on the wall, visitors should consult the alphabetical directories at either end of the memorial, or ask the staff for assistance.

The Vietnam Veterans Memorial is a tribute to the more than 58,000 men and women who died in service related to the Vietnam War and to those who fought and survived. It is a conscious attempt to separate the question of political and military policies that governed the conduct of that war from the men and women who served.

Authorized by act of Congress in 1980, the memorial is the design of Maya Lin, winner of a national design competition. Ms. Lin was, at that time, a 21-year-old architecture student at Yale University. The memorial was dedicated November 13, 1982, as the capstone of a weekend of events memorializing the survivors—as well as the dead—of the Vietnam War. The memorial serves as an act of national reconciliation in relation to the most controversial war America has fought.

It is no surprise, then, that the memorial design was, itself, controversial. Many observers saw Ms. Lin's design as a negative political statement. Two polished black granite walls, V-shaped, inscribed with the names of the dead, half-buried in the ground, reflect the faces of the viewers. Clearly, Ms. Lin had not created a traditional, soaring, white marble tribute of the kind we expect to see. The memorial is, on the contrary, an intensely personal and powerful experience in which each visitor is confronted with the names of the scores of thousands of victims of the war. Few come away unaffected.

Despite the controversy, the memorial was built as designed, with the later addition of Frederick Hart's heroic sculpture of three soldiers, which is set up and away from the memorial. The sculpture and memorial complement each other. All funds for the memorial were raised through private contributions.

Many visitors come to the memorial with the express desire of finding the name of a friend or relative and leaving a token of remembrance. Mementos are not thrown away; the National Park Service saves all of them. Names are inscribed in chronological order by the date of casualty, and alphabetically within date order. Next to each name is a diamond (confirmed death) or plus sign (unconfirmed, missing or unaccounted for). Visitors are permitted to make rubbings of names. See the park rangers for assistance.

VOICE OF AMERICA   485-6231
330 Independence Avenue, SW 20547
Hours: 8:30 A.M.–5:30 P.M. weekdays
          Closed legal holidays
Free Admission

M Federal Center SW stop (blue and orange lines).

🚌 30, 32, 34, 36, A4 (except when marked "Union Station").

🚗 Independence Avenue.

P Commercial parking lot at 4th and D Streets, SW; competitive parking on the Mall.

🍽 On premises. Cafeteria is in the basement.

👫 Not recommended for younger children.

The maximum tour size permitted is 25 people; call 485-6231 to let them know you're coming.

Fully accessible; bathroom and phones accessible.

Tours are given with advance notice.

Tours given to groups with advance notice if they bring their own signer.

As mentioned above.

A 35-minute tour of the Voice of America's extensive broadcasting operation is given on weekdays at 8:40, 9:40 and 10:40 A.M., and at 1:40 and 2:40 P.M. This tour, which is geared to adults, may prove boring to children. You can watch staffers at work in the newsrooms and listen to an actual broadcast on a shortwave radio as you observe its transmission.

The Voice of America is the radio network of the International Communication Agency (formerly the United States Information Agency); its job is to give the rest of the world a positive view of the United States. Radio shows, broadcast in 39 languages, are beamed to nations all over the globe.

WASHINGTON MONUMENT   **426-6839**
Constitution Avenue at 16th Street, NW
Mailing Address: National Park Service, Mall Operations,
                   900 Ohio Drive, SW 20242
Hours: April–Labor Day—8 A.M.–midnight daily (check first)
          September–March—9 A.M.–5 P.M. daily
Free Admission

Smithsonian stop (orange and blue lines).

13's, 50, 52; Tourmobile.

Constitution Avenue or 15th Street, NW.

Parking lot at 16th Street and Constitution Avenue; parking on the Mall. Both are likely to be very crowded during daylight hours.

None on premises. A kiosk near 15th Street sells snacks; street vendors across from the monument are on either side of the Ellipse.

 Recommended. Kids will enjoy the elevator ride and the view. There's lots of running room on the grounds.

 Groups of 20 can arrange to take a "step tour" by calling 426-6841 (see Tours below).

 Fully accessible. Accessible bathroom and phones at the bottom of the hill.

 Call 426-6841 in advance to make arrangements for a tour designed for those who are visually impaired.

 Call 426-6841 in advance to make arrangements for a tour in sign language.

 Stair tours are dependent on staff availability. Call 426-6841.

 For those of you who really can't bear the idea of not walking the stairs, the National Park Service conducts walking-down "step tours" for 20 people at a time weekends at 10 A.M. and 2 P.M. On this tour you'll get to see the 188 carved memorial stones that were given in the nineteenth century by private citizens, societies, states and nations. If you'd like to go on this walk be sure to be at the base of the monument at least 15 minutes before the tour begins; let the park ranger know then that you're interested in the walking tour. A free, informative pamphlet is available at the monument. Call 426-6841.

Pierre L'Enfant's idea of an equestrian statue to honor George Washington was long forgotten in 1847 when architect Robert Mills drew up his plans for an elaborate pseudo-Greek temple to serve as the Washington Monument. During the course of construction, Mills' design was honed down to the austere marble and granite obelisk we have today. The cornerstone of the monument to our first President was laid in 1848, but quarrels over construction and lack of private funds to support the project slowed work down; the Civil War finally halted it completely. When building resumed in 1880 with government funds and the War Department's Corps of Engineers in charge, the new marble came from a different part of the same Maryland quarry—you can see the color change about one fourth of the way up the monument's side.

The Washington Monument stands 555 feet 5⅛ inches high and

looms far above the rest of the city (since 1899, there has been a 90-foot limit on the height of buildings in Washington). When the monument opened in 1888, a steam-driven elevator took 10 minutes to reach the top. Because the contraption was not considered entirely safe, only men were allowed to ride; women and children had to walk so their lives would not be endangered.

Generations of Americans have prided themselves on their ability to climb the 897 steps to the top of the Washington Monument. Unfortunately, in recent years the National Park Service has had to close general access to the stairs because the trip proved too strenuous for many who attempted it, and because some of the memorial stones that line the stairs had been vandalized over the years and needed to be restored. (A special walking-down tour is offered for small groups—see the key.) Today you can ride the elevator to the top and take a look at the city spread out below. The view is especially lovely on summer nights. On summer days and holidays, the wait for the elevator is from 40 to 50 minutes.

Each year on the Fourth of July, Washington's big fireworks display is launched from the monument grounds. From time to time the grounds are used for various other events, such as kite-flying contests, concerts and boomerang exhibitions. One snowy winter the monument was even turned into a giant sundial by plowing the grounds around it to mark the hours. The service bands perform at the Sylvan Theater at 8 P.M. in season: Sunday, Marine Corps; Tuesday, Army; Thursday, Navy; Friday, Air Force. The Army Old Guard performs a Twilight Tattoo on Wednesdays at 7 P.M. on the Ellipse in the summer. Check the newspaper to see if anything is planned during your visit.

5

CAPITOL HILL

Capitol Hill houses the Congress, the Supreme Court, the massive Library of Congress, Union Station—and one of Washington's most charming residential and commercial neighborhoods. "The Hill" is unique in its contrasts: delicate town houses cozy up to enormous marble government buildings; rows of luxuriously renovated homes neighbor ghettos which have been crumbling for half a century; historic buildings stand next to modern edifices. These contrasts, and the presence of the Congress and the highest court, provide some of the most exciting scenes Washington has to offer.

This bustling community evolved slowly from L'Enfant's idea of locating the "Congress House" on Jenkins Hill. L'Enfant faced the Capitol east, since he expected the new capital city to grow first in that direction, around the deep, commercially promising Anacostia harbor. While he was wrong in his estimation of where the city would develop, the designer's use of the hill—"a pedestal awaiting a monument"—was exquisite. As you walk throughout the Capitol Hill neighborhood, and on the Mall, you're treated with new vistas of the Capitol with every turn.

When Congress opened in Washington in 1800, the Capitol was home to both houses of Congress, the Supreme Court and the Library of Congress; Capitol Hill consisted of eight boarding houses, a washerwoman, a shoemaker, a general store, an oyster house and tobacco farms. The neighborhood slept until after the Civil War, but the real boom didn't occur until the turn of the century. By 1935, the Library of Congress, Union Station, the Supreme Court and several thousand homes had taken their places near the Capitol.

The boom continues. Every year beginning in the 1960s several more blocks of renovated homes would claim to be part of "Capitol Hill" in order to reap status and escalated resale values for its houses.

Today the neighborhood is roughly defined as lying between H Street, NE, on the north, Robert F. Kennedy Memorial Stadium on the east, the Southwest Freeway on the south, and the Capitol on the west—but your sightseeing will take place in a much smaller area than this 1.5 mile square. Most of the government buildings and museums lie within several blocks of the Capitol. The only foray we suggest beyond these limits is a stroll along Pennsylvania Avenue, SE, to poke in the many fine restaurants, boutiques, bookstores and miscellaneous shops. Stop in at the Eastern Market and the adjacent shops on 7th Street, SE, or the antique shops on 8th Street, SE.

Some notes. Parking can be difficult on the Hill; it's a mixture of permit-only spaces, two-hour visitor spaces and limited meter parking. Crime is a problem on Capitol Hill, so restrict your nighttime travels to well-lighted Pennsylvania and Massachusetts Avenues (for restaurants and pubs) or as close as possible to the Folger Theater or Library of Congress if you're attending a concert or play (the Library of Congress allows parking in its lot for concertgoers). Finally, Capitol Hill street names can drive you mad. East Capitol Street divides the Northeast quadrant of the city from the southeast; C Street, NE, is six blocks from C Street, SE, so watch the quadrant indicators and proceed carefully.

Food choices abound on the Hill; check our recommendations at the end of this chapter.

CAPITAL CHILDREN'S MUSEUM   **638-5437 (tape)**
800 3rd Street, NE 20002   **543-8600**
Hours: 10 A.M.–5 P.M. daily
    Closed Easter, Thanksgiving, Christmas, and New Year's
Admission: $4; 60 years and over $1   Children—2 and under free

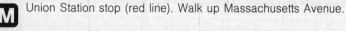 Union Station stop (red line). Walk up Massachusetts Avenue.

 D2, D4, D6, D8.

 3rd Street.

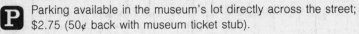

Parking available in the museum's lot directly across the street; $2.75 (50¢ back with museum ticket stub).

Snack vending machines. Picnic tables are available outside the museum; an eating room is provided indoors.

Highly recommended. Everything here is for kids; however, those under 16 must be accompanied by an adult.

Tours can be arranged in advance for groups of 10 or more by calling 675-4149 or by writing three weeks ahead.

Fully accessible.

No special services available, but since the museum is a "hands-on" place, those with impaired vision can still enjoy the facility.

While an interpreted tour can be arranged, staff feel that the tactile nature of the exhibits will allow those with hearing impairments to enjoy the museum fully without assistance.

As mentioned above.

Tours are given Monday to Friday at 10 and 11:30 A.M. and 1 P.M.

As its name would suggest, this is a wonderful place for kids although off the beaten path; the adults with them will find much of interest, too. All of the exhibits at the Children's Museum are made to be handled. A City Room, designed to help children learn how to use the city, has city workers' uniforms to dress up in, some cars and the front part of a bus to drive, a kitchen and a working switchboard connected to phones throughout the room. A permanent exhibit on Mexico includes an open-air market where kids can put on ponchos and straw hats and take a stroll to see what the market has to offer. In the Communications Room, visitors can learn how a printing press works and can actually print a poster. Compu-Tots (computer classes for kids four and up) are offered on several weekends throughout the year. All the exhibits are well designed to teach while they entertain and to encourage participation, even among the shiest of children. One temporary exhibit our adult reviewer especially liked was a room transformed into a large cardboard maze, challenging visitors to find their way in—and out!

The Dreamspree puppet company regularly appears at the theater, Thursday and Friday at 10:30 A.M., and Saturday and Sunday at 1 and 2:30 P.M. Admission is $2.50 ($2 with museum admission). Call 675-4124 for additional information and group reservations.

FOLGER SHAKESPEARE LIBRARY   **544-7077**
201 East Capitol Street, SE 20003
Hours: 10 A.M.–4 P.M. Monday–Saturday
          10 A.M.–4 P.M. on Sunday from April 15 through Labor Day
          Closed holidays
Free Admission

Ⓜ Union Station stop (red line); Capitol South stop (blue and orange lines).

🚌 13's, 30, 32, 34, 36, 52, 54.

🚕 East Capitol Street or 1st Street.

Ⓟ Limited two-hour street parking in daytime; at night (for special events) the Library of Congress lot can be used.

🍽 None on premises.

👫 Not recommended for young children. Group tours for older children can be arranged in advance by calling 544-7077. A Shakespeare Festival for elementary and secondary school-age kids is held in the spring. About one third of the Midday Muse events (free lunchtime readings and concerts) appeal to kids.

👥 Call 546-7077 or write to arrange for a group tour. Groups of 20 or more can get discounted theater tickets.

♿ Call or write to arrange access.

👁 No special services available.

👂 No special services available.

Ⓐ For special tours write or call 544-7077 at least two weeks in advance.

Ⓣ No scheduled tours are given. Volunteer docents are available to answer questions on a walk-in basis, Monday to Friday, 11 A.M. to 1 P.M.

If you have a special interest in Shakespeare and his times, the Folger Shakespeare Library is a worthwhile stop while you're touring Capitol Hill. The library houses the largest collection of Shakespeareana in the world and is a superb source of information on European life in the sixteenth and seventeenth centuries. The Great Hall, built and decorated to reflect Elizabethan taste, houses the museum exhibits. The rotating theater history and memorabilia exhibits include items such as scripts marked by the famous actors of the British and American stage who have played Shakespearean roles, as well as first editions of some Shakespearean plays and other items.

The Folger's building was designed by architect Paul Philippe Cret as an Art-Deco abstraction of Grecian architecture. The white marble façade is decorated with nine bas-relief panels by sculptor John Gregory, representing scenes from Shakespeare's plays. On the 2nd Street side of the building is a statue of Puck by another sculptor, Brenda Putnam.

The Shakespeare Library itself, which is under the trusteeship of Amherst College, houses the world's largest collection of Shakespearean literature. The library is only open to researchers who have obtained appropriate credentials in advance.

The theater in the building is modeled after an Elizabethan in-yard theater. Originally built to serve only as a model, it opened for public performances in the late 1960s and is the site of occasional performances.

The Folger presents a varied program of events, and it serves as a center of Washington's literary and cultural scene. We suggest you call or write for schedules of events; while most events are free and open to the public, many are extremely popular and tickets seem to disappear quickly.

This is home to the Folger Consort, an internationally acclaimed ensemble that performs vibrant medieval and Renaissance music.

The Midday Muse is an eclectic program of free lunchtime concerts, poetry readings and children's programs. The public is also welcome to attend the Evening Poetry Series of readings and seminars.

Top-notch contemporary fiction writers appear at the Folger throughout the year and read from their works. Part of the PEN/Faulkner Award for Fiction, to honor the best published works of fiction by contemporary writers, the readings are open to the public on a first-come, first-served basis.

LIBRARY OF CONGRESS 287-5000 (switchboard)
287-6500 (telephone inquiries for books)

1st and East Capitol Streets, SE 20540
Mailing Address: Library of Congress, Washington, DC 20540
Thomas Jefferson Building: 1st and East Capitol Streets, SE
Thomas Jefferson Annex: 2nd Street and Independence Avenue, SE
James Madison Memorial Building: 101 Independence Avenue, SE
John Adams Building: 2nd Street and Independence Avenue, SE
Hours: Exhibits in Thomas Jefferson Building and James Madison
Memorial Building:
8:30 A.M.–9:30 P.M. Monday–Friday
8:30 A.M.–5 P.M. Saturday
1 P.M.–5 P.M. Sunday
Exhibits in Thomas Jefferson Annex:
8:30 A.M.–9:30 P.M. weekdays
8:30 A.M.–5 P.M. Saturday
Closed Christmas and New Year's
Free Admission

M Capitol South stop (blue and orange lines).

13's, 30, 32, 34, 36, 52, 54; Tourmobile (use Capitol stop).

1st Street.

P Competitive street parking. The library has a parking lot available
for those attending special events in the evening.

On premises. The staff cafeteria, located on the sixth floor of the
James Madison Memorial Building, is open to the public from
7 A.M. to 3:30 P.M. on weekdays. There is a coffee shop located
on the ground floor of the same building, which is open from
8:30 A.M. to 4 P.M. on weekdays and from 8:30 A.M. to 2 P.M. on
Saturday. A snack bar is located on the ground floor of the
Thomas Jefferson Building and is open from 8:30 A.M. to 4:30 P.M.
weekdays.

Not recommended for young children, although an occasional
exhibit will appeal to them.

Tours available. Write to the Library of Congress, Educational
Liaison Office, Tour Coordinator, or call 287-5458 at least two
weeks in advance to arrange for a tour for more than 10 people.

Fully accessible.

None available, although books are available in Braille and on
tape (see text).

Several staff members can sign.

 As mentioned above.

 Tours of the Library of Congress begin in the Orientation Theater on the ground floor of the Thomas Jefferson Building with a 17-minute slide show, daily from 8:45 A.M. to 8:45 P.M. at 45 minutes past the hour. From 9 A.M. to 4 P.M. on weekdays, 45- to 60-minute guided tours of the Thomas Jefferson Building leave the ground-floor entrance lobby.

"There is . . . no subject to which a Member of Congress may not have occasion to refer," wrote Thomas Jefferson. In 1800, Congress, with these sentiments in mind, appropriated $5,000 to establish one room of the Capitol as the Library of Congress. The original library of 3,000 books was burned by the British in 1814, and Thomas Jefferson offered his personal library—for $24,000—to serve as a replacement. Congress accepted his offer. In 1870, the Copyright Office was assigned to the Library of Congress and its real growth began. Today, the library is a massive complex, housing more than 83 million items, including books, periodicals, maps, films, photographs and recordings stored on over 535 miles of shelving. The collection grows at the rate of more than 7,000 items each day, and has spread from the original building into two major adjacent annexes: the Thomas Jefferson Building, opened in 1939, and the James Madison Memorial Building, completed in 1980.

The original Library of Congress building, which opened in 1897, is a charming, yet grand, American version of the ornate style of the Italian Renaissance. It is still the heart of the library. The Great Hall is a beauty, with its enormous dome, towering columns, statues, murals and carved balustrades, which represent various aspects of civilized life. The Main Reading Room is equally impressive. The 160-foot-high dome looks down on 44,000 reference books and desks for 212 readers. The corridors of the main building house the exhibits, both temporary and permanent, which include one of the three remaining Gutenberg Bibles (the first great book to be printed with movable metal type), a collection of Stradivarius stringed instruments, maps, photos, rare books and prints. If you visit the library in the summer, you can see the White House News Photographers Association Annual Exhibit.

The Library of Congress is one of the world's great libraries and houses several special collections of interest to visitors. The Asian Division has the largest collection of Chinese and Japanese books outside their homelands; the European Room boasts the largest collection of Russian books in the West; the Music Division contains over 7 million items; and the Rare Book and Special Collections Division possesses such gems as what is left of the private libraries of Thomas Jefferson, Woodrow Wilson and, yes, Adolf Hitler.

Since this is the national library of the people of the United States, all adults are welcome to use the facilities for research, although books can't normally be borrowed. The library is heavily used, so the wait for books can be long, but it's fun to be part of this quiet hustle-bustle. A librarian is always available to explain how materials can be requested.

Through its Congressional Research Service, the Library of Congress fulfills its major task as the reference and research arm of Congress. A staff of over 800 compile reports and send materials to congressional representatives and their staffs.

The library offers several other services of note. An interlibrary loan program extends the use of books and other materials to researchers using public and academic libraries throughout the country. Through National Library Services for the Blind and Physically Handicapped, the library supplies books and magazines recorded on disc or tape, as well as conventional Braille materials.

The Library of Congress sponsors a concert series and a series of literary performances each year. The concert series usually runs from October to April. Performances, often of chamber music using the library's collection of fine antique instruments, are held in the library's 500-seat Coolidge Auditorium. Admission to concerts is now on a first-come, first-served basis. Doors open at 7:30 P.M. on concert nights. For concert schedule information call 287-5502. The literary performances run from October to June and feature poets and authors of national renown. The library's monthly calendar of events will provide you with information on concerts, readings and current exhibits. You can pick up a copy at the information desk when you get to the library or write ahead for one.

The information center sales counter on the ground floor includes a sales area where you can purchase publications, postcards, recordings (including those of the American Folklife Center) and posters. Occasionally, reasonably priced crafts are also sold.

NAVY YARD   **433-4882**
Navy Museum   **433-3840**
Marine Corps Museum
Submarine Annex
9th and M Streets, SE
Hours: Navy Memorial Museum:9 A.M.–4 P.M. weekdays
                                 10 A.M.–5 P.M. weekends and holidays
        Marine Museum:10 A.M.–4 P.M. Monday–Saturday
Free Admission

 Eastern Market stop (blue and orange lines). Walk east on Pennsylvania Avenue to 9th Street, then south to M Street.
50, 52.

M Street.

Free parking at site; enter at 11th and N Streets.

On premises. A snack bar is attached to the Navy Museum.

Highly recommended. This is a great place for kids! Literature for kids is available.
Special tours available by appointment. Call 433-4882.

Fully accessible (note: only Marine Museum has an accessible phone).
No special services available.

No special services available.

Reservations must be made to attend the Navy's Wednesday night performance by calling 433-2678. Reservations must be made three weeks in advance to attend the Marine Corps' Friday night ceremony by calling 433-6060.
No guided tours are given.

The Navy Yard is a great place to take kids since they can run and climb on the exhibits; the yard and museums are also entertaining for adults who have an interest in military history. Opened by the government in 1799, the Washington Navy Yard is the oldest naval facility in the United States. For a large part of its history it was known as the Naval Gun Factory and was the primary manufacturing site for naval weapons. The Navy Museum, housed in one of the old factory buildings, portrays 200 years of naval history in exhibits of warships, weapons and aircraft. Visitors can play on the movable gun mounts taken from fighting ships and can go exploring in the submarine room.

The Marine Corps Museum is a "time tunnel" of Marine history, displaying Marine weapons, clothing and battles presented in chronological order from 1775 to the present.

The Submarine Annex, opened in 1987, houses four World War II–vintage midget submarines from Axis countries, a submarine-launched Poseidon missile and various other underwater weapon systems.

From June to August, both the Navy and Marine Corps offer evening presentations that are great fun for everyone. On Wednesdays beginning at 8:45 P.M., the Navy gives a historical presentation accompanied by a film and a Navy band. On Friday nights at 8:20 at the Marine Corps Barracks, 8th and I Streets, SE, the Marines put on a 2½-hour parade complete with drill team, drum and bugle corps and a marching band. It's a thrill to see, but reservations must be made for both three weeks in advance.

SEWALL-BELMONT HOUSE   **546-1210**
(Headquarters—National Woman's Party)
144 Constitution Avenue, NE 20002
Hours: 10 A.M.–3 P.M. Tuesday–Friday
            Noon–4 P.M. weekends and holidays
Free Admission

Ⓜ Union Station (red line); walk up 1st Street to Constitution Avenue. Capitol South (blue and orange lines); walk uphill on 1st Street to Constitution Avenue; house is in first block of Constitution to right.

 16A, 16D, 16E, 40, 44, 54, 90, 91, 96, 98.

 1st Street, 2nd Street and Constitution Avenue.

P Competitive parking.

◯ None on premises.

👪 Recommended for older children with interest in history.

👥 Arrangements can be made for tours for small groups (up to 40) by calling 546-3989.

♿ Inaccessible.

👁 No special services available.

👂 No special services available.

A As noted above.

T Tours are given continually.

The Sewall-Belmont House, headquarters of the National Woman's Party, is an exquisite mansion contrasting delightfully with its massive neighbors, the Supreme Court, the Capitol and the Senate Office Buildings. The house, a National Historic Landmark and National Historic Site, is a museum of the women's rights movement. Contained within are the statues and portraits of leaders of the women's movement, as well as the possessions and memorabilia associated with the drives toward suffrage and the Equal Rights Amendment.

The house is historically of interest beyond its connection with the National Woman's Party. A portion of the house dates to 1680; it is thought to be the oldest house on Capitol Hill. The only resistance to the advancing British troops in 1814 originated in this house. In retaliation, the British soldiers set the front afire. The Sewalls repaired the damage, and the house remained in the family for 123 years.

Restored in 1922 by its owner, Senator Porter Dale, the house was sold to the National Woman's Party in 1929; the "Belmont" addition to its name was in honor of the party's chief benefactor (many of the furnishings were gifts from Alva Belmont).

Throughout its long life, the Sewall-Belmont House has had many additions and alterations. Consequently, it is of no one pure architectural style, but a blend of many, primarily Federal and Queen Anne.

SUPREME COURT OF THE UNITED STATES   479-3000
1st Street, NE 20543
(corner of 1st and East Capitol Streets)
Hours: 9 A.M.–4:30 P.M. weekdays
        Closed holidays
Free Admission

M Capitol South stop (blue and orange lines) or Union Station stop (red line). Each is about three blocks away.

🚌 13's, 30, 32, 34, 36, 52, 54; Tourmobile.

🚕 1st Street.

P Competitive two-hour parking in the neighborhood.

🍽 On premises. A good cafeteria in the building is open from 7:30 to 9 A.M. and from 11 A.M. to 2 P.M. (from noon to 12:15 and 1 to 1:15 P.M., Court employees have exclusive access). A grill is open from 10:30 A.M. to 3:30 P.M., with the same staff priority.

👨‍👧 Not recommended for small children.

👥 For information on group tours call 479-3499.

♿ Fully accessible; ramp is on the Maryland Avenue side of building.

👁 No special services available.

👂 Call 479-3499 to arrange for a special tour.

A None necessary.

T No guided tours are given.

One of the most exciting shows in town can be seen from the packed visitors' gallery of the Supreme Court. In these Court chambers, the laws of our land receive their ultimate interpretation with results that can touch, and have affected, us all. Alexis de Tocqueville, the nineteenth-century French political philosopher, observed of the U.S. Supreme Court: "A more imposing judicial power was never constituted by any people." Our highest court is unique in the history of justice; as noted in the Supreme Court's guidebook, few other courts in the world have the same authority of constitutional interpretation and none have exercised it for as long or with as much influence.

Today, the Supreme Court is an institution steeped in power and tradition. This is in sharp contrast to the Court in 1795, when John Jay, its first Chief Justice, resigned to become governor of New York, feeling the Court would never become the respected institution, shielded from day-to-day politics, that it needed to be to review the law effectively. At that time the Court was meeting in a cramped section of City Hall in Philadelphia.

The young Court floundered for its identity, incorporating some British legal traditions and forging some of its own. The justices decided to abandon the British practice of wearing wigs after being hooted at in the streets and in response to Thomas Jefferson's warning to "discard the monstrous wig which makes the English judges look like rats peeping through bunches of oakum."

It was John Marshall, the fourth Chief Justice, who used his powerful leadership abilities to strengthen the Court's self-concept and its doctrine of judicial review, thereby forcing the Court into a central role in the governing process alongside the Executive branch and the Congress. Through setting and observing precedents, the Court interprets the law. It has the final word on what an existing law means in practice, and its power rests in its respect for the law.

This respect for tradition is reflected in the design of the Supreme Court building. The Court has only been at its present location since 1935. Until that time it was a wandering branch of the federal government, spending the years from 1800 to 1935 in seven different locations within the capital. In 1932, Congress finally authorized architect Cass Gilbert to design for the Court what he called ". . . a building of dignity and importance suitable for its use."

The massive classical structure that houses the Court today pays homage to ancient Greece, the birthplace of democracy. Sixteen columns of Vermont marble support the main entrance, which is flanked by two enormous seated statues representing "The Contemplation of Justice" and "The Guardian, or Authority, of Law." The enormous bronze doors, each weighing more than six tons, depict famous scenes in the development of the law as sculpted by John Donnelly, Jr.

One enters the Great Hall, lined with more massive columns and busts of former Chief Justices. Straight ahead is the imposing Court

Chamber, with columns, walls and floors of Italian, Spanish and African marble. The furniture is rich mahogany, and the drapery and carpeting are dark-red velvet.

On the first Monday in October, the Supreme Court begins its yearly schedule, hearing oral arguments through the end of April. During this period, court is in session for two weeks and in adjournment for the following two weeks while the Justices deliberate the cases they've heard. When in session, the Court meets from Monday to Wednesday, hearing cases from 10 A.M. until 3 P.M., with a break from noon until 1 P.M. Beginning in May, the Court sits only on Mondays, when it hands down orders and opinions at 10 A.M. This schedule continues until the Court adjourns sometime in early July, depending on its workload.

The Court never announces in advance which opinions it plans to release on a given day, but its argument calendar is set a month in advance and printed in the newspaper daily. Since the gallery's limited seating is granted on a first-come, first-served basis, you'd do well to arrive no later than 9:30 A.M. If a very important case is before the Court or a historic decision is to be handed down, you may have to arrive even earlier. Call ahead or check the newspapers to be certain of the Court's schedule.

When the Court is not meeting, courtroom lectures are given every hour on the half hour from 9:30 A.M. to 3:30 P.M. These 15-minute talks provide a good introduction to the history of the Court and the building that houses it. When the Court is in session, these lectures are not given.

On the ground floor of the building are public exhibits and a continuous 27-minute film in which the Chief Justice, two Associate Justices and Court staff members explain the workings and history of the Supreme Court.

UNION STATION   **383-3078—Train Information**
50 Massachusetts Avenue, NE
Hours: Building is open 24 hours
        Store hours:
        10 A.M.–9 P.M. Monday through Saturday
        Noon–6 P.M. Sunday
Free Admission

M Union Station stop (red line).

[bus] D2/4/6/8; 40, 42, 44; X2/4/5/8; 80, 81, 87, 96

[car] Building entrance.

P 1,450 space parking garage in rear; very limited metered parking on street.

[food] Extensive food court; cafés; fancy restaurants.

[kids] Some retail stores that kids will love.

[group] For arrangements, call The National Trust for Historic Preservation at Union Station. (Phone number not available at press time.)

[wheelchair] Fully accessible. Equipped bathrooms.

[eye] No special services available.

[ear] No special services available.

A Call the Trust Kiosk.

T Call the Trust Kiosk.

With a collective sigh of relief, federal officials and members of the public-private partnership formed to save Union Station reopened the rejuvenated building in September 1988 after close to three decades of fighting and fiascoes. The station rises in splendor above the memory of falling plaster, cost overruns, and mismanaged and ill-conceived schemes. Union Station has been, at last, beautifully and painstakingly restored to its original state.

Washington's first train station was located on the center of the Mall, but was moved to its present site in the early part of this century in order to restore the Mall to L'Enfant's original vision. Union Station was designed as a monumental public entrance to the nation's capital at a time when rail travel was supreme. The architect, Daniel Burnham of Chicago, designed an enormous and grand edifice in Beaux-Arts style, complete with linked barrel-vaulted ceilings, statues, friezes, columns, and gold leaf galore. After years of neglect and decay, these elements have been meticulously researched and restored under a partnership including the Congressionally created Union Station Redevelopment Corporation, Amtrak, the federal government, Union Stations Venture Ltd., D.C.'s Historic Preservation Board, and several architectural and restoration firms.

Union Station still serves its original purpose as a train station, but that seems almost secondary in its new incarnation as an urban center. Over 100 upscale shops fill the concourse and main hall, including Benetton, Ann Taylor, The Narragansett, Nature Company, Brookstone, The Limited, Great Train Store, and many other bright and interesting retail outlets. AMC offers nine movie screens. A food court entices with possibilities to satisfy every member of your entourage. If your appetites are heartier or attracted to the more refined, five restaurants are sure to please, including Denver's transplanted Rattlesnake Club, housed in the elegant President's Suite, and America, serving over 100 American regional dishes.

The Station's spectacular interior is matched by its exterior setting. The center of Union Station Plaza is the lovely Columbus Memorial Fountain, designed by Lorado Taft in 1912; on hot days this is a favorite swimming hole for local kids.

UNITED STATES BOTANIC GARDEN   225-8333
1st Street and Maryland Avenue, SW 20024
Office: 1st and Canal Streets, SW 20024
Hours: Summer—9 A.M.–9 P.M.
          Winter—9 A.M.–5 P.M.
Free Admission

Ⓜ Federal Center SW (blue and orange lines). Walk up 3rd Street to Maryland Avenue, then east to 1st Street.

🚌 30's, 52, A2, A4, A6.

🚕 Maryland Avenue or Constitution Avenue.

Ⓟ Competitive parking on the Mall.

🍽 None on premises. The garden is close to cafeterias in other museums on the Mall and in the nearby Capitol. Picnicking is permitted in the park across the street. See the listing of restaurants on Capitol Hill.

Recommended. The guided tour is a favorite with kids; they can see growing bananas, pineapples and coffee.

Group tours are available. Write, or call 225-8333, to make reservations for a 30-minute guided tour. Call 225-7099 to see if special exhibits are on display during your stay.

Limited accessibility. The jungle room is not accessible to wheelchairs, but can be viewed from outside; the bathroom and phone are accessible.

No special services available.

The garden will provide tours to the hearing-impaired if they bring their own interpreter.

As noted above.

No scheduled walk-in tours are given.

The Botanic Garden is one of Washington's often-ignored treasures. A glass building situated on the eastern end of the Mall at the foot of Capitol Hill, the garden comes under the jurisdiction of the Architect of the Capitol. The Botanic Garden began in the 1820s as an outdoor garden on the Mall, but was allowed to wither when funds ran out. When a four-year exploratory trade expedition returned to the United States in 1842, they brought with them many exotic plants from the South Seas and the Pacific Northwest. This flora created quite a stir in Washington; the collection of plants was installed in the old Patent Office Building. When that building was slated to be torn down, the continuing interest in the exotic foliage caused Congress to appropriate money to have a conservatory built on the center of the Mall. In 1931, the plants were shifted again to the existing conservatory.

Today, the Botanic Garden houses a well-maintained permanent collection of both exotic and familiar plants. There are seasonal shows: spring flowers appear shortly before Easter; chrysanthemums are shown in November and poinsettias and Christmas greens go on display in mid-December. From September to June, the staff of the Botanic Garden offers one-hour horticultural classes on specific plants; call or write for a class schedule.

Across the street from the conservatory is a beautiful park, also part of the Botanic Garden. As its centerpiece it has a grand Victorian fountain that was part of the Philadelphia Centennial Exposition in

1876. This fountain was the creation of Frédéric Bartholdi, who also designed the Statue of Liberty.

The Botanic Garden is a wonderful retreat from the hustle of touring the Mall or Capitol Hill. An hour would give you ample time to see the plants and linger awhile.

UNITED STATES CAPITOL   224-3121
East end of the Mall on Capitol Hill
Hours: Summer—9 A.M.–3:45 P.M. daily
         Winter—9 A.M.–4:30 P.M. daily
         Closed Thanksgiving, Christmas and New Year's
Free Admission

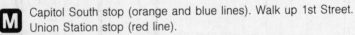 Capitol South stop (orange and blue lines). Walk up 1st Street. Union Station stop (red line).

13's, 30, 32, 34, 36, 52, 54; Tourmobile.

1st Street, Independence Avenue or Constitution Avenue.

Competitive two-hour parking in neighborhood. Nearby parking lot.

On premises. The restaurant in the Capitol is open to the public from 9 to 11:15 A.M. and from 1:15 to 2:30 P.M., as are restaurants in the Dirksen Senate Office Building and Rayburn and Longworth House office buildings. Also try the Refectory, a small public dining room in the Capitol with reasonably priced, better-than-most institutional fare.

Recommended. Kids will especially like the congressional subway ride.

Group tours available. Contact your members of Congress for a special early morning tour (see text).

Fully accessible. Handicapped people can request special parking from the parking guards; ramps are at the north and south entrances. There are special areas for the handicapped in the visitors' gallery for both the Senate and the House.

Special tours can be arranged for groups of people with visual impairments by calling 224-4048 in advance.

Special tours can be arranged for groups of people with hearing impairments by calling 224-4048 in advance. Make arrangements well in advance to schedule with a guide who signs. Call TDD 224-4049.

 A member of Congress or a senator can arrange for a special tour if you write in advance (see text).

 Free walk-in tours are conducted daily between 9 A.M. and 3:45 P.M. Write or call your congressperson's office well in advance to make arrangements for a special VIP tour. These tours are limited to families, and tickets go quickly. You can also walk many of the Capitol's impressive corridors on your own.

Pierre L'Enfant's plans for the capital city called for the "Congress House" to be built on the crest of what was then called Jenkins Hill. In 1792, a physician named William Thornton won $500 and a city lot for his design for the Capitol building. Because of difficulty in recruiting workmen in the new city, basic construction of the Capitol was accomplished in large part by slaves and the finishing work done by imported craftsmen. When Congress convened in November 1800, it met in a building that was but the palest foreshadow of the structure that stands today. This small building housed not only the House and the Senate, but the Supreme Court and the Library of Congress as well.

During the War of 1812, the British entered the city, and on August 24, 1814, set fire to the Capitol. Had there not been a heavy rainstorm, the building would have been destroyed. While the building was being rebuilt, Congress met once in Blodgett's Hotel under dismal conditions. In 1815, a group of Washington's leading citizens had a brick hall built nearly on the site of the present Supreme Court Building in order to house Congress in reasonable comfort until the official Capitol could be rebuilt. This "Brick Capitol" was built, it is suspected, to ensure that the government would not move from Washington, wiping out the investments the leading citizens had made in their new city.

The Capitol was ready for reoccupation in 1819. Additions have been made throughout the years, with the greatest enlargements coming in the 1850s and 1860s; these additions gave the Capitol the silhouette so recognizable today. The most recent structural change came in 1962 when the East Front was extended.

During the early months of the Civil War, the Capitol was used as a barracks for Northern troops. For about three months Union soldiers camped out in the hallways, parlors and legislative chambers. Eventually, some rooms were converted into bakeries to feed the men, and the Capitol was transformed into an emergency hospital to care for the wounded returning from Southern battlefields. Despite the troubles of the war, during 1863 the Capitol's nine-million-pound cast-iron dome was completed and the statue of Freedom raised to its top. Lincoln felt the completion of the dome to be an important symbol of faith in the endurance of the nation.

Start your tour of the Capitol by passing through Randolph Rogers' 10-ton bronze doors on the east side of the building. You are now in the Rotunda, the central portion of the Capitol that lies directly beneath the great iron dome. Many of our nation's leaders have lain in state here, including Lincoln and Kennedy. On the walls of the Rotunda are eight historical oil paintings depicting the struggle for independence. John Trumbull, a member of George Washington's war staff, did the four paintings of the Revolutionary War.

Looking up into the dome, you can see Constantino Brumidi's fresco, "The Apotheosis of Washington," an allegorical portrayal of an event in the nation's history where the founding fathers mingle with gods and goddesses. Brumidi was so in love with his adopted country that he devoted 25 years to working on the Capitol's interior.

Passing through the Rotunda, you enter Statuary Hall, which served as the House of Representatives' chamber until 1857. In 1864, each state was asked to contribute statues of its two most famous citizens; the inhabitants of the room are statues ranging from Robert E. Lee and Will Rogers to Dr. John Gorey, inventor of the ice machine.

Other historic sights in the Capitol are the restored old Senate and the Supreme Court chambers, both located in the north wing of the building, or the Senate side; Senate chambers and committee rooms are here. The southern wing of the Capitol is the House side. Within both chambers, Democrats sit to the right and Republicans to the left of the presiding officers—certainly an ideological switch!

The chambers, committee rooms and corridors and elevators in between can all be a hustle-bustle. When votes are about to proceed, bells are sounded, summoning members of Congress to the chambers for the calling of the roll. You'll be asked to clear the elevators and step to the side of corridors and stairways to facilitate their passage.

To observe a vote or debate from the chamber galleries, you must be on one of the tours or have a gallery pass. These passes can be obtained easily at your senators' and representatives' offices, and are good for the entire congressional session. Foreign visitors can enter the galleries by showing their passports and obtaining passes from the doorkeeper's office. Space is reserved for handicapped people in both galleries.

Whether or not you want a gallery pass, you can pay your representatives a visit. Staff members are always glad to see constituents, and can provide lots of information to help you enjoy your Washington visit. If you contact their offices well in advance of your trip, the staff can arrange special tours of the Capitol, the White House, the FBI building and other government agencies.

Members of Congress are located in the congressional office buildings adjacent to the Capitol. They consist of the Russell Senate Office Building (Delaware and Constitution Avenues, NE), the Dirksen Senate Office Building (1st Street and Constitution Avenue, NE), the Hart Senate Office Building (2nd Street and Constitution Avenue, NE), the Cannon House Office Building (New Jersey and Independence Avenues, SE), the Longworth House Office Building (Indiana and New Jersey Avenues, SE), and the Rayburn House Office Building (Independence Avenue and South Capitol Street, SW). If you don't know who your representatives or senators are, call the Capitol switchboard at 224-3121. A free miniature subway connects the Capitol to the three Senate office buildings and the Rayburn House Office Building; on this free ride you can rub elbows with politicians, lobbyists and media folks, as well as other tourists.

Be sure to plan to visit Congress while it's in session. It convenes the first Monday in January and adjourns in December, but has frequent recesses. To be sure of the schedule, call 224-3121, check *The Washington Post* daily "Activities in Congress" column, section A, or look for an American flag flying over the chamber you're interested in. A quaint method of telling when your members of Congress are working at night is to see if the lantern in the Capitol dome is lighted; if it is, one of the chambers is in session. To hear cloakroom tapes, which give daily accounts of the proceedings on the House and Senate floors, call 225-7400 (House, Democratic), 225-7430 (House, Republican), 224-8541 (Senate, Democratic) and 224-8601 (Senate, Republican).

Unlike other sights in Washington, the Capitol is at its liveliest in

December as the legislators try to cram through legislation to clean their desks and adjourn for the holidays. The lantern in the dome is often beaming well into the night; you can attend these busy nocturnal sessions with your gallery pass.

It's great fun to eat in the cafeterias at the Capitol, Dirksen Senate Office Building (with its gilt and marble surroundings) and Rayburn and Longworth House office buildings. You can surreptitiously peep at the lunchtime fare of congressional and TV news celebrities. Also be sure to enjoy the lovely 68-acre Capitol grounds designed by Olmsted.

During the summer, free evening concerts are given on the west terrace of the Capitol. (We advise you to check for details, for even traditions can change.) The National Symphony Orchestra gives 8 P.M. concerts on Memorial Day, July 4 and Labor Day. The U.S. Navy Concert Band performs each Monday, components of the U.S. Air Force Band entertain on Tuesday, the U.S. Marine Band performs on Wednesday and the U.S. Army Band plays on Friday; all concerts begin at 8 P.M.

FOOD ON CAPITOL HILL

Capitol Hill offers a variety of places to eat, many of which we recommend if only for the people-watching. Try the House of Representatives, Senate, Supreme Court or Library of Congress cafeterias and dining rooms. Food is generally more than adequate and prices reasonable. Public access to each facility sometimes changes abruptly—during congressional recesses, for instance—so double-check their hours before proceeding.

Capitol Hill's commercial restaurants are located along several main corridors:

- Pennsylvania Avenue, SE, between 2nd and 4th Streets, and then farther up the avenue between 6th and 7th Streets, which is a several-block walk from the House side of the Capitol
- 8th Street, SE, between Pennsylvania Avenue and G Street
- Massachusetts Avenue, SE, between 2nd and 3rd Streets, which is

a several-block walk from the Senate side of the Capitol to Union Station.

The spectrum spans carry-outs to glossy restaurants, with dozens of American and various ethnic restaurants in between. The hamburger-pub style seems to dominate: try *The Hawk'n Dove,* at 329 Pennsylvania Avenue, SE, 543-3300, and *Jenkins Hill,* 223 Pennsylvania Avenue, SE, 544-6600—between 2nd and 4th Streets—for hearty burgers and the hum of political chatter.

If the budget is tight, *Roy Rogers,* 317 Pennsylvania Avenue, and *McDonald's* are also on the Pennsylvania Avenue corridor. Street vendors sell inexpensive food in warm weather, and many of the neighborhood liquor stores sell submarines and other sandwiches.

Sherrill's, 233 Pennsylvania Avenue, SE, 544-2480, a bakery almost lost in time, and the *Tune Inn,* 331½ Pennsylvania Avenue, SE, 543-2725, a greasy spoon with stuffed deer and other game mounted on the wall, both stand out for their local color and their very lack of sophistication. Both restaurants are reasonably priced and offer a reprieve from the stylized trends most restaurants pursue.

For good pasta dishes—and their outstanding specialty of white pizza—try *Machiavelli's,* a relaxing Art-Deco restaurant at 613 Pennsylvania Avenue, SE, 543-1930.

Egg Roll King, 653 Pennsylvania Avenue, SE, 543-9336, is a fine source of remarkably inexpensive Chinese/Hunan food. Try not to be put off by the name and the glaring fast-food atmosphere: the food is a real find; we heartily recommend it, especially if you're looking to take out.

The *Broker,* 713 8th Street, SE, 546-8300, is a flashy, expensive, politically charged restaurant with consistently good food. The Broker features Swiss specialties—fondues of cheese and meat, roesti—and some new American dishes. It is famous for its sinful chocolate pâté, three kinds of chocolate in a raspberry and crème anglaise sauce.

Bullfeathers, at 401 1st Street, SE, 543-5005, offers a congenial neighborhood and rather politically charged atmosphere. It's handy for both Republican and Democratic national committee staffers; the food is quite fine.

Hunan on Capitol Hill, 201 D Street, NE, 544-0102, offers a wide variety of spicy and nonspicy Chinese dishes. It's a bit more expensive than many Chinatown restaurants, but you can rely on the quality of the food and service. *Hunan Dynasty,* 215 Pennsylvania Avenue, SE, 546-6161, offers wonderful Chinese food and almost always hosts congressmen and senators.

2 Quail, 320 Massachusetts Avenue, NE, 543-8030, with its warm, country-style decor, has a good range of offerings from sophisticated to simple fare.

The newly renovated Union Station offers a full range of eating opportunities, from an a la carte food court with over 20 choices to several very fancy establishments, including Denver's Rattlesnake Club.

Close to Union Station, you can find several worthwhile eateries: *The American Café and Market,* 227 Massachusetts Avenue, NE, 547-8500; *Café Capri,* 301 Massachusetts Avenue, NE, 546-5900; and for dessert, *Bob's Famous Ice Cream* has opened a Capitol Hill branch at 236 Massachusetts Avenue, NE, 546-3860.

An old-time favorite is *The Dubliner,* an Irish pub diagonally across from Union Station, at 520 N. Capitol Street, 737-3773. A crowd of regulars gathers there for live music and drink most evenings and an Irish country brunch, Sunday 11 A.M. to 4 P.M.

THE WATERFRONT RESTAURANTS

Washington's waterfront has come a long way in the past decade. What was merely a collection of take-away fish stands is now a several-block-long amalgam of hotels, restaurants, marinas and dock-side attractions. The restaurants tend to be large; they are good bets for buses and large groups. As with most superlarge restaurants, inventiveness is not their long suit. However, you can get consistently good food at reasonable prices at the major fish houses. *Hogates,* 9th Street and Maine Avenue, SW, 484-6300, welcomes groups and offers a special discount. Call 484-6305 for details. *Phillips Flagship,* 900 Water Street, 488-8515, is a similar operation, now run by a company that started by selling clams at a beach stand in Ocean City. Several blocks from the waterfront at 200 E Street, SW, is the *Market Inn,* 554-2100, which features a variety of homemade soups and seafood dishes in a festive atmosphere with walls laden with Washington memorabilia and other collectibles. Our favorite among the waterfront seafood houses is the smallest, *The Gangplank,* 600 Water Street, SW, 554-5000, located on a converted barge moored at the pier—good food, modest prices, nice view, decent service.

For two changes of pace, there are *El Torrito,* California-style Mexican at 700 Water Street, 554-5302 (try their semifrozen Margaritas), and *Negril,* 401 M (in the Waterside Mall), 488-3636, which serves Jamaican specialties, including baked goods and meat dishes.

6

DOWNTOWN

———

The Downtown section of Washington is perhaps the city's most disparate area, with its vital mix of federal and local government, international organizations, art museums, the Convention Center, major department stores and smaller retail operations, nonprofit organizations and associations, historic sites, parks, hotels, theaters, offices galore, every type of restaurant and bar imaginable—in fact, the only element Downtown lacks in quantity is residents, and that may change to an extent if the Pennsylvania Avenue Development Corporation's plans are fully implemented. This is Washington at work, with its shirtsleeves rolled up—or three-piece suit buttoned down.

The area is large; we define the borders as Capitol Hill (N. Capitol Street) to the east, the Mall (Constitution Avenue) to the south to 18th Street, along the diagonal of Pennsylvania Avenue to Georgetown and Foggy Bottom (23rd Street) on the west, and M Street to the north. The best modes of conveyance are Metro, buses and taxis; it's best to leave your car outside the city or in a parking lot, since street parking is difficult and driving is most challenging here (see the "Getting to and Around Town" chapter for details).

The Washington Convention Center, between 9th and 11th Streets, NW, and M Street and New York Avenue, hosts a variety of trade shows and conventions as well as occasional antique, home and auto shows open to the public.

Although several points of interest in Downtown aren't specific sites, we've included descriptions of them because they're part of Washington's essence: the Lafayette Square area, Pennsylvania Avenue, F Street and the Ellipse.

A myriad of eating establishments congregate in the Downtown area. We include a bunch of our favorites at the end of this section (it was difficult to contain ourselves)—but in fine weather, nothing can beat alfresco lunching on yogurt or cheese at Lafayette or Farragut Squares or the other small green patches of park that dot the area.

AMERICAN RED CROSS   737-8300
(National Headquarters)
431 17th Street, NW 20006
Hours: 9 A.M.–4 P.M. weekdays
      Closed holidays
Free Admission

  Farragut West stop (blue and orange lines).

 30, 32, 34, 36, X2, X4, G4, N2, N4, N6, 38C.

 17th Street.

 Competitive parking on 17th Street. Commercial lots on New York Avenue between 17th and 18th Streets.

 None on premises.

  Not recommended, although some dolls are displayed.

 Group tours must be arranged in advance; call 639-3335.

 Totally accessible. It's a long trek to get from the ramped entrance at 17th Street to the elevator.

 No special services available.

No special services available.

 As noted above.

No walk-in guided tours are given. A mimeographed brochure is available at the site for self-guided tours.

The home of the national headquarters of the American Red Cross is a lavish three-building wash of white marble (the main building is called, in fact, the Marble Palace), virtually blinding under a hot summer sun. The Marble Palace, constructed in 1917, contains displays and exhibits of Red Cross programs in the first- and second-floor lobbies, as well as paintings and sculptures. Three marble busts by American sculptor Hiram Powers—"Faith," "Hope" and "Charity"—crown the stairway to the second floor, and notable stained-glass windows by Louis Tiffany are in the second-floor assembly hall. Children may be interested in the small collection of dolls in native dress, including one very well dressed young lady of the nineteenth century who is displayed with her entire traveling wardrobe. The garden contains sculpture honoring American Red Cross workers who have lost their lives in service to others and a monument to Jane A. Delano, founder of the Red Cross Nursing Program, and to Red Cross nurses who died in World War I.

BETHUNE MUSEUM-ARCHIVES   332-1233

1318 Vermont Avenue, NW 20005

Hours: 10 A.M.–4:30 P.M. weekdays

       Weekend tours by appointment

Free Admission

M McPherson Square stop (orange and blue lines).

32, 34, 36, 42, X2, X4, G4, N2, N4, N6.

Generally available on Vermont Avenue, NW.

P Metered street parking and commercial lots nearby.

None on premises.

Exhibits may be of interest to kids.

Groups should make tour arrangements at least two weeks in advance.

Hoping to be accessible in 1989.

No special services available.

No special services available.

 None necessary.

 Call or write in advance to make arrangements for a tour. There is a $1 charge for a tour.

Mary McLeod Bethune, one of 17 children born to ex-slaves in South Carolina, achieved a good deal during her lifetime; the museum-archive celebrates her accomplishments and serves as an important repository.

Bethune founded Bethune-Cookman College in Daytona Beach, Florida, as well as the National Council of Negro Women. She also served as an adviser to President Franklin D. Roosevelt.

Two exhibitions are held each year exploring various issues affecting black women's history.

Housed here is the National Archives for Black Women's History, including Bethune's papers and those of other black leaders; documents from the National Committee on Household Employees; and several decades of records from the National Council of Negro Women. The archives are accessible by appointment only. In 1982, Congress designated this one of eight black National Historic Sites.

CORCORAN GALLERY OF ART   638-3211
17th Street and New York Avenue, NW 20006
Hours: 10 A.M.–4:30 P.M. Tuesday, Wednesday, Friday–Sunday
        10 A.M.–9 P.M. Thursday
        Closed July 4, Thanksgiving, Christmas and New Year's
Free Admission, Selected Special Shows Charge Admission

 Farragut West stop (blue and orange lines); use 17th and I Streets exit. Farragut North stop (red line); use Farragut Square exit. In both cases, walk south on 17th Street to New York Avenue.

 30, 32, 34, 36, X2, X4, G4, N2, N4, N6, 38C.

 New York Avenue.

P Metered parking on 17th Street and New York Avenue; commercial garage at 17th and New York; on-street parking further down 17th Street on side streets.

|O| None on premises.

👫 Recommended. The gallery is small enough to keep a child's interest. The Corcoran offers special events for kids, including occasional weekend workshops in printmaking and drawing for children as young as four. Special tours for children can be arranged by calling the Education Office at 638-3211. Ask what other events are on at the same time.

Call 638-3211 or write at least two weeks in advance to arrange for a tour.

♿ Limited accessibility. Call 638-3211 in advance to request special assistance to use the freight elevator; bathrooms and phones are accessible.

👁 Request a special tour in advance from the Education Office at 638-3211.

Make arrangements in advance for a signed tour with the Education Office at 638-3211.

A Arrangements for guided tours must be made with the Education Office at least two weeks in advance. Call at 638-3211.

T No walk-in guided tours are given.

The Corcoran Gallery of Art is the oldest and largest private art museum in Washington. Founded in 1869 by William Wilson Corcoran, a successful Washington banker turned philanthropist, the collection was originally housed in the building that is now the Smithsonian's Renwick Gallery, around the corner on Pennsylvania Avenue. When Corcoran's growing collection demanded more space, the banker commissioned the existing gallery. Completed in 1897, the building is considered by architectural historians to be one of the finest Beaux-Arts structures in the city.

Today the Corcoran Gallery houses a collection of American and European paintings, sculpture, prints, drawings and examples of the decorative arts. In fact, the American collection is among the country's best. Gilbert Stuart, John Singer Sargent, Mary Cassatt, Josef Albers and George Bellows are all represented as well as a more contemporary sampling. A European collection bequeathed to the gallery by Senator William Clark Andrews and the Walker Collection of French Impressionists have both enhanced the Corcoran's holdings. As one of the first museums to recognize photography as art, the gallery also has a fine collection of photographic prints, which is displayed in frequently changing exhibits.

The Corcoran is a local museum as well as one of national prominence. The gallery counts among its major purposes the display of works of artists from the Washington metropolitan area, and tries to fulfill that purpose with numerous exhibits and special events.

With the help of the museum's free map/brochure, available at the entrance, you can wander through the exhibits with knowledge and confidence. Be sure not to miss Samuel F. B. Morse's (yes, the inventor of the telegraph) famous painting "The Old House of Representatives" and Hiram Powers' sculpture "The Greek Slave," which was considered quite scandalous in the nineteenth century.

The Corcoran's impressive rotunda is the scene of frequent special events; check the newspapers, call the gallery or pick up the Corcoran's calendar of events while at the gallery to see if anything is scheduled during your visit.

Don't miss the Corcoran Gallery gift shop. One of the best in town, it sells fine crafts, unusually nice toys, jewelry and an excellent selection of cards and books.

DAR CONTINENTAL HALL   628-1776
(Daughters of the American Revolution)
1776 D Street, NW 20006
Hours: 8:30 A.M.–4 P.M. weekdays
Free Admission

M Farragut West stop (blue and orange lines); use Farragut Square exit. Walk south on 17th Street to D Street.

30, 32, 34, 36, X2, X4, G4, N2, N4, N6, 38C.

17th or 18th Streets.

P Competitive parking along 17th and 18th Streets.

None on premises.

Recommended. The New Hampshire Attic contains eighteenth- and nineteenth-century toys, games and amusements. The Touch

Program, designed for elementary-school children, lets kids physically explore objects from Revolutionary days. To arrange for this presentation, at the museum or at your local school, call 628-1776, ext. 241, at least two weeks in advance.

 Tours available. Groups must arrange for their tours two weeks in advance by calling 628-1776, ext. 238. Special-subject tours and lectures can also be arranged at that extension.

 Limited accessibility. The museum is accessible; there are no phones or bathrooms for those in wheelchairs.

 No special services available.

 No special services available.

 As noted above.

 Walk-in tours are given continually from 10 A.M. until 3 P.M.

In addition to their enormous genealogical archives, the Daughters of the American Revolution maintain a large decorative-arts museum at their national headquarters in Continental Hall. The building, housing both the museum and archives, was designed by John Russell Pope. Constructed in 1930 specifically for the organization's use, it completes the string of neoclassical buildings (with the Pan American Union and the Red Cross) envisioned by the McMillan Commission to surround the White House grounds. The 29 rooms in the museum are furnished with paintings, furniture, window hangings and other objects representing regional variations in American style and craftsmanship during the country's formative years. Perhaps the most charming of the exhibit rooms is the New Hampshire Attic, stocked with a mélange of dolls, games and toys that delighted children of other eras. For the most part, furnishings predate the Industrial Revolution, although one wonderful Victorian parlor displays Belter-style sofas and chairs.

Before your tour begins, roam through the first-floor displays of an excellent collection of ceramics (including an unusually fine selection of Chinese porcelain pieces), textiles, silver and glass. The small sales area has books, postcards and a few mementos, such as dolls in period costumes.

The DAR Genealogical Library is open to the public from 9 A.M. to 4 P.M., Monday to Friday. Nonmembers must pay a $5 user fee.

DECATUR HOUSE   673-4030
748 Jackson Place, NW 20006
Hours: 10 A.M.–2 P.M. Tuesday–Friday
      Noon–4 P.M. Saturday and Sunday
      Closed Thanksgiving, Christmas and New Year's
Admission: Adults—$2.50   Children and Senior Citizens—$1.25

 Farragut North stop (red line) or Farragut West stop (blue and orange lines); walk south on 17th Street to H Street; turn left to Jackson Place.

 30, 32, 34, 36, 42, X2, X4, N2, N4, N6.

 Pennsylvania Avenue or H Street.

 Very difficult street parking; commercial lots at 17th and H Streets or Connecticut Avenue and I Street.

 None on premises.

 Not recommended, unless a child is particularly interested in American history.

 Group tours available. Arrangements should be made in advance by calling 842-0920.

 Limited accessibility. You must call in advance at 842-0920 for a ramp to be placed at the H Street entrance. Once inside, there is an elevator to the second floor.

 No special services available.

 No special services available.

 As noted above.

 Walk-in guided tours given continually (30 minutes).

In 1819, Commodore Stephen Decatur, popular hero of United States sea battles against the Barbary pirates and in the War of 1812, moved into his imposing brick town house near the White House. Decatur House, the first private residence constructed on Lafayette Square, was designed by Benjamin Henry Latrobe, possibly the most prominent architect practicing in America at that time. It is an excellent example of the Federal style, with its very formal, simple façade and its square and sturdy but elegant shape. Unfortunately, neither architect nor owner long survived the construction of the house. A year after moving in, Decatur was killed in a duel with a fellow officer. In the same year, Latrobe succumbed to yellow fever without ever having seen the finished house. Immediately after Decatur's death, his widow left the house and never returned.

Decatur House became the residence of a succession of foreign diplomats and American politicians and statesmen, including Henry Clay, Martin Van Buren and Judah Benjamin (later to become secretary of state for the Confederacy). During the Civil War, Decatur House, like many other homes around Lafayette Square, was seized by the government for use as offices and storage. It was bought in the 1870s by General Edward Fitzgerald Beale, a colorful figure best known for his role in the settlement of the American West. In the 1940s, his daughter-in-law, socialite Marie Beale, restored the exterior of Decatur House to its 1820s appearance. She bequeathed Decatur House to the National Trust for Historic Preservation, and it served until recently as national headquarters of the trust. The new headquarters is in a beautiful and architecturally significant restored Beaux Arts–style building at 1785 Massachusetts Avenue, NW.

Of the two floors now open to the public, the first suggests the Decatur era and is furnished in the Federal style. The second floor, which contains two grand drawing rooms, commemorates the long period of Beale family ownership, with an eclectic blend of Victorian and twentieth-century furniture and objects. The house is frequently used for social events sponsored by nonprofit organizations and corporate members of the trust, but it is rarely closed completely to the visiting public during its advertised hours. A colonial crafts fair is held annually in late October.

The National Trust for Historic Preservation Shop is around the corner at 1600 H Street; it's a treasure trove of books, reproductions, classy T-shirts and wonderful gifts galore.

FBI   **324-3447**
(J. Edgar Hoover Building)
10th Street and Pennsylvania Avenue, NW 20535
(entrance on E Street)
Hours: 9 A.M.–4:15 P.M. weekdays
        Closed holidays
Free Admission

Federal Triangle stop (blue and orange lines); Gallery Place stop (red line); walk down 9th Street toward Pennsylvania Avenue.

 30, 32, 34, 36, 54, 60, 70, A2, A4.

 Pennsylvania Avenue.

 Commercial parking available along 9th Street.

 None on premises.

 Recommended, although fast pace of tour may cause kids to miss some information.

 Tours available for groups of 20 or more. Call ahead at 324-3447 to make a reservation, or ask the staff at your member of Congress's office to arrange a tour for you.

 Fully accessible.

 No special services available.

 No special services available.

 Contact your members of Congress well in advance of your trip for an FBI tour with no waiting.

Walk-in tours are given continually (one hour); the wait in line can be long. No admittance to the building except on the tours.

In one of the least attractive government buildings in town, the FBI presents a lively, fast-paced tour of its working space that has become one of Washington's most popular tourist attractions. A sure hit with children over kindergarten age, the tour (which is rigidly supervised by cheerful but firm FBI employees) takes visitors past exhibits that feature gangster paraphernalia and relics of some of the more prominent bad guys done in by federal agents, weapon displays, fingerprint and serology labs, a tape recording of an actual kidnap ransom demand, and J. Edgar Hoover's office desk and chair. The tour ends with a marksmanship demonstration using a standard FBI Smith and Wesson revolver and a Thompson machine gun that leaves the audience cheering.

FORD'S THEATRE   **426-6924**
511 10th Street, NW 20004   **TDD 426-1749**
THE HOUSE WHERE LINCOLN DIED   **426-6830**
(Petersen House)
516 10th Street, NW 20004
Hours: 9 A.M.–5 P.M. daily
        Closed Christmas
        Closed during matinees and rehearsals (call ahead to check)
Free Admission

M Metro Center stop (red, blue and orange lines); use the 11th Street exit. Gallery Place stop (red line); use 9th Street exit.
30, 32, 34, 36, 42, B6, G6, D2, D4, D6, D8.

F Street.

P Street parking is practically impossible. Commercial lots are in the neighborhood.

None on premises.

Recommended; kids love the museum and presentations.

No reservations necessary.

Limited accessibility. To enter, people in wheelchairs will need assistance. Call ahead at 426-6924. Phones and bathrooms are not accessible.

The Lincoln Museum has a sound presentation, and the rangers give a scheduled talk twice hourly. Visitors with visual impairments can enter the box where Lincoln was shot.

No special services available. Free printed brochures are available.

A None necessary.

T Presentations are given at 10 and 35 minutes after every hour, except when a play is in rehearsal.

At Ford's Theatre, where President Lincoln was shot in 1865, the National Park Service effectively interprets the event, both in performance and displays of artifacts. The recently restored building, which is once again functioning as a professional theater, is one of the busiest tourist sites in Washington. But don't despair; the theater seating is generous and there's rarely much of a wait for the tour. In the theater's basement, the Lincoln Museum houses glass cases displaying objects relating to the Lincolns and to the assassination. A "conspirator's exhibit" contains John Wilkes Booth's diary and one of his boots, among other treasures. Books, postcards and posters are sold at a small sales counter.

Upstairs in the restored auditorium, park rangers give a 15-minute presentation twice hourly on the events leading up to Lincoln's assassination. If you miss the talk, a well-written free brochure (available in six languages) can provide you with the background information that will make your visit to the theater meaningful. Visitors are invited to walk around the balcony and peer into the Presidential box from which Lincoln was watching *Our American Cousin* the night he was shot.

During past summers, short theatrical "informances" have been presented, in which professional actors portrayed characters from the Lincoln drama or performed programs of music from Lincoln's era. You'll probably want to follow your visit to Ford's Theatre with a trip across the street to the Petersen House, where Lincoln was taken after the shooting. This house has also been restored and furnished to re-create the way it was on April 15, 1865, the morning Lincoln died there.

See the "Entertainment" chapter for ticket information for Ford's Theatre's stage performances.

NATIONAL AQUARIUM   377-2825 (tape)
14th Street and Constitution Avenue, NW 20230
Commerce Department basement
Hours: 9 A.M.–5 P.M. daily
　　　　Closed Christmas
Admission: Adults—$1　Children and Senior Citizens—50¢

 Federal Triangle stop (blue and orange lines).

 30, 32, 34, 36, 50, 52.

 14th Street.

 Commercial parking across the street; lot is generally full by midday.

On premises. A cafeteria is open from 8:30 A.M. to 2 P.M. on weekdays.

 Recommended.

 No tours available. Groups welcome.

 Fully accessible.

 No special services available.

 No special services available.

 None necessary.

 No guided tours are given.

The National Aquarium, the oldest aquarium in the country, founded over 115 years ago, is a fine place to take children; while there are no guided tours and not much interpretation, the constant activity of more than 600 marine and freshwater animals, viewed through the bottle-green light of the tanks in Commerce's basement, seems to keep visitors of all ages happy. A tiny hands-on tidal pool should delight your small fry. The Commerce Department's cafeteria provides no-nonsense food at reasonable prices when the lure of the deep wears off. You can replenish your film at the aquarium's small bookstore.

Sharks are fed Monday, Wednesday and Friday at 2 P.M. Piranhas are fed Tuesday, Thursday and Sunday at 2 P.M.

While in the building, pop upstairs to see the census clock in the lobby of the Commerce Department. The clock's face shows the constant changes in our population, as we are born, die, immigrate and emigrate.

NATIONAL BUILDING MUSEUM   272-2448
F Street, Between 4th and 5th Streets, NW, 20001
Hours: 10 A.M.–4 P.M. weekdays
        Noon–4 P.M. Saturday, Sunday and Holidays
Free Admission, donations accepted

 Judiciary Square stop (red line); F Street exit.

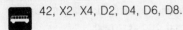 42, X2, X4, D2, D4, D6, D8.

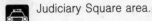 Judiciary Square area.

P Competitive street parking; some commercial lots.

|O| None on premises. Chinatown is nearby.

Recommended for older children.

Special group tours available, call 272-2448; advance reservations required.

Fully accessible. Construction is making access somewhat difficult. Some assistance may be required.

No special services available.

No special services available.

A None necessary.

T Tuesday to Friday at 12:30 P.M., weekends and holidays at 1 P.M. or by prior appointment.

The National Building Museum celebrates America's building heritage in grand fashion. Not only does it serve as a monument to the building arts, but it is housed in one of Washington's greatest works of public architecture, the U.S. Pension Building.

This massive structure, under construction from 1881 to 1887, is 400 feet long and 200 feet wide and is built of 15.5 million bricks; it's encircled by a 1,200-foot-long terra-cotta frieze representing a continuous procession of soldiers and sailors.

In an effort to promote a healthy work environment for the 1,500 clerks processing pensions, Montgomery C. Meigs, the architect, designed a single huge hall with plenty of light and air, and for added ventilation, he omitted three bricks below every window. Clearly, Mr. Meigs was ahead of his time with his concern for a healthy and productive workplace.

The Pension Building's Great Hall is a spectacular space, the size of a football field, soaring to 159 feet at its highest point—the height of a 15-story building. The massive central fountain and eight faux-marble Corinthian columns were, for many years, hidden and forgotten, and were only recently uncovered and restored.

As a young institution, the National Building Museum is just beginning to define its programs. And, as a private, nonprofit foundation, the museum faces the difficult task of building an endowment and locating funds to develop and support new exhibits. Finally, as a tenant of the federal government in a building under renovation by GSA, the museum must constantly juggle its physical environment. As renovations are completed, the museum is mounting new permanent and temporary exhibits. The first two permanent displays are *The U.S. Pension Building,* exploring the architectural inspirations and engineering innovations of the building itself, and *Washington: Site, Symbol & City,* bringing to life, through models, plans, and drawings, the architectural treasures of the capital city, from the early 1800s to the present.

Each spring and fall, the museum sponsors Construction Watch, a tour of various building sites around town. Call 272-2448 for reservations and specific dates. Every month (except the summer), the museum sponsors classical music concerts in the Great Hall at noon. Call 272-2448 for a schedule.

The museum shop (272-7706) offers a fine selection of books on architects and architecture, such special items as limited edition china reproductions of the Frank Lloyd Wright–designed china from the Imperial Hotel in Tokyo.

The Pension building is often used as the site of grand parties. The Great Hall can seat up to 1500; the Commissioner's Suite offers a more intimate setting. Non-profit and for-profit organizations are welcome. Call the Special Events Office at 272-3555 for details.

NATIONAL GEOGRAPHIC   **857-7000**
SOCIETY HEADQUARTERS
            Explorers Hall: 857-7588 (recorded information)
                      857-7700 (lecture information)
17th and M Streets, NW 20036
Hours: 9 A.M.–5 P.M. Monday–Saturday
       10 A.M.–5 P.M. Sunday
       Closed Christmas
Free Admission

M Farragut North or Dupont Circle stop (red line).

[bus] 42, 52, 54, D2, D4, D6, D8, N2, N4, N6, 38B.

[taxi] 17th Street.

P Difficult metered street parking; many commercial lots in area. On weekends, building parking lot is open free.

[restaurant] None on premises.

[family] Recommended. Although there is nothing specific for kids, the whole exhibit seems kid-oriented. Call 857-7689 to arrange for special school tours.

[group] To arrange a tour for 10 or more people, call 857-7689 and ask for the coordinator of Education and Special Tours.

[wheelchair] Limited accessibility. There's a ramp on the 17th Street side of the building; there's no phone but the bathroom is accessible.

[eye] Special tours can be arranged by contacting the coordinator of Education and Special Tours at 857-7689.

[ear] Special tours can be arranged by contacting the coordinator of Education and Special Tours at 857-7689.

A As noted above.

T No walk-in guided tours are given; the exhibits are self-explanatory.

The Explorers Hall exhibit area in the National Geographic Society's headquarters is an extension of the society's glossy, colorful magazine. Since the Society celebrated its centennial in 1988, the hall received a total facelift in 1987, with the addition of many new exhibits. Dramatic displays, often with audio accompaniment, inform visitors about some of the more exciting exploratory missions of the National Geographic Society. Permanent exhibits include a brand new free-standing globe—the world's largest, 11 feet from pole to pole; a theater of early man; and a variety of high-tech exhibits on geography. In addition, there will continue to be a variety of temporary exhibits. The Explorers Hall gift shop is the only place where Society publications may be purchased over the counter.

The National Geographic Society also houses a reference library that is open to the public from 8:30 A.M. to 5 P.M. weekdays. The society sponsors an ongoing lecture series that is open to members (if you subscribe to the magazine, you're a member). Call 857-7000 to find out what's on while you're in town.

NATIONAL MUSEUM OF AMERICAN ART   **357-1300**
8th and G Streets, NW 20560
Hours: 10 A.M.–5:30 P.M. daily
          Closed Christmas
Free Admission

M Gallery Place stop (red line); use 9th Street exit.

42, 80, 81, X2, X4, B6, G6, D2, D4, D6.

7th or 9th Streets.

P Limited metered street parking; commercial lots on 9th Street between F and H Streets.

On premises. Patent Pending, a small but notable cafeteria, offers "homemade" soups, breads, sandwiches, etc. In mild weather, you can eat at tables in the museum's courtyard. Cafeteria hours are 10 A.M. to 3:30 P.M. on weekdays and 11:30 A.M. to 3:30 P.M. on weekends.

Recommended for older children.

Arrangements for group tours must be made at least two weeks in advance by contacting the Education Office at 357-3111.

Fully accessible. Wheelchairs can be provided if advance notice is given; call 357-2247. A ramped entrance is at 9th and G Streets.

Special tours can be arranged by calling 357-3111 at least 48 hours in advance.

Special tours can be arranged by calling 357-3111 or TDD 357-1696 48 hours in advance.

A As noted above.

T Noon on weekdays; 1:45 P.M. on Sunday (60 to 90 minutes).

The National Museum of American Art shares elegant quarters with the National Portrait Gallery in the Old Patent Office Building, one of the great neoclassical buildings in the country. While the museum is part of the Smithsonian, the American Art collection predates the Institution's existence by 30 years—it's the oldest national art collection in the United States. The original collection was displayed in the Patent Office in the 1840s along with shrunken heads, the original Declaration of Independence, stuffed birds and Benjamin Franklin's printing press. The collection shifted locations throughout the years until it returned permanently to the Patent Office Building in 1968.

The museum holds over 25,000 works, primarily American paintings, graphics and sculpture dating from the eighteenth century to the present. Its smaller European and Asian collections contain objects from the eleventh to the eighteenth centuries. (The museum's collections of crafts and design are shown at the Renwick Gallery.) Among modern artists represented are Alexander Calder, Seymour Lipton, George Rickey, Franz Kline, Robert Rauschenberg and Helen Frankenthaler. Early American masters like Gilbert Stuart and Benjamin West vie for attention with a large collection of George Catlin's Indian paintings, Hiram Powers' plasters (models for his finished sculptures) and paintings by Winslow Homer and Albert Pinkham Ryder.

On the third floor are the Lincoln gallery—called by many "the greatest room in Washington"—and the Hampton Throne, the impressive and eccentric visionary work of Washingtonian James Hampton.

The Old Patent Office Building is worth a visit just for itself. Designed in the 1830s by William Parker Elliott and Robert Mills (who later designed the Washington Monument and the Treasury Building), the structure is an outstanding example of Greek Revival architecture. At that time, when Washington was still swampland with livestock roaming through the streets, the massive building was impressive indeed.

During the Civil War, the edifice was used as barracks, hospital and morgue for Union forces. Clara Barton—then a Patent Office clerk and later founder of the Red Cross—tended the wounded, who were visited by President Lincoln and Walt Whitman. In 1865, Lincoln's second inaugural ball was held on the third floor—now the Lincoln Gallery.

Various government agencies used the building until the 1950s, when it was slated to be razed for a new parking lot. Strong opposition convinced Congress to turn the historic site over to the Smithsonian for restoration and use as the home of the National Collection of Fine Arts—now the National Museum of American Art.

Postcards, catalogs and books are available in the museum shop, and the cafeteria (shared with the National Portrait Gallery) is a pleasant place to sort your thoughts and decide which gallery to visit next.

Occasional concerts and lectures are given at the museum. Check their calendar of events, which is available at the information desk, or call 357-1300 to see what's on while you're in town. You can make an appointment to see some of the museum's 24,000 paintings, sculptures, prints and drawings not on exhibit. Call 357-2593.

A library containing 40,000 volumes of art, history and biography is open to the public; for further information, inquire at the information desk. A slide-lending collection is also available; for information call 357-2283.

The Barney Studio House, at 2306 Massachusetts Avenue, NW, is yet another facet of the National Museum of American Art. Built by Alice Pike Barney in 1902, the edifice served as her home, studio and salon. Renovated recently, the studio house is filled with works by Barney and her contemporaries as well as with ornate furnishings typical of the early twentieth century. Appointments can be made to tour the building at 11 A.M. or 1 P.M. Wednesday, Thursday and one Sunday a month by calling 357-3111.

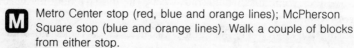

NATIONAL MUSEUM OF WOMEN IN THE ARTS 783-5000
13th Street and New York Avenue, NW 20005
Hours: 10 A.M.–5 P.M. Tuesday–Saturday (closed Monday)
     Noon–5 P.M. Sunday
Free Admission

M Metro Center stop (red, blue and orange lines); McPherson Square stop (blue and orange lines). Walk a couple of blocks from either stop.

30's along Pennsylvania; walk north on 13th Street for three blocks.

New York Avenue.

P Commercial lots nearby.

A restaurant on the premises is planned.

Recommended. A special family room and museum tours for kids are planned.

 Call or write in advance for information on tours.

 Fully accessible. Ramp and elevator at New York Avenue entrance; accessible restroom and telephone.

 No special services available.

 No special services available.

 Call or write for information on guided tours and special events.

 Call or write for tour schedule.

The National Museum of Women in the Arts is the first of its kind in the world (opened April 8, 1987). It celebrates the contributions of women to the history of art, a long-overlooked segment of the creative world.

The Holladay Collection, the nucleus of the museum, consists of more than 500 works by more than 180 artists from 19 countries. From the Renaissance to the present, European to Native American, the permanent collection includes paintings, drawings, sculpture, pottery, prints, books and photography. The earliest work is by Lavina Fontana, a leading artist in Bologna during the 1500s, a court artist to the Pope, painter of altarpieces in Bologna, and mother and supporter of 11 children!

The collection was started 20 years ago when the museum's founder and president, Wilhelmina Cole Holladay, and her husband, Wallace, began collecting art and took note of the dearth of information on women artists. "Painting by painting, artist by artist, we set out to track down great women artists who had been forgotten or ignored," explains Mrs. Holladay. "We found that some eras had been good to women artists and that others had been far more repressive," she adds.

"During the Renaissance, women artists flourished; they were court painters, papal painters, the heads of universities, but then, in the later ages, they were not even allowed to study," observes Mrs. Holladay.

The museum is housed in a 1907 Renaissance Revival building that was originally a Masonic temple; before the museum happened along, it hosted an adult movie theater.

The Library and Research Center is the world's most extensive collection of information on women artists. Scholars and students may consult the books, periodicals, slides and photographs by appointment.

State committees (comprised of volunteer museum members) work to encourage art by local women; their results are exhibited in the State Gallery.

Lectures, film and art seminars and musical, dance and theatrical performances are held in the auditorium (ask for a schedule). Don't miss the notecards, posters, scarves and other gifts available in the shop.

NATIONAL PORTRAIT GALLERY   357-1300
8th and F Streets, NW 20560
Hours: 10 A.M.–5:30 P.M. daily
        Closed Christmas
Free Admission

 Gallery Place stop (red line); use 9th Street exit.

 42, 80, 81, X2, X4, B6, D2, D4, D6, D8, G6.

 7th or 9th Streets.

 Limited metered street parking; commercial lots on 9th Street between F and H Streets.

 On premises. Patent Pending, a small but notable cafeteria, offers "homemade" soups, breads, sandwiches, etc. In mild weather, you can eat at tables in the museum's courtyard. Cafeteria hours are 10 A.M. to 3:30 P.M. on weekdays and 11:30 A.M. to 5 P.M. on weekends.

 Recommended—especially the Hall of Presidents.

 Group tours available. Make arrangements in advance by calling the Education Department at 357-2920.

 Fully accessible. Ramped entrance is at 9th and G Streets.

Special tours can be arranged by calling 357-2920 at least 48 hours in advance.

Special tours can be arranged by calling 357-2920 or TDD 357-1696 at least 48 hours in advance.

 As noted above.

 Walk-in guided tours are available from 10 A.M. to 3 P.M. on weekdays and 11 A.M. to 2 P.M. on weekends and holidays.

The National Portrait Gallery is the nation's official picture album. The best-known faces in American history—and some little-known ones as well—are represented here in paintings, sculpture, drawings, prints, silhouettes and photographs. The Hall of Presidents and the Gallery of Notable Americans are permanent exhibits. Temporary exhibits abound, offering frequent changes of pace and subject.

Slide and lecture programs are given throughout the year; call 357-2920 for information and scheduling.

The Portrait Gallery shares the building, cafeteria and gift shop with the National Museum of American Art. See that site report for the building's interesting history.

ORGANIZATION OF AMERICAN STATES   **OAS: 458-3000**
(Pan American Union Building)   **Art Museum: 458-6016**
17th Street and Constitution Avenue, NW 20006
Hours: OAS—9:30 A.M.–5 P.M. weekdays
     Museum of Modern Art of Latin America—10 A.M.–5 P.M.
     Tuesday–Saturday
Free Admission

 Farragut West stop (blue and orange lines); a *long* walk south on 17th Street.

 13's, 80, 81, A2, A4.

 Constitution Avenue.

 Metered parking spaces along 17th Street.

 On premises. The cafeteria is open to the public from 9 A.M. to 4 P.M.; it serves simple, but authentic, Latin American food, as well as standard Washington fare.

 Recommended.

Group tours available in English, Spanish and Portuguese. Arrangements should be made at least two weeks in advance by calling 458-3751.

 Fully accessible. The entrance accessible to those in wheelchairs is on C Street. Parking can be arranged for those with disabilities by calling 789-3000 in advance of your visit.

 No special services available.

 No special services available.

 As noted above.

 Tours are given weekdays by request or reservation.

Founded in 1890, the Organization of American States is the world's oldest international organization of nations; its members include 26 nations of the Western Hemisphere. Its home, the Pan American Union Building, was designed by Albert Kelsey and Paul Philippe Cret and constructed in 1910. The building is itself a symbol of the potential for happy coexistence among inhabitants of the Western Hemisphere, a conscious and felicitous blend of the architectural styles of both continents.

The Tropical Patio, a splendid interior courtyard and fountain ringed with banana, coffee, rubber and palm trees, welcomes visitors. You won't need a guide to visit the Hall of the Americas (displaying flags and sculpture) or the small art gallery on the first floor, where contemporary U.S. and Latin American artists are featured in exhibits that change every three weeks, but if you want to see the meeting rooms of the Permanent Council or the General Assembly, take the tour. The Aztec Garden, and indeed the whole complex, blossoms with sculpture, ranging from Queen Isabella of Spain to Cordell Hull, FDR's secretary of state and "Father of the United Nations." Xochipilli, Aztec god of flowers, keeps watch in the garden. (He is not as nice as he sounds, being intimately associated with hallucinogenic drugs and blood sacrifices!)

Generally, you may find the Pan American Union Building flooded with school groups in the fall and spring. The least-crowded season is summer, when you're likely to enjoy a more leisurely visit and the full attention of the tour guides. A small gift shop in the courtyard sells Latin American fabrics, pottery and other crafts.

In the former residence of the secretaries general, at the end of the Aztec Garden Court on 18th Street, is the world's first Museum of Modern Art of Latin America. The museum displays over 200 paintings, sculptures and other works of art.

RENWICK GALLERY 357-2531
17th Street and Pennsylvania Avenue, NW 20560
Hours: 10 A.M.–5:30 P.M. daily
Closed Christmas
Free Admission

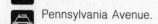 Farragut West stop (blue and orange lines) or Farragut North stop (red line); walk south on 17th Street.

30, 32, 34, 36, 37, 42, X2, X4, N2, N4, N6.

Pennsylvania Avenue.

P Practically no street parking; commercial lots on Pennsylvania Avenue between 17th and 18th Streets.

None on premises.

Recommended. A special "design experience" tour can be arranged for elementary-school children by calling 357-2531 two or three weeks in advance.

Tour available. Call 357-2531 three weeks in advance to make arrangements.

Limited accessibility. People in wheelchairs will need to use the ramp at the corner of Pennsylvania Avenue and 17th Street. Wheelchairs are available at the gallery.

Tours for visually impaired people can be arranged by calling 357-2531 two or three weeks in advance.

Tours for hearing-impaired people can be arranged by calling 357-2531 two or three weeks in advance.

A All tours are given by appointment only, conducted at 10 and 11 A.M. and 1 P.M. Monday to Thursday. Call 357-2531 to set up an appointment.

T No walk-in guided tours are given.

If you enjoy crafts, the Renwick Gallery will be a most exciting place to visit. The Renwick is the National Museum of American Art's exhibit of American crafts, decorative arts and design. Since opening in 1972, the gallery's exhibits have ranged from stark Shaker household goods to architectonic furniture and stained glass by Frank Lloyd Wright to Georg Jensen silver. Usually, the crafts and designs are even more up-to-the-minute, and contemporary craftsmen often get their first national showing here.

The setting is perhaps anachronistic, considering that the building is one of Washington's highest expressions of surpassingly high-style French Second Empire architecture. Constructed in 1859, the Renwick was originally designed to hold the art collection of William Wilson Corcoran. Look for his monogram and his portrait in stone on the building's front façade. Its architect and namesake was James Renwick, who also designed the Smithsonian "Castle" building on the Mall.

The Civil War intervened before Corcoran could move his collection into its new home, and the government seized the building for wartime use. The building was restored to Corcoran in 1874. Taking a cue from the octagonal gallery designed to show off the "Venus de Milo" at the Louvre, Corcoran raised Victorian eyebrows by building his own Octagon Room to display Hiram Powers' nude and graceful statue, "The Greek Slave."

By 1897, Corcoran's collection had grown too large for the Renwick and was moved to its present quarters, the great Beaux-Arts structure on 17th Street that bears Corcoran's name (see site report). The U.S. Court of Claims took possession of the Renwick and used it for the next 65 years.

When its demolition was contemplated in the 1960s, the Smithsonian rescued the building and meticulously restored it to a purpose more compatible with its origins. Corcoran's times, if not his collection, are evoked in the Renwick's plush second-floor Grand Salon and Octagon Room, hung with nineteenth-century European and American paintings and dotted with sculpture of the same period. The rest of the exhibit space is devoted to changing displays of design and crafts, both from the U.S. and abroad.

The gift shop is terrific, often offering crafts that have been created by the artists currently on exhibit in the gallery. In addition there is an excellent selection of books and publications devoted to design and crafts, as well as postcards, toys and games.

Twice a month at lunchtime the Renwick offers "The Creative Scene" film series. The subject of the films usually reflects what's on exhibit; check the monthly calendar, mentioned below. The gallery also hosts occasional concerts, lectures and crafts demonstrations. Call the gallery to see what's scheduled during your visit, or request the monthly calendar of events for the National Museum of American Art, of which the Renwick is a part. Send your name and address to Office of Public Affairs, Room 178, National Museum of American Art, Smithsonian Institution, Washington, D.C. 20560.

ST. JOHN'S CHURCH   **347-8766**
Lafayette Square, at 16th and H Streets, NW 20006
Hours: 8 A.M.–4 P.M. daily
Services: 8 A.M., 9 A.M., 11 A.M., 4 P.M. (in French) Sunday
            12:10 P.M. Monday, Tuesday, Thursday, Friday
Free Admission

McPherson Square or Farragut West stops (blue and orange lines); Farragut North stop (red line).
30, 32, 34, 36, 42, X2, X4, G4, N2, N4, N6.

16th Street—cross the street to Hay-Adams Hotel.

Commercial lots at 17th and H Streets and 16th and I Streets.

None on premises, except Wednesday "Déjeuner Français." A light lunch (under $7) begins promptly at noon in the parish house—only French is spoken. Call ahead for reservations at 347-8766.

Recommended for a brief visit. Nursery care is provided from 9 A.M. to noon for infants and toddlers whose parents are attending Sunday services.

Tours available. Make arrangements two weeks in advance by calling 347-8766.

Accessible.

No special services available.

Call in advance to arrange for signer at 347-8766.

As noted above.

T Walk-in tour is given after the 11 A.M. Sunday service.

Benjamin Henry Latrobe was so pleased with his design for St. John's Episcopal Church in 1816 that he not only donated his architectural services to the church, but he also wrote a hymn to celebrate its opening and performed as its first organist. Latrobe's small but elegant Greek Revival design is now obscured by additions made by other architects in the 1820s and later. James Renwick, architect of the Smithsonian's popular "Castle" on the Mall, supervised the installation of the stained-glass windows, designed by Madame Veuve Lorin, curator of stained-glass windows at Chartres Cathedral. Several other windows were installed in later additions to the church. One was given by President Chester Arthur in memory of his wife, who had been a member of St. John's choir. The President requested that the window be placed on the south side of the church so that he might see its light from his study in the White House. A 16-page booklet, which can be purchased in the vestibule, describes the church windows in detail and reproduces some in color.

Often called the Church of the Presidents, because every President since James Madison has worshiped there on some occasion, St. John's has designated Pew 54 as the traditional seat of worship for the First Family.

Next door on H Street, the Parish House (also known as the Ashburton House) is a pleasant companion to the little yellow church. Built as a private residence in 1836, it was the home of Lord Ashburton, the British minister, in 1842 when he negotiated the boundary between the U.S. and Canada with his friend Daniel Webster (who lived just down H Street where the Chamber of Commerce now stands). Aside from its historical interest, the house is a fine example of French Second Empire architecture in a relatively modest residential form. For grander examples, look at the Old Executive Office Building and the Renwick Gallery, both on Pennsylvania Avenue.

Free organ recitals are presented on Wednesdays at 12:10 P.M., except during Lent.

LILLIAN AND ALBERT SMALL   **Museum: 789-0900**
JEWISH MUSEUM
701 3rd Street, NW 20001

Hours: Weekdays by appointment
11 A.M.–3 P.M. Sunday
Free Admission

 Judiciary Square Stop; four-block walk.

 42, X2, X4, D2, D4, D6, D8.

 Difficult on Sundays; moderately easy weekdays.

 Noncompetitive street parking Sunday; competitive weekdays.

 None on premises. Reasonably close to carry-outs serving the nearby courthouses. Nothing open Sundays.

 Exhibits designed to appeal to all ages; principal interest to children sharing the cultural and historical context.

 Up to 40. Call two weeks in advance, 881-0100. Guide will be provided.

 First floor, which houses exhibits, is accessible. Balcony is not. No bathroom.

 No special services available now. Tapes planned.

 No special services available.

For weekday tours, call 881-0100 two weeks in advance.

Walk-in tours provided by docents on premises.

This building served as the original home of Adas Israel Synagogue, and was dedicated by President Ulysses S. Grant in 1876. When the congregation moved to larger quarters, it served as a Greek Orthodox church, an Evangelical Church of God, a grocery and a carry-out. Moved from its original site in 1969, the structure is a good example of nineteenth-century religious architecture—simple, unadorned, functional. The modest displays offer a glimpse of Jewish life in the Washington community over the last 100 years, including old photographs, ritual objects, letters and congregational records. The Holocaust is memorialized with a contemporary work of art by local artist Herman Perlman.

THE WASHINGTON POST COMPANY   **334-7969**
1150 15th Street, NW 20005
Hours: 10 A.M.–3 P.M. Monday and Thursday
    Tours by appointment only
Free Admission

M McPherson Square stop (blue and orange lines).

S1, S2, S3, S4—all on 16th Street.

15th Street.

P Difficult street parking; commercial lots in neighborhood.

IOI None on premises.

For insurance reasons, kids must be either in the 5th grade or 11 years old.

Group tours available. A maximum of 50 can take the tour at one time. Reservations must be made in advance.

Limited accessibility. Tour can be taken in wheelchair but phones and bathrooms aren't accessible.

No special services available.

Tours can be given in sign language; arrange at least a day in advance by calling 334-7969.

A As noted above.

T All tours are by appointment only.

The Washington Post gained national prominence in 1972 with its investigative reporting on Watergate by Carl Bernstein and Bob Woodward, which led to the resignation of President Richard Nixon. On an informative one-hour tour, you can see how this big-city newspaper gets put together each day; you'll see the newsroom and printing plant and learn of the *Post*'s history since it first published in 1877.

WHITE HOUSE   **456-7041**
1600 Pennsylvania Avenue, NW 20500

Hours: 10 A.M.–noon Tuesday–Saturday
      Closed Christmas and New Year's
Free Admission

M Farragut West stop (blue and orange lines) or Farragut North stop (red line); take Farragut Square exit. Walk south on Connecticut Avenue.

🚌 30, 32, 34, 36, 42, X2, X4, G4, N2, N4, N6.

🚗 Pennsylvania Avenue.

P Commercial lots at 17th and H Streets, along Pennsylvania Avenue between 17th and 18th Streets. Competitive metered street parking on Ellipse.

🍽️ None on premises.

👫 Recommended.

👨‍👩‍👧 No group tours available.

♿ Fully accessible. People with disabilities need not wait in line for the White House tour; go directly to the Northeast Gate on Pennsylvania Avenue for immediate admittance.

👁️ People with handicaps need not wait in line for the White House tour; go directly to the Northeast Gate on Pennsylvania Avenue for immediate admittance.

👂 No special services available.

A Visitors who plan ahead may be able to arrange for special "VIP" tours through their members of Congress. Six months is not too far in advance for residents of nearby states (Virginia, Maryland, Pennsylvania, New York, New Jersey, etc.), since congressional offices are deluged with requests for tickets virtually year-round. Bear in mind that senators receive only three passes per day, representatives only two, so they are not equipped to handle large groups or last-minute requests. Foreign visitors may be able to pick up VIP tickets at their embassies.

T Tours are given Tuesday to Saturday between 10 A.M. and noon. Because of the number of visitors who pass through the White House during this tight schedule, sightseers who want a tour of the executive mansion should be prepared for long lines and, at times, long waits. In the summer, admission is by ticket only, and tickets must be picked up in person; they are good only on the day issued and at the time specified. The tickets indicate the approximate time of your tour. They are distributed on a first-come, first-served basis beginning at 8 A.M. (often all tickets have been distributed by 9 A.M.) on the Ellipse (the park south of the White House); from Labor Day through Memorial Day, tickets are not necessary; line up at the East Gate by 10 A.M. Indoor seating is usually available for elderly people after they have obtained their tickets. While tours aren't available in foreign languages, free brochures are printed in Spanish, French, Italian, Russian, Chinese and Japanese. Tours are not conducted during state visits, so call ahead.

Each year more than a million and a half visitors pay their respects to the White House, home to every President and his family since 1800. When you catch sight of the lines waiting to see the White House in July and August, you may think a good part of those visitors have chosen the same day as you to view the "President's Palace"—so named by the city's first planner, Pierre L'Enfant. Since your visit in the White House may be as short as 10 minutes during peak tourist time, and since the tours aren't guided, it's wise to study what you'll be seeing before you arrive. For a detailed description, try an excellent guidebook to the White House and grounds, the White House Historical Society's *The White House: An Historic Guide,* available at the end of the tour or in many of Washington's bookstores.

In 1792, Thomas Jefferson announced a national design competition for the presidential residence. Jefferson himself submitted a design—anonymously—and lost. The winner, James Hoban, was an Irish architect practicing in Charleston, South Carolina, who proposed a building similar to Leinster Hall in Dublin.

John Adams found the house habitable, but not comfortable, when he became its first resident in 1800. Mrs. Adams hung her laundry to dry in the drafty and unfinished East Room—Theodore Roosevelt's children later roller-skated here. And Jefferson, who had grumbled at Hoban's Anglo-Palladian design as too grand for the chief executive of a new republic ("Big enough for two emperors, one Pope and the grand Lama," he sniffed), nevertheless became the first in the long succession of Presidents who have altered, added to, repaired or redecorated the mansion when he took up residence in 1807. He added the low service wings on either side of the main block of the house.

The executive mansion was nearly burned to the ground by British troops in August 1814. In 1902, Theodore Roosevelt found the mansion in such sad disrepair that he moved to a house on Jackson Place across Lafayette Square while the White House was repaired and enlarged. Harry Truman also found it necessary to leave his home in the White House when, in 1948, he found the structure so unsound—"standing up purely from habit"—that it had to be virtually rebuilt around a new steel frame. During the renovation, the Truman family lived across the street at Blair House, where visiting dignitaries now stay.

On your tour, you'll see only a few of the mansion's 132 rooms, but they're among the most historic. Visitors enter through the East Wing Lobby; through the windows you can see the Jacqueline Kennedy Rose Garden. Portraits of Presidents and their First Ladies hang in the hallway. As you pass through the Colonnade, enclosed with handmade antique glass, to the East Room, you can admire the changing exhibit of gifts presented by foreign governments to the U.S.

You'll undoubtedly recognize the East Room as the site of Presidential press conferences. The portrait of George Washington that hangs here is the oldest original White House belonging; Dolley Madison saved it as she and President Madison fled from the advancing British fires. The East Room has been the site of great moments in history: four First Family weddings (Nellie Grant, Alice Roosevelt, Jessie Wilson and Lynda Bird Johnson), the funerals of six Presidents (Harrison, Taylor, Lincoln, Harding, Franklin Roosevelt and Kennedy), as well as Richard Nixon's farewell address to his staff. The East Room today looks much as it did after the 1902 renovation, and is used to present plays, concerts and receptions.

The Green Room is a parlor that has been bedecked with some shade of green since James Monroe refurnished the White House after the 1814 fire. Of note are: an English cut-glass chandelier, 1790; furniture pieces by Duncan Phyfe, particularly the window benches, 1810; the New England sofa, once owned by Daniel Webster; and the English Empire marble mantel, installed by President Monroe after the 1814 fire.

The most formal of the parlors is the Blue Room, Hoban's "elliptical saloon," which now sports French Empire furnishings that date from—or are facsimiles of the furnishings of—Monroe's postconflagration decorating. The "blue" tradition of the room began in 1837 with President Van Buren. In this room, the President and First Lady officially receive their guests for receptions and state dinners.

The final parlor, the Red Room, is furnished in the American Empire style, popular between 1810 and 1830. Perhaps the best example of this style is the small, round, inlaid mahogany and fruitwood table opposite the fireplace.

The elegant gold and white State Dining Room, where 140 dinner guests can be seated, is next on the tour. George Healy's portrait of Abraham Lincoln hangs above the marble mantel, which is inscribed with President John Adams' prayer: "I pray Heaven to Bestow the Best of Blessings on THIS HOUSE and on ALL That shall hereafter Inhabit It."

The tour concludes in the Cross Hall and North Entrance Halls, passing the main stairway to the Presidential living quarters.

For relatively uncrowded, unhassled viewing, the best visiting time is from October until March, excluding December. The spring is usually heavy with school groups, summer with vacationing families, and December with those who want to see the White House Christmas decorations.

Several special tours are held each year. In December an evening candlelight tour of the seasonally decorated White House is given. In spring and fall an afternoon garden tour is conducted. The schedules for these tours are determined anew each year, so call 456-7041 to check if one is planned during your visit.

THE WILDERNESS SOCIETY'S ANSEL ADAMS COLLECTION 842-3400

1400 Eye Street, NW, 10th Floor, 20005

Hours: 10 A.M.–5 P.M. weekdays
Closed weekends and holidays

Free Admission

 McPherson Square stop (orange and blue lines), 14th Street exit.

 30's.

Available nearby.

Metered parking on street and commercial lots nearby.

 None on premises.

 Recommended for older kids, especially those interested in photography.

 For groups of 20 or more, call or write at least one week in advance to make arrangements.

 Fully accessible, including restrooms and water fountain.

 No special services available.

 No special services available.

 Not necessary.

 None available.

Seventy-five of Ansel Adams' most important landscape photographs are on permanent display in the Wilderness Society's new gallery. A visit here serves as a superb respite—a gentle reminder of the beauty of America's public lands, far indeed from the capital.

A gift from Adams, the prominent twentieth-century landscape photographer, the photographs have played a critical role in the evolution of American attitudes toward nature and conservation. Adams, long committed to wilderness preservation, decided several months before his death in 1984 that his work would best express its message in a permanent home where environmental policy is made.

Included in the collection is "The Minarets and Iceberg Lake, from Volcanic Ridge," a 1935 view of a spectacular wilderness section in the California High Sierra. Congress recently named the 226,000-acre area the Ansel Adams Wilderness.

A STROLL DOWN THE MAIN STREET OF THE NATION—PENNSYLVANIA AVENUE

Pennsylvania Avenue is undergoing a major fix-up campaign intended to complete, once and for all, L'Enfant's conception of a grand boulevard extending from the White House to the Capitol. While the Mall blossomed into L'Enfant's original vision, Pennsylvania Avenue deteriorated, becoming the home of Washington's red-light district. (During the Civil War, General Hooker attempted to control the ever-increasing number of ladies of the night who were attracted to Washington by the permanent presence of thousands of soldiers. He created a red-light district south of Pennsylvania Avenue from 7th to 14th Streets. The ladies became known as "Hooker's Division"—later shortened to "hookers.") On his inaugural ride from the Capitol to the White House in 1961, President Kennedy viewed Pennsylvania Avenue's plight—tired retail shops, abandoned lots and buildings, dreary federal offices—as a national disgrace, planting the seed of its renaissance.

The Pennsylvania Avenue Development Corporation (PADC) has drawn a master plan for the avenue that, when completed, will provide the area with 1,400 hotel rooms, 1,500 residential units, a slew of retail spaces, acres of offices, 700 trees, 300 benches and four new parks. Many of the architectural gems that remained on the avenue have been renovated for modern use. Concentrated on the north side of the avenue, the plan fills in the gaps left by two centuries of sporadic and unplanned development. Construction is underway—there's no telling what you'll encounter on your visit.

From the White House, follow the avenue east one block to the Treasury Building, considered to be one of the finest Greek Revival civic structures in the United States. The entire building, which covers five acres, is now faced with granite, but original wings were constructed of aquia sandstone, like the White House. The existing edifice is the third Treasury Building on this site. The first one suffered two disastrous fires, one accidentally in 1801, the other in 1814 at the hands of British troops. The second building also burned, in 1833. The present structure was designed by Robert Mills, Thomas U. Walter, Ammi B. Young, Isaiah Rogers and Alfred Bult Mullet (yes, *all* of them—but not all at once) and took 31 years to complete. Congress mandated that *this* building be fireproof. The east and center wings were constructed between 1838 and 1842, the south wing in 1860, the west wing in 1863, and the north wing in 1869—this addition required the demolition of the State Department Building and blocked forever the unobstructed vista from the White House to the Capitol.

The statue to the north of the building is of Albert Gallatin, the fourth secretary of the treasury, who served in that office longer than anyone else (1801–1814); the one to the south is of Alexander Hamilton, the first secretary of the treasury (1789–1795). The park directly south is Sherman Park, an imposing memorial to the Civil War general.

Along the way around the Treasury, you'll see Washington's financial district, which sprang up in the late nineteenth century. American Security and Trust Co. and Riggs National Bank—both in the Greek Revival style—are testimony to the fact that, at the turn of the century when banks often failed, investors wanted their bank to look solid. The red brick National Savings and Trust Company Building, designed in the 1880s, is a bit less imposing than its neighbors—indeed, even quirky in its ornamentation.

The 15th Street leg connecting the two diagonals of Pennsylvania Avenue has undergone a massive face-lift: Metropolitan Square houses the new Old Ebbitt Grill in cosmopolitan flair; the Hotel Washington has had its elegant sgraffito ornamentation restored by artisans from Italy and throughout the United States.

At the northwest corner of 14th Street and Pennsylvania Avenue, take a look at the Willard Hotel, an impressive Beaux-Arts structure built in 1901. Designed by Henry Hardenbergh, noted also for the Plaza Hotel in New York, the Willard was often called the Hotel of Presidents because many stayed here at one time or another. In an earlier hotel on this site, Julia Ward Howe wrote "The Battle Hymn of the Republic." The Willard has been lushly and faithfully restored to its turn-of-the-century opulence.

Pershing Park, in the middle of the avenue, is one of the new parks in the PADC scheme. It's an enticing spot for lunch on a sunny day (there's a food kiosk) or for ice-skating on a winter afternoon. Don't overlook what you're walking on as you traverse Western Plaza; it's an intriguing granite map of the area adorned with historic quotes.

To the north of the Plaza is the National Theater, which forms the base of the new National Press Building and The Shops at National Place. The Shops, a lively and elegant urban mall, connect to the sparkling new flagship of the Marriott hotel chain.

To the south of the avenue is the Beaux Arts–style District Building, Washington's city hall. At this point begins the Federal Triangle, the bureaucratic center of the nation. Facing 14th Street from the west is the Department of Commerce Building (which houses the National Aquarium in its basement—see that site report—and the Visitor's Information Center). When built, it was the largest office building in the world. Its semicircular neighbor to the east is the Post Office

Department, which looks out on an enormous parking lot and a fountain commemorating Oscar S. Straus, first secretary of the Department of Commerce and Labor. The parking lot was intended to become the Great Plaza, a landscaped crown for the western head of the Triangle; it's in the plans to rid the plaza of cars once again.

The Triangle proper stretches from 14th to 6th Streets, in the wedge of land formed by Pennsylvania Avenue on the north and Constitution Avenue on the south. With the exception of the Old Post Office Building and the District Building, which early twentieth-century planners expected to be demolished, all the buildings were designed in the neoclassical style and were constructed between 1928 and 1938. Their façades are more coherent, but no less intimidating, from Constitution Avenue.

At 12th Street, the Old Post Office, with its 315-foot clock tower, survives as one of Washington's few major examples of the Richardsonian Romanesque style popular in the 1890s. The Old Post Office, despite periodic schemes to tear it down and complete the Pennsylvania Avenue façade in a more compatible Greek or Roman style, has been restored and renovated as The Pavilion at the Old Post Office, a collection of shops, restaurants and food carts, with federal offices above. The National Park Service offers tours of the tower, which is the second-highest building in Washington. The view is splendid, with less of a wait than at the city's tallest structure, the Washington Monument.

The National Archives, between 9th and 7th Streets, is the repository of such venerable documents as the Declaration of Independence, the Bill of Rights and the Constitution (see site report in the "Mall" chapter). On the north side of the avenue is the massive, unwelcoming FBI building. To the north and east respectively are Market Square and Indiana Plaza, planned by PADC as a public park, pedestrian shopping area and condominium. At Market Square resides the U.S. Navy Memorial and a bandstand, which is the permanent home of the U.S. Navy Band. On the south side of the avenue you will find the only public monument in Washington to Franklin D. Roosevelt, the most influential President of this century. The Triangle tapers to a close at the Andrew Mellon Memorial Fountain, at the intersection of Pennsylvania and Constitution, across 6th Street from the rounded façade of the Federal Trade Commission Building. The Canadian Embassy is at 6th Street and Pennsylvania Avenue.

A WALK AROUND LAFAYETTE SQUARE

Lafayette Square, directly across Pennsylvania Avenue from the north entrance of the White House, began its official life in 1790 as part of the President's front yard in L'Enfant's plan for the federal city. Thomas Jefferson found the seven-acre plot too imposing for the use of a republican Chief of State; he declared the area a public park, and Pennsylvania Avenue was cut through to separate it from the Presidential grounds. The park came to be called Lafayette Square after an enormous public reception was held there in honor of the Marquis de Lafayette during his final visit to the United States in 1824.

The park in those days was hardly the landscaped gem we see today. An orchard when it was acquired for use by the federal government, it served as the site of brick kilns and laborers' huts during the construction of the White House. In the early nineteenth century, a racetrack ran along its western edge. The park was generally neglected as a young nation tended to its more pressing business.

Things began to look brighter in the 1850s when a planting program was devised by the brilliant young landscape architect Andrew Jackson Downing. In 1853, the dashing statue of Andrew Jackson— the first equestrian monument produced in America by a home-trained sculptor—was erected in the center of the park. The statue was a rousing public success, and for a time the park was renamed Jackson Square.

In the 1890s and the early twentieth century, other statues commemorating foreign military leaders who aided in the Revolution were added at the corners of the square. Lafayette came first, taking his position at the southeast corner (nearest the Treasury) in 1891. His compatriot, Major General Comte Jean de Rochambeau (the commander of the French Expeditionary Force), followed in 1902 at the southwest corner. Brigadier General Thaddeus Kosciuszko, the gallant Pole who built the fortifications at West Point and Saratoga before returning to fight in his own country's war of independence, occupies the northeast corner, and the Prussian hero who trained America's troops at Valley Forge, Baron von Steuben, stands at the northwest corner.

A less obvious memorial to a twentieth-century noncombatant is located near Jackson's statue—the Bernard Baruch "Seat of Inspiration," a park bench from which the noted philanthropist is said to have contemplated the world and mulled over his advice to his friend in the White House, Franklin D. Roosevelt.

The park still attracts lunchtime philosophers—as well as chess-players and sun-worshipers—since Lafayette Square is one of the most popular lunch sites for brown-baggers. You may recognize the park as the locale of past demonstrations shown on the nightly news; its proximity to the White House makes it popular with protesters.

Today the buildings around Lafayette Square are occupied almost exclusively by governmental or quasi-governmental agencies. The square's delightful present appearance is the result of a federal decision in the late 1960s to preserve as many of the older residential buildings as possible while still adding the huge amount of office space needed for federal workers.

Start your tour of the square area at the White House or Treasury Building. Then, cross Pennsylvania Avenue at the east end of the block onto Madison Place. The Treasury Annex (1921; Cass Gilbert, architect) will give you an idea of how early twentieth-century planners intended the area around the White House to look—plans and tastes changed later. In the middle of the block you'll find the red-brick, modern entrance to the new Court of Claims complex, constructed in the 1970s on a design by California architect John Carl Warnecke and Associates. Look behind you, across the square, and see its twin, the New Executive Office Building. Both buildings are set well back from the street behind low entrance courts to keep them from overpowering the smaller buildings around them. Farther down the street are the 1820s Tayloe House and the Dolley Madison House (properly, the Cutts-Madison House—Dolley lived there after her husband died, but it was built by her brother-in-law). Both are part of the Court of Claims complex, and the Tayloe House has a pleasant and charming government cafeteria—complete with chandeliers and antique-glass windows.

Across H Street, where 16th Street meets the square, is St. John's Church (see site report), with its parish house next door. Look up 16th Street and you'll see the carillon tower of a very different church—the Third Church of Christ Scientist—designed by modern architect I. M. Pei in the 1970s.

Starting at Decatur House (see site report) on the square's northwest corner, walk along Jackson Place (the western boundary of the square) and notice that many of the buildings are "in-fill" architecture—that is, structures designed simply to fill the spaces between existing ones without changing the character of the block. Decatur House, built in 1819, is the oldest residence remaining; it was the first building on the square constructed after the White House. Down the block are Victorian buildings dating from the 1860s to the 1890s. Theodore Roosevelt lived in one of them while the White House was being remodeled in 1902.

Take a right at the corner onto Pennsylvania Avenue. The Blair and Lee houses are in the middle of the block. They are the home-away-from-home for high-ranking foreign dignitaries on official visits to the United States. President Truman lived in Blair House while the White House underwent its massive restoration from 1948 to 1952. A plaque on the fence notes the attempt on his life by Puerto Rican fanatics and commemorates the life of a White House guard who died in that attack.

Next door is the Renwick Gallery, now part of the Smithsonian Institution (see site report). The Renwick is in the elaborate Second Empire style. Across Pennsylvania Avenue, you confront the Old Executive Office Building (formerly State, War and Navy), a mammoth Victorian edifice also in the Second Empire style popular during President Grant's administration. Grant insisted that no general should have to function in the cramped space then allotted to the Army Department, so he ordered construction in 1871 of what Harry Truman would fondly refer to as "the greatest monstrosity in America."

THE ELLIPSE—BACKYARD TO THE WHITE HOUSE

Immediately south of the White House, the Ellipse—now officially called the President's Park South—is a 54-acre oval of lawn bounded by 15th and 17th Streets and Constitution Avenue. In L'Enfant's 1791 plan for the city, the Ellipse was the southernmost portion of the grounds of the President's palace, but like much of the early capital, it remained marshland through most of the nineteenth century. The Ellipse was bounded on the south by the Tiber Canal, the present-day site of Constitution Avenue. Unfortunately, the canal, which was never a great success, had become an open sewer flowing past the White House by the time of the Lincoln administration. At the same time, the Ellipse itself served as a military campground and a corral for mules, horses and cattle; to avoid the stench, Lincoln spent many

summer nights at the Old Soldiers' Home. After the completion of the
Washington Monument (originally planned for the Ellipse but moved
because of the unstable soil conditions), the Army Corps of Engineers
filled and graded the land; with plantings designed by the great landscape architect Andrew Jackson Downing, the Ellipse took its present
form in 1880. During the summer, on Wednesdays at 7 P.M. components of the U.S. Army Band perform on the Ellipse. Call 696-3399
for information.

VISITING F STREET—A SMALL PIECE OF HISTORY

A visit to Ford's Theatre, the National Portrait Gallery or the National Museum of American Art (see site reports) affords an opportunity to look in on Washington's downtown shopping district. It's
easily accessible by Metrorail, via the Metro Center or Gallery Place
stops. Many of the buildings between 7th and 11th Streets on F Street
date from the nineteenth century, including the fine classical revival
structures of the Old Patent Office (between 7th and 9th Streets—now
the home of the aforementioned art galleries) and the LeDroit Building, a pre–Civil War office building at 8th Street, which the PADC
will renovate.

Architecture buffs will want to see the only Mies van der Rohe
building in Washington—the Martin Luther King, Jr., Memorial
Library at 901 G Street, with yet another pedestrian mall fronting it.

Washington's tiny Chinatown, between 6th and 8th Streets on G
and H Streets, is under intense development pressure because of the
Convention Center, bounded by 9th and 11th Streets, H Street and
New York Avenue and Mount Vernon Place. You can still find some
of the city's best Chinese restaurants here (see recommendations at
the end of this chapter) as well as numerous Oriental import shops
and groceries.

SAMPLING DOWNTOWN DINING

Downtown now has so many restaurants that to make sense of the
possibilities, from the fancy Continental through a bazaar of ethnic
foods to the countless carry-outs and fast-food vendors, we've divided
the area into a number of logical eating areas: Old Downtown (closest

to the Mall attractions), Chinatown, the White House area, New Downtown (north and west of the White House), and The West End (a newly developed area west of Washington Circle on Pennsylvania Avenue stretching to Georgetown).

Old Downtown—The Capitol to the White House

As Pennsylvania Avenue has been renewed and new office buildings have brought many more thousands of eaters to the area, restaurants have appeared. The best bets are located in the Old Post Office pavilion, at 15th Street and Pennsylvania Avenue, NW, and The Shops at National Place, 13th Street and Pennsylvania Avenue. Both feature sit-down restaurants and food halls. Families might try *Club LT* at National Place; its menu starts with peanut butter and jelly sandwiches . . . and goes on from there. The Pavilion has three major restaurants: *Hunan* (Chinese), *Fitch, Fox & Brown* (American) and *Blossoms* (salads, burgers, light fare). National Place has the *American Café* (soups, sandwiches, new American cuisine) and *Boston Seafood* (seafood and more). Both malls have an assortment of fast-food establishments serving just about everything—hot dogs, hamburgers, pizza, deli, barbecue, fresh fruit salads, you name it. Of special note in the Old Post Office pavilion is the Indian food stand; at National Place you can even get sushi to go!

Worth mentioning is the carry-out in Pershing Park, at 14th Street and Pennsylvania Avenue. It has a very limited menu of hot dogs, burritos and the like, but the park is lovely, an oasis of trees and water. Moreover, the park has nice public facilities and is accessible to those in wheelchairs.

The Willard Intercontinental Hotel (at 14th Street) deserves a look. Its restaurants: the *Willard Room*—formal, expensive American cuisine (637-7440)—and the *Café Espresso*—a more casual and moderately priced restaurant. The Hotel Washington next door to the Willard has undergone extensive renovation and now boasts a seasonal outdoor café with sandwiches, cold plates and salads. The hotel's rooftop *Terrace* restaurant has one of the best views in the city, a perfect setting for an evening drink in good weather. Across the street from the Willard is the flagship hotel of the Marriott chain; it connects directly to National Place. *The National Café* in the Marriott is pretty and moderately priced at lunch. The *Celadon* is fancy and a bit more expensive.

Around the corner at 675 15th Street, NW, is the new *Old Ebbitt Grill,* a Washington institution. The new facility is richly appointed; the atmosphere is lively, the service friendly (but we have found it slow) and the food hit or miss. Reservations are necessary, call 347-4800.

A number of other downtown hotels have restaurants worth mentioning. Close by the Marriott and Willard is *Occidental,* 1475 Pennsylvania Avenue, NW, 783-1475, which has received consistently excellent reviews for its updated versions of classic American dishes (expensive). *Herb's,* at the Holiday Inn, 1661 Rhode Island Avenue, NW, 333-4372, can be counted on for decent salads, burgers and inventive specials. The Jefferson Hotel, 1200 16th Street, NW, houses *The Hunt Club,* 347-2200, which serves expensive American cuisine in a formal, clublike setting favored by many power brokers. We had the best crab cakes we ever tasted there. In the Vista International Hotel, 1400 M Street, NW, you will find *American Harvest,* 429-1700, another rather expensive, but excellent, dining room for regional American food—New England to Southwest.

The *K Street Eatery,* 1411 K Street, NW (again, no credit cards), offers a variety of sandwiches, pizzas, salads and more—quality fast food. In the National Portrait Gallery, at 8th and F Streets, you will find a good, small cafeteria called *Patent Pending.*

In the same neighborhood, convenient to the Convention Center, is *Café Mozart,* 1331 H Street, NW, 347-5732, with Viennese and German specialties, and some of the best desserts in town—Sacher torte, Black Forest cake, strudel. There is live music daily. *Los Planes de Renderos,* 908 11th Street, NW, 347-8416, is an inexpensive South American restaurant with excellent food in a very plain setting.

The *Morrison-Clark Inn,* Massachusetts Avenue and 11th Street, NW, 898-1200, is a meticulously restored townhouse built in 1865; the Inn's dining room and fare are exquisite, New American cuisine at its finest.

A bit further afield are *A-V Ristorante Italiano,* 607 New York Avenue, NW, 737-0550 and, next door, the *Marrakesh,* 617 New York Avenue, 393-9393. A-V used to be a premier restaurant, but has gone through some changes. You can still get excellent food, however, if you hit it on the chef's good days. It's an old-fashioned, family-run place loaded with the feel of Italy. Marrakesh is fun. Open for dinner only (they will open for lunch for groups of 10 or more with advance notice) it is a multicourse, multihour dining experience, serving Moroccan cuisine in a traditional style—on low tables surrounded by cushioned banquettes. A stylish (and tasteful) belly dancer provides nightly entertainment. Terrific for an evening with a large group of friends.

Chinatown

Among the many impacts of the Convention Center is the revitalization of Washington's small Chinatown. Its borders are expanding, and its restaurants multiplying. Our old favorites, the *Szechuan,* 615 I Street, NW, 393-0130, and the *Ruby,* 609 H Street, 842-0060, have been joined by several restaurants of note. *Big Wong,* at 610 H Street, serves Cantonese food and dim sum all day in a small, crowded basement location—very cheap and very good. *The China Inn,* 631 H Street, 842-0910, has a wide variety of all styles of Chinese cuisine. *Ms. Tao,* 817 7th Street, 289-4144, offers excellent seafood.

As is true with most Chinese restaurants, you will usually find good, inexpensive food wherever you go in Chinatown. For conventioneers, Chinatown is a good bet.

Several large new developments are under construction in the Chinatown/Convention Center area—among them, Techworld, due for completion in 1991 and the new Grand Hyatt hotel at 1000 H Street. The Hyatt has three restaurants, from informal to fancy.

The White House Area—16th to 22nd Streets, Pennsylvania Avenue

Among the inexpensive eateries, a good bet is *Metro Market,* 18th and I Streets, with more than 20 varied fast-food stands—Italian, Greek, Chinese, bagels, barbecue, fish, chicken, etc. The *Paramount Coffee Shop,* 18th and I Streets, has a wide variety of sandwiches, salads, Greek specialties and daily specials at reasonable prices. *The Lunch Box* carry-outs can be found throughout downtown, including 825 20th Street, 1622 I Street, 1721 G Street, 1700 Pennsylvania Avenue. *Yummy Yogurt,* also in various downtown locations, including 1337 F Street, 1801 H Street, 1724 M Street, 2119 L Street, 1106 Vermont Avenue and 1010 17th Street, has salads, pita bread sandwiches and yogurts.

The Esplanade Mall, 20th and I Streets, has a variety of restaurants, plain to fancy: *Roy Rogers,* pizza, Chinese, *Swenson's* and *Sholl's Colonial Cafeteria,* a Washington landmark for solid, inexpensive food. *Vie de France* (659-0055), a French café, has an outlet in Esplanade and at 1723 K Street, too.

If you are in the mood for French, try *Le Gaulois,* 2133 Pennsylvania Avenue, 466-3232. It's one of our favorites; unpretentious, moderately priced. The "Red Lion Row," the block of Pennsylvania Avenue between 20th and 21st Streets, has several fine choices, including *Wolensky's* (463-0050), for burgers and salads; *Devon Grill* (833-5660), for mesquite-grilled chicken, fish and meats; and *Le Café,* a French café with excellent filled croissants, sandwiches and desserts.

New Downtown
Where to start? The area north and northwest of the White House, up to M Street, has almost too many choices. Along the K Street corridor, we can recommend *China Express* (223-4139) (cafeteria style, inexpensive) and *Thai Kingdom* (835-1700) (spicy, moderate). Many of the city's most expensive restaurants are found in these blocks, including *Tiberio* (452-1915), *Jean-Pierre* (466-2022), *Prime Rib* (466-8811); *Mr. K's* (331-8868) and *Sichuan Pavilion* (466-7790) are perhaps two of the fanciest Chinese restaurants to be found anywhere. All are excellent, elegant and expensive.

Moderately priced choices include *Café Marché* (293-3000), 1810 K Street; *Health's-a-Popping* (466-6616), 2020 K Street; *Ziggy* (331-0860), 1015 18th Street.

Along the numbered streets—18th, 19th and 20th from I Street north to Dupont Circle—you will find an assortment to suit any taste. Among the best (and most expensive, sorry) are *Il Giardino,* 1110 21st Street, NW, 223-4555, with exquisitely prepared and presented Northern Italian food; *Shezan,* 913 19th Street, 659-5555, for Indian and Continental; *Le Lion D'Or,* 1150 Connecticut Avenue, at 18th Street, 296-7972, the grande dame of haute cuisine French restaurants; *Cantina d'Italia,* 1214A 18th Street, 659-1830, another landmark of Northern Italian cuisine; and *Gary's,* 18th and M Streets, in the courtyard, 463-6470, for what many consider the best steaks in town. At a more reasonable price level, try *The Great Wall* (Chinese), 1120 19th Street (296-4956), and *Luigi's* (331-7574), 1132 19th Street (famous for their pizza).

M Street from Connecticut Avenue west to 22nd is chockablock with restaurants. *The Astor* (331-7994), 1813 M Street, offers no-nonsense Greek food at reasonable cost. *Bacchus* (785-0734), 1827 Jefferson Place (a half block north of M), is a Washington institution, serving basic Lebanese food.

7

GEORGETOWN/ FOGGY BOTTOM/ THE WEST END

GEORGETOWN—AN INTRODUCTION

Georgetown is history, trendy boutiques, crowded cobblestoned streets, peaceful and staid grand estates, a watering hole for the "in crowd," canal walkers/joggers, galleries, music, fine and frilly food— and much, much more. It's a hustle, steeped in times gone by, and the contrasts lead to delight and entertainment at every turn. If there's one place in Washington where folks just go to walk around, day or night, it's Georgetown.

Georgetown began as an Indian trading center. The earliest recorded description of the confluence of the Potomac River and Rock Creek was written by Captain John Smith, who sailed up the Potomac in 1608, noting several tribes of farming Indians. In 1703, Lord Baltimore ceded most of the Georgetown area to Ninion Beall, who established a plantation, and George Gordon, a merchant who made a fortune by founding a tobacco-inspection station. In 1751, the State of Maryland recognized the town of George as a major tobacco port; the Potomac was wide and deep enough to be navigable by ships, and the town of George was the last port point before the river's Great Falls.

The town boomed, and was incorporated in 1789 as "George Town." In the same year Georgetown University was founded as the first Roman Catholic university in the United States. Wealthy merchants and middle-class tradesmen resided in town, and sneered at their uncultured country cousins setting up the new city of Washington just down the river. While L'Enfant envisioned the capital growing eastward, it expanded west—many feel as a result of Georgetown's civilized attractiveness.

The glory days were soon over, however, as the railroads, steam-powered ships and river silt destroyed Georgetown's usefulness as a port. Despite the construction of the Chesapeake and Ohio Canal and the diversification into flour, munitions and paper industries on the waterfront, Georgetown declined, losing its charter in 1871 when it was officially annexed by the capital city.

From 1880 through 1890, a multitude of brownstone Victorian houses were built for the benefit of federal workers. Today, almost half of Georgetown's houses date from that period or before. By the 1920s, more than half of Georgetown's population were poverty-stricken blacks who had few means to repair the deteriorating housing stock—but Georgetown's charm was still visible. Though some restoration began in the 1920s, the New Dealers gentrified the area; today Georgetown is one of the city's most exclusive—and expensive—places to live.

Beyond the sites noted in this chapter (Dumbarton Oaks, a marvelous Georgian estate, and Old Stone House, a humble middle-class residence dating from the 1760s), Georgetown is a delight in itself. Shopping opportunities abound (see the "Shopping" chapter), eating possibilities boggle the mind (see our recommendations at this chapter's end), nighttime entertainment potentials challenge the hardiest (see the "Entertainment" chapter) and the peacefulness of the restored C&O Canal beckons (see the site report in the "Nearby Maryland" chapter).

Of course, explore the main drags of Wisconsin Avenue and M Street—but don't stop there. The real charm of Georgetown lies in its shaded, elegant back streets, so stroll about for as long as your feet hold out to savor its flavor. If you're here in April, check the newspapers for the schedules of the annual Georgetown House and Garden Tours for a more intimate view.

Don't overlook a stroll through Georgetown's new waterfront development, Washington Harbor. After many years, this area has finally become an attraction deserving of its capital views. It's also great fun to take a barge trip on the C&O Canal (see the "Outdoor Washington/Sports" chapter).

There are no Metro stops in Georgetown (the Citizen Association of Georgetown, an extremely powerful civic group, rejected the idea), but buses run along M Street and Wisconsin Avenue (30, 32, 34 and

36). You can also view M Street on an Old Town Trolley Tour, as part of an 11-stop tour of the city. Riders can get off, explore the area and reboard later (call 269-3020 for details).

Parking in Georgetown is incredibly difficult, especially on weekends, so it's best to leave your car behind (with the possible exception of your trip to Dumbarton Oaks, which is a healthy uphill distance from Georgetown's commercial center).

DUMBARTON OAKS   **338-8278 (recorded information)**
                              342-3200 (main number)
                              342-3212 (guided tours)

1703 32nd Street, NW 20007 (museum entrance)
31st and R Streets, NW (garden entrance)
Hours: Gardens: 2–6 P.M. daily
          Byzantine and Pre-Columbian collections:
          2–5 P.M. Tuesday–Saturday
          Closed holidays
Admission: $2

 No Metro stop.

 D2 and D4 on Q Street, even-numbered 30's or any other Wisconsin Avenue bus.

 Wisconsin Avenue.

 Competitive two-hour parking in neighborhood; especially difficult on weekends.

 None on premises; picnicking in Dumbarton Oaks is not permitted. Picnic tables can be used in Montrose Park on R Street; from Wisconsin Avenue, enter through the gate near the end of the Dumbarton Oaks fence.

 Gardens are recommended, though visitors must stay on paths. Public playgrounds are next door to Dumbarton Oaks.

Group tours available. Tours of the Byzantine collection can be arranged by calling 342-3212.

 Inaccessible to people in wheelchairs without assistance. Steps must be traversed, and the garden has gravel/cobblestone paths that could be difficult. Bathroom and phone are not accessible.

No special services available.

No special services available.

 Call recording at 338-8278 to find out when museum tours are
being offered, and what's in bloom in the garden.
 No walk-in guided tours are given.

Though it's just around the corner from Georgetown's heavily
trafficked Wisconsin Avenue, Dumbarton Oaks feels like a well-
mannered country retreat. Ten acres of formal gardens surround a
museum that houses two collections, one of Byzantine art and the
other of Pre-Columbian artifacts.

The gardens of Dumbarton Oaks manage to be both lush and
formal, with fountains and benches amid meticulously planned flower
beds and borders. Even on the most crowded weekend you can have
a peaceful moment in a private garden cul-de-sac. Allow yourself
enough time for a leisurely stroll.

The Dumbarton Oaks Byzantine and Pre-Columbian collections
were assembled by Mr. and Mrs. Robert Woods Bliss, who acquired
the property of Dumbarton Oaks in 1920. The beautifully displayed
Pre-Columbian pieces, housed in a pavilion designed by Philip Johnson, are arranged according to culture in a generally geographical and
chronological sequence. The Byzantine collection, dealing primarily
with the minor arts, includes jewelry, metalwork and textiles.

The Dumbarton Oaks land was part of the original 1702 grant by
Queen Anne of what was to become the thriving port of Georgetown,
then part of Maryland. The original house was built in 1801 by
William Dorsey. In 1940, the Bliss family gave the Dumbarton Oaks
collections and research libraries to Harvard University, which still
owns and oversees the property. It was here in 1944 that the conferences were held that led to the formation of the United Nations.
Today, Dumbarton Oaks serves as a research center on Byzantine and
Pre-Columbian studies, and landscape architecture. It houses the museums and libraries on the Pre-Columbian and Byzantine periods. It
also contains a large garden library. The libraries are open only to
scholars, though the rare-book room of the garden library is open for
viewing on weekends from 2 to 5 P.M.

Occasionally, concerts are performed on the grounds; in the winter,
concerts in the music room of the house emphasize seventeenth- and

eighteenth-century pieces. Call 342-3200 to find out if there will be any music when you plan to visit.

A sales shop sells a few good, inexpensive replicas of pieces in the museums as well as postcards and scholarly publications on the collections.

Formal gardens border on Rock Creek Park and Montrose Park, where there is a playground. A paved path runs along the eastern edge of the Dumbarton Oaks gardens; if you follow it to its end you'll wind up on Massachusetts Avenue just above the Islamic Center (see site report). Even though the path is paved, about halfway through you may begin to feel you're in a forest far from the city.

OLD STONE HOUSE   426-6851
3051 M Street, NW 20007
Hours: 9:30 A.M.–5 P.M. Wednesday–Sunday
          Closed Thanksgiving, Christmas and New Year's
          Garden open 9:30 A.M.–5 P.M. daily
Free Admission

 No Metro stop.

 30, 32, 34, 36, 38, 5K, 55.

 M Street.

 Competitive parking; commercial parking lots on M and Jefferson Streets.

 None on premises. Picnic tables available.

 Recommended.

 Small group tours can be arranged by calling 426-6851.

 Limited accessibility. The first floor and garden are accessible; a photo album of the second floor, which is inaccessible, is available for viewing. There are no bathrooms or phones.

 "Seeing" tour available at all times.

A staff member who is hearing-impaired is always at Old Stone House and is available for signed tours and questions.

As noted above.

A narrated slide show is being developed. A candlelight tour is given at 7 P.M. on Wednesday during the second week of each month from October to May; the tour is followed by a presentation of eighteenth-century music in the parlor.

This, the oldest house originally built in Washington, is a charmer. Built in 1765, and added on to by subsequent tenants, Old Stone House was owned by a cabinetmaker; it's quite representative of middle-class dwellings of the late eighteenth and early nineteenth centuries, and, as such, provides pleasant contrast to the grand houses of the Washington wealthy that are also open to the public.

The house's five rooms include a shop where craft demonstrations are given by women garbed in eighteenth-century costume. Those who give the demonstrations are extremely knowledgeable on the house and are quite pleased to answer questions. A small but lovely colonial garden is in back of the house. Together the house and garden provide an appealing respite from one of the busiest streets in the city.

FOGGY BOTTOM—AN INTRODUCTION

Belying its humorous name, Foggy Bottom is an impressive place these days, the locale of the Kennedy Center for the Performing Arts, George Washington University, international monetary organizations, the Departments of State and Interior and swanky retail/residential complexes. It wasn't always so. When Jacob Funk purchased 130 acres in this area in 1765, much of the land was malarial river marsh. Initially incorporated as Hamburg, and known as Funkstown, this land was included in the planned capital in 1791. The area became Washington's industrial center, with a glass factory, gas works, coal depot and brewery—the foul industrial emissions led to the nickname Foggy Bottom. Irish, Italian and German immigrants lived and worked here, west of 23rd Street; to the east, the middle-class civil servants made their homes. The university, founded in 1821, has been expanding ever since. Federal agencies began their influx to Foggy Bottom after World War II, and redevelopment of the area followed.

The area today is roughly defined by the following borders: 18th

Street on the east; Constitution Avenue on the south; the Potomac River and 26th Street on the west; and Pennsylvania Avenue on the north. Street parking, of course, is difficult, but you can appreciate the essence of the area by driving through—although traffic can also be horrendous. The Kennedy Center has ample parking.

INTERIOR DEPARTMENT MUSEUM 343-2743
18th and C Streets, NW 20240
Hours: 7:45 A.M.–4:15 P.M. weekdays
      Closed holidays
Free Admission

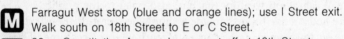 Farragut West stop (blue and orange lines); use I Street exit. Walk south on 18th Street to E or C Street.

80 or Constitution Avenue buses; get off at 18th Street.

18th Street.

Competitive, metered street parking. Commercial parking lots on 18th and 19th Streets above E, and New York Avenue between 17th and 18th Streets.

On premises. The Interior Department cafeteria is open from 7 to 8:15 A.M. and 11:00 A.M. to 1:45 P.M.

Recommended. Kids like the dioramas and Native American handicrafts and clothing.

Call 343-2743 to arrange for group tours.

Fully accessible. Use the E Street entrance.

No special services available.

No special services available.

As noted above.

No scheduled walk-in tours are given.

The Interior Department Museum is a microcosm of the myriad activities of the enormous composite of the National Park Service, the

Bureau of Land Management, the Bureau of Reclamation, the Geological Survey, the Bureau of Indian Affairs and other agencies. The museum consists of 10 exhibit galleries that include paintings, dioramas, Native American handicrafts, maps, aerial surveys, scientific models and a wealth of other specimens, artworks and artifacts. A particularly fascinating aspect of the museum is its portrayal of the opening of the West, illustrated by original land grants, bounties, patents and other documents, as well as through paintings and photos.

Next to the galleries is the Indian Crafts Shop, where authentic handmade Native American objects are sold.

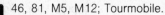

JOHN F. KENNEDY CENTER   254-3600
FOR THE PERFORMING ARTS
New Hampshire Avenue
and Rock Creek Parkway 20566
Hours: 10 A.M.–1 A.M. daily
Free Admission

M Foggy Bottom stop (blue and orange lines); walk west on
H Street, then south on New Hampshire Avenue.
🚌 46, 81, M5, M12; Tourmobile.

🚗 Building entrance or Virginia Avenue.

P Commercial parking lot in basement. Half-hour free parking
before 6 P.M. to pick up tickets. $1.50 for first hour; $1 per hour
thereafter with $5 maximum. $3 flat fee at night.

🍽 On premises. The Rooftop Terrace offers three separate
restaurants catering to different budgets. The Encore Cafeteria
has hot entrées (in $3 range), fruit and vegetable salads, soups
and desserts; it's open daily from 11 A.M. to 8 P.M. Curtain Call
Café is open daily from 5 to 8 P.M. and offers quiche, burgers,
casseroles and the like in the $6 range. The Roof Terrace
Restaurant and Hors D'Oeuvrerie (833-8870) has expensive
French cuisine; you'll need reservations. Light snacks are
available at the Hors D'Oeuvrerie from 5 P.M. until midnight. In
warm weather, Encore has seating outside on the terrace with a
splendid view of the Potomac River, Georgetown and the Mall.

👪 Recommended. The Kennedy Center has some terrific
entertainment series for kids. Free programs for children and

youth are presented on a dozen Saturdays throughout the year; these wonderful productions include dance, plays, musicals, puppets, music and mime. Call 254-3600 to see if one's on while you're in town.

 No special group tours available. Groups can be accommodated in regular tours, 10 A.M. to 1 P.M.; call 254-3643.

Fully accessible. For performances, reserve wheelchairs one hour before curtain by calling 254-3774. Contact the usher to be guided to special theater entrances. Half-price tickets are available to most performances.

Braille in elevators; half-price tickets are available to most performances. Call 254-3774 to find out if audio descriptions are available for a particular performance.

The Eisenhower Theater, Opera House and Terrace Theater are equipped with 25 receiver headsets and five hearing-aid receivers. Half-price tickets are available for most performances.

A limited number of half-price tickets for most performances are available for students, senior citizens, low-income patrons, people with handicaps and enlisted military personnel (E1-4). Coupons for these tickets must be picked up and validated at the Friend's Volunteer Desk in the Hall of States before purchasing tickets at the box office.

The best way to see the Kennedy Center is on one of the free 45-minute tours which leave daily from 10 A.M. until 1 P.M. from Motor Lobby A. You'll see much more on these tours than you can on your own, including the exquisite theater lounges, housing gifts of various nations. Written tour scripts in German, Italian, Spanish, French, Portuguese and Japanese are available at the beginning of the tours.

———————————————

Before the Kennedy Center for the Performing Arts opened in 1971, Washington was considered by many to be culturally anemic; with the center's advent, however, the capital has become a national—and, indeed, international—cultural force. The finest opera, dance, music and theater companies in the world perform in the center's four theaters, and classic and contemporary films are shown in the American Film Institute.

The center is far more than a cultural bonanza, however; it is the sole official memorial to President John F. Kennedy in the nation's capital. A seven-foot-high bronze bust of the slain President stands in the center of the Grand Foyer, and many of his quotations are carved into the center's river façade, clearly visible from the River Terrace. In JFK's memory, many nations gave exquisite gifts which have been incorporated into the building.

The marble structure (the marble was a gift from Italy), designed by Edward Durell Stone, commands a spectacular view of the Potomac River, Georgetown and bits of the Mall. An elegant Entrance Plaza (the bronzes were gifts from West Germany) fronts the building's two entrances, one to the Hall of States wherein flags of America's states and territories are flown, and one to the Hall of Nations, wherein flags of all nations officially recognized by the U.S. are displayed. These halls lead to the 630-foot Grand Foyer, where 18 Orrefors crystal chandeliers sparkle (a gift from Sweden) in front of enormous mirrors (gifts from Belgium). The Grand Foyer opens onto the River Terrace, a lovely and romantic composite of marble, fountains and willow trees.

The three major performance stages are entered from the Grand Foyer: the gold-and-white Concert Hall, which seats 2,750, has fine acoustics—and elegant chandeliers (from Norway); the Opera House, which seats 2,300, is designed for opera, ballet and musical-theater presentations (note the gold silk stage curtain from Japan and starburst chandelier from Austria); the Eisenhower Theater seats 1,200 and is paneled with East Indian laurel (the stage curtain was a gift from Canada). The entrance to the American Film Institute Theater is in the Hall of States.

The Rooftop Terrace often has notable exhibits. The Terrace Theater, a bicentennial gift to the center from Japan, opened in 1979. This small, 500-seat theater is ideal for chamber music, poetry readings and theater performances. Also on this level is the Theater Lab, offering free performances, often for children. Ticket information for the various stages can be obtained by calling: Concert Hall—254-3776; Opera House—254-3770; Eisenhower Theater—254-3670; American Film Institute—785-4600; and Terrace Theater—254-9895. Telephone ticket sales are handled by Instant Charge at 857-0900. For more information about entertainment possibilities at the Kennedy Center, see the "Entertainment" chapter.

The Rooftop Terrace offers a grand view. To the center's north is the Watergate complex, home of exceedingly expensive apartments, a hotel, exclusive shops and offices (you'll recall the Watergate break-in of the Democratic National Committee offices, which eventually led to President Richard Nixon's resignation).

The Performing Arts Library is open to the public from 11 A.M. to 8 P.M. Tuesday to Saturday, and Wednesday and Friday evenings. As well as housing a wealth of information on the performing arts, the library has changing exhibits of manuscripts and visual displays supplied by the Library of Congress. For information, call 254-9803.

Christmas is a particularly exciting time at the center; check the newspapers or call 254-3600 to see what's on—especially the enormous Christmas caroling fest.

The Kennedy Center has two gift counters, one in each hall of the main level. Souvenirs appropriate to the center and its performances are sold.

THE OCTAGON   **638-3105**
1799 New York Avenue, NW (at 18th Street) 20006
Hours: 10 A.M.–4 P.M. Tuesday–Friday
         1–4 P.M. weekends
         Closed Thanksgiving, Christmas and New Year's
Donations Requested

Farragut West stop (blue and orange lines); use 18th Street exit.

52, 80, 81, S1 (during rush hour only).

New York Avenue.

Competitive street parking on side streets in area; commercial lots on New York Avenue.

None on premises.

Not recommended for kids under 12.

Tours available. Reservations must be made at least two weeks in advance for groups of 10 or more. Fee charged for groups: $2 for adults, 50¢ for senior citizens and kids.

Limited accessibility. Only the first floor is accessible to people in wheelchairs; enter through the garden. The bathroom is not accessible; there is no phone.

No special services available.

No special services available.

As noted above.

 Walk-in tours are given continually.

The Octagon, built in 1798, is one of the few central Washington buildings that survived the British entry into the capital during the War of 1812. A fine example of Federal-style architecture, the Octagon was built as the town home of the John Tayloe family. Tayloe, a Virginia plantation owner, was persuaded by his friend, George Washington, to build his home in the new capital rather than in Philadelphia. The house was designed by William Thornton, who served as the first architect of the Capitol.

When the British burned the White House and the Capitol, the Octagon was spared—perhaps because the French minister who was residing there prominently flew his nation's flag from the house. When President James Madison and his wife, Dolley, returned to the city to find their house in ruins, they stayed at the Octagon. It was here, in the second-floor study, that Madison signed the Treaty of Ghent that ended the War of 1812. The table on which the document was signed is on display, along with other appropriate Federal-period furnishings.

Today, the Octagon is operated as a historic house museum by the American Institute of Architects Foundation; not only can visitors tour the house with its intriguing basement kitchen, but they can also see changing architectural and historical exhibitions in the second-floor exhibit area.

The Octagon is reported to harbor a number of Tayloe family ghosts, but this is a topic not stressed in the architecturally oriented tours. Visitors are treated very graciously. A small sales area in the entrance hall offers books and pamphlets of architectural interest.

The American Institute of Architects headquarters building is located behind the Octagon; occasional exhibits are presented in the first- and second-floor lobbies of that building.

THE WEST END—AN INTRODUCTION

The West End is a neighborhood just coming into its own. North of Pennsylvania Avenue between Washington Circle and Georgetown, the West End, until recently, was something of a neglected stepchild, never really part of Downtown and shunned by nearby Georgetown.

Now it has become a lively neighborhood in its own right. Glitzy new office buildings dot the area, and many restaurants, hotels and cinemas have ushered in new life. Although there are no specific sights of note, you may want to try a restaurant here and then explore the neighborhood starting at 23rd Street.

GEORGETOWN/FOGGY BOTTOM/THE WEST END —THE EDIBLE FARE

Georgetown is tricky. Every time you look, new restaurants have appeared and those you thought would last forever are gone. So it goes in the food business. And Georgetown, too, is under pressure in a sense; other areas of the city are blooming with new restaurants and diners are being lured away from old Georgetown haunts. But don't get us wrong; you can still eat at a different restaurant every day and not repeat yourself for several seasons of the year.

To make sense of this area of town, we will work our way west from Washington Circle on Pennsylvania Avenue, down a few blocks toward the Kennedy Center and then westward-ho to Georgetown.

The West End

A small nest of restaurants can be found on the west side of Washington Circle along Pennsylvania Avenue. *The Bristol Grill,* 2430 Pennsylvania Avenue, 955-6400, is expensive; try the mesquite-grilled meats. *Marshall's West End,* 2525 Pennsylvania Avenue, 659-6886, is a pleasant bar/restaurant serving standard but highly edible fare. The *One Step Down,* 2517 Pennsylvania Avenue, 331-8863, offers jazz, live and canned, along with bar food. Other choices in the immediate area include *Donatello* (Italian) and *Brasil Tropical.*

Foggy Bottom

The Foggy Bottom Café, 924 25th Street, 338-8707, remains a charming place, serving a mix of new American cuisine and eclectic Continental. Convenient to the Kennedy Center, it is a popular spot for before- and after-theater dining. Moderately expensive.

The Kennedy Center itself has a number of food facilities, from cafeteria style to tablecloth elegant. See site report for details.

The Watergate complex has several restaurants, ranging from the ultra-expensive and culinarily exploratory *Jean-Louis,* 2650 Virginia Avenue, 298-4488, to a favorite for after-theater light fare, *Les Champs,* 600 New Hampshire Avenue, 338-0700 (try their blintzes!), especially as a way to avoid the post-performance parking lot crunch.

Georgetown

The "entrance" to Georgetown is guarded by the *Four Seasons Hotel,* 2800 Pennsylvania Avenue, 342-0444, which we can heartily recommend for high tea (scones, clotted cream, the works). Close by you can find fine Mexican at *Enriqueta's,* 2811 M Street, 338-7772. For pizza and other light Italian fare, *Gepetto's,* 2917 M Street, 333-2602, is a good bet. You may often find lines and the service may match the crush.

On Georgetown's waterfront, at Washington Harbor, you'll find a stylish Southwestern restaurant in *Jaimalito's,* 3000 K Street, 944-4400. At 3223 K Street is *River Club,* 333-8118, delicious food and dancing in a gorgeous Art Deco setting.

Up along M Street, you will find two of Washington's better Vietnamese restaurants, *Viet Huong,* 2929 M Street, 337-5588, and *Vietnam Georgetown,* 2934 M Street, 337-4536. Both are good; spring rolls are a real delicacy. Continuing in an ethnic vein, *Apana,* 3066 M Street, 965-3040, is a wonderful and elegant Indian restaurant. The flavors are subtle, the service quiet and careful and the surroundings beautiful. *Bistro Français,* 3128 M Street, 338-3830, is an attractive café/restaurant with a menu that has strengthened over time. Open until 4 A.M.

Down 31st Street are several attractive eateries. *La Ruche,* 1039 31st Street, 965-2684, still offers decent food at attractive prices, as does *Tout Va Bien,* 1063 31st Street, 965-1212. Neither offers memorable food, but you won't likely be disappointed; service is attentive and the surroundings pleasant.

Hamburger Hamlet, 3125 M Street, 965-6970, conforms to the menu of this national chain, with burgers, omelettes, sandwiches and salads. *Chadwicks,* 3205 K Street, 333-2565, tries hard to please with a family-style pub atmosphere and decent burgers. *Clyde's,* 3325 M Street, 333-0294, is yet another Washington landmark, famous for its brunch, burgers and Bloody Marys. It is the quintessential bar/restaurant.

El Caribe, 3288 M Street, 338-3121, is one of the city's excellent Latin American restaurants (with a branch on Columbia Road). Chicken, shrimp, pork—and mountains of black beans and rice. A real treat awaits you at *Bamiyan,* 3320 M Street, 338-1896. If you have never tried Afghani cuisine, now is the time. (Bamiyan has two sister locations—Old Town Alexandria and Connecticut Avenue and Calvert Street, NW.) The food is a cross between Middle Eastern (shish kebabs) and Indian subcontinental (yogurt, mint and Indian spices). Delicious. Be sure to try the noodles stuffed with meat in a tomato/meat sauce and the sauteed pumpkin.

Morton's, 3251 Prospect Street, 342-6258, is a superb steakhouse and very expensive. At 1226 36th Street, 965-1789, *1789* offers classic French cuisine in elegant surroundings. Downstairs from 1789 is *The Tombs,* a college burger-and-brew bar. Turning up Wisconsin Avenue at M you'll find the *American Café and Market,* 1211 Wisconsin Avenue, 944-9464: soups, sandwiches and enticing desserts, eat-in or carry-out. Two blocks up is *Aux Fruits de Mer,* at 1329 Wisconsin Avenue, 333-2333, emphasizing fish and seafood. Its cohort next door, *Au Pied de Cochon,* 1335 Wisconsin Avenue, 333-5440, is a French bistro, inexpensive and crowded. *Sarinah Satay House,* 1338 Wisconsin Avenue, 337-2955, serves carefully prepared Indonesian food at moderate prices.

In the upper reaches of Georgetown are five restaurants worth mentioning. First, the *Japan Inn,* 1715 Wisconsin Avenue, 337-3400, for a broad variety of Japanese cuisine; *La Niçoise,* 1721 Wisconsin Avenue, 965-9300, where the waiters whirl about on roller skates and provide raucous songs and skits; good, clean fun . . . and the food isn't bad either, but it is expensive. Washington's first sushi bar, *Sushi-ko,* 2309 Wisconsin Avenue, 333-4187, is a tiny gem with a gentle atmosphere. It has nonsushi items, too. *Germaine's,* across the street, 2400 Wisconsin Avenue, 965-1185, serves food of several Asian countries—Vietnam, China, Korea—but with an emphasis on the fresh and natural tastes of the "new" cuisines. Finally, and save this one for when you have a big hunger, is *Old Europe,* 2434 Wisconsin Avenue, 333-7600, stolid fare from schnitzel to strudel. *Sehr gut.*

A few good carry-outs: *Uno Pizzeria,* 3211 M Street, 965-6333; *Ikaros,* 3130 M Street, 333-5551—terrific "airborne" pizza, souvlaki and gyros. For ice cream, try *Bob's Famous,* 2416 Wisconsin Avenue (one of the very best anywhere) or *Häagen-Dazs,* 1438 Wisconsin Avenue.

8

NORTHWEST

The Northwest quadrant of Washington is a collection of distinct—and distinctive—neighborhoods. Because of their unique and concentrated nature, Downtown and Georgetown/Foggy Bottom/The West End have been discussed as separate chapters; here we cover the rest of Northwest.

The city grew slowly in this direction; few houses stood along the dirt roads in Northwest until after the Civil War, and even then this section of Washington remained a vast picnic grove for most of the city until well into the twentieth century. With the exception of a few major commercial arteries (Massachusetts, Connecticut, Georgia and Wisconsin Avenues, and Columbia Road), the area is predominantly residential.

A major expansion into Northwest occurred at the turn of the century when the city's rapidly growing wealthy class built their ornate homes in the Dupont Circle and Kalorama neighborhoods; many of the sights you'll want to see in Northwest are in these restored mansions (Anderson House, the Columbia Historical Society, the Phillips Collection, the Textile Museum, the Woodrow Wilson House and Embassy Row).

While the remaining points of interest are widely scattered, they include at least two of Washington's most impressive sites: the National Zoo and the Washington Cathedral.

Because the attractions are dispersed in the Northwest quadrant, the best means of transportation is a car, although parking will be difficult. Buses can also take you to within a few blocks of most of your destinations. Old Town Trolley Tours (see the "Getting to and Around Town" chapter) also provides access to the area.

There are many, many restaurants in Northwest; at the end of this chapter we recommend some of our favorites.

ANDERSON HOUSE—SOCIETY OF THE CINCINNATI   785-2040
2118 Massachusetts Avenue, NW 20008
Hours: 1–4 P.M. Tuesday–Saturday
     Closed Saturdays in August and holidays
Free Admission

M Dupont Circle stop (red line).

🚌 46, D2, D4, D6, D8, N2, N4, N6, L4, L6.

🚕 Massachusetts Avenue.

P Competitive street parking.

🍽 None on premises.

👪 Not recommended for younger children.

👥 Tours available for groups of 20 or more. Make reservations in advance by calling 785-0540.

♿ Limited accessibility to ground floor (two front steps). Elevator to upper floors may prove too small for some wheelchairs.

👁 No special services available.

👂 No special services available.

A As noted above.

T No scheduled tours. A very good free pamphlet is available to facilitate a self-guided tour.

Anderson House is a delight that even many longtime Washingtonians don't know about, although it's right off heavily trafficked Dupont

Circle and practically across the street from the well-known Phillips Collection (see site report). The Georgian mansion was built in 1902 for Ambassador and Mrs. Larz Anderson—he was a special envoy to Belgium from 1911 to 1912 and ambassador to Japan from 1912 to 1913, and she was one of the wealthiest young women in the country. Anderson was a member of the Society of the Cincinnati, an organization of male descendants of officers who served in the Continental Army or Navy during the Revolutionary War; the Andersons bequeathed their mansion to the society.

Today the mansion serves two purposes. The ground floor holds the society's collection of Revolutionary War memorabilia and a reference library of over 10,000 volumes on our war for independence; the library is open to the public from 10 A.M. to 4 P.M. on weekdays. The second floor is furnished much the way it was when the Andersons lived there, complete with their fine art collection and the treasures they collected while serving abroad. Since the ambassador entertained lavishly, the house portrays life in wealthy Washington society in the early twentieth century. A glance across the street at the exclusive Cosmos Club and at the corner of 20th Street and Massachusetts Avenue to the Evalyn Walsh McLean mansion (now the Indonesian Embassy) will give you a further idea of what the neighborhood was like in its heyday.

B'NAI B'RITH MUSEUM   857-6583
640 Rhode Island Avenue, NW 20036
Hours: 10 A.M.–5 P.M. Sunday–Friday
        Closed legal and Jewish holidays
Free Admission

M Farragut North stop (red line); walk north on 17th Street.

🚌 42, 52, 54, D2, D4, D6, D8, N2, N4, 38B.

🚕 17th or M Streets.

P Limited metered street parking; parking garages next door and across the street.
🍽 None on premises.

Recommended. A special tour for kids is available on request (call 857-6583); it may include hands-on activities.

 Call 857-6583 one week in advance to arrange for a tour.

 Fully accessible. A special tour for those confined to wheelchairs is available on request; call 857-6583. The bathroom is accessible.

 No special services available.

 No special services available.

 Call 857-6583 to arrange for a tour; also arrange in advance to have the tour conducted in Hebrew, Yiddish, German or French. No walk-in guided tours are given.

The B'nai B'rith Klutznick Museum has on permanent display over 500 objects relating to Jewish ceremony and daily life dating from earliest times. The museum also conducts a series of shows each year dealing with specific themes from modern art to archaeological findings. Though the museum is probably of greater interest to Jewish visitors, its offerings appeal to people of all backgrounds. Exhibits are well labeled, but a tour might be helpful for visitors who have little knowledge of Jewish traditions.

The museum shop sells books on Judaism and Judaica, as well as Israeli crafts, ceremonial pieces, posters and cards.

COLUMBIA HISTORICAL SOCIETY   **785-2068**
(Christian Heurich Memorial Mansion)   **TDD 877-5785**
1307 New Hampshire Avenue, NW 20036
Hours: House: Noon–4 P.M. Wednesday, Friday, Saturday
        Library: 10 A.M.–4 P.M. Wednesday, Friday, Saturday
Free Admission

 Dupont Circle stop (red line); use Dupont Circle exit.

 46, L4, L6, D2, D4, D6.

New Hampshire Avenue.

 Competitive street parking; several commercial lots in neighborhood.

 Small café in the garden.

 Not recommended.

 Arrangements should be made one week in advance for groups of 10 or more by calling 785-2068.

 Wheelchair entrance under construction.

 Interpretive notebooks—large-print highlights of tour—in development.

 No special services available.

 As noted above.

 All visitors must go on guided tours, given continually during museum hours (45 minutes).

The Christian Heurich Mansion is the headquarters of the Columbia Historical Society, Washington's local historical association, but most out-of-town visitors will be interested in the 1894 Romanesque Revival mansion near Dupont Circle as the home of a successful Washington burgher. Christian Heurich, a German immigrant, made his fortune in beer and spent it lavishly on his elaborate, 31-room brown sandstone mansion. The superb, if overpowering, interior woodwork, an airy conservatory, a pretty garden (with a small café) and many of the original furnishings suggest the opulence of turn-of-the-century life among the nation's rising merchant class.

The Library, open to the public, houses an excellent collection of prints, photographs, books and other materials about Washington's history.

Visitors should note that most historic houses in Washington keep their doors locked as a security measure. No need to feel put off by the practice—they still want you. Ring the bell, wait patiently and, provided you have arrived during advertised hours, someone will appear.

HILLWOOD MUSEUM
686-5807

4155 Linnean Avenue, NW 20008

Hours: Grounds open 11 A.M.–4 P.M. Monday, Wednesday–Saturday

Admission: $7 house and grounds $2 grounds only

No Metro stop.

Significant walk from Connecticut Avenue bus routes L2, L4.

It's best to telephone for a taxi from the mansion.

Free parking; buses may enter the gates.

Light luncheon fare served at Movable Feast at Hillwood café, 10 A.M. to 4 P.M. Reservations suggested, 686-8893.

Children under 12 years old (including infants) are not permitted.

Arrangements can be made for a group tour by calling 686-5807 or by writing well in advance of your trip; a maximum of 25 people are allowed on each tour.

Limited accessibility. The first floor and bathrooms are accessible; the second floor is not.

No special services available.

No special services available.

As noted above.

Tours of Hillwood are given at 9 and 10:30 A.M., noon and 1:30 P.M. (2 hours). You must make a reservation to go on the tour; because the tour is popular and limited in size, call three weeks in advance in summer and winter, and one or two months ahead in spring and fall.

Built in 1926, this opulent Georgian 40-room mansion houses many fine artworks and furnishings. Hillwood's collection of Russian icons, gold and silver pieces, porcelain and Fabergé eggs has been called the most representative outside the Soviet Union. A newly opened part of the house displays a collection of jewelry and fine seventeenth-century Belgian lace. For many years the home of Mrs. Marjorie Merriweather Post, cereal heiress and grande dame of Washington society, Hillwood is a grand estate. The 25 acres of land bordering

Rock Creek Park contain Japanese and formal French gardens, a small dacha or Russian summer house, an American Indian building to house Mrs. Post's Indian collection on loan from the Smithsonian and a greenhouse with over 5,000 orchids. The gardens were designed primarily by Perry Wheeler, who helped establish the White House Rose Garden.

INTELSAT   944-7500
(International Telecommunications Satellite Organization)
3400 International Drive, NW
Hours: By appointment
Free Admission

Van Ness Center stop (red line).

L2, L4.

Connecticut Avenue.

Metered street parking.

None on premises. A wide variety of restaurants and carry-outs are located along Connecticut Avenue.

Recommended for older children, particularly school groups.

The tour can accommodate up to 30 people. Call 944-7500 at least one month in advance.

Fully accessible.

No special services available.

No special services available.

As mentioned above.

Tours, lasting approximately 45 minutes, are offered during business hours by advance arrangement only.

INTELSAT, the International Telecommunications Satellite Organization, owns, maintains and operates the global satellite system used for public international telecommunications services. It was formed in 1964 when 11 nations joined to establish an international communications network; there are now 112 member countries. If you've watched a live broadcast of an international Olympic competition, athletic match, royal wedding or other event, it's reached your TV thanks to the INTELSAT network.

The INTELSAT tour begins with an 11-minute film about the organization, moves on to the operations center—a fascinating beehive of electronic activity—and to an electronic question and answer board. Kids will enjoy Blast Off, an electronic quiz game. The striking building was designed by John Andrews, architect of the Sydney Opera House.

ISLAMIC CENTER   **332-8343**
(The Mosque)
2551 Massachusetts Avenue, NW 20008
Hours: 10 A.M.–5 P.M. daily; closed to groups on Friday 1–2 P.M.
Free Admission

M Dupont Circle stop (red line); a half-mile walk up Massachusetts Avenue.

N2, N4, N6.

Massachusetts Avenue.

P Difficult street parking in neighborhood.

None on premises.

Recommended for older children.

Call 332-8343 to make arrangements for group tours.

Inaccessible.

No special services available.

No special services available.

A As mentioned above.

T Tours are offered on a walk-in basis.

The Islamic Center, a Moorish jewel on Embassy Row, transports you from the buzz of Washington streets to the peace of a Muslim house of worship. The mosque, which faces Mecca, has a striking exterior and a lush interior: thick Persian carpets provide a place for the devout to pray (Muslim tradition bars chairs—and shoes, which you must leave at the entrance), and wonderfully ornate Turkish tiles grace the walls. The interior designs are outstanding examples of Islamic craft. A muezzin calls the devout to prayer from the minaret five times a day.

Women are asked to cover their heads before entering the mosque; head coverings are provided. Visitors should not wear shorts or other brief attire.

Religious services are held on Friday from 1 to 2 P.M. During this period groups are not allowed in the mosque; individual visitors, however, are invited. Women must wear head coverings, long skirts or slacks and long-sleeved tops.

Those visitors with a special interest in Islamic religion might want to investigate the library in the center, which is open to the public the same hours as the mosque. The Islamic Center also houses a gift shop that sells prayer rugs, books on Islam, incense and postcards.

NATIONAL   **673-4800 (recorded visitor's information)**
ZOOLOGICAL PARK   **673-4717**
3001 Connecticut Avenue, NW 20008
Hours: May 1–September 15—Buildings 9 A.M.–6:30 P.M.
Grounds 8 A.M.–8 P.M.
September 16–April 30—Buildings 9 A.M.–4:30 P.M.
Grounds 8 A.M.–6 P.M.
Closed Christmas
Free Admission

M Woodley Park/Zoo stop (red line).

H2, H4, L2, L4, 96 to Connecticut Avenue entrance; H2 to Adams Mill Road entrance.

 Connecticut Avenue.

 Limited parking in zoo lots for $3 (free to FONZ members); during peak times, lots are often filled by 10 A.M. Street parking in the area is very difficult. Areas are set aside for bus-passenger discharge, pickup and free parking.

 On the grounds. The Mane is a cafeteria/snack bar open year-round for lunch. The fare is limp burgers, hot dogs and fries. In warm weather, food choices expand to include the Panda Garden, selling German beer-garden food and beverages at reasonable prices; the kiosk near the birdhouse offers cold-cut sandwiches. In the summer months, several stands throughout the zoo sell soda and ice cream. The zoo is a great place to picnic.

 Highly recommended. The National Zoo is a terrific place for kids, even if they're not interested in animals. There's lots of room to run, hills to roll down, etc. Special tours can be arranged for children's groups on weekdays by calling 673-4954. Strollers can be rented in the spring and summer for $3 per day; you must leave your driver's license at the rental booth.

 Guided tours can be scheduled one month in advance for groups of 10 or more. In the summer, tours are given only on weekends. Call 673-4954 to make arrangements.

 Fully accessible. Special parking is reserved in Parking Lots B and D; all exhibit space is wheelchair-accessible, as are phones and bathrooms. While the zoo is accessible, it is on a very steep hill.

 Special tours for the visually impaired are not standard, but can be arranged one week in advance by calling 673-4954. Beepers have been installed at the Connecticut Avenue traffic light to assist crossing for those who are visually impaired.

 Sign-language tours can be arranged by calling 673-4955.

 As noted above.

 No scheduled tours.

If you like zoos, you'll love our National Zoo—it's among the finest in the world. The zoo is just about everything it should be: spacious (over 160 acres, originally designed by Frederick Law Olmsted) with an extensive variety of fauna (over 2,500 animals of 650 species) that are comfortably lodged for study, preservation and enjoyment. Well-designed and beautifully marked pathways allow you to meander through the exhibit areas, which mimic the animals' natural habitat wherever possible. An extensive rebuilding program has been under-way for the past decade: some of the truly lovely results include the 1.5 acre Lion-Tiger exhibit, the Great Ape House and the 90-foot-high Great Flight Cage, wherein visitors mingle with birds among waterfalls, foliage and pools. An invertebrate exhibit and gibbon envi-ronment are the newest exhibits. Both the Small Mammal and Reptile houses are now renovated.

Exotic treasures abound. Hsing-Hsing and Ling-Ling, gifts to the nation from the People's Republic of China in 1972, are the only giant pandas in the U.S. Literally millions of visitors have come to see them waddle through their compound, pensively chew bamboo or, most often, lie on their backs fast asleep. Many endangered species—orang-utans, polar bears, pygmy hippopotami and bald eagles among them—are zoo inhabitants. More common creatures are just as charming: a prairie-dog village is always lively and amusing, as are the large pools for seals and sea lions.

If you can arrange it, the best time to see the animals is early morning or late afternoon; at midday the animals tend to snooze. The only scheduled feeding times are for the giant pandas, 11 A.M. and 3 P.M. Other animals are fed on a varied schedule. "Birdlab" is conducted in the beautifully refurbished Bird House, Friday to Sun-day, noon to 3 P.M.; visitors learn about birds by participating in lab activities. "Zoolab" is conducted in the education building Tuesday to Sunday, noon to 3 P.M. "Herplab" in the Reptile House is open the same hours.

Two gift shops sell zoo souvenirs—panda mugs and so forth. A gallery and gift shop in the education building offers classier memen-tos (at higher prices), including books, cards and handcrafted articles with animal motifs. These shops and the food operations are operated by Friends of the National Zoo, and proceeds benefit the zoo's pro-grams.

PEIRCE MILL   426-6908
Tilden Street and Beach Drive in Rock Creek Park
Mailing Address: Park Manager, 5000 Glover Road, NW 20015
Hours: 8 A.M.–4:30 P.M. Wednesday–Sunday
       Closed holidays
Free Admission

M No Metro stop.

No Metrobus service.

It's best to telephone for a taxi from this location.

P Free parking in lot.

None on premises; picnic tables are available in a lovely setting within view of the creek.

Recommended.

Make arrangements for group tours three weeks in advance by calling 426-6908.

Inaccessible.

Special tours can be arranged for those who have visual impairments; call 426-6908 at least three weeks in advance.

Special tours can be arranged for those with hearing impairments; call 426-6908 at least three weeks in advance.

A As noted above.

T While no formal guided tours are given on a walk-in basis, the staff is eager to answer questions and explain the mill's mechanics.

Peirce Mill began grinding grain into flour in the 1820s, harnessing its power from Rock Creek. At its peak in the 1860s, the mill ground about 70 bushels a day of corn, wheat, buckwheat and rye. Gradually the water-powered mill and its like were superseded by newer, more efficient, steam-powered mills which could produce whiter, finer flour more cheaply. In the 1890s, the mill became part of the newly created Rock Creek Park, ceased operation as a mill, and was refurbished as a teahouse. It's undergone restoration as a mill twice since then—in the 1930s as a public-works project and again in the 1960s under the jurisdiction of the National Park Service.

Today, the mill is back in business, grinding wheat and corn and selling its products to visitors. It's a fascinating process to watch, and the small, helpful staff are glad to answer questions and demonstrate each step of the milling process.

The mill was built by Isaac Peirce, who owned a large piece of land along the creek. In addition to the mill, Peirce erected a springhouse, barns, a sawmill and a house; the springhouse and carriage barn still stand.

Across the street from the mill is the Art Barn (426-6719; open 10 A.M. to 5 P.M. Wednesday to Saturday; closed holidays). Displayed here are changing exhibits of works by local artists.

PHILLIPS COLLECTION   387-0961
1600–1612 21st Street, NW 20009
        (21st and Q Streets)
Hours: 10 A.M.–5 P.M. Tuesday–Saturday
        2–7 P.M. Sunday
        Closed July 4, Thanksgiving, Christmas and New Year's
Free Admission, donations requested

M Dupont Circle stop (red line).

46, N2, N4, N6, D2, D4, D6, L4, L6.

Massachusetts or Connecticut Avenues.

P Limited street parking; several commercial lots in neighborhood.

Suzanne's, a nearby local restaurant, runs a café open 10 A.M. to 4 P.M. Tuesday to Saturday, 2 P.M. to 4:30 P.M. Sunday. A fixed-price concert supper is available on Sundays. Call 483-4633.

Recommended for a short visit or if a child has a particular interest in art.

Arrangements for group tours should be made at least two weeks in advance by calling 387-2151 during business hours.

Fully accessible. Enter at 1612 21st Street; a wheelchair is available.

No special services available.

 No special services available.

 As noted above.

 Tours are given Wednesday and Saturday at 2 P.M.

Beyond the rather funereal atmosphere of the entrance hall, the Phillips Collection is one of the true delights of Washington. The collection, gathered by the late Duncan Phillips and his artist-wife, Marjorie, and donated—along with Phillips' family home—as a public museum in 1921, is composed largely of twentieth-century paintings, along with those of earlier artists who influenced their modern counterparts. The house itself is a late-Victorian brownstone, an unexpected setting for what was, in fact, the first museum of modern art in the United States. Although the exhibit is small (of about 2,000 paintings, only 250 can be displayed at any one time), it is choice, and the opportunity to view it in the intimate surroundings of parlors and sitting rooms furnished with armchairs and couches is a further enticement. Among works on display are Daumier's "The Uprising"; Cézanne's 1877 "Self-Portrait"; Renoir's "Luncheon of the Boating Party"; O'Keeffe's "Red Hills and the Sun"; Eakins' "Miss Van Buren"; a whole roomful of small but wonderful Klees; major works by Rothko; an impressive collection of Braques and Bonnards; and paintings by Van Gogh, Degas, Monet and Manet.

For many years the museum has sponsored a series of free concerts Sundays at 5 P.M. Museum talks are given Thursdays at 12:30 P.M.

TEXTILE MUSEUM   667-0441
2320 S Street, NW 20008
Hours: 10 A.M.–5 P.M. Tuesday–Saturday, 1–5 P.M. Sunday
      Closed holidays
Free Admission   Suggested Donations: Adults—$3   Children—50¢

 Dupont Circle stop (red line); use Q Street exit. Walk up Connecticut Avenue and turn left at S Street (half mile).

N2, N4, N6—walk one block off Massachusetts Avenue on S Street.

Massachusetts or Connecticut Avenue.

Difficult street parking.

None on premises.

Not recommended unless child has a particular interest in design and handicrafts.

Call 667-0441 to make arrangements for group tours.

Limited accessibility. Call ahead on the day of your visit for staff assistance in negotiating the one-step entrance and the several steps to one exhibit room.

No special services available.

No special services available.

As noted above.

Walk-in tours are given Sunday from 2 to 4 P.M. Tours in French, German and Italian may be arranged in advance—call 667-0441. Also call 667-0441 to arrange tours at other times.

The Textile Museum is located on a quiet, elegant residential street northwest of Dupont Circle. Founded in 1925 with the collection of George Hewitt-Myers, the museum houses over 12,000 woven pieces of both artistic and archaeological significance; only a fraction of the works can be displayed at one time. The house itself was designed by John Russell Pope. If you have an interest in Oriental rugs or Navajo blankets or any of the more obscure aspects of fine weaving, you'll want to make a stop here; it is one of only two museums in the world devoted entirely to handwoven rugs and fabric, and has the world's finest collection of Peruvian weavings.

For visitors without a background in textiles, we recommend the museum tour because, although the works are well displayed and labeled, there is very little explanatory text to inform you of the various processes or significance of the exhibits.

The Museum Arts Library is divided into sections on fine arts, decorative arts, techniques, costumes and textile processes, all organized by nationality. The library is open to the public Wednesday to Friday from 10 A.M. to 5 P.M. and on Saturday from 10 A.M. to 1 P.M. The museum also has a very fine shop with books on every conceivable variety of textile work, as well as yarn, rugs, scarves, beads and handcrafted gift items.

The Textile Museum mounts three to four major exhibits a year that are accompanied by a series of lectures and luncheon seminars. Occasional workshops and demonstrations are also given. Saturday morning is rug morning: at 10:30, discussions on scheduled topics are held and visitors bring in pertinent textiles for examination by experts. The first Saturday each month is a potpourri; not bound by a topic, folks bring in any textile with which they're having conservation problems for expert advice. Call 667-0441 for a copy of the museum's newsletter.

UNITED STATES NAVAL OBSERVATORY
653-1543 (taped message)

34th Street and Massachusetts Avenue, NW 20390
Hours: Open only for tours—see below
Free Admission

M No Metro stop.

N2, N4, N6.

Massachusetts Avenue.

P Very limited neighborhood street parking off Massachusetts Avenue; no parking on grounds. Buses for groups and the elderly or handicapped may park on grounds if arrangements are made in advance; call 653-1541.

None on premises. Soda machines.

Special tours can be arranged that are suited for children. Advance notice is required for school groups; call 653-1541.

Night tours are considered inappropriate for children under seventh-grade level.

 Contact the superintendent at 653-1541 in advance for groups of 15 to 35 people.

 Inaccessible.

 No special services available.

 No special services available.

 If you wish to go on an evening tour, reservations must be made in writing to the superintendent one or two months in advance, providing names of all who wish to attend and indicating the date and time preferred.

 Evening tours are scheduled every Monday night, except federal holidays. Tours, up to 100 people, are on a first-come, first-served basis. Gates open at 8:30 P.M. during daylight saving time; 7:30 P.M. during standard time.

The Naval Observatory is a fascinating place generally overlooked by tourists. Since it's very near Washington Cathedral, these two places could make a good afternoon of sightseeing.

The observatory's work is to provide the accurate time and astronomical information necessary for safe navigation in air and space as well as at sea. Established in 1844, the observatory moved to its present site in 1893 to avoid the bustle of the city and the malarial swamp air of its location in Foggy Bottom.

Visitors can view the observatory only by going on a tour. The tour is fascinating, even for those who never thought they had an interest in astronomy. On these tours you'll see the atomic clocks that keep the most accurate time on the planet. The tour also includes the telescopes used to track the positions of the sun, moon, stars and planets. A word of warning: the buildings are not climate-controlled; also the tours of the observatory are fairly strenuous and should not be undertaken by people who have difficulty climbing stairs.

During the Ford Administration, the admiral's house on the observatory grounds was made the official residence of the Vice-President.

WALTER REED MEDICAL MUSEUM   576-2418 or 576-2348
(Armed Forces Medical Museum)
6825 16th Street, NW 20306
Hours: 9:30 A.M.–4:30 P.M. Monday–Friday
     11:30 A.M.–4:30 P.M. weekends
     Closed Christmas
Free Admission

M No Metro stop.

[bus] S2, S4, 16th Street buses unless they are marked ''Carter Barron.''

[taxi] Difficult to find. Best bet is Georgia Avenue.

P Free parking available in front of museum.

[food] Cafeteria on grounds of Walter Reed open to the public only on weekdays; otherwise drive up Alaska Avenue to Georgia Avenue and head into Silver Spring.

[family] Not recommended.

[groups] Groups of up to 100 can be handled, but 20 to 30 people at a time are preferred. Make arrangements one week in advance by calling 576-2348 or writing to: Tour Coordinator, Walter Reed Medical Museum, 6825 16th Street, NW, Washington, D.C. 20306.

[wheelchair] Fully accessible. The bathroom is accessible but there is no phone.

[vision] No special services available.

[hearing] No special services available.

A Appointments must be made in advance for tours–call 576-2348 or write the tour coordinator at above address.

T No walk-in tours are given.

———————————————

The Armed Forces Medical Museum caters to a specialized audience: those persons interested in the history of military medicine and the history of the study of pathology (the museum is part of the Army Pathology Institute). In the museum, a single room on the concourse level of the building, you will find many examples of the results of disease on the human body. There is an exhibit about teratology—that is, congenital malformations at birth. The Lincoln and Garfield assassinations are covered in other displays. So as you can see, this is a place for those of stout heart and strong stomach (or morbid curiosity). On the lighter side, the museum boasts one of the world's largest collections of microscopes, from sixteenth-century Dutch to the most modern electron microscopes. Also of note is the historical survey of military medicine from the Civil War to Vietnam.

WASHINGTON CATHEDRAL   537-6200
(The Cathedral Church of St. Peter and St. Paul)
Wisconsin Avenue at Woodley Road (Mt. St. Alban) 20016
Hours: Main Floor: 10 A.M.–4:30 P.M.
Pilgrim Observation Gallery: 10 A.M.–3:15 P.M. daily
12:30–3:45 P.M. Sunday
Free Admission, donations accepted

No Metro stop.

N2, N4, N6 (Massachusetts Avenue); 30, 32, 34, 36 (Wisconsin Avenue).

Wisconsin Avenue.

Free parking on cathedral grounds.

None on premises.

Recommended. Special tours dealing with subjects of interest to kids can be arranged; call 537-6207. Kids like the massive scale, ornate decor and the gardens. Note the new gargoyle, winning entry in the national Children's Competition.

Call to request group tours at 537-6207.

Accessible. Wheelchairs are available and can go on tour, though steps may limit unassisted wheelchair access to the main nave area. Phones and bathrooms are accessible.

Tours can be arranged for the visually disabled by calling 537-6207.

No special services available.

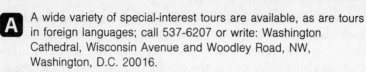

A A wide variety of special-interest tours are available, as are tours in foreign languages; call 537-6207 or write: Washington Cathedral, Wisconsin Avenue and Woodley Road, NW, Washington, D.C. 20016.

T Walk-in tours are given from 10:15 A.M. to 12:30 P.M. and 2 to 3:15 P.M., Monday to Saturday (30 minutes).

The glorious Washington Cathedral is a twentieth-century church in fourteenth-century form. This massive Gothic structure, designed by Philip Hubert Frohman and under construction since 1907, is near completion; consecration is scheduled for September 29, 1990. It is the sixth-largest cathedral in the world, and second only in size in the U.S. to New York's Cathedral of St. John the Divine. Though under the jurisdiction of the Episcopal Church, the cathedral acts as the national church envisioned by George Washington, hosting many interdenominational services and events.

Even for those not interested in worship, the Washington Cathedral is a fascinating place to visit. Modeled after the churches of medieval Europe, the cathedral is perhaps one of the last pure Gothic buildings to be constructed. No structural steel is used; flying buttresses, adorned with gargoyles, balance the outward thrust of the Indiana-limestone walls. Still, it's distinctly modern: imbedded in the Space Window is a piece of moon rock retrieved by our astronauts. Everything in the Children's Chapel is scaled to a child's dimensions. The Pilgrim Observation Gallery provides a magnificent panoramic view of Washington from the area's highest point, 676 feet above sea level.

The 30-minute tours are very informative, providing the visitor with an understanding of the sources and meaning of Gothic architecture. Specialized tours dealing in more depth with the architecture, stained glass and the cathedral's tower can be arranged. If you prefer to tour by yourself, you can purchase the excellent *Guide to the Washington Cathedral* at the cathedral gift shop. This booklet is available in German, Japanese, Spanish and French, as well as in English.

The grounds of the cathedral, designed by Frederick Law Olmsted, Jr., are lovely. The Bishop's Garden, with its roses, perennials, boxwood, medieval herbs and flowers, is an especially peaceful place; its entrance is a twelfth-century Norman arch. A greenhouse, open Monday to Saturday, 8:30 A.M. to 4:30 P.M., sells annual, perennial and herb plants; an herb cottage (open 9:30 A.M. to 5 P.M. weekdays, 12 noon to 4 P.M. Sundays) sells dried herbs and gift items. A brass-rubbing center is located in the gift shop crypt; visitors can see an exhibit of rubbings and do their own for a nominal fee. The gift shop itself sells cards, books, miniature gargoyles and toys, as well as information about the cathedral; it is open from 9:30 A.M. to 5 P.M. daily. A rare-book library is open to the public from noon to 4 P.M. Tuesday to Saturday.

On Sundays at 5 P.M. free organ concerts are given, and a carillon concert can be heard beginning at 4:30 P.M. on Saturdays.

On Wisconsin Avenue just north of the cathedral are several places to eat. If you want a snack, the *University Pastry Shop* is famous locally for its homemade ice cream and other sweets. A nationally celebrated ice-cream emporium, *Bob's Famous,* is several blocks below the cathedral on Wisconsin Avenue.

WOODROW WILSON HOUSE 387-4062
2340 S Street, NW 20008
Hours: 10 A.M.–4 P.M. Tuesday–Sunday
    Closed Thanksgiving, Christmas and New Year's
Admission: Adults—$3.50   Children, Students and Senior Citizens—$2

M Dupont Circle stop (red line); use Q Street exit.

N2, N4, T2, T3, T4, T6 (exit at 24th Street and Massachusetts Avenue).

Massachusetts Avenue.

P Competitive street parking.

None on premises.

Recommended for a brief visit: kids who are collectors may enjoy seeing a President's sports and vaudeville collection in his bedroom.

Make reservations for group tours two weeks in advance by calling 387-4062. No discounts are available.

Partially accessible. Staff will assist in navigating the two front steps if necessary

Large-print cards available.

 No special services available.

 As noted above.

 Walk-in guided tours (45 minutes) are given as needed. Last tour at 3:30 P.M.

Of all the American Presidents, only Woodrow Wilson chose to make his retirement home in Washington. Wilson and his second wife, the former Edith Bolling Galt, came directly from the White House to this brick Georgian Revival house (designed by Waddy Wood) in what was, in 1921, a quiet, wooded neighborhood. Wilson, tired, ill and disillusioned after the defeat of his campaign to bring the United States into the League of Nations, lived here for only three years until his death in 1924. Mrs. Wilson continued to live in the house for another 37 years, leaving it at her death to the National Trust for Historic Preservation as a permanent Washington memorial to the former President. Not surprisingly, the house often presents a stronger picture of the tastes and times of Edith Wilson than those of her husband. Nevertheless, it is chockablock with the furnishings, gifts and memorabilia not only of Wilson's presidency but also of his earlier career as a college professor, president of Princeton University and governor of New Jersey. (An unexpected aspect of Wilson's personality: his avid interest in sports and vaudeville.)

On display are the President and Mrs. Wilson's bedrooms (and her bathroom), which contain many furnishings dating from the Wilsons' occupancy; the parlor, dominated by an enormous Gobelin tapestry presented as a personal gift to Mrs. Wilson by the French government; the library, from which Wilson made the first radio broadcast from a private house; the dining room; the wine cellar and—a real delight— the first-floor kitchen, restored to an early twentieth-century appearance with a combination gas-and-coal stove and a wealth of appropriate kitchen gear.

The house is sometimes used for large social gatherings sponsored by nonprofit organizations, but is rarely closed to the public during its advertised hours. There is no gift shop, but pamphlets and a few books may be purchased from the docents.

DUPONT CIRCLE

Dupont Circle, the largest circle park in the District of Columbia, is also one of the liveliest—and, many think, one of the loveliest. Its centerpiece, a large, graceful fountain designed in 1921 by Daniel Chester French (the sculptor of Lincoln in the Lincoln Memorial), is a tribute to Rear Admiral Samuel Francis Dupont, a naval hero of the Union cause during the Civil War. The figures supporting the fountain represent the Arts of Ocean Navigation—Sea, Wind and Stars. Today, the circle is a favorite gathering ground for brown-bag lunchers, chess players, children, dog walkers, jugglers and assorted colorful characters. Any day of the week you may find an impromptu concert or a protest demonstration in progress. (Demonstrations often start here and move down Connecticut Avenue to Lafayette Square.) The neighborhood around the circle is home to galleries, nontraditional retail operations and many nonprofit organizations.

The commercial bustle that surrounds the circle today gives little hint of its more elegant nineteenth-century beginnings. From the 1880s until the turn of the century, it was the most western—and the most expensive—residential neighborhood in the city. Architectural holdouts from that period, like the gleaming Patterson House (now the private Washington Club) at the eastern corner of Massachusetts Avenue and the circle (15 Dupont Circle), and the earlier, red-brick Blaine Mansion on the western edge (2000 Massachusetts Avenue) contrast sharply with modern high-rise office buildings (the most impressive of which is the Euram Building at 21 Dupont Circle).

Delightful shops and restaurants radiate generally north and south of the circle, and the enormous Beaux-Arts mansions of the traditional embassy section march west along Massachusetts Avenue. Night life is particularly active along Connecticut Avenue above and below the circle and south along 18th and 19th Streets. To the northeast lies Columbia Road, a vibrant ethnic mélange that provides some of the best Latin American food and the most spirited street life in Washington.

THE DIPLOMATIC WORLD—EMBASSY ROW

Washington's large, official diplomatic community clusters in Kalorama and along Massachusetts Avenue, from Scott Circle to

Wisconsin Avenue, giving the avenue its nickname—Embassy Row. The lower part of Embassy Row around Scott, Dupont and Sheridan Circles remained virtual countryside until the turn of the century; the upper part remained bucolic even longer. A few country estates were scattered through the area, but most Washingtonians viewed this as space for picnicking in the wilds for the adventuresome.

From 1900 until World War I, Massachusetts Avenue, as the southern border of Kalorama, became the residential neighborhood of the very wealthy. In contrast to much of the housing elsewhere in Washington, the houses here were large, detached and designed by architects—a great many in the Beaux-Arts style. Society was high, and entertaining was lavish in these palatial homes. As fortunes began to fade in the Depression and as the wealthy sought greater privacy elsewhere, some of the houses were demolished to make room for hotels and apartments, but many were sold to foreign legations to serve as their embassies and chanceries; others are now used and maintained by private organizations and clubs. New embassies have been built alongside the old residences, and the charm of Embassy Row is undiminished.

Most of the embassies are well marked with identifying plaques and national flags. Among those most easily recognizable are the Chancery of India (2107 Massachusetts Avenue) with elephants flanking its entrance; the Japanese Chancery (at 2520); the closed Iranian Embassy, decorated with blue and white ceramic tile (at 3005); the modernistic Brazilian Embassy (at 3006) and the British Embassy (at 3100), recognized for its stately Queen Anne architecture and its statue of a striding Winston Churchill. Also along the route are the Phillips Gallery (see site report), the Islamic Center (see site report), the U.S. Naval Observatory (see site report), Saint Sophia Greek Orthodox Cathedral and the Washington Cathedral (see site report).

If you're walking, focus on the Sheridan Circle area where the greatest concentration of these twentieth-century palaces remain.

Each spring, usually in early April, a half dozen of these elegant buildings are opened for tours to benefit area charities.

ELEGANCE PAST AND PRESENT IN KALORAMA

When you walk through the stately streets of Kalorama today, it's difficult to imagine that virtually no development had taken place in this neighborhood at the turn of the century. The neighborhood, bounded by Massachusetts Avenue, Rock Creek Park, Connecticut Avenue and Florida Avenue, didn't become part of the city of Washington until 1890; before then, all land beyond Florida Avenue (then called Boundary Avenue) was part of Washington County, true wilderness to most of those who lived in the civilized city.

Kalorama was the name of the area's first estate, part of a colonial patent granted by Lord Baltimore to John Langworth in 1664. Joel Barlow, a diplomat, built his large country house in 1807, coining its name from the Greek word for "beautiful view," since the site looked out across the capital and Potomac River to northern Virginia. Until the 1890s, fewer than a dozen other residences were built—and by that time, the original Kalorama manor house had been demolished.

By 1890, Washington was beginning to boom with post–Civil War fervor. The population expanded—particularly the wealthy class—pushing the physical bounds of the city westward. Massachusetts and Connecticut Avenues were extended beyond Florida Avenue, Rock Creek Valley was preserved as a park for all to enjoy, bridges were constructed across Rock Creek, and the very rich moved beyond Dupont Circle. During the next 20 years, the houses built in Kalorama were palatial, custom designed in Beaux-Arts manner for elegant entertaining. Presidents, members of Congress, Supreme Court Justices and the very wealthy lived in this neighborhood.

Fortunately, a good sampling of these sumptuous houses survive, though many are no longer private homes. Many of the grand estates now serve as embassies, chanceries, museums and private clubs.

The best representation of Kalorama at its prosperous peak is Sheridan Circle; if you can block out today's hustle, it's easy to imagine the heyday.

COLUMBIA ROAD—A TOUCH OF SALSA

The Columbia Road/Kalorama Triangle/Adams-Morgan neighborhood forms the most diverse residential area of the city—economically, racially and ethnically. Columbia Road itself is one of the oldest thoroughfares in Washington, and has long been a commercial center for small businesses and trades. Today, it has a particularly Latin flavor, since Columbia Road is the heart of Washington's Latin American community. Restaurants and carry-outs abound, offering paella, chorizo, sangria, black beans and other Spanish/Latino delicacies. Latino groceries share Columbia Road and 18th Street with community art galleries, dance and art studios, discount clothing stores, antique shops, a farmers' market and the city's best collection of African restaurants—it's a thriving, vital spot.

The joys of urban life are shadowed by its sorrows here; the area was "rediscovered" in the 1960s, attracting many young, white professionals who have restored houses to their original charm, but have displaced residents from their lifelong homes. As a result, the neighborhood is politically concerned, active and vocal—and one of Washington's more vibrant places.

In recent years, what was a local celebration of the area's diversity has become "the biggest block party in the world," according to the organizers of Adams-Morgan Day. Held in mid-September, this vivid street fair draws over 250,000 visitors. Music fills the air from multiple stages around the neighborhood, and hundreds of vendors sell food and merchandise.

NOSHING IN NORTHWEST

For Northwest, we will begin at Dupont Circle, and follow some major arteries away from the circle—Connecticut Avenue, 18th Street and Wisconsin Avenue (which doesn't intersect the circle, but is in Northwest and does have noteworthy restaurants).

Dupont Circle

P Street, from 19th to 22nd Streets, will serve all tastes, from subs, *Subway,* 2008 P Street, and fast food, *Burger King,* 2010 P Street, to unusual international selections at *Bootsie, Winkey and Miss Maud,* 887-0900, 2026 P Street, and moderately expensive Northern Italian cuisine at *Donna Adele,* 2100 P Street, 296-1142, a particularly pretty place with a nice, covered sidewalk café. Across the street, at 2111 P, you will find the stylish *Café Beaux Arts,* 956-6690, with a big bar, raw bar, pizza, fish and meats. The best of the P Street bunch is undoubtedly *Galileo,* at 2014, 293-7191, serving Italian food of exceptional range and quality. The variety of antipastos is mouth-watering (and satisfying), and their grill produces superb meats and fish. The pastas are out of the ordinary. It's small, so call for reservations.

Just above the circle is *Kramerbooks & afterwords,* 1517 Connecticut Avenue, 387-1462, a lively bookstore/café combination, which is open all night Friday and Saturday. The menu runs from sandwiches and salads to a variety of pastas, chicken and fish. *Suzanne's,* 1735 Connecticut Avenue, 483-4633, a wine bar/carry-out/restaurant, serves attractive, light food. *Odeon Café,* 1714 Connecticut Avenue, 328-6228, could be called "California-Italian." Individual pizzas, pastas, good fried squid (hard to find, really) and the most heavenly blackberry-chocolate chip gelato. *Café Patitto,* 1724 Connecticut Avenue, 462-8771, features artfully presented pastas and pizzas and has an antipasto salad bar.

Washington's best fish restaurant, *Vincenzo's,* 1606 20th Street, 667-0047, is expensive but totally committed to its work. *Timberlake's,* 1726 Connecticut Avenue, 483-2266, is a good neighborhood bar with typical bar food.

New Orleans Creole cooking can be found at *Lafitte,* 1310 New Hampshire Avenue, 466-7978; spicy food, not for the faint of heart or stomach. *The Iron Gate Inn,* 1734 N Street, 737-1370, serves mild Middle Eastern food—indoors and outdoors in a nice carriage house courtyard. *Trattu,* 1823 Jefferson Place, 466-4570, is a small trattoria; well-prepared food, served Italian.

Several blocks north, around the Shoreham and Sheraton Park hotels, you have a multitude of choices. *Khyber Pass,* 2309 Calvert Street, 234-4632, is sister to *Bamiyan* in Georgetown, and serves superb Afghani food. *New Heights,* 2317 Calvert Street, 234-4110, is a popular new entry in the "New American Cuisine" sweepstakes. People are passionate about this place—both for and against. Some people object to the unusual combinations of flavors. Expensive, but one of the most beautiful restaurants in the city.

Petitto's, 2653 Connecticut Avenue, 667-5350, serves Italian pastas, vegetarian and with meat sauces, and some veal and lamb dishes; *The Tandoor,* 2623 Connecticut Avenue, 483-1115, serves good Indian food; *Mont Martre,* 2655 Connecticut Avenue, 667-5115, serves French cuisine; and *Thai Taste,* 2606 Connecticut Avenue, 387-8876, serves delicious Thai fare.

Near the zoo try *Mrs. Simpson's,* 2915 Connecticut Avenue, 332-8300; new American food, but not too far out. *Csiko's Hungarian Restaurant,* 3601 Connecticut Avenue, 362-5624, is an old-world, 1930s experience. In a high-ceilinged room, among widely spaced square tables, with white tablecloths, courtly waiters serve moderately priced Continental cuisine. The strolling gypsy violinist is almost a superfluous touch.

The Thai Room, 5037 Connecticut Avenue, 244-5933, was the first and is still one of the best Thai restaurants around. Thai food can tend to the very spicy, so be careful; the chef will be glad to tone things down if you ask. *The Fishery,* 5511 Connecticut Avenue, 363-2144, is expensive (considering the spare decor) but reasonably reliable for simply prepared fresh fish.

18th Street/Columbia Road

Starting back down at Dupont Circle, you could head up 17th or 18th Streets and run into a number of new neighborhood restaurants of note. One of the prettiest is *Sushi Taro,* upstairs at 1503 17th Street, 462-8999; sushi and cooked Japanese cuisine.

At 17th and R Streets, you can choose Mexican, *La Fonda,* 232-6965, or Spanish, *El Bodegon,* 667-1710. Both are moderately priced. *Helen's,* 1805 18th Street, 483-1813, serves new American food with an Oriental accent. Their appetizers and desserts are excellent. *Lauriol Plaza,* 1801 18th Street, 387-0035, is a noisy, attractive place with hearty Latin and continental offerings, all consistently good.

In the several blocks around Columbia Road and 18th Street, there are no less than 60 (count 'em) restaurants, including (are you ready?) 9 (!) Ethiopian, 5 Chinese, 16 Latin American, 4 Caribbean, 4 Italian, 3 French, one Creole and the rest a varied bunch, from gourmet carry-out to neighborhood bars. Just around the corner, in the 1800 block of Columbia, are five more Latin American and several others. Take a walk; enjoy the crowds; pick a menu that suits your mood. Adams-Morgan is among the most vibrant neighborhoods in D.C. Part of the fun is the social scene. We have another suggestion: with so many interesting restaurants in such a small area, why not do as the Spanish do; nibble, sip, talk, look—visit half a dozen or more restaurants, sampling the wares? Order some Jamaican appetizers at *Negril;* try an Ethiopian dish at *Addis Ababa,* some dumplings at *Guang Dong,* shrimp at *El Tazumal* and pâté at *La Fourchette*—a different way to eat.

Two new restaurant/disco/nightspots have opened in the past year, and they have accelerated the gentrification of Adams-Morgan. They are *Cities,* 2424 18th Street, 328-7194, and *Dakota,* 1777 Columbia Road, 265-6600. Cities transforms itself every four months into a new "city" decor, and changes the menu accordingly. You can always count on reasonably priced appetizers, pastas and pizzas. Dakota offers what has become known as "eclectic" American food— a nice mishmash. Count on both places being packed, lively, Yuppie and noisy.

Wisconsin Avenue

We left Wisconsin Avenue at the top of Georgetown, just below the Washington Cathedral. Between the cathedral and the District-Maryland line in Friendship Heights (an excellent shopping area), there are a number of mentionables. *Armand's Chicago Pizzeria,* 4231 Wisconsin Avenue, 686-9450, so the story goes, rifled the trash cans of a Chicago pizzeria for clues to their deep-dish recipes; the results speak for themselves—lines form early, no reservations. *The Dancing Crab,* 4611 Wisconsin Avenue, 244-1882, caters to a boisterous crowd—talent and technicians from nearby WUSA-TV studios, and jocks. The menu is simple—seafood—the surroundings plain and the prices moderate. At *The Mikado,* 4707 Wisconsin Avenue, 244-1740, kimonoed waitresses pad softly through the room with sushi, sashimi, tempuras, teriyakis and soups—a gentle place.

In Friendship Heights, the *American Café,* 5252 Wisconsin Avenue, 363-5400, is a fancier version of its Georgetown and Capitol Hill locations, but with the same fresh, American look to the food. The *Pleasant Peasant,* 5300 Wisconsin Avenue, 364-2500, has a definite look—black and white (decor inherited from its predecessor). It has an elevator, too, that takes you up from the street-level bar to the dining room. The food is Continental, the prices moderately steep and the service friendly. The desserts are highly touted and live up to their billing, for the most part. If imagination fails, *Hamburger Hamlet,* 5225 Wisconsin Avenue, 244-2037, will fill the void. For cheap eats, you can't go wrong at *El Tamarindo,* 4910 Wisconsin Avenue, 244-8888, for no-frills Mexican. At the other end of the Tex-Mex spectrum is *Tila's,* 2 Wisconsin Circle (at the District line), 652-8452, a moderately expensive, funky-but-upscale specialist in eclectic Southwestern fare.

9

OTHER

D.C. AREAS

This chapter is a catchall for points of interest that fall outside the usual tourist areas in the capital city. While these sites aren't among the most spectacular of Washington's offerings by any means, each provides an interesting change of pace which might be welcome in an otherwise hectic trip.

Since these sites are scattered throughout Northeast and Southeast Washington, driving is the best way to get to them; parking won't be a problem, because these areas are well off the usual tourist circuit. While the National Shrine of the Immaculate Conception has a cafeteria, none of the other sites has eating facilities, and restaurants are few and far between. Accordingly, spend your mealtimes in other parts of the city.

ANACOSTIA NEIGHBORHOOD MUSEUM   **287-3369**
1901 Fort Place, SE 20560   **TDD 357-1696**
Hours: 10 A.M.–5 P.M. daily
       Closed Christmas
Free Admission

 No Metro stop.

 92, 94, A2, A4, A6, A8, B5, B7.

 Martin Luther King, Jr., Avenue, though it's best to telephone for a cab.

P Street parking available.

|O| None on premises.

Recommended. There is a Children's Room where kids can participate in demonstrations.

Guided tours for groups of 10 or more can be arranged by calling 287-3369 at least two days ahead of time.

Fully accessible. One wheelchair is available at the museum.

Audio tape tours are available. Special tours can be arranged by calling 287-3369 at least 48 hours in advance.

Special tours and educational programs are available for the hearing-impaired; call 287-3369 or TDD 357-1696 at least 48 hours in advance. With one week's notice an interpreter is available for any of the museum's programs.

A As noted above.

T No walk-in tours are given. A 30-minute, self-guided recorded tour is available.

The Anacostia Neighborhood Museum, a branch of the Smithsonian Institution, is geared toward serving the educational and cultural needs of Washington's black community. Exhibits, which change monthly, deal largely with black history, urban problems, arts and crafts and have included displays on achievements of black women, Harlem photography, Frederick Douglass and Anacostia. The museum serves as an educational center for the neighborhood, providing programs and workshops; exhibits invite participation. A portion of the museum's exhibits consists of work from members of the community. A half-hour, self-guided recorded tour is available on a walk-in basis. A monthly calendar of events is available from the museum.

FRANCISCAN MONASTERY   **526-6800**
1400 Quincy Street, NE 20017
Hours: Tours—9 A.M.–4 P.M. Monday–Saturday
1–3:30 P.M. Sunday
Services: Sundays and Holy Days—Mass at 7, 8:30, 10:30 A.M. and noon.

Spanish service at 4:30 P.M.
Vespers at 3:30 P.M.
Weekdays—Mass at 6, 7 and 8 A.M.; confessions on request
Free Admission

M Brookland-CUA stop (red line).

🚌 80, 81, H2, H4, R4, R6, G4, G6.

🚕 10th Street, though it's best to telephone for a cab.

P Plenty of free parking.

🍽 Snack bar on premises.

👫 Recommended.

👪 Group tours available. Call 526-6800.

♿ Fully accessible.

👁 No special services available.

👂 No special services available.

A None necessary.

T Walk-in tours leave hourly—except noon—from the visitor center (30 minutes).

The Franciscan Monastery is also the official "Commissariat of the Holy Land for the United States"; its function is to preserve and maintain shrines in the Holy Land by raising funds in the United States. The monastery, which was founded in 1899, occupies 44 acres of wooded land and gardens just a few blocks from the Shrine of the Immaculate Conception (see site report).

The central part of the monastery is the Memorial Church, which was completed in 1899 in the Byzantine style. The church houses a number of reproductions of sacred shrines from the Holy Land. Underneath the church is a reproduction of a small portion of the miles of catacombs under Rome where in order to escape persecution, early Christians worshiped.

The monastery grounds are one of the overlooked glories of Washington. Throughout the year, bulbs, dogwood, flowering cherry trees, fabulous roses and shaded walkways (along which are found reproductions of Holy Land shrines) reflect the constant and loving attention they receive.

FREDERICK DOUGLASS NATIONAL HISTORIC SITE
(Cedar Hill)   House: 426-5961
                                          Visitor Center: 426-5960

1411 W Street, SE 20020
Hours: October–April—9 A.M.–4 P.M.; May–September—9 A.M.–5 P.M. daily
        Closed Thanksgiving, Christmas, New Year's
Free Admission

M No Metro stop.

🚌 B2, B5, 94, A2, A4, A6.

🚗 Martin Luther King, Jr., Avenue, though it's best to telephone for a cab.

P Street parking available.

🍽 None on premises; picnic area on grounds.

👪 Recommended if related to schoolwork.

👥 Groups of five or more are asked to schedule their visit in advance. Call 426-5961.

♿ Limited accessibility. Only the first floor is accessible; bathroom in visitor center.

👁 No special services available.

👂 Captioned film.

A As noted above.

T Walk-in tours given on the half hour; a film of Douglass' life is shown on the hour. Self-guided tour of exhibits and audio-visual programs in visitor center.

The fiery black abolitionist Frederick Douglass lived in this house from 1877, when he was 60 years old, until his death in 1895. Douglass was an escaped slave who became one of the country's most eloquent spokesmen for the abolition of slavery. By the time Douglass moved to this house, he was a prosperous man who had held high positions in the government.

Cedar Hill is a comfortable house that overlooks the city from the far side of the Anacostia River. The house has been restored to appear much as it did when Douglass lived here, and it contains many of his personal effects as well as his large library. Congress designated it the first Black National Historic Site.

KENILWORTH AQUATIC GARDENS   426-6905
Kenilworth Avenue and Douglas Street, NE 20019
Hours: 7 A.M.–sundown daily
Free Admission

M Deanwood stop (blue and orange lines); about a half-mile walk to the gardens.
U2, M16.

Kenilworth Avenue, but it's best to telephone for a cab.

P Free parking in lot; driving provides best access to this site.

None on premises or in immediate area; picnic tables are available on the grounds.
Recommended.

Call 426-6905 or write one week in advance to arrange for a group tour.

Limited accessibility. Gardens accessible, but phone and bathrooms are not.

No special services available.

No special services available.

A Call 426-6905 on Wednesdays, one week in advance, to arrange a tour on weekdays.

T 9 and 11 A.M., 1 and 3 P.M. on weekends and holidays.

The Kenilworth Aquatic Gardens are hidden along the Anacostia River well away from Washington's mainstream. Over 100,000 water-lily, lotus, water hyacinth, bamboo and other water plants grow here in ponds formed by diking the Anacostia's marshland along this stretch of its shoreline. Turtles, frogs, waterfowl, muskrats, raccoons and opossums thrive here among the exotic flora.

The Aquatic Gardens were started in 1882, when W. B. Shaw, a Civil War veteran who was working in Washington as a government clerk, brought some waterlilies from his native Maine to plant on his land along the Anacostia River. Shaw added to his collection regularly and eventually became a leading authority on water plants. When the federal government purchased the gardens in 1938, they had become a large commercial enterprise stocked with exotic water plants from around the world, as well as with the new varieties of lilies Shaw and his daughter had developed over the years.

The flowers are in bloom from June through August. Visit the Aquatic Gardens early in the morning, since many of the blossoms close in the heat of the day.

NATIONAL ARBORETUM   **475-4815**
24th and R Streets, NE 20002
Hours: 8 A.M.–5 P.M. weekdays
          10 A.M.–5 P.M. weekends and holidays
          Bonsai collection—10 A.M.–2:30 P.M. daily
          Closed Christmas
Free Admission

M No Metro stop.

🚌 B2, B4, B5.

🚕 In front of administration building, but it's best to telephone for a cab.

P Plenty of parking except when the azaleas are blooming; driving is best for this site.

🍽 None on premises; no eating permitted on grounds.

👪 Recommended. There's lots of wide open spaces to run in.

For groups of 10 or more, a guided tour will be provided. Set up an appointment at least three weeks in advance by calling 475-4815.

 Roads wind through and much can be viewed from your car; footpaths are difficult to navigate. Japanese Garden and National Herb Garden (both with gravel paths) are accessible, though no bathroom is accessible. Administration building is accessible.

 No special services available.

 No special services available.

 As noted above.

 No walk-in tours given.

No matter what season you visit Washington, try the National Arboretum for a breath of fresh air. The facility's 444 hilly acres abound with herbaceous plants, shrubs and trees that you can enjoy as you drive along the 9.5 miles of roadway or stroll on one of the many pleasant footpaths. Since the arboretum includes the second-highest point in the city, the hillsides offer dramatic views of the Capitol, Washington Monument and Anacostia River, as well as changing vistas of flowers and foliage.

The arboretum is most famous for its collection of 70,000 azaleas that usually bloom from the end of April until mid-May. When the azaleas are at their peak, as many as 20,000 people may visit the arboretum in a single day. This may be the arboretum's flashiest hour, but each month has its special offerings. The conifers and hollies dominate the winter; one of the most significant collections is over 1,500 dwarf and slow-growing conifers assembled on a five-acre hillside. Winter's conclusion is marked by the jasmine and camellia blossoms. Spring presents bulbs, the azaleas, wildflowers, ornamental cherries, crabapple and an extensive array of dogwood. Fern Valley and the National Herb Garden are delightful summer spots, as are the collections of peonies, daylilies and crepe myrtle. The autumn foliage is spectacular.

A year-round treat is the National Bonsai Collection and Japanese Garden, a stunning bicentennial gift to our country from the Nippon Bonsai Association of Japan. The pavilion garden is a work of art;

some of the treasured specimens are over 350 years old. This garden's cultivated compactness contrasts beautifully with the arboretum's hills and dales, and is worth a trip on its own.

The arboretum, in its role as a major research and education facility, offers special demonstrations, lectures, films and flower shows in the Administration Center throughout the year. Call 475-4815 to find out what's offered—and what's blooming—while you're in town.

A car is just about essential to enjoy the arboretum thoroughly.

NATIONAL SHRINE OF THE IMMACULATE CONCEPTION   526-8300

4th and Michigan Avenue, NE 20017

Hours: November 1–April 1—7 A.M.–6 P.M. daily
       April 2–October 31—7 A.M.–7 P.M. daily

Free Admission

M Brookland-CUA stop (red line).

80, 81, H2, H4, G4, G6.

Michigan Avenue.

P Ample free parking.

On premises. A cafeteria-style dining room is open from 7:30 A.M. to 4:30 P.M. year-round.

Nothing here to appeal especially to children.

Groups of 50 or more should notify the shrine at least a week in advance of their visit; call 526-8300.

Limited accessibility.

No special services available.

No special services available.

A As noted above.

T Walk-in tours given every half-hour from 9 to 11 A.M. and 1 to 3 P.M. (40 minutes); Sunday tour schedule varies, so call ahead.

The National Shrine of the Immaculate Conception is the largest Roman Catholic church in the United States and the seventh largest religious building in the world. The shrine seats over 3,000 people, and will have 55 chapels when completed. Located right off the campus of Catholic University, the shrine's architecture is a blend of the contemporary, Byzantine and Romanesque styles. Work on the building, which is shaped like a Latin cross, began in 1920; while it is structurally complete today, decorative work continues. The structure is noted for its statuary, stained-glass windows and beautiful mosaics. A gift shop is on the lower level.

The National Shrine Music Guild gives frequent musical performances; call 526-8300 for their schedule.

10

SUBURBAN

VIRGINIA

The sites in suburban Virginia are primarily historic and/or military in nature, and many are associated with the activities of the Washington and Lee families. In Old Alexandria, the many noteworthy historic homes and commercial buildings include Robert E. Lee's boyhood home, the Lee-Fendall House, Carlyle House, Gadsby's Tavern and the Stabler-Leadbeater Apothecary, as well as Christ Church. Within 15 miles are Mount Vernon, Woodlawn Plantation and George Washington's Grist Mill, with their rich details of eighteenth-century life. Arlington National Cemetery, the Iwo Jima Memorial and the Pentagon, all of which are in Arlington, appeal to many beyond the military buffs among us.

If your sightseeing exhausts you, retreat with a picnic to one of the several parks in the area, including Great Falls Park or Theodore Roosevelt Island. If your food tastes run more to restaurant fare, check our recommendations at the end of this chapter.

ARLINGTON HOUSE   **(703) 557-3154**
(The Custis-Lee Mansion)
On the grounds of the Arlington National Cemetery
Mailing Address: Arlington House
                  George Washington Memorial Parkway
                  McLean, VA 22101
Hours: April–September—9:30 A.M.–6 P.M.
           October–March—9:30 A.M.–4:30 P.M.
Free Admission

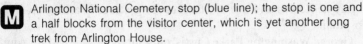

M Arlington National Cemetery stop (blue line); the stop is one and a half blocks from the visitor center, which is yet another long trek from Arlington House.

🚌 The Tourmobile will take you right up to the house.

🚗 Arlington National Cemetery visitor center.

P Two-hour parking is available near the National Cemetery visitor center, which is a long hike from the house.

🍽 None on premises. It's best to eat in D.C. or Alexandria.

👫 There are extensive educational programs for school groups, geared toward the fourth-grade level and above. Call 557-0613 or write at least one week in advance to make arrangements for a tour for children.

👥 Groups can make advance arrangements for the standard tour by calling 557-3154.

♿ Accessible to first floor. No bathroom, phone or fountain.

👁 The staff will try to arrange a special tour if called at least one week in advance at 557-3154.

👂 The staff will try to arrange a special tour if called at least one week in advance at 557-3154.

A As noted above.

T Walk-in tours are given during slow months (i.e., nonsummer, nonholiday). Brochures are always available.

Arlington House is located on the grounds of Arlington Cemetery, overlooking the Potomac River. The history of the mansion centers around the two most powerful families in Virginia—the Washingtons and the Lees—and the roles they played in the history of their country.

The original enormous tract of land was purchased in 1778 by George Washington's stepson, John Parke Custis, as the site where he intended to build his estate. But before he could build his home, Custis died at Yorktown during the Revolutionary War. In 1802, Custis' son, George Washington Parke Custis (who had been raised by his grandparents, George and Martha Washington), actually began construction on the Greek Revival mansion that we see today. When Custis finally completed the mansion in 1820, he filled it with Washington family heirlooms and made it famous for gracious Washington-style hospitality.

George Washington Parke Custis' only surviving child, Mary Ann, married the dashing Lt. Robert E. Lee in 1831. The Lees lived in Arlington House for 30 years, until the Civil War. In his bedroom in Arlington House on April 20, 1861, Lee wrote his letter resigning his commission from the United States Army upon the secession of Virginia from the Union. The next day Lee left the house to assume command of the Confederate Army in Richmond; he never returned to Arlington House. Mrs. Lee departed the mansion soon after her husband.

The Union Army found Arlington House to be of prime importance because of its strategic position overlooking the Potomac River; during the Civil War the mansion and its grounds became an armed Union camp. Many of the Washington heirlooms remaining in the house were moved to the Patent Office for safekeeping. Most are now at Mount Vernon (see site report).

In 1864, when Mrs. Lee failed to appear in person to pay her property taxes, the house and land were confiscated by the federal government for back taxes, and 200 acres were set aside to serve as a national cemetery. The Supreme Court restored the property to the Lee heirs after the war, but in the 1880s the Lees sold it back to the government for $150,000.

In 1925, Congress approved funds for the restoration of the house, which had been neglected for many years. The house you see today is as it was when the Lees lived here in the nineteenth century.

ARLINGTON NATIONAL CEMETERY   **(703) 692-0931**
Arlington, VA 22211
Hours: April–September—8 A.M.–7 P.M.
       October–March—8 A.M.–5 P.M.
Free Admission

 Arlington Cemetery stop (blue line); visitor center is one-and-a-half-block walk.

 Tourmobile.

 Visitor center.

Free two-hour parking in lots near visitor center. Directly across Memorial Bridge from D.C.

 None on premises or in the area; picnicking on the grounds is forbidden.

 Older children with an enthusiasm for history will enjoy walking among the graves of famous soldiers. Younger children can stretch their legs.

 No special services.

 Limited accessibility. Park information desk will give special car passes to handicapped visitors who want to visit particular gravesites. Special parking is available at various sites on the grounds. Phones and bathrooms are inaccessible.

 No special services available.

 No special services available.

 None necessary.

 Tours of areas of interest in the cemetery are available through the Tourmobile concession in the visitor center. Since cars are not allowed in the cemetery, the Tourmobile is the best way to see all the points of interest, which are scattered throughout the cemetery.

Arlington National Cemetery is located on 420 acres of land, about half of which was once part of the estate of Mrs. Robert E. Lee. The land was acquired by the federal government during the Civil War for use as a burial ground for Union dead. The first man buried here, however, was not a Union soldier, but a Confederate prisoner of war who had died in a local hospital.

Among the more than 60,000 American war dead buried here are soldiers who served in the Revolutionary War, the War of 1812, the Civil War, the Spanish-American War, World Wars I and II, the Korean War and the war in Vietnam. Burial in the cemetery is reserved for those who have served in the military, Medal of Honor recipients, high-level government officials and their dependents. New graves are added to the rows of markers at the rate of 75 a week.

Pierre L'Enfant, Washington's first planner, is buried south of the Custis-Lee Mansion (see Arlington House site report) on a slope overlooking the city that he designed. Mary and George Washington Park Custis, the builders of the mansion, are also buried here.

On a slope below the mansion is the grave of President John F. Kennedy, marked by a slate headstone, covered with Cape Cod fieldstone and surrounded by marble inscribed with quotations from Kennedy's Inaugural Address. Nearby, in a grass plot, is the grave of Senator Robert F. Kennedy.

The simple, marble Tomb of the Unknown Soldier is inscribed, "Here rests in honored glory an American soldier known but to God." In the tomb are the remains of an unidentified soldier slain in World War I; crypts at the head of one tomb contain the remains of unknown military personnel who died in World War II and the Korean War. The tomb is guarded by a single soldier from the 3rd U.S. Infantry; the watch is changed in a simple yet impressive ceremony every hour on the hour from October to March and every half hour from April to September.

If you're visiting the cemetery on a Saturday or holiday afternoon from April to September, you should stop at the nearby Netherlands Carillon. Carillon concerts are given at 2 and 4 P.M., sponsored by the National Park Service. Also visit the Marine Corps Memorial (see site report).

CARLYLE HOUSE HISTORIC SITE (703) 549-2997
121 N. Fairfax Street, Alexandria, VA 22314
Hours: 10 A.M.–5 P.M. Tuesday to Saturday
Noon–5 P.M. Sunday
Admission: Adults—$2 Groups of 10 or more—$1.50 Students (6–17)—$1 Youth and student groups of 10 or more—50¢ Senior Citizens—$1.50

 King Street stop (yellow line); DASH to Old Town.

 DASH to Old Town; 60¢, exact fare required.

 Expensive from Washington; take the Metro to National Airport and catch a taxi there.

 On-street parking. From D.C., take the 14th Street Bridge. Take the second right onto the George Washington Memorial Parkway south to Alexandria. The parkway becomes Washington Street once you enter Alexandria. Turn left on Cameron Street and drive four blocks to Fairfax Street where you should turn right. The house is on the left.

 None on premises.

 Recommended for older children; the restoration of the house is illustrated in interesting detail.

 Call at least one week in advance, so the staff can arrange for extra guides to be on hand. Group rates noted above.

 Limited accessibility. The ground and first floors are accessible to someone in a wheelchair, but the top floor is inaccessible. The bathroom is accessible.

 No special services available.

 Written guidebook available.

 As noted above.

 Tours are given every half hour (30 minutes).

When John Carlyle built his colonial mansion in 1751, the Potomac River lapped at the garden gate. Today the house is landlocked, bordered by modern row houses and a factory. Because of restoration by the Northern Virginia Regional Park Authority, however, the grandeur of the house, if not its grounds, has been reinstated. While the furnishings of the house aren't Carlyle family pieces, they are representative of the period. Of particular note are the painted-canvas floor coverings—"poor man's marble"—and the 200-year-old broom that was carved from one piece of wood—bristles and all.

Carlyle, a Scottish immigrant, was one of Alexandria's founding fathers. A leading figure in northern Virginia, he was a merchant, customs collector of the port of Alexandria, commissary for the Virginia militia, and a justice of the Fairfax County Court.

In 1755, General Edward Braddock, Commander-in-Chief of His Majesty's Forces in North America, met with colonial leaders in Carlyle House to discuss plans for financing the French and Indian War. The recommendations of the meeting led to the passage of the Stamp Act, one of the sparks that ignited the American Revolution.

CHRIST CHURCH   (703) 549-1450
118 N. Washington Street, Alexandria, VA 22314
Hours: 9 A.M.–5 P.M. Monday–Friday
           9 A.M.–noon Saturday
           2–5 P.M. Sunday
Free Admission

King Street stop (yellow line); DASH to Old Town.

DASH to Old Town; 60¢, exact fare required.

Expensive from Washington; take Metro to National Airport and get a cab there.

Pay lot and curb parking on Columbus Street. From Washington, take 14th Street Bridge. Take second right onto the George Washington Memorial Parkway south to Alexandria. Once in Alexandria, the parkway becomes Washington Street; the church is on the right at the corner of Cameron and Washington Streets.

None on premises.

Older children may be interested in the historical significance of the church and in the fact that both George Washington and Robert E. Lee worshiped here.

No special arrangements are required.

Inaccessible without help; one step up into the church; staff member is always there to help. Bathroom is inaccessible.

No special services available.

No special services available.

None necessary.

Walk-in tour given (5 minutes).

Christ Church, designed by James Wren and built in 1773, is typical of early Georgian church architecture, much like an English country church. Christ Church features a well-lighted interior emphasized by stark white walls, woodwork and furnishings. The church was constructed of local red brick and trimmed with white stone from a local quarry. Most of the interior is also original although the gallery, tower and cupola were added in later years.

Christ Church was the first Episcopal church in Alexandria. General and Mrs. Washington had a pew here, as did Robert E. Lee, who was confirmed as a youth and later worshiped here with his family. Both pews are marked with silver plates. The quiet, shaded churchyard is a pleasant place and provides the visitor with a short break from the strain of sightseeing.

Every Saturday at 5 P.M. in July and August organ recitals are given in the church. The church choir also performs on occasion. Other special events are posted on the gates of the church.

CLAUDE MOORE COLONIAL FARM AT TURKEY RUN (703) 442-7557

6310 Old Georgetown Pike, McLean, VA 22101
Hours: April–December—10 A.M.–4:30 P.M. Wednesday–Sunday
Admission: Adults—$1   Children—50¢

M No Metro stop.

No Metrobus service.

Too expensive to be feasible.

P Free lot. Take Capital Beltway (I-495) to Exit 13. Turn south on Virginia Route 193 and go 2.3 miles to Claude Moore Colonial Farm sign. Go left and follow signs to lot. Take care not to confuse the Farm with Turkey Run Park.

None on premises; picnic area near parking lot.

Highly recommended. Schoolchildren from preschool on up can participate in Colonial Experiences for a modest fee. They can dip candles, spin yarn and make toys. Call three months in advance.

Due to limited parking, groups should call in advance at 442-7557 to reserve space and time, so the farm does not become overcrowded.

Limited accessibility. The path to the farm is hilly and hard to pass with a wheelchair. With a day's advance notice, the farm staff will allow people to enter a special gate near the cabin. Call 442-7557. Bathrooms are inaccessible.

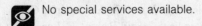

No special services available.

No special services available.

A As noted above.

T No walk-in tours are given, but the costumed "family" is always on hand and very willing to answer questions.

The Claude Moore Colonial Farm at Turkey Run is an 11-acre working farm operated by a private foundation. A "family" of volunteers re-creates the life of a low-income, rural family in the 1770s. You may find this especially interesting after visiting some of the larger, more prosperous historical plantations in Virginia and Maryland.

The family grows tobacco and works in two kitchen gardens and an apple orchard. The daily routines of the farm include cooking lunch over a log fire, washing dishes in a wooden tub, planting buckwheat and weeding the gardens. Such domesticated animals as guinea hens, ducks, quarter horses, cattle and razorback hogs roam the farm. And if you keep a sharp eye out, you are likely to see white-tailed deer, opossums, skunks and migratory geese and ducks nearby.

Special programs, featuring music and crafts, are conducted on some weekends. Call 442-7557 to find out what's on while you're in town.

COLVIN RUN MILL   **(703) 759-2771**
Virginia Route 7 (Leesburg Pike), 5 miles west of Tyson's Corner
(Capital Beltway (I-495) Exit 10B; Route 7 west for 5 miles)
Mailing Address: Fairfax County Park Authority
                            4030 Hummer Road
                            Annandale, VA 22003
Hours: April–December—11 A.M.–5 P.M. Wednesday–Monday
                January–March—noon–4 P.M.
                Last tour begins at 4 P.M.
                Closed Thanksgiving, Christmas Eve and Christmas and New
                Year's
Admission: Adults—$3   Children—$1

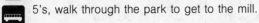

M Not served by Metro.

🚌 5's, walk through the park to get to the mill.

🚕 An extraordinarily expensive taxi ride from Washington.

P Free parking lot.

🍽 You can picnic in the park by the ponds. The general store sells penny candy and sodas.

👪 Kids are impressed by the enormous workings of the mill, and they can feed the ducks in the two nearby ponds. There are occasional weekend crafts demonstrations of spinning and blacksmithing. Tours can be arranged for school groups.

Call or write two or three weeks in advance to arrange for special tours.

♿ Inaccessible.

👁 No special services available.

👂 No special services available.

A None necessary.

T Call a few days ahead to arrange for a special tour. No walk-in tours.

This water-driven grist mill, dating back to the early 1800s, makes for a captivating and rather humbling visit. For most people, bread is something bought in plastic bags at the grocery store. Here, however, powerful wooden gears work away to stone-mill whole wheat and buckwheat flour and meal. If inspired, you can even buy some flour and meal at the general store for home baking.

GADSBY'S TAVERN MUSEUM   **(703) 838-4242**
134 N. Royal Street, Alexandria, VA 22313
Hours: 10 A.M.–5 P.M. Tuesday–Saturday
          1–5 P.M. Sunday
          Closed Thanksgiving, Christmas and New Year's

Admission: Adults—$2   Senior Citizens—$1.75   Kids (6–17)—$1
Group Rates: Ten or more adults—$1.50   Ten or more kids—50¢

M   King Street stop (yellow line); DASH to Old Town.

🚌   DASH to Old Town; 60¢, exact fare required.

🚕   Expensive from Washington. Take Metro to National Airport and catch a cab there.

P   On-street parking. From D.C. take 14th Street Bridge; take second right, George Washington Memorial Parkway south to Alexandria. The parkway becomes Washington Street once you are in Alexandria. Turn left onto Cameron Street; go three blocks, and turn right onto Royal Street.

🍽   None on premises. Gadsby's Tavern Restaurant, 548-1288, which is next to the museum, is open from 11:30 A.M. to 3 P.M. and 5:30 to 10 P.M.; waiters wear period costumes.

👪   See special rates above.

👫   Recommended. See special rates above. Advance notice required.

♿   Limited accessibility. First floor of the City Tavern Museum is accessible. The bathroom is inaccessible.

👁   No special services available.

👂   No special services available.

A   None necessary.

T   A tour is given every 30 minutes.

Gadsby's Tavern Museum in Alexandria combines the two-story pre-Revolutionary City Tavern, built in 1752, with the larger City Hotel, added in 1792. The tavern was described by many as the finest public house in America. Both buildings were well known to George Washington, who came here often; he used the City Tavern as his headquarters several times during the French and Indian War. He and Mrs. Washington often danced in the ballroom of the hotel. Other well-known visitors to the tavern included John Paul Jones, Aaron Burr, George Mason, Francis Scott Key, Henry Clay and the Marquis de Lafayette.

In the City Tavern, a guest could enjoy a meal and a drink in the taproom, or visit the gaming room across the hall. Upstairs in the assembly room one could take dancing lessons or attend lectures or club meetings. Above, under the gabled roof, one might find primitive lodgings. The addition of the hotel provided more commodious sleeping arrangements plus a lovely ballroom. After the Civil War, the buildings fell into decay and the hotel closed in 1879.

The beautiful woodwork that you see in the ballroom is a reproduction; the original is in the American Wing of the Metropolitan Museum of Art in New York. While you are in the ballroom, note the musicians' gallery. The "honesty box" in the taproom used to dispense tobacco by the pipeful if a coin was dropped into its slot; the user was expected to close the box after his pipe was filled.

At Christmas, the staff gives a lovely candlelight tour of the tavern. Call 549-0205 for the time and date of this event.

GEORGE WASHINGTON'S GRIST MILL   (703) 780-3383
5514 Mount Vernon Memorial Highway, Alexandria, VA 22309
Hours: Memorial Day–Labor Day—9 A.M.–5 P.M.
          Labor Day–Memorial Day—by appointment only to groups
Admission: Memorial Day–Labor Day   Adults—$1   Children—75¢

M No Metro stop.

No Metrobus stop.

Impractical; the fare would be exorbitant.

P Parking is available on the shoulder of Route 325 where it is possible to get cars well away from the traffic flow.

None on premises, but picnicking is permitted on the grounds.

Recommended. Kids will enjoy watching a working grist mill. They can climb the steep steps to the floors above the mill where the grain was stored and processed.

Make arrangements for group tours by calling (703) 339-7265 two weeks in advance.

Limited accessibility. The staff will help the wheelchair up the three steps to the ground floor. Other floors are inaccessible. The bathroom is accessible.

No special services available.

 No special services available.

 From Labor Day to Memorial Day you must make an appointment at least two days in advance to go inside the mill. Call 339-7265 to make arrangements.

 No walk-in tours are given, but there is a slide show on the entry level and the ranger will give you a free brochure.

George Washington had this grist mill built in 1770–1771 to replace an inefficient and badly located mill he had inherited along with Mount Vernon. The new mill produced two grades of flour and bran that were good enough to be sold commercially. Washington took great interest in the operation of his mill and would occasionally walk from Mount Vernon to inspect it. In 1799, Washington gave the mill to his nephew, Lawrence Lewis, and Martha Washington's granddaughter, Nellie Custis, as a wedding gift. No one knows how long the mill continued to operate, but in 1850 the walls finally collapsed, and over the years the stones were carted away to be used for other buildings.

Restored from 1932 to 1934, the present building is a close replica of George Washington's much-prized mill. The reconstruction, which was undertaken by the Civilian Conservation Corps and local architects and craftspeople, was based in part on a drawing done by a nineteenth-century surveyor who, upon realizing that the mill was collapsing, sketched it from memory and collaborated with local residents to make sure that his drawing was accurate. Further details about the original appearance of the mill were found in Washington's personal papers and through excavations made on the site. The mill is a part of Mason Neck State Park.

GREAT FALLS PARK   **(703) 235-3884**
9200 Old Dominion Drive, Great Falls, VA 22066
Hours: 8 A.M.–dark daily
Free Admission

 No Metro stop.

No Metrobus service.

 Too expensive to be feasible.

 Parking lot is at visitor center. Drive out Canal Road; take Chain Bridge and turn right onto Route 123. Turn on 193W (also Georgetown Pike); go past Claude Moore Colonial Farm at Turkey Run and the Capital Beltway (I-495), and look for the park signs. The park is 15 miles from D.C. and seven miles from Chain Bridge.

 Snack bar at the visitor center is open daily from Memorial Day to Labor Day. Restaurants can be found in Great Falls, two miles away. Picnicking is allowed.

 Recommended, in the presence of attentive adults.

 The park staff will arrange guided tours of the park with two days' notice. Call 235-3884.

 Limited accessibility. The visitor center has long ramps and accessible phones and bathrooms. The third overlook of the falls is accessible to someone in a wheelchair.

 No special services available.

 No special services available.

 As noted above.

 No walk-in guided tours are given.

Great Falls Park is aptly named, for it is here that the Potomac River plunges 76 feet over a series of huge boulders through the mile-long Stephen Mather Gorge. The river is a quarter-mile wide in this gorge and, at places, up to 50 feet deep. At the height of the spring melt, up to 480,000 cubic feet of water pour over the falls every second, a flow even greater than that of Niagara Falls.

The wooded park lends itself to hiking, picnicking and bird watching. In addition, it is possible to see a great deal of wildlife, including beaver, skunks, opossum, red fox, white-tailed deer and cottontail rabbits.

The park encompasses the relics of George Washington's ill-fated dream of operating a canal on the Virginia side of the river to bypass the unnavigable sections of the Potomac. Washington founded the

Potowmack Canal Company (an Indian word meaning "trading place") in 1785 and the canal was completed in 1802. Light-Horse Harry Lee, the father of Robert E. Lee, founded a town nearby named Matildaville. Within 26 years, however, trade declined, the canal company folded and the town fell into ruins. The remains of the canal and of Matildaville lie north and east of the visitor center. You will find two of the five canal locks still standing; the National Park Service is reconstructing the entire system. Note the beaten marks of the proud stonemen's "signatures." Only a few vine-covered foundations and the chimney of Dickey's Tavern remain to mark the town of Matildaville.

One final word of warning about visiting Great Falls Park: the park rangers insist with good reason that you stay off the rocks near the water's edge and neither swim nor wade near the falls. Many people drown in this part of the river every year.

GUNSTON HALL PLANTATION   (703) 550-9220
Route 242 (4 miles east of Route 1), Lorton, VA 22079
Hours: 9:30 A.M.–5 P.M. daily
     Closed Christmas
Admission: Adults—$3   Children (6–15)—$1   Senior Citizens—$2.50

 No Metro stop.

 No Metrobus service.

 Impractical; fare would be exorbitant.

 Parking at visitor center. Take US-1 South to Virginia Route 242; go left on Route 242 to Gunston Hall.

 None on premises; picnic tables on grounds. Fast food is available on Route 1; nearest restaurants are in Alexandria. Meeting Room in new building is rentable for catered affairs.

 A special "Touch It Museum" is open to school groups only with advance notice; call 550-9220. Kids will also enjoy the nature trail where they may see deer, wild turkeys, bald eagles and other wildlife (one-and-a-half miles round-trip to river and back).

Discount rate ($2.50 per adult) and special tours are available to 12 or more; call 550-9220 to make arrangements or stop at desk.

Limited accessibility. Visitor center and grounds are fully accessible. The gardeners will help you enter the house but the upper floors are inaccessible.

 No special services available.

 No special services available.

 Special-interest tours on furniture, architecture, needlework and so forth are available with two weeks' notice; call 550-9220 to make arrangements.

 Walk-in guided tours are given continually. The guides are well versed in the historical and domestic details of the house. French, Spanish, Portuguese, Russian, Japanese and Italian language brochures are available.

Gunston Hall was the home of George Mason, the person Thomas Jefferson called "the wisest man of his generation." Mason is best known as the father of the Bill of Rights of the United States Constitution. A visit to Gunston Hall (now administered by the National Society of Colonial Dames of America) and its 550 acres of gardens and woodlands will reward you with an unparalleled view into the life, architecture and horticulture of the era when Mason lived.

When you begin your tour of the first floor of this early Colonial mansion (construction began in 1755), note the handcarved woodwork in the Palladian drawing room off the central hall. The intricate carving is the work of the English carpenter William Buckland, an indentured servant who worked at Gunston Hall from 1755 to 1759. A portrait of Mason's first wife, Ann Eilbeck, also hangs in this room, while a portrait of Mason rests over the dining-room fireplace. The first-floor study contains the table on which Mason penned the Virginia "Declaration of Rights," which was later used as the model for the Bill of Rights.

From the window of the upstairs bedroom you can look down on the formal gardens. These gardens, which are comparable to those at the Governor's Palace in Williamsburg, are divided by a boxwood hedge planted by Mason more than 200 years ago. All the plants and shrubs in the garden are varieties actually found in colonial times. A three-quarter-mile nature trail leads down to the Potomac River.

In addition to the house and the grounds, take time to visit the restored kitchen and schoolhouse, for they provide an excellent view of everyday plantation life.

Gunston Hall Plantation is 20 miles southwest of Washington.

LEE'S BOYHOOD HOME   (703) 548-8454
607 Oronoco Street, Alexandria, VA
Mailing Address: The Lee-Jackson Foundation
                          450 Citizens Commonwealth Building
                          Charlottesville, VA 22901
Hours: 10 A.M.–4 P.M. Monday–Saturday
          Noon–4 P.M. Sunday
          Closed December 15 through January 31, except by
          appointment
Admission: Adults—$2   Children—$1

M King Street stop (yellow line), DASH to Old Town.

DASH to Old Town; 60¢, exact fare required.

Very expensive from D.C.; take Metro to National Airport stop and a taxi from there.

P On-street parking. From D.C. take the 14th Street Bridge; take the second right onto the George Washington Parkway south. This becomes Washington Street in Alexandria. Take a left onto Oronoco.

None on premises.

Recommended for older children. Groups of 10 or more kids pay 50¢ each.

Admission is lowered to $1.50 for groups of 10 or more. The staff requests several days' notice for groups of 40 or more so they can arrange for extra guides; call 548-8454 to notify staff of your plans.

Inaccessible.

No special services available.

No special services available.

As noted above.

 Walk-in guided tours are given continually (45 minutes).

The Revolutionary War hero, Light-Horse Harry Lee, leased this early-Federal–style house in 1812. When Lee died in 1818, Mrs. Lee kept the house and raised her five children here until 1825. The young Robert E. Lee attended the Quaker School next door; he left in 1825 to attend West Point and begin his military career.

The house is full of charming Lee memorabilia and rare antiques. As you enter, take the time to note the low mirror in the entrance hall where the ladies once paused to inspect their boots and skirts before entering the parlor. You will also see that the table in the breakfast room is laid out for a game of cards, complete to the detail of the long-stemmed clay pipe that was passed from man to man during the game; each broke off the tip of the stem before passing it on.

Several special events take place during the year: in January the birthdays of Light-Horse Harry Lee and Robert E. Lee are celebrated; in March a "Living History Weekend" presents demonstrations of daily life from the early nineteenth century; in October a celebration honors the visit of General Lafayette to Mrs. Lee in 1824 and in December candlelight tours of the house are conducted. Call 548-8454 to find out the precise times of these events; the dates change each year.

LEE-FENDALL HOUSE   **(703) 548-1789**
429 North Washington Street, Alexandria, VA
Mailing Address: 614 Oronoco Street, Alexandria, VA 22314
Hours: 10 A.M.–4 P.M. Tuesday–Saturday
          Noon–4 P.M. Sunday
          Closed Christmas and New Year's
Admission: Adults—$2 Children (6–17)—$1

 King Street stop (yellow line), DASH to Old Town.

 DASH from Metro; 60¢, exact fare required.

Very expensive from D.C.; take Metro to National Airport stop and a taxi from there.

 Parking lot off Oronoco Street. Take 14th Street Bridge from D.C.; take second right onto George Washington Memorial Parkway. The parkway becomes Washington Street in Alexandria—the Lee-Fendall house is on the left.

 None on premises.

 Recommended because of dollhouse collection.

Tours and special rates ($1.50 per person) can be arranged with two weeks' notice.

 Inaccessible.

 No special services available.

No special services available.

 As noted above.

Walk-in guided tours are given continually of the first and second floor.

A long line of Lees lived in this house from the time it was built in 1785 until 1903. The Federal-style house was built by Philip Fendall for his second wife, Mary Lee, who was the sister of the Revolutionary War hero, Light-Horse Harry Lee, and the aunt of Robert E. Lee.

The first two floors of the house contain a mélange of the furnishings of all the eras when Lees resided here and present an unclear picture of what life in the house was like at any given time. The third floor of the house, however, shelters a delightful treat: a fine collection of dollhouses. Because the third floor is not air-conditioned, it may be closed off in very hot weather.

At least one famous person who was neither a Lee nor a Fendall lived here, too; John L. Lewis, president of the United Mine Workers, resided in the Lee-Fendall House from 1927 until his death in 1969.

For those who are interested in learning more about the Lee family and how they lived, we recommend a visit to Lee's boyhood home across the street (see site report).

THE LYCEUM (703) 838-4994
201 S. Washington Street, Alexandria, VA 22314
Hours: 10 A.M.–5 P.M. daily
     Closed Thanksgiving, Christmas and New Year's
Free Admission

 King Street stop (yellow line), DASH to Old Town.

 DASH to Old Town; 60¢, exact fare required.

 Expensive from Washington. Take the Metro to National Airport and catch a cab from there. Telephone from the center for a return taxi.

 Free parking lot. Take the 14th Street Bridge from Washington. Make the second right after the bridge onto the George Washington Memorial Parkway. In Alexandria this will become Washington Street. Turn right after Prince Street into the center's lot.

 None on premises.

 Exhibits may be of interest to older children with an enthusiasm for history.

 One month's notice is required to arrange any special-interest program. Subjects range from fashion to architecture.

 Fully accessible.

 No special services available.

 With advance notice the staff will arrange special tours; call 838-4200 to make arrangements.

 As noted above.

 No walk-in tours given.

The Lyceum is a brick and stucco Greek Revival–style house that was built 1839–1840. After serving as a Civil War military hospital, a private home and an office building, the Lyceum was bought by the City of Alexandria in 1969. These days it acts as a center for state travel information and as a museum.

    The staff of the Lyceum can make hotel, campground and dinner reservations for you, help you plan an itinerary and inform you of special events in the state.

The building is available to rent for all kinds of events. Call the office for details.

MARINE CORPS WAR MEMORIAL   (703) 285-2600
(Iwo Jima Memorial)
Adjacent to the Arlington National Cemetery
Mailing Address: George Washington Memorial Parkway
                      Turkey Run Park, McLean, VA 22101
Hours: Open 24 hours daily
      (Night visits are not advised)
Free Admission

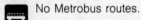 Rosslyn stop (blue and orange lines); it's a three-block walk to the memorial.

No Metrobus routes.

Take the Metro to Rosslyn and catch a cab from there.

Free lot. Take the Roosevelt Bridge from D.C. to Virginia. Follow the signs for Route 50 (you will see the memorial to your left once you are on 50). Take the first exit off 50 to the right—it's marked ''Rosslyn/Key Bridge,'' and a second smaller sign says ''Fort Myer.'' Take a left at the top of the ramp onto Meade Street. Continue on past the memorial, which you will pass again on your left, and take the first left onto Jackson Avenue. Take the first left after the Netherlands Carillon and follow the drive to the parking lot.

None on grounds. Nearest restaurants are in D.C. or Rosslyn.

Recommended for a quick visit.

No special services.

Limited accessibility. Ramps lead from parking lot to sidewalks around monument; steps go up to the monument. No bathrooms or phones.

No special services available.

No special services available.

None necessary.

 No tours given.

Better known as the Iwo Jima statue, the Marine Corps War Memorial commemorates all the marines who have died in the defense of the United States since the Corps was founded in 1775. Designer Horace W. Peaslee based the statue on Joseph Rosenthal's photograph of five marines and one sailor raising the U.S. flag on Mount Suribachi after a bloody World War II battle in the Pacific. Sculptor Felix W. de Weldon created this 78-foot-long piece, the largest bronze statue ever cast. The flag incorporated into the monument is a real flag, which flies day and night by Executive Order. The Marine Sunset Parade occurs Tuesdays, June to August, at 7 P.M.

Try to plan your visit to the memorial to coincide with the concert given adjacent to the memorial at the Netherlands Carillon, a 49-bell musical instrument presented to the United States by the people of the Netherlands after World War II. The free concerts are given on the carillon from April to September on Saturdays and national holidays, 2 to 4 P.M.

MOUNT VERNON PLANTATION   (703) 780-2000
Southern terminus of the George Washington Memorial Parkway
Mailing Address: Ladies Association
            Mount Vernon, VA 22121
Hours: March–October—9 A.M.–5 P.M. daily
        November–February—9 A.M.–4 P.M. daily
Admission: Adults—$5   Senior Citizens over 62—$4
          Kids (6–11)—$2

 No Metro stop.

 Tourmobile stop from June 1 to September 15 only.

 Not practical; the fare would be quite high.

 Free, but a very crowded lot. The walk from the lot to the house is long. Mount Vernon is eight miles south of Alexandria and 16 miles south of Washington on the George Washington Memorial Parkway.

None allowed on premises. The Mount Vernon Inn, just outside the gates, offers both restaurant and snack-bar fare. Alexandria offers many restaurants as well.

 Special rates for student and youth groups of $2 for grades one to 12. Write or call 780-2000. The house and grounds are a lot for a kid to cover, but history buffs will enjoy the details of eighteenth-century plantation life.

 For groups of 20 or more, admission is $4.50 for adults, $3.50 for seniors. Call 780-2000.

 Limited accessibility. Ramps can be placed on the ground floor with advance notice. Write or call 780-2000. First floor and museum are accessible. A few wheelchairs are available at the main entrance on a first-come, first-served basis. The Mount Vernon Inn, bathrooms and phone are accessible.

 No special services available.

 No special services available.

 As noted above.

 No walk-in tours are given, but guides are stationed throughout the mansion to answer questions. A free brochure is available as you enter the grounds; an excellent guide, *Mount Vernon, An Illustrated Handbook,* can be purchased for $2 at the gift shop.

If you can manage to arrive at Mount Vernon early in the day, you will be rewarded with a parking space on the lot that will be crowded by midday, a tour of the house after only a short wait and the pleasure of visiting George Washington's estate without having to contend with too many of the up to 10,000 people who visit the mansion each day during the tourist season.

The 5,000 acres of land that originally comprised the Mount Vernon estate were granted to George Washington's great-grandfather, John Washington, in 1674. George Washington lived here from 1754 until his death in 1799. Washington had to spend many of those years away from his beloved estate, however, to serve as Commander-in-Chief of the Continental Army, delegate to the Constitutional Convention and first President of the United States. Despite his long absences from Mount Vernon, Washington directed the enlargement of the house from 1½ to 2½ stories and increased the estate's size to 8,000 acres. Of the five independently operating farms that thrived on the estate during the years of Washington's management, only the mansion house farm remains intact today.

As you walk up the path to the mid-Georgian–style mansion, you pass nine outbuildings, all of which are original, with the exception of the coach house and the greenhouse-slave quarters. Before you enter the mansion, stop to enjoy the unspoiled view of the Potomac River from the porch; the view is probably very much as it was when Washington gazed out over the same fields.

You can see 14 rooms of the house; the third floor is closed. Some of the main points of interest in the mansion are the Palladian window in the banquet room, the decorated ceiling and Washington family coat-of-arms above the mantel in the west parlor, and Washington's library where the President wrote in his diary, kept the farm's records and carried on his tireless correspondence. Upstairs are five bedrooms.

Wander around the 30-acre grounds; visit Washington's tomb, the lovely gardens, the museum and outbuildings.

A lovely way to see the mansion and grounds is to take the cruise from the Mount Vernon dock for a 45-minute ride on the Potomac or the four-hour round-trip cruise from Pier 4 in Washington. See the "Outdoor Washington/Sports" chapter for details.

A small gift shop is located on the grounds; a larger shop is outside the entrance gate.

PENTAGON　　　　　　　　　　　　　**(703) 695-1776**
Right off I-395
Mailing Address: Pentagon, Washington, D.C. 20301
Hours: 10:30 A.M., 1:30 and 3:00 P.M. Monday–Friday
　　　　　Closed holidays
Free Admission

Pentagon stop (blue line). The stop is inside the Pentagon.
Follow the arrows at the top of the escalator to the tours.
13's.

Telephone for a cab to pick you up at the south parking entrance.

 Pay lot. From D.C. take the 14th Street Bridge, which will lead you to I-395. Follow the signs to the Pentagon.

 Limited food available on the concourse.

 Not recommended. The tour is fast and there is little except pictures to see.

 If possible, give one week's notice by phone (695-1776), or write to Pentagon Tour Director's Office, 20301.

 Limited access. Bathrooms are accessible, phones are not.

 No special services available. People with visual impairments can bring their own guides but must give the staff 48 hours' notice at 695-1776.

 No special services available. People with hearing impairments who want to bring their own interpreters must notify the tour staff at 695-1776.

 As noted above.

 Tours are given at 10:30 A.M., 1:30 and 3:00 P.M. The tours are confined to certain corridors and the guide walks backward to make sure that you do not stray into secured areas. Among the points of interest on the tour are the cases of models of past and present aircraft and the corridor of Time-Life World War II paintings.

The Pentagon, one of the world's largest office buildings, is the head-quarters of the Defense Department. It took only 16 months to build and was finished in January 1943. Most people are familiar with its five-sided shape. Within those five walls are five concentric inner-to-outer rings connected by 10 spokelike corridors. Although there are 17.5 miles of corridors, no office is any further than a seven-minute walk from any other office.

The Pentagon houses the secretaries of defense, Army, Navy, Air Force and Coast Guard, as well as the Joint Chiefs of Staff. The military and civilian employees who work here are concerned both with making policy decisions and with housing, training, feeding, equipping and caring for the members of the armed services.

POHICK CHURCH   (703) 550-9449
9301 Richmond Avenue, Lorton, VA 22079
Hours: 8:30 A.M.–4:30 P.M. daily
Free Admission

 No Metro stop.

 No Metrobus service.

 Too expensive to be feasible.

 On-street parking. From Washington, take I-395 south to the Fort Belvoir exit. Turn right onto Backlick Road and then turn right onto Old Telegraph Road, where you will see the church. The church is 19.5 miles south of Washington.

 None on premises.

 Recommended for older children for a brief visit.

 No special arrangements necessary.

 Inaccessible without assistance; there are four steps up to the church and no ramp. Bathroom is inaccessible.

 No special services available.

 No special services available.

 None required.

 No walk-in guided tours are given.

Pohick Church, completed in 1774, is located equidistant from Mount Vernon and Gunston Hall (see site reports). Both George Washington and George Mason were members of the church's building committee: Washington surveyed the site and drew the plans for the brick building and Mason designed the interior. A notable feature is the box pews, similar to those in English churches of the time; the boxed enclosures kept out drafts and retained the heat of footwarmers and hot bricks used by parishioners in winter.

During the Civil War, one wall, the interior and all the furniture except the marble font were destroyed by Union troops who stabled their horses inside the church and carved their names into the sandstone around the entrance. Since then the church has been renovated twice, in 1874 and again in 1906.

POPE-LEIGHEY HOUSE   **(703) 780-4000**
9000 Richmond Highway (Route 1)
Mailing Address: Woodlawn Plantation
                    Mount Vernon, VA 22121
Hours: March–October—9:30 A.M.–4:30 P.M. weekends
        By appointment throughout the year for all other times
Admission: Adults—$4   Children—$3   Senior Citizens—$3
Students—$3   *Ticket rate reduced if Woodlawn ticket purchased jointly*

M King Street stop (yellow line), DASH to Old Town.

🚌 DASH from Metro; 60¢, exact fare required.

🚕 Too expensive to be feasible.

P Plenty of free parking.

🍽 None on premises.

👪 Recommended for older children with an interest in architecture.

👥 Groups of 15 or more must schedule their visit one week in advance by calling 780-4000. Slightly reduced rates are available.

♿ Inaccessible.

👁 No special services available.

👂 No special services available.

A If you wish to visit the house at times other than those listed above, call 780-4000 or write to make arrangements.

T Walk-in guided tours are given continually (30 minutes).

The Pope-Leighey House, designed by Frank Lloyd Wright in 1940, reflects the architect's belief that living in well-designed space should not be a privilege reserved for the wealthy. This house is one of five built by Wright on the East Coast in what he called the Usonian style, which involved the use of available industrial technology to create modest homes.

Built for the Loren Pope family, the house contains many architectural features that, although commonplace today, were revolutionary in 1940. For instance, Wright designed a carport instead of an enclosed garage, a flat roof rather than a sloped one, built-in furniture; he also placed heating coils in the floors.

In 1964, when the construction of a highway threatened the house's existence, the National Trust for Historic Preservation dismantled the Pope-Leighey House and reassembled it here on the grounds of the Woodlawn Plantation (see site report).

RAMSEY HOUSE   (703) 838-4200
(Alexandria Tourist Council)
221 King Street, Alexandria, VA 22314
Hours: 9 A.M.–5 P.M. daily
        Closed Thanksgiving, Christmas and New Year's
Free Admission

King Street stop (yellow line); DASH to Old Town.

DASH from Metro; 60¢, exact fare required.

Take Metro to National Airport and catch a cab there. Catching a return cab is facilitated by telephoning from Ramsey House.

On-street parking. From D.C., take the 14th Street Bridge and exit on the second right after the bridge onto the George Washington Memorial Parkway. This will become Washington Street once you are in Alexandria. Since you can't go left onto King Street, go left on Cameron the block before and then right onto Fairfax Street. Ramsey House is on the corner of Fairfax and King Streets.

None on premises.

Not recommended.

The Ramsey House staff can make group arrangements with sufficient notice; call (703) 548-0100.

Inaccessible. Ramsey House has steep stairs from the street.

No special services available.

No special services available.

As noted above.

No walk-in tours given. Staff will help you arrange tours of other historic sites in town.

Ramsey House is the home of Alexandria's Tourist Council. The origin of this, Alexandria's oldest house, is uncertain, but most historians believe that this frame-over-brick structure was built in Dumfries in 1724 and moved to its present location in 1749–1750 by William Ramsey, the city's first postmaster. Over the years the house has seen duty as a tavern, grocery store and rooming house.

If you can manage the steep climb up the stairs to enter Ramsey House, you will find a library of brochures on Alexandria's restaurants, motels, hotels, antique and art galleries and specialty shops. The staff will provide you with a calendar of events listing house and garden tours, candlelight tours and celebrations of historical events. In addition to a "Bruncher's Guide to Alexandria" and a guide to the city's nightlife, the staff has compiled a helpful book containing menus from neighborhood restaurants. You may find that the most helpful aid here is the guide-map to walking through Alexandria, which is available in 15 languages in addition to English. It provides a ready overview of the city.

The staff will provide free parking passes for out-of-town visitors for the metered zones of the city, and will make group reservations for restaurants, hotels and entertainment.

STABLER-LEADBEATER APOTHECARY SHOP
(703) 836-3713

107 S. Fairfax Street, Alexandria, VA 22314

Hours: 10 A.M.–4 P.M. Monday–Saturday
Closed Thanksgiving, Christmas and New Year's
Free Admission

 King Street stop (yellow line); DASH to Old Town.

 DASH to Old Town; 60¢, exact fare required.

 Expensive from Washington; available at National Airport, which is much closer.

 On-street parking. Take the 14th Street Bridge from Washington, turning at the second right onto the George Washington Memorial Parkway. Follow to Alexandria. Take a left on Cameron Street, and continue four blocks to Fairfax Street, where you will turn right and continue 1½ blocks. The apothecary is on the right.

 None on premises.

 Recommended for older children for a brief visit.

 No special arrangements necessary.

 Limited accessibility. There are two steps up into the shop and another step up into the museum. The woman in the shop will open both doors and lend a hand with the wheelchair.

 No special services available.

No special services available.

None necessary.

No walk-in tours given, but there is a 15-minute recording that explains the items in the museum as you wander through it.

The Apothecary Shop, founded by Edward Stabler, operated continuously as a pharmacy from 1792 to 1933. Included among the prominent customers of the shop were the Washington, Lee, Custis and Fairfax families. Account books also show that drugs were sold to Henry Clay and Daniel Webster. Robert E. Lee was in the shop making a purchase when Lieutenant J. E. B. Stuart handed him his orders to suppress the John Brown uprising at Harper's Ferry.

The Apothecary Shop museum, which opened in 1939, exhibits a collection of approximately 800 early hand-blown glass containers, antique mortars and pestles, scales and thermometers. Here, too, are the original account books and prescription files.

SULLY HISTORIC HOUSE   (703) 437-1794
Route 28, between U.S. 50 and the Dulles Toll Road, Chantilly, VA (4 miles from Dulles Airport)
Mailing Address: Fairfax County Park Authority
                   4040 Hummer Road, Annandale, VA 22003
Hours: 11 A.M.–5 P.M. Wednesday–Monday
           January–March weekends only—11 A.M.–4 P.M.
Admission: Adults—$3   Children—$1   Seniors—$1.50

M No Metro stop.

No Metrobus service.

An exorbitant taxi ride from Washington.

P Free parking lot.

None on premises. Picnicking is allowed.

There are lots of special events for kids. Sunday afternoon family activities include open-hearth cooking, craft demonstrations and music (included in the price of admission). During the summer, there is an eighteenth-century–type round-robin of activities for kids. School groups and scout troops can arrange for special tours.

Call or write several weeks in advance to set up a tour.

Grounds are accessible using the brick walkway. There are eight steps leading to the house.

No special services available.

No special services available.

A As noted above.

T Docent tours available.

An excursion to the Sully Historic House is an enjoyable escape from the city. This Federal-period plantation house was built in 1794, and is authentically furnished. It stands as an intriguing example of Federal architecture, handsome and pleasing to look at yet lacking the symmetry so characteristic of its period.

Richard Bland Lee, a member of the first U.S. Congress, a judge of the District of Columbia Orphans Court and brother of Revolutionary War hero Light-Horse Harry Lee, the father of Robert E. Lee, once lived here. It was continuously lived in until the government bought the land for Dulles Airport in 1958.

You may be interested in the program of special events (call or write for a schedule), which includes Spring on the Farm, an antique auto show in June, an August quilt show, an October Harvest Festival and a Christmas celebration.

THEODORE ROOSEVELT ISLAND   (703) 285-2600

In the Potomac River between Roosevelt and Key bridges
Mailing Address: George Washington Memorial Parkway
                McLean, VA 22101
Hours: 8 A.M.–dusk daily
Free Admission

 No Metro stop.

 No Metrobus service.

 Difficult to get a cab for a return trip.

 Free lot on the Virginia shore. Access to the park is from the northbound lane only of the George Washington Memorial Parkway.

 None on premises. Picnicking is permitted but no tables are provided and no fires allowed.

 Highly recommended. This is a great place for kids—lots of trails and different sorts of ecosystems.

 The park rangers will give a combined nature and historical walk with seven days' advance notice; call 285-2598 to make arrangements.

 Limited accessibility. The island is accessible by wheelchair, but the trails are not paved. The bathroom is inaccessible and there is no phone.

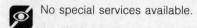

No special services available.

TDD number is 285-2620.

As noted above.

None offered.

Theodore Roosevelt Island is an appropriate memorial for the nature-loving President who created the national park system. Although the island is within sight and sound of D.C., it is a home to wildlife and a tranquil haven for humans as well. No cars are allowed on the island, which is accessible only by a footbridge from the parking lot.

The memorial itself, designed by Paul Manship, consists of a 17-foot bronze statue of the President in a familiar speaking pose and four 21-foot granite tablets inscribed with Roosevelt's philosophy on citizenship.

If you're feeling energetic, take the time to hike the 2.5 miles of nature trail. The island provides examples of marsh, swamp, upland wood and rocky shore ecosystems. You may even spy some of the wildlife that lives on the island, including pileated woodpeckers, wood ducks, red and grey fox, deer, kingfishers and marsh wrens.

WOODLAWN PLANTATION   **(703) 780-4000**
9000 Richmond Highway (Route 1), Mount Vernon, VA
Mailing Address: P.O. Box 37, Mount Vernon, VA 22121
Hours: 9:30 A.M.–4:30 P.M. daily
          Closed Thanksgiving, Christmas and New Year's
Admission: Adults—$4 Senior Citizens—$3 Students (through high school)—$3   *Joint tickets with the Pope-Leighey House are less expensive*

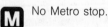

No Metro stop.

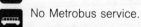

No Metrobus service.

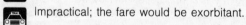

Impractical; the fare would be exorbitant.

P Plenty of free parking.

|O| None on premises.

Recommended for the Touch and Try exhibit in museum room and the Audubon nature trail. School tours should be arranged one week in advance by calling 780-4000.

Groups of 15 or more must schedule a visit in advance and will receive slightly reduced entrance rates; call 780-4000 or write to make arrangements.

Limited accessibility. A ramp can be provided to the first floor only with one day's notice; call 780-4000. Ramps are also provided to the needlework workshop in March. Bathrooms are inaccessible.

No special services available.

No special services available.

A As noted above.

T A guide will give you introductory historical background of the plantation. Brochures are available for a self-guided tour and a sheet posted at each door points out the highlights of that room.

Woodlawn Plantation provides an excellent picture of the life of the Virginia gentry in the early nineteenth century. Woodlawn's 2,000 acres of land were once a part of George Washington's estate, Mount Vernon (see site report); our first President gave the land as a wedding gift to his step-granddaughter, Nellie Custis, when she married his favorite nephew and secretary, Lawrence Lewis.

Construction of the Georgian-style mansion, which was designed by Dr. William Thornton (who was the first architect of the Capitol), lasted from 1800 to 1805. The spacious sophistication of the plantation mansion contrasts with the house at Mount Vernon, which is much more like a farmhouse. From the porch at Woodlawn you can see Mount Vernon in the distance; it's said that Nellie Custis Lewis kept a tract of land between the two houses clear all the years she lived at Woodlawn so she could sit in her "catch-all" room on the second floor and look at her childhood home through a telescope.

In keeping with the standards of the National Trust for Historic Preservation, which maintains the plantation, all of the lovely furnishings in the house are from the Lewis' period and some of them are the pieces the family actually used. Of special interest are the music room with its pianoforte and two harps and the children's bedroom, well stocked with period toys.

After touring the house and visiting the exhibit area and gift shop in the basement, take the time to stroll through the handsome formal gardens, with a rest on one of the many shaded benches. If you want to walk the nature trails as well as view the mansion and its gardens, allow yourself at least two hours at Woodlawn.

Each year Woodlawn Plantation sponsors three special events: a needlework exhibit is held in March; on a weekend in July the plantation is open in the evening for music, champagne, picnicking and dancing on the green; and there is caroling by candlelight in December. Since these events are rescheduled each year, write or call 780-4000 to find out the exact dates they'll be held.

Visit the Pope-Leighey House (see site report) while you're at Woodlawn; it's one of five houses on the East Coast designed by Frank Lloyd Wright.

OLD TOWN RAMBLE

Founded in 1749 by Scottish merchants and named for John Alexander, a principal original landowner, Alexandria is today reminiscent of its colonial origins. Many of Virginia's most influential families settled around the new port city—among them the Washington, Lee, Mason and Fairfax clans. George Washington, then an apprentice surveyor, helped lay out many of the city's streets.

Alexandria thrived as a tobacco port; many merchants and sea captains built comfortable homes which survive today. Most of the streets in Old Alexandria are still lined with attached row houses that are flush with the sidewalks; behind many of these charming houses, out of view of the casual stroller and beyond earshot of the clatter of carriage on cobblestone, are lovely gardens and patios.

In Revolutionary days and through the mid-1800s, Alexandria was a political, commercial and cultural center in addition to its role as a leading seaport (surpassed in importance only by Boston). In 1846, Virginia successfully petitioned Congress to grant Alexandria back to the state, which, from the 1790s, had been an official part of the new nation's capital.

Alexandria was spared the destruction of the Civil War because Union troops occupied it from the first and cut it off from the rest of the South. Soon thereafter, however, the advent of the railroad caused Baltimore to become the dominant port in the area. With its economy slowed by the loss of commerce, Alexandria became a sleepy if genteel little city.

Only during the first administration of Franklin Roosevelt was the city rediscovered and appreciated for both its proximity to the capital city and its historic examples of Colonial, Revolutionary and Greek Revival styles of architecture. In the past 20 years, historic-preservation groups have slowly restored the old sites, and the attention that they have paid to accurate historical detail today delights visitors.

Old Town—the restored center of Alexandria—lies roughly between Oronoco Street on the north, the Potomac River on the east, Gibbon Street on the south, and Washington Street on the west. The heart of the commercial development, which is quite charming, is King Street; start your tour here, at Ramsey House, which is the excellent tourist information center. Ramsey House also offers 1½-hour walking tours of the historic district; call 838-4200 for times, which change throughout the year.

Old Town boasts many fine restaurants and shops. Check our eating recommendations at this chapter's end, and shopping tips in the "Shopping" chapter.

VIRGINIA VITTLES

Being city folk, the authors have to overcome some provincialism when considering the Maryland and Virginia suburbs, especially with regard to restaurants. In point of fact, it wasn't so long ago that you could not find a truly outstanding meal outside of the city, but, happily, that is no longer the case. Even the "restaurants with a view" have become gastronomically ambitious.

Rosslyn/Arlington

Just across the river from D.C., facing Georgetown, is Rosslyn. What used to be a motley collection of pawnshops and bus depots is now a forest of high-rises. While not attractive at ground level, Rosslyn boasts a bunch of restaurants with spectacular views of the Washington skyline. The very best, and one of the area's most adventuresome restaurants, is *Windows,* 1000 Wilson Boulevard, 527-4430. Windows serves California-style new American cuisine; inventive, intriguing, usually hitting the mark. It's expensive. *Tivoli,* 1700 N. Moore, 524-8900, serves a marvelous variety of Italian food, with a strong emphasis on seafood. Their clams and mussels are invariably delicious; the appetizers excellent.

The *Pawnshop Restaurant,* Lee Highway at N. Moore, 522-7400, serves up a combination of singles, lobster and quiche. For Mexican, try *El Sombrero,* 5401 Lee Highway, 536-6500. Among Oriental restaurants, the *China Garden,* 1901 N. Moore, 525-5317, is moderately priced and good; the *Szechuan Gourmet,* 1812 N. Moore, 528-8188, is competent and reliable and the *Bangkok Gourmet,* 523 S. 23rd Street, 521-1305 (Crystal City), is a consistent, bargain-priced place. A word about Crystal City: it is a world unto itself, with grocery stores, restaurants, hotels, theaters and an underground shopping mall. If you find yourself at the Pentagon or Arlington Cemetery with a major hunger, head to Crystal City—there is plenty to satisfy, but little to write home about.

Alexandria

La Bergerie, 218 N. Lee, 683-1007, still ranks as one of the area's best, presenting a Basque menu, hearty and piquant; expensive. *Geranio,* 724 King, 548-0008, is a nice neighborhood restaurant—but with downtown prices—and has a varied Italian menu. *Henry Africa,* 607 King, 549-4010, boasts handsome decor as well as moderately priced Continental cuisine. *The Old Club,* 555 S. Washington, 549-4555, continues a 200-year-old tradition of Southern cooking. For well-prepared Greek food in a striking restaurant setting, try *Taverna Cretekou,* 818 King, 548-8688. Seafood of respectable origin and presentation can be found at *The Wharf,* 119 King, 836-2834. Authentic Creole cuisine can be enjoyed at *219,* 219 King, 734-1901.

Tyson's Corner/McLean

Other than the shopping malls, or friends, there is little to take you out Tyson's Corner way, but, just in case, here are a few places to take note of. *Clyde's,* 8322 Leesburg Pike, 734-1900, is a multimillion-dollar facility with original murals, plenty of panache and acceptable, if not memorable, food of the sophisticated bar variety. Far from the twentieth-century glitz of Clyde's is *Evan's Farm Inn,* which trades on its eighteenth-century setting and country cooking—Smithfield ham, duck, beef, lamb and seafood. Pretty, with plenty of colonial charm, go for the ambiance, not especially the food.

More Suburbs/The Country

In the reaches of northern Virginia, you will find two Turkish restaurants, *Kazan,* 6813 Richmond Drive, McLean, 734-1960, and *Nizam,* 523 Maple Avenue W., Vienna, 938-8948. If you are eager to explore this cuisine, a cross between Greek and Middle Eastern, here is your opportunity. Both are good and moderate in price. In Annandale, head for *Duck Chang's,* 4427 John Marr Drive, 941-9400, and as the name implies, do duck. Mesquite has come to Annandale at *Caldwell's,* 7131 Little River Turnpike, 750-0778—meats and seafood on the grill; no additives or preservatives in any of their food, they say.

For a country dining experience, Virginia offers a number of good bets. *L'Auberge Chez François,* 332 Springvale Road, Great Falls, 759-3800, serves excellent French country cooking (with an Alsatian accent). The surroundings are pleasant, the service gracious and the food always top-drawer. Call well ahead for reservations. The *Inn at Little Washington,* Washington, Virginia, (703) 675-3800, may be 90 minutes from the city, but its heart is several thousand miles away in the gentle valleys of the Loire. Classic French haute cuisine is served up in simple, but elegant, style. A newcomer to the country scene is *Leathercoat,* The Plains, Virginia, (703) 471-5327, which offers gourmet American and Continental in a formal dining room, or casual food—soups, salads, pizza—in a café setting.

11

NEARBY

MARYLAND

Glimpses into the past, portents of the future and events of the day will be found at different suburban Maryland points of interest. The only tie that binds these sites is the family car necessary to see just about all of them—they're scattered from 20 miles north to 16 miles south of downtown Washington, and virtually none is served by public transportation.

Historical sites include the National Colonial Farm, a working replica of a modest eighteenth-century plantation; Fort Washington Park, a fortress surviving from the 1820s; the C&O Canal, a national historic park celebrating canal life from the mid-1800s; Oxon Hill Farm, a functioning replica of a farm from the turn of the twentieth century; Clara Barton House, the restored home of the founder of the American Red Cross; the National Trolley Museum; and Glen Echo Park, an old-time amusement park that has been converted to offer creative leisure-time pursuits. NASA, the National Bureau of Standards and the Agricultural Research Center offer views of the government at work in space, in laboratories and on the land. Finally, Wheaton and Cabin John Regional Parks let the whole family relax, exercise, picnic and play.

The sites are scattered, and most are well off the beaten path. At the end of the collection we list a few of our favorite Maryland restaurants.

AGRICULTURAL RESEARCH CENTER   **(301) 344-2483**
Route 1, Beltsville, MD 20705

Hours: 8 A.M.–4:30 P.M. weekdays
   Closed holidays
Free Admission

M   No Metro stop.

🚌   Shuttle bus service from the Department of Agriculture at 14th
   Street and Independence Avenue, NW. Since the schedule
   varies, call 344-2483 to find out when the bus leaves on the day
   you're planning a visit. No Metrobus service.

🚗   Impractical; fare would be exorbitant.

P   Free parking. Capital Beltway (I-495) to Exit 27 north (Route 1);
   bear right on Powder Mill Road. The visitor center is on the left.

🍽   Picnic tables are available. There are a number of restaurants
   and fast-food operations along Route 1.

👫   Regular tour not recommended unless child is really interested in
   farming. Special tours can be arranged two weeks in advance
   for schoolchildren, fifth grade and up, that concentrate on the
   animals. Call 344-2483 to arrange a tour.

👥   Make arrangements two weeks in advance for group tours by
   calling 344-2483.

♿   The tour is taken on a bus; however, if arrangements are made
   in advance, a tour guide will accompany a person with impaired
   mobility in that person's vehicle.

👁   No special services available.

👂   Arrangements can be made for a signing interpreter by calling
   344-2483 at least two weeks in advance.

A   As noted above.

T   Guided tours are by appointment only (1½ hours). Call 344-2483
   or write: Visitor Center, Building 186, BARC-East, Beltsville, MD
   20705.

———————————————

The Agricultural Research Center of the U.S. Department of Agriculture covers more than 7,500 acres of experimental pastures, orchards,
gardens, fields and woods, and has over 1,000 buildings, including
research laboratories, greenhouses, barns, poultry houses, mechanical
shops and other laboratories. The tour of this complex is mobile: you
can guide yourself in the family car (maps are available in the Visitor
Center, Building 186) or you can call ahead to schedule a guided tour,

which is given on an air-conditioned bus. We recommend the guided tour, since you'll learn about the experiments being conducted at the center and have someone to answer your questions.

The tours are popular with farmers and foreign visitors but would be of interest to most people. Young children might be bored by the tour, although about a quarter of the trip has to do with animals.

The center is 15 miles northeast of Washington.

CABIN JOHN REGIONAL PARK (301) 299-4555
7400 Tuckerman Lane, Rockville, MD 20852
Hours: 9 A.M.–sunset daily
Free Admission

 No Metro stop.

 No Metrobus service.

 Telephone for a cab.

 Free parking in lot. From Washington, drive along MacArthur Boulevard. In Cabin John, take a right on Seven Locks Road. Go right on Tuckerman Lane to the park entrance.

 Summer snack bar at train station. An 8.5-acre picnic area has over 100 tables and 45 charcoal grills. Bring your own food and charcoal.

 Highly recommended. There's lots of equipment for climbing, swinging and playing, as well as Noah's Ark (complete with farm animals), a small train, sports fields and a nature center.

 From May 1 to October 15, groups of up to 175 people can reserve picnic sites and play equipment for a $175 fee. Call 495-2525 for details and reservations. Small groups and families can use free picnic facilities.

 Limited accessibility. There are no accessible bathrooms or phones; no special play equipment for kids with physical handicaps.

 No special services available.

No special services available.

As noted above.

None given.

Cabin John Regional Park is a family recreation oasis. The park has numerous ballfields, tennis and handball courts, a small train (fee), Noah's Ark Farm with farm animals and structures, a picnic area, campsites, an ice rink, 365-2246 (fee), a nature center, a terrific play area and hiking trails. Before setting out, call the park at 299-4555 to ascertain the schedules and regulations of the part of the park you wish to use.

Public transportation to the park is impractical; you'll need to drive your car, but parking is no problem.

C&O CANAL NATIONAL HISTORIC PARK   (301) 789-4200
Great Falls   HQ 739-4000
11710 MacArthur Boulevard, Potomac, MD 20854
Hours: Park—dawn to dusk
          Tavern Museum—9 A.M.–5 P.M.
Free Admission

No Metro stop.

No Metrobus service.

Not practical; the fare would be astronomical.

Free parking in lot. From Washington, take Canal Road to its end; go left on MacArthur Boulevard. Take your first left, which is Falls Road; this leads to Great Falls Park.

Food concession open in summer; picnic sites are available.

Recommended.

Groups can charter the *Canal Clipper*, a mule-drawn barge, for day or evening trips from April to October by calling 299-2026.

Fully accessible. Both museum and towpath are accessible to someone in a wheelchair. Bathrooms are accessible.

No special services available.

 Special tours can be arranged for the hearing-impaired by calling 299-3614.

 As noted above.

 No scheduled walk-in tours given.

The Chesapeake and Ohio Canal, which stretches 184 miles from Georgetown to Cumberland, Maryland, is a great deal more successful today as a recreational experience than it ever was as a commercial venture. Constructed between 1828 and 1850, the canal was rendered obsolete—even before its completion—by the B&O Railroad, which was built concurrently. The aim of both projects was to link the abundant resources of the frontier with the cities and commercial ventures of the East, but the railroad accomplished this feat more cheaply and with greater speed. While the canal never achieved great economic success, it served as a conduit for grains, furs, lumber, coal and flour until it was destroyed by a flood in 1924.

Today the canal prospers as a National Historic Park. On the 12-foot-wide dirt towpath next to the canal, barge-towing mules have given way to hikers, joggers, bikers and casual strollers (see "Outdoor Washington/Sports" chapter for bike- and canoe-rental facilities). Wildlife abounds: we've spotted beaver, snapping turtles, families of Canada geese, snakes, osprey, indigo buntings and bass, to name a few.

At Great Falls, you can get a fine sense of life on the canal's barges. The tavern, built circa 1830, has been turned into a lovely little museum; numerous ranger-conducted walks and evening programs start here (call 299-2026 for a schedule of activities). The museum also is the starting point for a 1½-hour mule-drawn barge trip on the *Canal Clipper;* on these trips, the park staff, dressed in period clothes, demonstrate typical canal tasks, such as guiding the mules and working the water locks, and lead the group in song. Tickets are $4 for adults, $3 for senior citizens and $2.50 for children 12 and under. Civic and educational groups can reserve the barge for daytime trips. For around $400, anyone can charter the barge for an evening trip. Call 299-2026 for the barge's schedule and chartering information. The Canal Clipper runs from mid-April to mid-October, with weekend trips at 10:30 A.M., 1 P.M. and 3 P.M. (and sometimes 5 P.M.).

While you don't even have to get near the Potomac's rushing waters to enjoy the park thoroughly, many people ignore the park's warning signs, scramble onto the river's rocks, and slip into the falls. Because of this, Great Falls, tiny as it is, has the highest annual fatality rate of any of the national parks.

CLARA BARTON NATIONAL HISTORIC SITE

(301) 492-6245

5801 Oxford Road, Glen Echo, MD 20768
Hours: 10 A.M.–5 P.M. daily
       Closed holidays
Free Admission

 No Metro stop.

  N4, N5.

 Impractical.

 Free parking in lot. Drive out MacArthur Boulevard to Glen Echo Park; the historic site shares its parking lot.

 None on premises.

 Recommended. Park rangers here delight in talking to youngsters. Also, the site is next door to Glen Echo Park, a boon for children (see site report).

 Group tours available. Call 492-6245 to make arrangements.

 Inaccessible.

 No special services available.

 To arrange for a tour in sign language, call 492-6245.

 As noted above.

 Walk-in tours given continually.

The Clara Barton National Historic Site was home to Clara Barton, founder of the American Red Cross. Built in 1891 as a warehouse for

American Red Cross supplies, the building was modified in 1897 and became the organization's national headquarters and Barton's home. The charming home is furnished with furniture and gifts she received from countries throughout the world in recognition of her work. In addition, a 20-minute film on Barton's life is available to be shown to groups. Call 492-6245 to make arrangements.

FORT WASHINGTON PARK (301) 763-4600
Fort Washington, MD
Mailing Address: Fort Washington Park
National Capital Parks—East
1900 Anacostia Drive, SE
Washington, D.C. 20020

Hours: Summer—8:30 A.M.–8 P.M. daily
Winter–8:30 A.M.–5 P.M. daily
Closed Christmas
$3 per car

No Metro stop.

No Metrobus service.

Impractical; fare would be exorbitant.

Free parking. Capital Beltway (I-495) to Exit 37 south onto Indian Head Highway (Route 210); follow signs to the park, which is 16 miles south of downtown Washington.

None on grounds. Picnic tables abound.

Recommended. Kids will especially enjoy the Sunday military demonstrations from noon to 5 P.M.

Group tours available upon request. Call 763-4600 to make arrangements.

The fort and information center are inaccessible. The visitors center is fully accessible.

No special services available.

No special services available.

As noted above.

Tours are given on the hour, noon to 4 P.M.

Fort Washington was originally built in 1808 to protect the new capital city from enemy intrusions up the Potomac River. During the War of 1812, however, the British overran the facility and burned it. A new fort was designed in 1824 by Pierre L'Enfant, and that garrison survives today. Fort Washington was an active Army post until 1945, but now it is administered by the National Park Service as a piece of Washington's history.

Visitors enter the fort on a drawbridge over a dry moat. A film is shown in the visitors center; there is also a bookstore that sells history and nature books as well as souvenirs.

On Sundays noon to 5 P.M., volunteers in period clothing conduct tours of the facility and musket-firing demonstrations are given. During the summer months, torchlight tours are given of the fort one evening each month; call 763-4600 to find out the schedule.

Consider combining your visit to Fort Washington Park with a trip to either the Oxon Hill Farm or the National Colonial Farm, both of which are nearby (see site reports).

GLEN ECHO PARK   (301) 492-6229
MacArthur Boulevard, Glen Echo, MD 20768
Hours: Always open
Free Admission

 No Metro stop.

 N4, N5.

 Impractical, since the fare would be exorbitant.

 Free parking in lot. Follow MacArthur Boulevard out to Glen Echo.

 Food offered in conjunction with weekend festivals. Shaded picnic tables are available.

 Highly recommended. The carousel is a delight on summer weekends; there's also a nice play area with play equipment.

Children's workshops and classes are given in crafts and drama; the Adventure Theater presents excellent children's entertainment. Call 320-5331 for class and theater schedules.

 The Adventure Theater offers group rates; call 320-5331 for information.

 The park is fully accessible but individual buildings may not be. Bathrooms are accessible. Call 492-6229 for a special pass to drive a car into the park.

 No special services available.

 No special services available.

 None necessary.

A Thursday tour is available by reservation, call 492-6229.

Glen Echo Park is unique in the Washington metropolitan area, perhaps even in the entire country. Administered since 1971 by the National Park Service, the park offers creative leisure experiences for everyone—from arts-and-crafts classes to ethnic festivals to a ride on an antique merry-go-round.*

Glen Echo began in 1891 as a National Chautauqua Assembly, a center "to promote liberal and practical education, especially among the masses of people; to teach the sciences, arts, languages, and literature." Some of the Chautauqua structures survive, but most of the park activities take place in buildings from the park's next incarnation—an amusement park. The House of Mirrors is now a dance studio, and the penny arcade is a children's theater. Other artist-in-residence programs include woodworking, stained glass, ceramics, photoworks, a writers' center and a consumer-interests program. Year-round classes are offered by all of the artists.

A 50-year-old, hand-carved and hand-painted Dentzel carousel operates Wednesday (10 A.M. to 2 P.M.) and Saturday and Sunday afternoons (noon to 5 P.M.) during the summer. The park also has a play area with swinging and climbing apparatus. Concerts, crafts demonstrations, workshops, festivals and children's theater presentations are held on Sunday afternoons during the summer; call 320-5331

---

* In 1987, the Glen Echo Park Foundation was established to raise funds in support of the activities of artists and craftsmen at the park, and to work toward the eventual transfer of the park from public to a private, nonprofit organization.

for a schedule of activities. The Chautauqua Tower Gallery displays changing exhibits of Glen Echo's artists.

While you're at Glen Echo, visit the park's neighbor, the Clara Barton National Historic Site (see site report).

MORMON TEMPLE   (301) 587-0144
(Washington Temple of the Church of Latter-Day Saints)
9900 Stoneybrook Drive, Kensington, MD 20795
Hours: Visitors Center—10 A.M.–9:30 P.M. daily
Grounds—7 A.M.–9:30 P.M. Tuesday–Friday
6 A.M.–3 P.M. Saturday
2–6 P.M. Sunday
Free Admission

M No Metro stop.

No Metrobus service.

It's best to telephone for a taxi from the visitors center.

P Free parking in lot. Take Connecticut Avenue north from Washington. Turn right on Beach Drive (just north of the Capital Beltway) and left on Stoneybrook Drive to the temple entrance on the left.

None on premises.

Not recommended for younger children.

Group tours can be arranged by calling 587-0144 one to two weeks in advance.

Fully accessible.

No special services available.

Some of the films shown at the visitors center are captioned; arrangements can be made in advance for a tour in sign language.

A Call ahead at 578-0144 to find out what's in bloom on the temple grounds.

T Visitors center: tours are given continually from 10 A.M. to 9:30 P.M. (1 hour).

Since its dedication in 1974, the Washington Temple of the Church of Latter-Day Saints has been closed to non-Mormons, but the visitors center and temple grounds are open to the general public. The visitors center has exhibits and displays that explain the church's history and doctrine, as well as interior shots of the imposing temple. The 57 acres of grounds have won national landscaping awards, and present lovely seasonal displays.

NATIONAL AERONAUTICS AND　　　　　**(301) 286-2000**
SPACE ADMINISTRATION
(Goddard Space Flight Center)
Greenbelt, MD 20771
Hours: 10 A.M.–4 P.M. Wednesday–Sunday
　　　Closed Thanksgiving, Christmas and New Year's
Free Admission

M No Metro stop.

No Metrobus service.

Impractical.

P Free parking. Capital Beltway (I-495) to Exit 29 north; bear right and follow signs to NASA.

Picnic area.

Recommended.

Advance arrangements are requested for groups of 20 or more; call 286-8103.

Fully accessible.

Tour objects can be handled.

No special services available.

A As noted above.

T Walk-in guided tours of NASA's tracking and communication center are given Thursdays at 2 P.M.

At the Goddard Space Flight Center visitors center, you can see spacecraft and rockets and watch film clips of NASA's space feats. Access to the tracking and communications center is by tour only on Thursdays at 2 P.M.

Local rocket clubs launch their models at Goddard on the first and third Sundays of every month from 1 to 2 P.M.; if weather looks ominous, call 286-8981 to check if the launch is on.

NATIONAL CAPITAL TROLLEY MUSEUM   (301) 589-4676

P.O. Box 4007, Colesville Branch,
Silver Spring, MD 20904

Hours: Noon–5 P.M. weekends, Memorial Day, July 4 and Labor Day
      Noon–4 P.M. Wednesdays in July and August
      Closed December 15–January 1

Free Admission

M No Metro stop.

No Metrobus service.

Impractical; the fare would be exorbitant.

P Free parking. North on Georgia Avenue. Bear right on Layhill Road, and right again on Bonifant Road; the museum is on the left.

None on premises.

Recommended. School tours (a short lecture followed by trolley rides) are accommodated on Fridays when the museum is not open to the public. Schedule a tour by calling 589-4676 between 9 A.M. and 5 P.M.

Call 589-4676 to make arrangements for group tours.

Limited accessibility. Museum accessible; bathrooms and phone are not.

No special services available.

No special services available.

A As mentioned above.

No walk-in guided tours are given.

_____

The big treat this museum offers is a trolley ride through the countryside. The small museum, filled with trolley memorabilia, is built in the form of an old train station. The trolleys, exhibited outdoors, come from Austria, Germany and Washington itself (trolley tracks are still evident throughout the city). A slide show is presented 15 minutes before each hour, and a small gift counter sells assorted memorabilia.

This site is way out in the country; it might be wise to combine the outing with a picnic at Wheaton Regional Park, which is 15 minutes away. Ironically, a car is the only practical means of transportation to this site.

_____

NATIONAL COLONIAL FARM   (301) 283-2113
3400 Bryan Point Road, Accokeek, MD 20607
Hours: 10 A.M.–5 P.M. Tuesday–Sunday
          Closed Thanksgiving, Christmas and New Year's
Admission: Adults—$1   Children under 12—free

 No Metro stop.

 No Metrobus service.

 Impractical; the fare would be exorbitant.

 Free parking. Capital Beltway (Route 95); take Exit 3A south (Indian Head Highway) for 10 miles; bear right on Bryan Point Road, continuing four miles to farm.

 None on grounds. The Saylor Memorial Picnic Grove is across the street from the farm.

 Recommended. Seeing the farm in action will please children; demonstrations are given on weekends.

 Group tours available. Make arrangements by calling 283-2113.

 Accessible. A vehicle is available for those with physical handicaps; call 283-2113 to make arrangements.
Special tours for the visually impaired can be arranged by calling 283-2113.

Special tours for those who are hearing-impaired can be arranged by calling 283-2113.

 As noted above.

 Walk-in guided tours are given on a casual basis, as needed, if a staff member is free.

The National Colonial Farm ushers you back to a modest Tidewater plantation of 1750; crops, livestock, agricultural methods, farm structures and farmers' garb are all from the mid-eighteenth century. Tobacco, corn, wheat, vegetables, fruits and herbs are grown; these crops provided both cash and food for the colonial farm family. A smokehouse, barn and kitchen are all open, and demonstrations of farm activities are given on weekends.

This lovely farm is operated by the Accokeek Foundation in cooperation with the National Park Service. It's situated across the Potomac River from Mount Vernon, George Washington's estate, about 15 miles south of downtown Washington. Consider combining your visit to the National Colonial Farm with a stop at Fort Washington Park, which is nearby (see site report).

OXON HILL FARM   (301) 839-1176
6411 Oxon Hill Road, Oxon Hill, MD 20021
Hours: 8:30 A.M.–5 P.M. daily
          Closed Thanksgiving, Christmas and New Year's
Free Admission

 No Metro stop.

 No Metrobus service.

 Impractical.

 Free parking. Capital Beltway (Route 95); Exit 37 south; bear right onto Oxon Hill Road. The farm is on the right.
None on grounds. Picnic tables are available.

 Recommended. Kids will enjoy seeing farm tasks—milking cows and threshing wheat. They can also ride on the farm's hay wagon, plant corn and take part in other activities.

Group tours available. Call 839-1176 to make arrangements.

 Call ahead at 839-1176 to arrange to drive beyond the parking lot onto the farm. The farm and visitors center are accessible; the bathroom and phone are not.

 No special services available.

 A staff member can communicate in sign language.

 Call 839-1177 to hear a recording of scheduled events.

 No walk-in guided tours are given, but the friendly staff welcomes questions and conversations.

This delightful working farm, run by the National Park Service, is a replica of those in the Washington area at the turn of this century. The family cow is milked at 4 P.M.; the horse team plows the fields and hauls crops (you're welcome to hop aboard when the horses are pulling the hay wagon); and other farm animals are available for petting and observing. Check in at the visitors center when you arrive to ascertain the day's activities; they may include planting, harvesting, cooking, sheep-shearing, spinning or cider pressing, depending on the season. The farm's woodlot has a self-guided nature trail.

Consider combining your trip to Oxon Hill Farm with a stop at Fort Washington Park, which is nearby (see site report).

WHEATON REGIONAL PARK

Brookside Gardens tape (301) 949-8230
Nature Center (301) 946-9071
Park Manager (301) 946-7033

Shorefield Road or Glenallen Avenue, Wheaton, MD 20902

Hours: Park—dawn until dusk daily
Brookside Conservatory Greenhouse—9 A.M.–5 P.M. daily
Closed Christmas

Free Admission

 No Metro stop.

 No Metrobus service.

Telephone for cab.

 Free parking in lots.

 None on grounds, although there are picnic facilities aplenty.

 Highly recommended. Terrific play area, small train, playing fields and Old McDonald's Farm are a few of the treats.

 Group tours of the Brookside Gardens and Conservatory can be arranged by calling 949-8230. Group tours of the Nature Center can also be arranged; call 946-9071.

 Fully accessible. Some play equipment is specifically designed for children in wheelchairs.

 A touch garden with Braille labels has been planted behind the Brookside greenhouse.

 No special services available.

 As mentioned above.

 No walk-in tours given.

This 500-acre regional park offers a bonanza of recreational opportunities for the whole family: a large, creative play area, picnic space, a small train (fee), stables and horseback-riding trails (fee), an ice rink (fee), a nature center, tennis courts and bubbles (fee for indoor facility), hiking trails and the Brookside Gardens and Conservatory. The 50 acres of gardens are serenely beautiful, ranging from formal beds and fountains to a hillside of azaleas and rhododendrons to a Japanese pavilion overlooking a small pond. The Conservatory Greenhouse houses banana, cacao, bird-of-paradise trees, coffee bushes and many other exotic plants.

The park is enormous; the family car is your best mode of transportation to and around the grounds. Call 946-7033 to check the hours of the park facility you plan to use.

A DASH THROUGH ANNAPOLIS

Annapolis, an easy 30-mile drive from Washington, makes for a fun day-trip. First settled in 1649, Annapolis retains its impressive historic charm. This was a thriving center of political, commercial and social life in the eighteenth century, thanks to a booming tobacco trade. The commercial district now consists of gracious and carefully restored buildings facing brick-lined streets, a thriving collection of shops, eating spots and intriguing nooks and crannies.

Historic sites are plentiful. We suggest you first check in with the Visitors Information Center at the City Dock, (301) 268-TOUR, from April to October; the State House Visitors Center is open November to March, (301) 974-3400. Free brochures and maps are available. You may even want to park free at the Navy–Marine Corps Stadium and take the shuttle bus to the nearby historic district, since parking is tight there.

Any visit to Annapolis should include the Naval Academy and the State House. The U.S. Naval Academy is open to visitors Monday to Saturday, 9 A.M. to 4 P.M.; Sunday, 11 A.M. to 4 P.M. Guided tours ($2 for adults, $1 for children under 12) are given frequently from early spring through Thanksgiving, and by appointment at other times; call (301) 267-3363. The State House is the oldest state capital building in continuous use in America. Free tours, given six times daily, begin in the restored Old Senate Chamber, where the Continental Congress met in 1783–1784 when Annapolis was the nation's capital. The building is open 9 A.M. to 4 P.M. daily, except Thanksgiving, Christmas and New Year's.

There are three State Historic Buildings of interest: the Victualling Warehouse, an eighteenth-century building now serving as a colonial maritime history museum (77 Main Street, 628-5576); The Barracks, restored to show how Revolutionary War soldiers lived (43 Pinckney Street, 267-8149); and The Tobacco Prise House, with exhibits of Maryland's historic tobacco trade, located in an eighteenth-century warehouse (4 Pinckney Street, 267-8149).

Annapolis boasts numerous historically and architecturally significant houses and mansions. The Hammond-Harwood House (19 Maryland Avenue, 269-1714) is one of the country's finest examples of Georgian architecture; it was designed by William Buckland of Gunston Hall fame (see site report). Thomas Jefferson was apparently so impressed by its magnificent proportions and ornate decorative trim that he sketched it in his diary. Don't miss the William Paca House (186 Prince George Street, 263-5553) or the magnificent gardens at the Chase-Lloyd House (22 Maryland Avenue, 263-2723).

Annapolis features a variety of festivities and special events, such as the Marine Trades Exposition (April), the Maryland Seafood Festival (September) and the U.S. Sailboat and Power Boat Show (October). "Christmas in Annapolis" is a six-week-long celebration, and it includes an exhausting roster of events, from wreath-hanging and tree-lighting to candlelight touring of the State House to festive feasting.

James Michener, in his novel *Space,* called Annapolis "the most beautiful state capital in America . . . with an enchanting harbor right in the heart of town and small craft lining its shores." Alex Haley traced his roots here to Kunta Kinte's arrival by slave ship in 1767; look for the commemorative plaque by the dock.

To get to Annapolis, take New York Avenue, NW, out of Washington, which connects to Route 50.

Annapolis is a fine place to wine and dine. Nestled along the shores of the Chesapeake Bay, the town is, as you might guess, noted for its seafood. Even if you don't manage a full day in the town, we can certainly recommend Annapolis for a dinner, a stroll along the City Dock, and some boat-watching.

Restaurants

Crate Cafe, 49 West Street, (301) 268-3600, moderately priced, with a convenient downtown location. Especially good for lunch. Make-your-own salads and sandwiches from broad selection of ingredients. *Fran O'Brien's,* 113 Main Street, has seafood, steaks, burgers, bar and dancing. *Old Towne Seafood Shoppe,* 105 Main Street, (301) 268-8703, offers absolutely fresh, inexpensive seafood in simple surroundings (no credit cards). Three bar/restaurants are located in Market Square, which encloses three sides of the Annapolis harbor: *Middleton's Tavern* at #2, (301) 263-3323; *McGarvey's* at #8, (301) 263-5700; and *Riordan's* at #26, (301) 263-5449. All are pleasant environments, convivial and relaxed.

Restaurants outside of downtown, but worth the effort: *Busch's Chesapeake Inn,* Route 50 between Annapolis and the Bay Bridge; D.C., phone 261-2034, reservations recommended. This is an institution; it's a large place with an enormous selection of seafood, prepared just about any way you want it. *Steamboat Landing,* 4850 Riverside Drive, Galesville, (301) 867-4600, is a favorite of locals. It is situated on an old river steamboat and serves moderately expensive, but excellent, French cuisine. Tends to be extremely crowded on weekends; reservations recommended at all times.

Music
King of France Tavern, Maryland Inn, Church Circle, (301) 263-2641, a pleasant spot with live jazz; cover. *Fran O'Brien's,* 113 Main Street, (301) 268-6288, has dancing in a bar/restaurant setting.

Harbor/Bay Cruises
Chesapeake Marine Tours, City Dock, slip 20, (301) 268-7600, offers a narrated bay cruise aboard an authentic oyster boat, weather permitting, from mid-May to Labor Day, Wednesday to Sunday, at 1:30 and 3:30 P.M. Other cruises—from a 45-minute harbor tour to a full-day Bay outing—are offered.

Walking Tours
Historic Annapolis, Old Treasury Building, State Street, (301) 267-8149, provides a variety of walking tours, both standard and custom-designed. The same service is also offered by Three Centuries Tours of Annapolis, (301) 263-5401, with tours departing from the Hilton Inn from April to October. Annapolis, being small and charming, lends itself nicely to walking tours.

A COOK'S TOUR OF BALTIMORE

Baltimore, about 35 miles north of Washington on I-95, has been undergoing an impressive rebirth. It's well worth a day-trip to have a look (or make a detour en route to or from Washington) to take in the lively harbor, wonderful ethnic food festivals, many sporting events and the general goings-on. We strongly suggest you call (301) 837-INFO to get a copy of *Baltimore! Good Times,* an excellent free publication on the city's sites and events.

Many attractions* are clustered around the glass-enclosed pavilion of shops and restaurants known as Harbor Place. Make it your first stop—it's where most of the action is. The Visitor Information Center

---

* Bear in mind that, unlike Washington, *everything* in Baltimore costs money—museums, exhibits. Be prepared to spend freely.

at Pier 4 has a 15-minute video on the city, as well as sightseeing literature galore. A quick rundown of must-sees in this area includes the National Aquarium, a seven-level complex with 6,000 mammals, reptiles, fish, amphibians and birds in their natural habitats. The aquarium has replicas of coral reefs, tropical rain forests and even a hands-on Children's Cove.

The World Trade Center has a 27th-floor observation level and museum for a stunning view of the area. Visitors are also welcome at the frigate U.S.S. *Constellation,* the oldest navy warship afloat. The Maryland Science Center and Davis Planetarium make for an edifying—and fun—stop, too.

The Rash Field Flower Garden is enormous (an entire square mile), filled with an impressive assortment of international flowers. The area's newest attraction is the Six Flags Power Plant, a super-fantasy world of family entertainment.

If you've got any energy left after touring these sites in the harbor area, Little Italy's array of wonderful ethnic restaurants is just a short walk away.

North from the harbor is Charles Street, the city's grand boule-vard, lined with magnificent homes, shops, art galleries, antique shops and restaurants. The Museum of Art, near Johns Hopkins University, has one of the country's finest collections of works by Matisse. An impressive small museum deserving of a visit is the Walters Art Gallery, located at the George Washington Monument on Charles Street.

All in all, Baltimore has become a strong area attraction in its own right; do try to visit, and make sure to sample the fare.

MARYLAND RESTAURANTS

Since suburban Maryland encompasses such a large area, we'll tackle our restaurant recommendations geographically.

Silver Spring
Sakura Palace, 7926 Georgia Avenue, 587-7070, is an excellent Japanese restaurant, offering everything from sushi to tempura. *Crisfield,* 8012 Georgia Avenue, 589-1306 (no reservations or credit cards), serves up fresh seafood—clams and oysters, fish, shrimp—in very

plain surroundings. There are some booths, a few tables and a large raw bar. Lines form early, so expect to wait at normal lunch and dinner times. Closed Mondays.

Bethesda

Once a sleepy suburb, Bethesda is now a growing, bustling commercial center, bristling with new high-rise offices and condominiums. As a result, eateries have multiplied rapidly. Several well-known downtown establishments have either opened branches or moved entirely. *Joe & Mo's,* 7345 Wisconsin Avenue, 656-8501, is a good place for a business lunch, with reliable pastas, meats and salads. *La Posada,* 8117 Woodmont Avenue (in the American Inn—Wisconsin Avenue), 656-9588, is a new entry in the Mexican food competition. Moderate prices, pleasant surroundings and consistent, if a bit unexciting, food.

Pines of Rome, 4709 Hampden Lane, 657-8775, offers excellent Southern Italian food at inexpensive prices in a casual, red-checked tablecloth atmosphere. Try their white pizza for a real treat. If you're in the mood for seafood, try *Bish Thompson's,* 7935 Wisconsin Avenue, 656-2400, or, four blocks further, *O'Donnell's Sea Grill,* 8301 Wisconsin Avenue, 656-6200. Both offer well-prepared food at moderate prices, and cater to groups and families. The *North China,* 7814 Old Georgetown Road, 656-7922, has grown from a small local favorite to a large and somewhat sumptuous (for Chinese) restaurant that still packs them in. Their fried dumplings are superb. *China Coral,* 6900 Wisconsin, 656-1203, emphasizes seafood; it's a perennial winner of praise from critics and diners alike. You can count on a good charbroiled steak, or a thin plank of prime rib at any of the *Sir Walter Raleigh Inns,* 8001 Woodmont Avenue, 652-4244 (locations in upper Georgetown, College Park, Gaithersburg, Wheaton, Alexandria, Falls Church); excellent salad bar, besides. If you are in the mood for barbecue, you won't do better in the Washington area than any of the *O'Brien's Barbecue Pits,* 7305 Waverly Street, 654-9004, and 1314 E. Gude Drive, Rockville, 340-8596. Ribs, pork, chicken and chili top the menu; plain surroundings, modestly priced.

For pizza, try *Panetteria,* 4921 Cordell Avenue, 951-6433, or its neighbor, *Il Forno,* 4926 Cordell Avenue, 652-7757. Panetteria, by the way, offers an early-bird special, a complete meal for $7.95, from 4 to 6:30 P.M. A Bethesda institution, the *Tastee Diner,* 7731 Woodmont Avenue, is no place to go for a romantic meal, but it's open 24 hours a day and serves traditional diner fare at extremely reasonable prices. *La Champagne,* 5027 Wilson Lane, 657-3383, is the working arm of L'Academie de Cuisine next door, and can be counted on for carefully and faithfully prepared French cuisine; moderately expensive. *Kabul West,* 4871 Cordell Avenue, 986-8566, one of the area's Afghani restaurants, is agreeable and moderately priced. *Tia Queta,* 8009 Norfolk Avenue, 654-4443, has decent Mexican food, and something new for Bethesda, an outdoor café.

Rockville
Hamburger Hamlet, 10400 Old Georgetown Road, 244-2037, a California transplant, offers an amazing variety of burgers, etc., in a non-fast-food atmosphere at non-fast-food prices. *Seven Seas,* 1776 E. Jefferson Street, 770-5020, and *The Eatery,* a fast-food extravaganza in White Flint Mall, 11301 Rockville Pike, may also suit your fancy.

12

A SHORT HISTORY

OF WASHINGTON

1608   Captain John Smith sails up the Potomac, probably as far as Little Falls above Georgetown.

1663–1703   All of present-day District acquired through grant or purchase by private landowners.

1751   Founding of Georgetown.

c. 1765   "Old Stone House" (3051 M Street, NW, in Georgetown) front portion built; one of the oldest buildings in D.C., now a historic-house museum.

1789   Georgetown University founded; first Catholic institution of higher learning in the United States and first university in Washington.

1790   The first Congress, sitting in New York, strikes a deal between New England and the South: the new government will assume the North's heavy war debts and the new capital will be in the South.

1791   Pierre Charles L'Enfant's plan for the city of Washington "unite[s] the useful with the commodious and agreeable" but he can't (or won't) produce a map. Andrew Ellicott and Benjamin Banneker (a free black) undertake survey.

1792   L'Enfant dismissed (dies in poverty, 1825).

The White House begun in 1792 utilizing design of architect James Hoban, who won a competition over several entries, including an anonymous one submitted by Thomas Jefferson.

1793   The Capitol begun in 1793, when George Washington lays the cornerstone using a silver trowel and with proper Masonic ceremonies. William Thornton (a doctor and amateur architect) wins design competition.

1797   "Chain Bridge" (the first of many) is the first bridge across the Potomac.

1799   Rhodes Tavern built at 15th and F Streets; serves as home of Pierre L'Enfant.

1800   Mrs. John Quincy Adams arrives to find the Executive Mansion unplastered, short of firewood; hangs the family wash in the East Room.

        Library of Congress created by Act of Congress and founded with 3,000 books (possibly chosen by Jefferson); the Library is in the Capitol.

        Bill is presented in the House which would strip Washington residents of vote and representation in Congress.

1808   Washington's first black code (moderate by Southern standards) sets 10 P.M. curfew.

        Debate on moving capital from Washington rages in Congress. Congressmen decry the excessive living costs, innumerable inconveniences and the "debasement" of citizens willing to sacrifice their political freedom for pecuniary gain.

1812   First guidebook to Washington published.

1814   British burn White House and Capitol.

1815   Washington businessmen build "Brick Capitol" (current Supreme Court site) for Congress and end, for the moment, talk of moving the capital from Washington.

Columbia Typographical Union formed, one of the first workingman's organizations in the U.S.

1820s   Washington is notorious for slave trade, but Congress refuses to grant city's request to bar trade from city.

1820   D.C. City Hall (451 Indiana Avenue, NW), George Hadfield, architect; 1916, reconstructed—stuccoed brick exterior replaced with limestone.

1853–1863   Washington Aqueduct brings water from Great Falls, Maryland; water supply for Georgetown and D.C. had become critically inadequate, depending solely on natural springs, wells and rainwater cisterns for drinking as well as for fire-fighting.

1857   Gallaudet College founded (as Columbia Institution for Deaf, Dumb, and Blind) through efforts of Jackson's Postmaster General Amos Kendall; campus designed by Frederick Law Olmsted. Edward Gallaudet heads school for next 53 years.

1858   Mathew Brady sets up photography studio in Gilman's Drug Store.

1859   Congressman Daniel Sickles, after learning of his wife's infidelity, shoots her lover, Philip Barton Key, son of Francis Scott Key, in Lafayette Park; he is acquitted amid courtroom cheers, convincing many of "the unparalleled depravity of Washington society," according to the *Star* newspaper.

1860s   Walt Whitman serves as a customs clerk, and tends to wounded soldiers in the building now housing the National Portrait Gallery, along with Louisa May Alcott (author of *Little Women*) and Clara Barton, founder of the American Red Cross.

1861   Inauguration of Abraham Lincoln; he comes into town quietly and possibly in disguise (there are threats of assassination) and stays at the Willard Hotel.

Francis Preston Blair, Sr., editor of the *Washington Globe,* offers Robert E. Lee command of the Union Army on Lincoln's behalf; conversation takes place in Blair House, 1651 Pennsylvania Avenue, NW (built 1824).

Railroad bridges to the North are burned one week after Fort Sumter, leaving Washington isolated and nervous until Northern troops arrive.

Battle of Manassas—first great battle of the Civil War. Lincoln awaits news at Army headquarters in the Winder Building.

Julia Ward Howe, watching Union soldiers from the Willard Hotel, is inspired to write "The Battle Hymn of the Republic."

Washington's mayor refuses to take loyalty oath and is thrown in jail until he has a change of heart.

1862   Congress outlaws slavery in D.C.; the only place in the country where owners are legally compensated (but not above $300) if they will take the oath of allegiance to the Union; many refuse and leave town.

1863   Thomas Crawford's statue, "Freedom," placed on top of Capitol dome; Lincoln continues construction during Civil War as a symbol to the Union.

Municipal garbage carts begin regular rounds.

1864   General Jubal Early, with 15,000 Confederate troops, marches toward capital but is repulsed at Fort Stevens, only five miles from the White House.

1865   Lincoln's second inaugural ball; blacks take part for the first time; held in Patent Office (now the National Portrait Gallery), built 1849–1867; largest government office building in the nineteenth century.

Lincoln is assassinated by John Wilkes Booth in Ford's Theatre (theater was later converted to government offices; front wall collapsed in 1893 killing 22 employees; restored 1964–1968 as museum and theater).

Four people are hanged as Booth's conspirators in the courtyard of the Washington Penitentiary (built in 1826 and mostly razed by 1903, on site of present Fort McNair, 4th and P Streets, SW).

1867   Blacks get the vote in D.C.

Howard University is founded by General Oliver O. Howard, head of Freedmen's Bureau.

1868   Horace Greeley on Washington: "The rents are high, the food is bad, the dust is disgusting, the mud is deep, and the morals are deplorable."

1870s   Colonel Henry Robert, a District engineer commissioner, drafts *Robert's Rules of Order.*

1870   City Council prohibits racial discrimination in restaurants, bars, hotels and places of amusement.

Petitions in Congress from Midwest ask that capital be moved to Mississippi Valley, now the center of the country.

Laws against livestock running free within the city are to be enforced.

Prevost Paradahl, Napoleon III's minister to the U.S., shoots himself at the outbreak of the Franco-Prussian War; some surmise that the excessive heat of the town had unhinged his mind. Washington is not a popular post among foreign diplomats.

Washington Canal, mostly an open sewer, is covered by Constitution Avenue.

1871   Frederick Douglass comes to Washington to be an editor of the *New National Era,* Marshal of District, Recorder of Deeds, Minister to Haiti. First lives at 316–318 A Street, NE. In 1877 moves to a house on Cedar Hill, built 1855 (1411 W Street, SE), now preserved as a memorial to Douglass.

District Territorial Act provides an appointed governor, bicameral legislature (half elected), nonvoting delegate to Congress, and appointed Board of Public Works; three blacks, including Frederick Douglass, serve on Governor's Council.

"Boss" Alexander Shepherd and the Board of Public Works create a new Washington; plant trees, build sewers, pave streets, lay sidewalks, provide water facilities and parks, and spend money that isn't there.

1872   British Legation built near Dupont Circle (Connecticut Avenue and N Street, NW); first foreign-owned legation built in Washington; also the first significant structure built near Dupont Circle. Its location influenced development of area in late nineteenth century as most elegant residential area in Washington. Demolished in 1931, but portions incorporated in British Embassy today.

1875–1876 Adas Israel Synagogue built at 6th and G Streets, NW; oldest synagogue in Washington. Moved to 3rd and G Streets, NW, when threatened with demolition (1969); now a museum.

1874   Patrick Healy is first black man to head major white university (Georgetown).

Congressional investigation of Governor Shepherd and his buddies results in disgrace of territorial government and in its dissolution.

1875   Civil Rights Act forbids segregation in public places of entertainment, churches and cemeteries.

1877   The Potomac floods; high water 10 feet at 17th Street.

Henry Adams comes to Washington to be "stable-companion to statesmen."

1878   The Organic Act strips the last vestiges of home rule from D.C., but acknowledges, for the first time, congressional responsibility to share equally with the local population the burden of expenses to maintain the capital city. Never mind that, in 180 years, Congress has never once provided 50 percent of the city's funds.

President and Mrs. Hayes begin tradition of egg rolling for children on the White House Lawn on Easter Sunday.

Bathrooms built in the White House.

1880   John Philip Sousa becomes director of Marine Corps Band; gives concerts on White House and Capitol grounds.

119 telephones in government offices.

1882   A newspaper estimates the personal fortunes of 17 senators at over $600 million (total city budget, 1881: $3.7 million). It is a common practice for congressmen and senators sitting on District committees to arrange to benefit financially from their legislation affecting the District.

1882–1897 Redemption of Potomac Flats (filling in of tidal marshes).

1884   Belva Lockwood, Washington lawyer and first woman to be admitted to practice before the Supreme Court, is first woman to be nominated for President; she gets 4,149 votes.

Aluminum capstone of Washington Monument is set in place.

1888–1897 Library of Congress built at northeast corner of 1st Street and Independence Avenue.

1890   Electricity installed in the White House.

1891   Augustus Saint-Gaudens' sculpture, "Grief," dedicated in memory of Mrs. Henry Adams in Rock Creek Cemetery.

1894   Coxey's Army of 300 unemployed marches to Washington where President Cleveland and Congress refuse to see them; Coxey is arrested for walking on the grass.

Cairo Hotel, 1615 Q Street, NW, at 165 feet, is the tallest private building in the city; the debate it creates leads to imposition of height restrictions (1910); converted to apartments and then condominiums.

1896   First automobile driven down Pennsylvania Avenue.

1899–1901   Washington redesigned by Frederick Law Olmsted, Jr. (McMillan Commission), including park systems and sites for the Lincoln and Jefferson memorials, Memorial Bridge, George Washington Parkway.

1904–1908   District Building constructed southeast corner 14th and E Streets, NW, Beaux-Arts–style building housing municipal government of D.C.

1904   Roosevelt elected; swims in Potomac through floating ice.

1909   Statue of Alexander Shepherd erected, first outdoor statue in honor of a native Washingtonian (removed without explanation in 1980 by Pennsylvania Avenue Development Corporation and supposedly next seen at Blue Plains Sewage Treatment Plant).

1911–1912   Mrs. Taft receives 2,000 cherry trees, a gift from the mayor of Tokyo, for planting around the Tidal Basin.

1912   Griffith Stadium opens; President Taft is the first President to throw out the first ball.

     President Taft's cow, Pauline, and sheep graze on White House grounds.

1921   Wilson retires to private life at 2340 S Street, now a museum. He was the only President to retire to Washington.

1922   At Lincoln Memorial dedication, blacks are relegated to a segregated section, across a road. Chief Justice Taft provides the weak defense that the arrangement was not "officially sanctioned."

1924   C&O Canal, seriously damaged by storm, is closed as commercial waterway.

     Washington Nats beat the New York Giants in the World Series; Walter Johnson pitches.

1928	British Embassy is first to be built on Embassy Row.
1932	Bonus March: 10,000 jobless World War I veterans asking for immediate payment of bonus due in 1945; they camp out peacefully, but Hoover sends MacArthur and the Army in with tear gas, bayonets, sabers and torches.
1935	Supreme Court building completed.
1939	The DAR refuses to let black singer Marian Anderson perform in Constitution Hall, so she sings at the Lincoln Memorial; the public outcry does much to advance the cause of civil rights.
1940	President Roosevelt issues executive order prohibiting racial discrimination in plants with defense contracts; represents the first presidential action since the Emancipation Proclamation in 1863 to protect the rights of blacks. Action taken after A. Phillip Randolph, head of Brotherhood of Sleeping Car Porters, calls for march on D.C.
1943	Pentagon completed.
	Jefferson Memorial opened, John Russell Pope, architect.
1950	Attempt on Truman's life by Puerto Rican nationalists in front of Blair House.
1963	March on Washington; Martin Luther King, Jr., delivers "I have a dream" speech to 200,000 at Lincoln Memorial.
1967	Reorganization Act establishes an appointed mayor and an elected nine-member city council.
	Allen Ginsberg and several thousand protesters try to levitate the Pentagon; first of the large antiwar demonstrations.
1968	Riots follow assassination of Martin Luther King, Jr.
	District residents vote in presidential election for the first time in 168 years.

1971   Walter Fauntroy is elected D.C.'s first representative in Congress in 100 years; nonvoting except in committee.

Texas steals the Washington Senators and makes them the Texas Rangers.

1972   Pandas arrive at the Washington Zoo.

Watergate break-in; five arrested in the Watergate while E. Howard Hunt watches from the Howard Johnson Motel across Virginia Avenue.

1974   Richard M. Nixon resigns as President, the first ever to do so.

1975   District of Columbia Self-Government Reorganization Act provides an elected mayor and city council.

1976   University of the District of Columbia is founded.

Metrorail service inaugurated.

Washington serves as center of Bicentennial celebration.

1981   Pershing Park opens as cornerstone of Pennsylvania Avenue Development Corporation's rebuilding of the "Avenue of Presidents."

1982   Vietnam Veterans Memorial dedicated.

1983   Convention Center opens.

Redskins win the Super Bowl.

1986   Restored Willard Hotel opens.

1988   Navy Memorial opens at Market Square, 7th and Pennsylvania Avenue.

Redskins win the Super Bowl again.

Restored Union Station opens.

13

ENTERTAINMENT

LET US INTRODUCE YOU...

Washington's nightlife is concentrated in a few areas of town, with some lonesome surprises scattered here and there. Your best resource for nightlife is the *Washington Post* Friday pull-out, *Weekend,* with reviews, lists, ads and more.

Georgetown

The best-known area of the city is Georgetown. Sophisticated in part, trendy in part, old-style hippie in part, Georgetown can scratch just about any entertainment itch. It has excellent jazz clubs, nightclubs with rock bands, elegant ethnic or down-home restaurants and enough bars and saloons to satisfy the thirstiest sailor.

You can find live theater and both first-run and classic films. If your idea of entertainment runs to the more interpersonal, there are any number of spots to meet members of the opposite—or same (this is Washington, remember)—sex. In short, if you wander enough in Georgetown, you'll find it all.

Be prepared to spend money. Everything costs—and Georgetown merchants have a knack for making you want to buy something. Free street parking is hard to come by. In fact, parking along Georgetown's main streets—M and Wisconsin—is prohibited weekend evenings. Cars are towed. In clubs with live music, expect to pay a cover and a minimum. (And you may have to guard your drinks in bars with dancing. Many a customer has returned from a spin on the dance floor to find his half-full drink gone, and strangers at the table.)

The Georgetown area is geographically small, and it's crowded, especially on pleasant summer evenings and weekends. Narrow streets have many nighttime attractions crammed along them. Just walking the sidewalks on a weekend evening can be a form of entertainment in itself, or a sublime form of torture, depending how claustrophobic you are.

Because of the intensive street traffic, many retail stores and boutiques stay open late at night. It is certainly possible to have dinner, dance the night away and, when you're done, still be able to buy a book, record or pair of jeans!

Georgetown attracts all types—young and old, straight and gay, black and white. But it is our feeling that Georgetown, except for a few expensive clubs, hotels and eateries, is preeminently a young person's place. Youth and high spirits dominate—at least at night.

Dupont Circle

The Dupont Circle area—Connecticut Avenue from the Washington Hilton to K Street—is experiencing a major boom. Some of the best, not just the most expensive, restaurants in town are here. Movie theaters are plentiful. And it is centrally located, easy to walk to from major hotels, and readily accessible by Metro (Farragut and Dupont Circle stations).

As the city grows, it is becoming harder to define the borders of any area. Right now, Dupont Circle and Georgetown are spreading their wings toward each other—meeting in an area known as the "West End." In a few years the West End will become a major entertainment center on its own, thus forming a seamless web of nighttime attractions from Key Bridge in Georgetown to Dupont Circle.

Capitol Hill

Legislators and their staffs have long supplied Capitol Hill restaurateurs and pubkeepers with a good living, but in recent years new elements have been added to the scene. The residential neighborhoods surrounding the Capitol have been among the hottest markets for housing in the metropolitan area. Young professionals have moved in; the Metro has aligned the Hill with the rest of the city, encouraging non-Hill people to explore the neighborhood; and many older facilities—such as fresh-air markets and warehouses—have been renovated or recycled to new areas. As a consequence of this activity, a number of new enterprises have appeared, including restaurants, theaters and discos, catering to a diverse neighborhood market.

Historically, Hill entertainments have been discreet, not for the uninitiated. The legislators wanted it that way; no sense in letting stories leak back to the home district. By and large, the new businesses have followed this pattern. They do not advertise themselves over-much, so gay bars for men and women go virtually unnoticed—no big signs, no advertising; restaurants rely on word of mouth and night-clubs are small and expensive. In some ways, Capitol Hill is a town-within-a-city; it likes the rest of us, but is perfectly happy on its own, thank you.

Virginia Suburbs

The only concentrated center of nightlife activity in Virginia is Old Town, Alexandria, which boasts an impressive array of restaurants, bars and nightclubs, especially along King Street toward the water.

With its Federal architecture and cobbled streets, Old Town is a pleasant experience—Georgetown without the frenzy. Old Town is considerably more sedate and aims to keep it that way. You may find that Old Town restaurants and bars are somewhat more formal than their Georgetown counterparts; "appropriate attire" may be the by-word of the evening.

Maryland Suburbs

Bethesda, once a quiet bedroom community, is booming with the opening of Metro. Lots of new restaurants are opening, and the estab-lished bars and clubs are advertising more heavily. The area's offer-ings are mixed—everything from live rock and bluegrass to recorded disco in elegant surroundings. Bethesda is peppered with lots of movie theaters, too.

Wisconsin Avenue is the main drag. Most of the attractions will be found right on—or close to—the avenue. Wisconsin Avenue leads to Rockville in what is now a continuous strip of malls, shops, car dealers, pizza parlors—the works. If shopping is your kind of night-time entertainment, one of the area's most elegant malls—White Flint—is on the avenue in north Bethesda (see the "Shopping" chap-ter).

LIVE MUSIC

While Washington is no Chicago for jazz or New York for rock, it has a live music scene that can keep you hopping or tapping all night long. We try to highlight here some of the spots that feature live entertainment—not just recorded music. We have attempted to pick out a wide variety of music—from new wave to classic jazz to hard-driving rock. The live-music scene being what it is, changes in format, the appearance of new places and the disappearance of old ones make it wise for you to check the local papers for a rundown of current happenings when you are actually in town. The city paper will have the most complete listings of live entertainment.

The Smithsonian Performing Arts Division is designed around museum programs, and offers a series of concerts, mostly by major names in American music and theater, as well as performance in dance, jazz ensembles, gospel groups and country music. Performances are given in various Smithsonian museums. The Performing Arts Division also sponsors the Twentieth Century Consort and the Smithsonian Chamber Players, who use antique instruments from the museum collection. Check local papers for details and prices, or call the Smithsonian at 673-4800.

Folk/Acoustic/Country

Birchmere, 3901 Mount Vernon Avenue, Alexandria, 549-5919. The Birchmere has moved away from straight country to include traditional folk as well. Many nationally known artists perform.

Bosco's, 8210 Piney Branch Road, Silver Spring, 588-4440.

Dubliner, 4 F Street, NW, 737-3773. Irish music.

Flanagan's, 7706 Woodmont Avenue, Bethesda, 986-1007.

Grog & Tankard, 2408 Wisconsin Avenue, NW, 333-3114.

Ireland's Four Provinces, 3412 Connecticut Avenue, NW, 244-0860.

Kalorama Café, 2228 18th Street, NW, 667-1022.

Kramerbooks & afterwords, 1517 Connecticut Avenue, NW, 387-1462.

Mr. Henry's Alexandria, 1319 King Street, Alexandria, 836-3377.

Mr. Smith's, 3014 M Street, NW, 333-3104.

Murphy's D.C., 2609 24th Street, NW, 462-7171.

Takoma Café, 1 Columbia Avenue, Takoma Park, 270-2440.

Tiffany Tavern, 1116 King Street, Alexandria, 836-8844.

Whitey's, 2761 Washington Boulevard, Arlington, 525-9825.

Jazz

Blue's Alley, Wisconsin Avenue and M Street (rear alley), 337-4141. Washington's premier jazz showcase for a generation. Shows 8 and 10 nightly, plus a midnight show Friday, Saturday and Sunday. Cover. Creole cuisine on the dinner menu. Nationally known acts.

Cates, 600 Franklin Street, Alexandria, 549-4460.

Hazel's, 1834 Columbia Road, NW, 462-0415.

Henry Africa, 607 King Street, Alexandria, 549-4010.

Joe & Mo's Old Town, 1101 King, 548-0111. Weekends.

King of France Tavern, 16 Church Circle, Annapolis, (301) 263-2641.

Lenny's of Washington, 1025 Vermont Avenue, NW, 638-1313. Local jazz musicians Wednesday to Saturday. Cover.

Marley's in the Henley Park Hotel, 926 Massachusetts Avenue, NW, 638-5200.

One Step Down, 2517 Pennsylvania Avenue, NW, 331-8863.

Rock/Dancing

Bayou, 3135 K Street, NW, 333-2897, under the parkway in Georgetown. Local and national talent, rock to country to new wave. Cover and minimum varies.

Club Soda, 3433 Connecticut Avenue, NW, 244-3189. Oldies live and recorded.

Crazy Horse Saloon, 3529 M Street, NW, 333-0400. Bar bands, college crowd.

d.c. space, 443 7th Street, NW, 347-4960 (recorded message), 347-1445 (reservations). A downtown multimedia environment; some theater, mostly music for the hard-core young.

Déjà Vu, 2119 M Street, NW, 452-1966. A large (capacity 2,000) emporium devoted to the music of the '50s and '60s, for dancing.

Ibex, 5832 Georgia Avenue, NW, 726-1800. Live R & B dance music in the Marvin Gaye Room.

Kilimanjaro Restaurant-Nightclub, 1724 California Street, NW, 328-3838. Sophisticated, cosmopolitan dining and entertainment. Music includes African, Calypso, Latin and American.

Nightclub 9:30, 930 F Street, NW, 393-0930. Local and national bands, rock from the familiar to the far-out.

Roxy Restaurant, 1214 18th Street, NW (at Connecticut Avenue), 296-9292. Dinner club with mixed styles—reggae, rock, blues; some local, some national acts.

Tracks DC, 1st and M Streets, SE, 488-3320. Dancing and fun, with dee-jays and vee-jays.

Other

Anton's 1201, 1201 Pennsylvania Avenue, NW, 783-1201. Dinner and entertainment provided by such notables as Mel Torme, Tony Bennett, and Bobby Short.

Astor Restaurant, 1813 M Street, NW, 331-7994. Greek music and belly dancing nightly.

The Dandy, Zero Prince Street, Alexandria, 683-6076. Luncheon and dinner cruises in climate-controlled riverboat, with taped music after dinner for dancing. Reservations essential.

F. Scott's, 1226 36th Street, NW, 965-1789. Nostalgia for the elegant crowd.

Marquee Lounge, Shoreham Hotel, 2500 Calvert Street, NW, 234-0700. A Washington landmark, former home of Mark Russell. Popular entertainment.

Piano Bars/Lobby Music

Grand Hotel, 2350 M Street, NW, 955-4404 or 429-0100. One of the new luxury West End hotels. Chamber music during Sunday brunch.

Hyatt Regency Hotel, 400 New Jersey Avenue, NW, 737-1234. Capitol View Room.

Sheraton-Carlton, 16th and K Streets, NW, 638-2626. Allegro Bar.

Ritz-Carlton, 2100 Massachusetts Avenue, NW, 293-2100. Fairfax Bar.

Vista Hotel, 1400 M Street, NW, 429-1700. Music in the Federal Bar.

COMEDY CLUBS

Comedy Café, 1520 K Street, NW, 638-5653. Weekends. Cover.

Comedy Late Nite, Bethesda Cinema & Drafthouse, 7719 Wisconsin Avenue, Bethesda, 656-3337. Midnight shows, weekends.

Garvin's Comedy Club, 420 S. 23rd Street, Crystal City, 684-3354.

Ibex, 5832 Georgia Avenue, NW, 726-1800.

Lafayette Comedy Spot, 1621 H Street, NW, 347-9845.

A note on comedy clubs: they tend to be ephemeral. If we, the authors, are lucky, most of the above-mentioned clubs will still exist on publication date. We don't make any promises for six months after that.

CLASSICAL MUSIC, BALLET AND OPERA

The Kennedy Center (see "Theaters" for a full description of the facilities) is the principal site for classical music, opera and ballet, as the home of the National Symphony, and the Washington home for the New York City Ballet, the American Ballet Theatre and the Washington Performing Arts Society, which brings many orchestras, soloists and dance troupes to town.

Lisner Auditorium, 21st and H Streets, NW, on the campus of George Washington University, 994-6800, has been the home of the Washington Ballet, a fledgling dance company now receiving national attention for the efforts of its late gifted choreographer, Coo San Goh, and as the training ground for Amanda McKerrow, winner of the Gold Medal in Moscow in the summer of 1981. Lisner is a rather plain but well-constructed hall, with excellent sightlines and acoustics. Four wheelchairs can be accommodated at each performance.

DAR Constitution Hall, 18th and D Streets, NW, 638-2661, is a cavern of a hall, owned and operated by the Daughters of the American Revolution. Less used than in past years (because of the Kennedy Center), Constitution Hall still attracts such visiting artists as Luciano Pavarotti. Accessible to wheelchairs.

Coolidge Auditorium at the Library of Congress, 1st Street and Independence Avenue, SE, 287-5502, hosts concerts by the resident string quartet using the library's invaluable collection of Stradivarius stringed instruments. In recent years, the Julliard Quartet has had this honor. Concerts are given Friday nights, from October to May. Admission is on a first-come, first-served basis in the week before a concert.

East Garden Court at the National Gallery of Art, 6th Street and Constitution Avenue, NW, 737-4215, is a handsome place, although the acoustics can be a bit spotty. The Gallery Orchestra, under George Manos, has been playing Sunday evening concerts (7 P.M.) for over 20 years. Season from September to June. Free admission.

The Folger Library has a Renaissance musical group that performs periodically.

Corcoran Gallery of Art Auditorium, 17th Street and New York Avenue, NW, 638-3211, is newly refurbished and will no doubt have music on a regular basis.

Phillips Collection, 1600 21st Street, NW, 387-2151, runs a chamber music series, Sunday afternoons at 5, from September to May. To wander among the French Impressionists and to bathe in music at the same time is a refreshing and relaxing experience.

The Smithsonian Institution museums have very active programs throughout the year. Each museum is responsible for its own schedule, and listings of current events will be posted at each museum. Often exhibits at the museums will generate special events. Budget uncertainties will cause substantial changes in programs, so check at each museum.

The Museum of American History has a variety of programs. Jazz workshops are held twice a month from fall to spring, Sunday afternoons in the Palm Court. The Smithsonian Chamber Orchestra offers two sets of concerts winter and spring. The Smithsonian String Quartet has a series of four concerts at the Renwick Museum. The Chamber Players uses old instruments from the Smithsonian's collection in the Hall of Musical Instruments at four sets of concerts.

The Black American Culture Program at the Museum of American History sponsors a series of major performance programs in jazz, gospel, dance and theater.

THEATERS

For convenience, we have divided area theaters into two groups—first, those theaters that present performances by either a resident or touring professional company of national stature or serve as the Washington home for national productions, and second, decidedly local companies, both professional and amateur. We also mention local children's theater.

Theaters survive on their ability to attract an audience. Any reasonably organized company will advertise itself extensively (or at least to the limit of its financial capability) during a run. Therefore, scan the local papers for announcements of what's playing, ticket prices, times of performances and, given the fluid nature of some theater productions in this city, where the theater is located. *The Washington Post* "Guide to the Lively Arts" in the "Style" section usually has a comprehensive listing, and the *Washingtonian* magazine has a rundown of area entertainments in the front of each monthly issue.

Ticketplace, 842-5387, located in a kiosk on the F Street Plaza between 12th and 13th Streets, NW, offers half-price tickets on the day of performance for most area theaters, including most music, dance and stage productions. The half-price tickets must be paid for in cash. Full-price tickets, for future performances, are also available, and can be paid for with credit cards. For further information, write Ticketplace, c/o Cultural Alliance, 805 15th Street, NW, Suite 45, Washington, D.C. 20005.

Tickets can also be purchased at: Ticket Center, various locations, full-price tickets, 432-0200; Ticketron, various locations, 659-2601; and Premiere Theater Seats, "preferred seating" service for individuals and corporations, 963-6161.

A note to students, senior citizens, people with disabilities and military personnel E-4 and below: the Kennedy Center and National Theater offer discounts on tickets. Discounts vary with the size of group, length of run and so on. For information, call the group-sales number, where listed, or the main number given. People with handicaps should also refer to the "Tips for Visitors with Disabilities" chapter.

ARENA STAGE　　　　　　　　　　Information: 554-9066
6th Street and Maine Avenue, SW　　Charge-A-Ticket: 488-3300
　　　　　　　　　　　　　　　　　Group Sales: 554-9066

 Fully accessible.

 Interpreters for some performances; earphones for people who are hard of hearing. Phonic Ear.

This is actually three theaters under one roof. The Arena Stage is a theater-in-the-round with its own repertory company of national stature. New plays by major playwrights often have their premiere here; old standards are often given new life. The Kreeger Theatre is a proscenium stage in a smaller, more intimate setting. The Old Vat Room often presents one-man shows and small-cast reviews.

SHAKESPEARE THEATER AT THE FOLGER　　546-4000
201 E. Capitol Street

 Accessible with 48 hours notice.

Performances are given in the Folger Shakespeare Library's recreation of an Elizabethan Innyard-style theater. As you might expect, Shakespeare dominates, but the company has become well known for its vibrant productions of classics and new plays as well.

FORD'S THEATRE　　　　　Information: 347-6262
511 10th Street, NW　　　　Ticket Center: 432-0200
　　　　　　　　　　　　　Group Sales: 638-2367

Limited accessibility—call for use of ramp.

The theater in which Lincoln was shot is now the site of many dramatic plays, musical shows, reviews and dance. Touring companies often appear.

THE JOHN F. KENNEDY
CENTER FOR THE PERFORMING ARTS
2700 F Street, NW

General Information:
254-3600
Offices: 872-0466

 Fully accessible

The Kennedy Center is not only a complex for the performing arts, it is a major tourist attraction on its own. An extensive description of the building and its furnishings is in the "Foggy Bottom" section of this *Guide*. The center now houses five locations for the arts, each with a different purpose. Taken together, they form the most complete arts center in the city, rivaling Lincoln Center in New York City and the South Bank arts complex in London. On any given day you can feast on a wide assortment of cultural goodies. Ample parking is usually available in the underground garage for $4.50. A free shuttle bus runs from Columbia Plaza at 2400 Virginia Avenue to the center every night. The Watergate garage, just across the street from the center, is also convenient. Thirty minutes free parking is allowed for ticket buyers before 5 P.M.; be sure to get ticket stamped at box office. Here is a brief summary of what you may find at the center:

Concert Hall

Information: 254-3776
Instant Charge: 857-0900
Group Sales: 634-7201

Designed for concert performances, the hall hosts a wide variety of performers from jazz to pop, and serves as the principal stage for visiting orchestras and soloists. The Concert Hall is the home of the National Symphony, which presents a full season from September to June and summer concerts elsewhere in the city.

Opera House   Information: 254-3770
                                         Instant Charge: 857-0900
                                         Group Sales: 634-7201

More opulent and somewhat smaller than the Concert Hall, the Opera House offers opera, ballet and musicals. Both the American Ballet Theatre and New York City Ballet present their Washington seasons on this excellent dance stage.

Eisenhower Theater   Information: 254-3670
                                         Instant Charge: 857-0900
                                         Group Sales: 634-7201

 Special amplification earphones.

This is the Kennedy Center stage for plays and small reviews. Original productions and Broadway-bound shows often make their first appearance here; this is a comfortable and rather intimate house.

Terrace Theater   Information: 254-9895
                                         Instant Charge: 857-0900
                                         Group Sales: 634-7201

 Special amplification earphones.

A gift of the Japanese people, the Terrace is an attempt to provide a showcase setting for new dance, experimental theater and small musical reviews in an intimate theater with professional facilities.

American Film Institute Theater   Box Office: 785-4600

A bow in the direction of the cinematic arts, the institute runs a never-ending series of films, each presented only one night, in a small, rather tacky (for the Kennedy Center, anyway) room off the Hall of Nations. Talk is that a new screening room will be constructed soon.

NATIONAL THEATER
1321 E Street, NW

Information: 783-3371
Teletron: 1-800-233-3123
TDD 554-1900
Group Sales: 628-6166

 Theater accessible. No accessible bathroom.

 Special amplification earphones.

Washington's oldest continuously operating theater (founded 1835), the National is now under the booking management of the Shubert Organization. As the National is free now to compete directly for top bookings with the Kennedy Center (under whose management the theater operated for several years), Washington will likely enjoy a boom in topflight shows. Free theater and music are presented in the Helen Hayes Gallery on Monday nights; call 783-3372 for information and reservations. Special note for parents: the National is conducting a series of Saturday-morning entertainments for kids, including mime, magic and music. Call 783-3372 for information.

WARNER THEATER
513 13th Street, NW

Information: 626-1050
Teletron: 1-800-233-3123
Group Sales: 626-1075

 Theater accessible. No accessible bathroom.

This former vaudeville palace is now most often the setting for one-night concerts and short-run touring company shows. It is a well-designed and rather ornate reminder of the golden years of vaudeville and movies.

LOCAL THEATERS

It is the nature of local theater to defy classification. Indeed, some energy is expended in modern theater to achieve that very situation.

So much as we would like, we cannot, in some cases that follow, give you a very clear picture of what it is each of the theaters listed actually does. Your best bet is to consult local papers for reviews of the current shows. Bear in mind that many of the small theaters are in recycled buildings. Limited budgets do not often permit the construction of facilities with access for people confined to wheelchairs, or modern restrooms or efficient air-conditioning systems. If you are concerned with any of these issues, you should call the theater and check.

A final word on local theater: some, maybe many, of the companies listed here may have disappeared, or been renamed, or moved, by the time this book is published. The best guide to the local theater scene is the daily paper.

Gala Theater, 1625 Park Road, NW, 234-7174. A bilingual theater troupe, performing in English and Spanish on alternate nights.

Hartke Theater, Catholic University of America, Harwood Road, NE, 529-3333. The respected home of CUA college dramatics. Several cuts above your ordinary college fare.

Living Stage, 1901 14th Street, NW, 554-9066. Community outreach theater program.

New Playwright's Theater, 1742 Church Street, NW, 232-4527. A nonprofit educational institution and theater, devoted to presentation of new works by American playwrights. Script readings and rehearsals of works in progress are open to the public as performances for nominal charges. Full performances of five plays a season.

Olney Theater, Route 108, Olney, MD, (301) 924-3400. A professional summer theater offering old favorites.

Roundhouse Theatre, 12210 Bushey Drive, Silver Spring, MD, (301) 468-4234. A Montgomery County–sponsored professional theater which often performs at local festivals as well as in its home—a converted elementary school.

dc space, 7th and E Streets, NW, 347-4960. An artists' cooperative venture. Mixed media, music, dance, video and dramatic theater.

Source Theater Company, 1809 14th Street, NW, 462-1073.

Studio Theatre, 1333 P Street, NW, 265-7412.

Washington Project for the Arts, 400 7th Street, NW, 347-8304. A young, experimental, changing arts organization that seeks to incorporate and integrate the arts—from music and dance to video and three-dimensional art.

Wooly Mammoth, 1401 Church Street, NW, 393-3939. The productions of this small company have met with rave reviews.

CHILDREN'S THEATERS AND ATTRACTIONS

Adventure Theater, Glen Echo Park, Glen Echo, MD, (301) 320-5331. Performances Saturday and Sunday, 1:30 and 3:30 P.M. Group rates; reservations recommended.

BARNSTORM! The Barns at Wolf Trap Farm Park, 1624 Trap Road, Vienna, VA (703) 938-2404. On Saturdays at 11 A.M. and 1 P.M., October through May, performers ranging from folksingers to mimes, storytellers, and puppeteers regale youngsters.

Bob Brown Puppet Productions, 1415 South Queen Street, Arlington, VA, 920-1040. Performances at various theaters around town. A professional and highly competent, sophisticated and entertaining troupe. Catch them if you can.

Discovery Theater, Smithsonian Institution, Arts and Industries Building, 900 Jefferson Drive, SW, 357-1300. See site report for details.

National Theater, 1321 E Street, NW, 783-3371. The National conducts a series of Saturday morning entertainments for kids, including mime, magic and music.

B&O Railroad Station Museum, Main Street and Maryland Avenue, Ellicott City, MD, (301) 461-1944. Admission fee. Tuesday to Sunday, 11 A.M. to 4 P.M. Station house (c. 1831) with authentic model of the 13 miles of the original system.

Washington Dolls' House and Toy Museum, 5236 44th Street, NW, 244-0024. Admission fee: Tuesday to Saturday, 11 A.M. to 5 P.M. Sunday, noon to 5 P.M. This wonderful private museum, founded by author and dollhouse authority Flora Gill Jacobs, exhibits antique dollhouses, dolls and other toys from all over the world.

DINNER THEATERS

Burn Brae, 3811 Blackburn Road, Burtonsville, MD, (301) 384-5800. Broadway musicals. Full-course dinners from varied menu. Tickets from $14.95 to $24.95. Group rates. Limited accessibility due to stairs; call ahead for assistance. Bathrooms accessible.

PERFORMANCES:

	Open	*Dinner*	*Show*
Tuesday to Thursday	6 P.M.	6:15 P.M.	8 P.M.
Friday	6:30	6:45	8:30
Saturday	6:15	7:30	8:15
Sunday	4	4:15	6

Harlequin, 1330 Gude Drive, Rockville, MD, (301) 340-8515. Musicals. Buffet with varied entrées, salads and desserts. Tickets from $28.50 to $29.95. Group rates. Theater and bathroom accessible.

PERFORMANCES:

	Open	*Dinner*	*Show*
Tuesday to Sunday	6 P.M.	6:30 P.M.	8:30 P.M.
Wednesday matinee	11 A.M.	11:30 A.M.	1 P.M.
Sunday matinee	11:30 A.M.	noon	1:30 P.M.

Hayloft, 10501 Balls Ford Road, Manassas, VA, (703) 631-0230. Musicals, plays, reviews. Buffet with international dishes, especially French and Mediterranean. Tickets from $22.50 to $28. Group rates. Theater accessible. No accessible bathroom.

PERFORMANCES:

	Open	*Dinner*	*Show*
Tuesday to Sunday	6 P.M.	7 P.M.	8:30 P.M.
Sunday brunch	11 A.M.	11:30 A.M.	1 P.M.

Lazy Susan, Route 1, Woodbridge, VA, (703) 550-7384. Musicals. Varied menu with many home-style dishes. Tickets: $16.95 to $23.95. Group rates. Theater and bathroom accessible.

PERFORMANCES:

	Open	*Dinner*	*Show*
Tuesday to Saturday	6 P.M.	7 P.M.	8:30 P.M.
Sunday	5	6	7:30

Petrucci's Main Street, 312 Main Street, Laurel, MD, (301) 725-5226. Comedies, musical mysteries. Varied international cuisine. Tickets: $22 to $28. Group rates. Theater and bathroom accessible.

PERFORMANCES:

	Open	Dinner	Show
Wednesday, Thursday, Saturday and Sunday	6 P.M.	6:30 P.M.	8 P.M.
Friday	6:30	7	8:30
Wednesday and Sunday matinee	11:30 A.M.	11:45 A.M.	1

Toby's, Columbia, MD, (301) 730-8311. Musicals. Buffet with varied entrées, salads and desserts. Tickets: $16 to $18.50. Group rates, except Saturday. Theater accessible. No accessible bathroom.

PERFORMANCES:

	Open	Dinner	Show
Tuesday to Saturday	6:15 P.M.	6:45 P.M.	8:30 P.M.
Sunday	5:15	5:45	7:30

OUTDOOR MUSIC AND PAVILIONS

Carter Barron Amphitheatre, 16th and Kennedy Streets, NW, 829-3202. Theater and bathroom accessible.

A 4,500-seat open amphitheater, owned by the National Park Service and leased to local entrepreneurs and promoters, Carter Barron presents a varied program of popular entertainments.

Wolf Trap Farm Park, 1624 Trap Road, Vienna, VA, (703) 255-1800. Group Sales: (703) 255-1851. Theater and bathroom accessible.

A gift to the nation by a generous benefactor, Catherine Jouett Shouse, Wolf Trap is one of the loveliest settings for a summer's evening of entertainment. Through the season—which goes from early June to early September—one can enjoy the widest possible array of entertainment. The Metropolitan Opera, a bluegrass music festival, the National Symphony, Bill Cosby, the Alvin Ailey Dance Theater and many, many more have delighted the more than 500,000 people a season who come to enjoy not only the performance but the acres of grassy slopes for serene picnicking. Wolf Trap hosts an International Children's Festival every August.

From October through May, a variety of entertainments take place in The Barns at Wolf Trap. Folk singers, jazz performers, and chamber musicians can be seen on a varying schedule of Friday and Saturday nights in this more intimate setting.

Merriweather Post Pavilion, Columbia, MD, (301) 982-1800. The pavilion offers a summer season of mostly popular music, including rock and roll, folk and jazz. Located about 45 minutes from D.C. up Route 29.

FREE MUSIC AND THEATER

Throughout the year, but especially during the warm months, residents and visitors are treated to a wide variety of free music and entertainment. The various armed forces bands—Army, Navy and Marine Corps—can be found somewhere around the city almost every day. Regular performances are given on the West Terrace of the U.S. Capitol, at the Jefferson Memorial, the White House Ellipse and the Marine Barracks (8th and I Streets, SE). Reservations are required for the Marine evening parades, and should be made in advance by calling 433-4681. The list of organizations sponsoring free music and entertainment is ever-changing, but the following have participated substantially in the past few years:

National Theater, 1321 E Street, NW. Free music and theater, Monday nights. Free entertainment for children, Saturday mornings.

Folger Shakespeare Library, 201 E. Capitol Street.

Library of Congress, 1st Street and Independence Avenue, SE.

National Gallery of Art, Constitution Avenue at 6th Street, NW.

D.C. Government Summer in the Parks Program, various locations around the city.

National Symphony, summer concerts on the West Terrace of the Capitol and on the Mall.

Foundry Shopping Mall, Georgetown, summer jazz series.

Washington Cathedral, Massachusetts Avenue at Wisconsin Avenue, NW.

Carter Barron Amphitheatre, 16th and Kennedy Streets, NW.

Kennedy Center, a varied program of seasonal music at Christmas-time and free kids' series throughout the year.
Glen Echo Park, Maryland; folk and ethnic music.
Smithsonian Institution, most museums.

Free music will be announced and promoted through the local papers. The "Calendar of Events" in the *Washingtonian* magazine is a good source of information as is "Weekend," *The Washington Post* Friday supplement.

THE BAR SCENE

Washington is not a trend-setter where bars are concerned. It takes a while for new styles to filter their way through the country to D.C. For example, the first Western-style bar just opened in the area in late 1980, several years after the trend had started. But what Washington lacks in pace-setting, it makes up for in numbers. The city is packed with bars, lounges, saloons, pubs, drinking holes—call them what you will. And the scene is lively and diverse. You can sip your way through an evening at wine bars, like *Suzanne's,* 1735 Connecticut Avenue, NW, 483-4633, a rather informal spot above Dupont Circle, or relax in the elegant surroundings of *Flutes,* 1025 Thomas Jefferson Street, NW (between K and M), with over 100 kinds of champagne ($5 a glass and up), caviar, foie gras, oysters and smoked salmon. If you want to catch the eye of a stranger or make new friends, the options are almost limitless. In Georgetown, *Annie Oakley's,* 3204 M Street, NW, 333-6767, offers a DJ, big screen videos and dancing to top 40. *Clyde's,* 3236 M Street, NW, 333-0294, has developed a national reputation for its elegant decorations and respectable food. *Mr. Smith's,* 3104 M Street, NW, 333-3104, is a casual and friendly place, and *Nathan's,* corner of M Street and Wisconsin Avenue, 338-2000, has the best view of the passing parade on the busiest corner in town. *Champions,* "The American Sports Bar," 1206 Wisconsin Avenue, 965-4005, is *the* jock hangout these days. It's the sort of place that sponsors 10K races, fitness contests and bikini contests. As we have noted earlier, wherever you go in Georgetown you can find something to suit your mood.

Dupont Circle has a considerable number of excellent places to pass an evening, especially at the numerous outdoor cafés that ring the circle. One of the best is *Kramerbooks & afterwords,* 1517 Connecticut Avenue, NW, 387-1462, a combination bookstore/café, with a comfortable indoor/outdoor café out its back door, on tree-lined 19th Street. Around the corner at 1739 N Street, you'll find the *Tabard Inn,* 785-1277, a country inn tucked into the heart of the city. Down 19th Street from the circle is an endless array of bars, restaurants and discos. Work your way down to *Flaps* for a drink with a very lively crowd, 1207 19th Street, 223-3617; stop by *Rumors,* 1900 M Street, 466-7378, for a breath of California ferns, or *The Sign of the Whale,* 1825 M Street, 223-4152, and you still will not even have scratched the surface of this teeming area.

Up on Capitol Hill, you will find a relaxed crowd—lots of Hill staffers, and the occasional congressman or senator. Favorite hangouts include the *Hawk and Dove,* 329 Pennsylvania Avenue, SE, 543-3300; *Duddington's,* 319 Pennsylvania Avenue, SE, 544-3500; *Jenkins Hill,* 223 Pennsylvania Avenue, SE, 544-6600; and the *Tune Inn,* 331½ Pennsylvania Avenue, SE, 543-2725, called by many the best neighborhood bar in town.

Pennsylvania Avenue, just a few blocks from the Capitol, is the main strip of bars and restaurants. On the Senate side of the Capitol, along Massachusetts Avenue, the tempo is a bit slower, and you will find some good restaurants, including the *American Café and Market,* 227 Massachusetts Avenue, NE, 547-8500.

Several area hotels have spectacular panoramic views of the city. *The Hotel Washington,* 15th Street and Pennsylvania Avenue, NW, 638-5900, has a popular rooftop restaurant with what is acknowledged to be the best view from within the city. The *Marriott Key Bridge Hotel,* in Rosslyn, just across Key Bridge from Georgetown, has a revolving rooftop restaurant, with a slowly changing view of the city and Virginia suburbs. Since these two establishments specialize in views, we recommend them for drinks rather than dinner.

MOVIE THEATERS

The grand movie palaces may all have been torn down, and first-run films fled to the suburban multiscreen theaters, but Washington can still boast of many well-run movie houses, including first-run, second-run and classic film houses. Check the local papers, especially the "Style" section of the daily *Post* and the pullout "Weekend" section of the Friday *Post,* for complete movie listings. Here are a few out-of-the-ordinary movie theaters that merit your attention:

American Film Institute Theater, Kennedy Center, 785-4600. The AFI runs series of all kinds: stars, directors, love stories, westerns, etc. Usually there are two shows per day, an early show, between 5 and 6, and another between 8 and 9. The only drawback to AFI is that films come and go in a single day. Members of AFI are admitted for $1.75; nonmembers for $3.50.

The Biograph, 2819 M Street, Georgetown, 333-2696. A repertory format; well programmed.

Spanish-language films play fairly often at the Ontario Theater, 462-7118.

Good areas for movies:

Georgetown/The West End: Cerberus, Biograph, Circle West End, K-B Foundry.

Dupont Circle: Janus, Circle Embassy, K-B Fine Arts.

Upper Northwest: Circle Avalon, Circle Uptown, Circle Tenley, K-B Paris and Studio, Outer Circle, Jennifer Cinema.

Union Station: 9-screen American Multi-Cinema.

BOAT RIDES

The Dandy, Zero Prince Street, Alexandria, VA (804) 683-6076. Luncheon and dinner cruises in climate-controlled riverboat, with taped music after dinner for dancing. Built low to the water, the *Dandy* is the only excursion boat that can go under all the river bridges, so its range is somewhat more extended than others. Luncheon cruises leave at 12:30 and return at 3 P.M.; $25 per person, plus tips, tax and bar. There are always luncheon cruises Saturday and Sunday in season; call for midweek schedule. Dinner cruises Sunday to Thursday are $40, from 7:30 to 10:30 P.M.; Friday and Saturday $45, 7:30 to 11 P.M. All meals on the *Dandy* are big and hearty. Discounts are offered on midweek luncheon cruises for groups of 40 or more.

Spirit of Washington, Pier 4, 6th and Water Streets, SW, 554-8000.

Mount Vernon Cruise. Departs daily in season at 9 A.M. and 2 P.M.; one-hour-45-minute stopover at Mount Vernon. Adults $14, children 2 to 11, $8; includes Mount Vernon admission.

Evening Dinner Cruise. Boards 6:30 P.M. daily. Dinner and dancing until 10 P.M.; $24.95 weekdays, $28.95 Fridays and Saturdays.

Moonlight Party Cruise. Departs 11 P.M. Friday and Saturday in season; $12 per person. Live bands, snacks and cocktails.

Lunch Cruise. Thursday, Friday and Saturday, departs at noon, returns at 2 P.M.; $15.95 per person.

City Lights Cruise. Sunday nights 8 to 10 P.M. Arlington/Georgetown shoreline; $8 per person.

AMUSEMENT PARKS

King's Dominion, Doswell, VA 23047, (804) 876-5000. Located 75 miles south of Washington on Route 95. The 1988 entrance fee was $16.95, children two and under, free. Fee good for all rides. Open weekends from late March to Memorial Day, daily Memorial Day to Labor Day, weekends to mid-October. In full season, open 9:30 A.M. to 10 P.M., closes at 8 P.M. between seasons.

Major rides: White Water Canyon, Diamond Falls, Haunted River; roller coasters include Grizzly, Rebel Yell, Scooby Doo (for little kids); monorail, lots of small rides for kids, arcade games (not included in fee).

Food: several food kiosks throughout park. Several sit-down restaurants.

Play area for kids includes climbing apparatus, slides, chutes, ball bounce.

Wild World, 13710 Central Avenue, Mitchellville, MD 20716, 249-1500. Capital Beltway (I-495) to Exit 15A or 17A, to Route 214 east (Central Avenue) 4 miles, park on left. The 1988 entrance fee was $12.50 for ages 10 and above; $10.50, 3 to 10; free to children two and under. Open weekends mid-May to Memorial Day, daily Memorial Day to Labor Day, weekends in September. Hours: 10 A.M. to 10 P.M.

Major attractions: world's largest wave pool, swimming, rides, shows.

Major rides: roller coaster called Wild One, the only wooden roller coaster on the East Coast; Rampage and Rainbow Zoom, water rides; major new rides.

Shows: six major shows daily, including magician, high dive, puppets and others, to be announced.

Food: pizza, hamburgers, hot dogs, chicken, ribs, shrimp.

Play area for kids includes climbing apparatus, slides, ball bounce.

14

SHOPPING

Washington shopping opportunities are enough to make the eyes glaze over, whether you're looking for a major purchase or just a few trinkets. As the federal city, Washington is home to a variety of government and nonprofit cultural organizations that sell unusual and often reasonably priced goods. At the same time, during the 1970s and 1980s, several nationally known retailers suddenly discovered the area and descended to tap its affluent residential and tourist market. Yet the city is still down-to-earth enough to support countless street vendors.

You name it, and chances are you'll find it in Washington. Streets are lined with clothing and gift shops, bookstores, jewelry and antique stores, galleries and restaurants. New, upscale shopping malls dot Washington, often housing the city's most exclusive shops.

While we note gift shops and special finds in the *Guide*'s site reports, this chapter gives an overview of shopping opportunities, pointing you in the general direction of places to buy and highlighting out-of-the-ordinary wares. Although there are plenty of things to do in Washington without even going near a store, you'll probably want to sample the fare and bring a piece of your visit back home.

FEDERAL FINDS

The *Smithsonian Institution* shops offer a true feast for the consumer. Shoppers can find gems, astronaut freeze-dried ice cream, handcrafted dinnerware, African artifacts and robots among the endless treasures for sale. The *Guide*'s individual site reports will alert you to shopping opportunities in various parts of the Smithsonian.

The *Indian Craft Shop,* tucked away in the Department of the Interior Building at 18th and C Streets, NW, has a wonderful selection of jewelry, rugs, baskets, pottery and other handicrafts made by Native Americans. Since the shop is in a government building you'll have to sign in; the hours are Monday to Friday, 8:30 A.M. to 4 P.M.

The *Library of Congress* sells cards, exhibition catalogs and posters, recordings and other items based on its vast collection of Americana. The photographs here are a real find. You can buy a copy of a photograph by Walker Evans, Charles H. Currier or Dorothea Lange, or unmatted lithographic reproductions of masterful photographs for rock-bottom prices. Explore the shop and lobby display areas thoroughly; often there are examples of regional crafts for sale, including rag rugs and basketry.

The *Government Printing Office* bookstore sells nearly all of the literature the federal government prints for the public on everything from national parks to foreign affairs, Social Security, cooking, health and fish diseases. You can also pick up copies of the daily *Congressional Record* and *Federal Register,* as well as patriotic and nature posters. Everything is reasonably priced. Located near Union Station, at 710 North Capitol Street, NW (between G and H Streets), it may not be worth a trip unless you're looking for something special. You can call 783-3238 to order a particular item, and GPO can send it to you. The general bookstore number is 275-2091.

While the next two suggestions aren't under the auspices of the federal government, they offer similar high-quality goods.

The *National Trust for Historic Preservation* shop, located at 1616 H Street, NW, has a large selection of books on architecture and historic preservation, as well as gifts such as glass, ceramic and silver objects, dolls, T-shirts, ties, stationery and posters. Some are reproductions while others are modern interpretations of traditional crafts.

The shop at the *Corcoran Gallery* has a variety of unusual cards and other stationery items, art books and posters and slides. A few special items made by gifted hands are usually available. On a recent visit we found exquisite glassware, hand-painted pillows and unique jewelry.

DEPARTMENT STORES

You'll find a staggering variety of stores in Washington. The major home-grown department stores are Garfinckel's, a classic store with high-quality men's, women's and children's clothing, and home furnishings; Hecht's, a large department store with a full line of clothing, accessories and furniture; and Woodward & Lothrop, affectionately dubbed "Woodie's," which has a wide variety of clothing, furniture and household items. Garfinckel's, Hecht's and Woodward & Lothrop have main stores downtown and are also located in various shopping centers and malls throughout the area. Several large retailers from other parts of the country are here, too, such as Bloomingdale's, I. Magnin, Neiman Marcus, Lord & Taylor and Saks Fifth Avenue.

ART GALLERIES

The Washington art scene is thriving, and artists from the city, metropolitan area and region are well represented in the District's 70-plus commercial art galleries. With a few exceptions, the galleries emphasize twentieth-century works, and many specialize in contemporary art.

Local artists have often voiced resentment at a lack of support for their work in the Washington area: they are in "competition" of sorts with pieces exhibited in the national museums here; also, serious art collectors are lured away by New York's dazzle and proximity. Despite this, D.C. galleries give vibrant display to a wide range of artistic talent. The two primary commercial gallery areas in the city are Dupont Circle and 7th Street, NW, between D and E Streets. The Takoma Metro Arts Center is a vibrant collection of studios, workshops, a gallery and offices located three blocks from the red line Takoma stop on the Metro. The Orange Crush Factory on Capitol Hill is a brand new "arts colony," promising gallery and studio space for visual and performing artists. The Torpedo Factory Art Center is a cornerstone of Old Town, Alexandria, cultural life. The block-long, two-story building was originally used for the manufacture of torpedoes during both world wars. It has been renovated and now houses galleries and artists' studios. The center is located on the waterfront, at King and Union Streets. The invaluable guide to gallery-goers is *Galleries: A Guide to Washington Area Art Galleries,* published monthly and available for free in most galleries. It is also available as a subscription. Another excellent publication is *Museum & Arts,* a bimonthly magazine discussing museum shows and the Washington art scene.

Among the finest galleries are:

Franz Bader Gallery, 1701 Pennsylvania Avenue, NW
Jane Haslem, 406 7th Street, NW, and 2025 Hillyer Place, NW (by appointment)
Middendorf Gallery, 2009 Columbia Road, NW
Mickelson Gallery, 707 G Street, NW
Gallery K, 2032 P Street, NW

STREET VENDORS

Pounding the pavement may provide an afternoon's amusement, as well as fill your shopping needs. The sidewalks in certain areas around town are transformed into bazaars, as eager street vendors set up shop. The goods piled high on their tables run the gamut, including baskets, purses and briefcases, Chinese canvas shoes, clothing, plants, framed posters and prints, crafts and, of course, food.

Street food abounds. You can find nearly anything you'd like, including falafel, giant chocolate-chip cookies, gourmet lunches and ice-cream concoctions, in addition to the classic hot dog and soda. Do indulge, and then head to the nearest vest-pocket park for a mini-picnic.

The best area for street-shopping is the corridor around Connecticut Avenue and K Street, NW; the scene continues along Connecticut Avenue toward Dupont Circle.

The Mall, too, becomes a cacophony of street vendors, particularly on bright, warm days. The trailers here offer T-shirts, postcards and other souvenirs, as well as snacks. We found the best T-shirt prices in town here.

The Capitol Hill lunch crowd is usually greeted by some local vendors, especially along Independence Avenue, SE, between 2nd and 4th Streets.

Georgetown also boasts a lively commercial street scene. Vendors sell T-shirts, crafts, jewelry and more. They generally won't pack up their goods until late, so plan to stroll and browse after dinner.

MAIN SHOPPING AREAS

There are several main shopping areas where you can simply window shop or join the hustle and bustle of Washingtonians in hot pursuit of a purchase.

Downtown

The *F Street Plaza,* between 7th and 14th Streets, NW, has been the heart of the Downtown shopping area for years, and it has undergone a recent rejuvenation. Here you can shop at *Woodward & Lothrop,* which has direct access from the Metrorail stop at Metro Center. If you're traveling aboveground, Woodie's is at 10th and 11th Streets, NW, between F and G Streets. *Hecht's* glittery new flagship store— the only urban free-standing department store built in this country since World War II—is located at 12th and G Streets, NW, while *Garfinckel's* is at 14th and F Streets, NW.

The Shops at National Place stretch between F Street and Pennsylvania Avenue in the 1300 block, bringing pizzazz to the refurbished National Press Building. Over 85 shops and eateries offer a full array of goods, from computerized clock radios to lacy underpinnings and Chinese fast food to complete seafood dinners. The shops connect to the elegant lobby of the new Marriott Hotel.

A block down Pennsylvania Avenue is yet another stunning renovated retail space, *The Pavilion at the Old Post Office.* The shopping is less serious here, with knickknacks and casual jewelry stores outweighing clothing operations, but eating possibilities vary from snack to sumptuous. (You might also want to take the elevator to the top of the 315-foot clock tower for a great view of the city. Tours start from the elevator on the stage level.)

After years of neglect and more years of bad planning and fiscal mismanagement, Washington's grand railroad terminal, Union Station, has been reborn—this time as a railroad/Metro station combined with a major urban shopping/dining mall. Several significant retailers are present—The Limited, Cignal, Brookstone, Nature, Company, Ann Taylor—and more than 100 others. Cafés and five major restaurants complete the space, along with a food court featuring varied cuisines and a nine-screen movie house. If it works, it could vitalize the Capitol Hill area as a shopping district. To date, stores on the Hill cater only to the neighborhood. So, if you are on the Hill to sightsee, it will certainly be worth a look.

Georgetown

Georgetown offers a smorgasbord of amusement, among which are its shops, which range from chic (and expensive) boutiques to consummate punk. The streets teem with restaurants and fast-food outlets. You can start at the intersection of Wisconsin Avenue and M Street, NW, and head off in any direction, sure to find lots of ways to spend money. Your best bet is to walk as long as your feet can take it, exploring the nooks and crannies. Here are some specific suggestions. Be forewarned: the Georgetown retail scene is ephemeral; shops come and go with the blink of an eye.

Along M Street:

American Hand, 2906 M Street; stunning ceramics and architect-designed dinnerware, serving pieces and kitchen implements.

Antiques, 31st Street above M Street; several antique shops.

earl allen, 3109 M Street; elegant dresses, suits and sweaters for women.

Urban Outfitters, 3111 M Street; casual, trendy clothes and toys for adults and kids; brightly colored plastic housewares.

door store, 3146 M Street; assemble-it-yourself furniture.

Banana Republic, M Street at Wisconsin Avenue; safari-, tropics- and Egyptian-inspired clothing for urban adults with adventure in their hearts.

Georgetown Park, 3222 M Street; Washington's largest mall, this is a fancy neo-Victorian collection of almost 100 shops and restaurants. A number of Georgetown's most elegant retailers moved here when it opened in 1981. Some examples of the stores include *Abercrombie & Fitch, Ann Taylor, Conran's, Davison's of Bermuda, F. A. O. Schwarz, Godiva Chocolatier, Liberty of London, Mark Cross, Pappagallo* and *Scan Furnishings.*

Laura Ashley, 3213 M Street; women's clothing, fabrics and accessories in the English-country tradition.

Georgetown Leather Design, 3265 M Street; brand-name leather goods and their own designs.

Along Wisconsin Avenue:

Indian Craft Shop, 1050 Wisconsin Avenue; a newly opened branch of the Interior Department's retail outlet of fine crafts made by Native Americans.

Pleasure Chest, 1063 Wisconsin Avenue; erotica in a nonthreatening environment. Adults only.

Red Balloon, 1073 Wisconsin Avenue; toys, clothes and other children's goodies.

The Coach Store, 1214 Wisconsin Avenue; fine leather accessories.

Esprit, 1229 Wisconsin Avenue; trendy women's wear.

Olsson's Books and Records, 1239 Wisconsin Avenue; an excellent selection of discounted books and tapes.

Georgetown Court, 3251 Prospect Street; a small, exclusive mall of 25 shops, galleries and restaurants, including *Casini, Jaeger* and *Carroll Reed.*

Rodolpho's, several locations on Wisconsin Avenue; elegant and fashionable Italian clothing and shoes for men.

The Nature Company, 1323 Wisconsin Avenue; globes, minerals, posters, T-shirts, books—all with a focus on nature.

Commander Salamander, 1420 Wisconsin Avenue; an emporium of the latest punk regalia.

Audubon Bookshop, 1621 Wisconsin Avenue; nature-related books, posters, toys and T-shirts.

Appalachian Spring and Marblehead Handprints, 1655 Wisconsin Avenue; lovely, high-quality regional handcrafted items.

Watergate/Les Champs

The Watergate Complex, at the intersection of Virginia Avenue, NW, and Rock Creek Parkway, offers ample opportunities for conspicuous consumption. From the choicest of chic to South American handicrafts to the famous Watergate pastries, it's all here. To give you some idea of the tone and price tags, though, shops include *Gucci.*

Connecticut Avenue

The Connecticut Avenue corridor from K Street to Dupont Circle aims primarily for a well-heeled professional clientele. *Burberry's* (1155 Connecticut Avenue), *Elizabeth Arden* (1147 Connecticut Avenue) and *Camalier & Buckley* (1141 Connecticut Avenue) share the promenade with numerous jewelry stores. The less-than-wealthy will feel right at home here, as well, in a variety of lower-ticket shops.

Eddie Bauer is around the corner on M Street for urban campers.

Connecticut Avenue in the area of Dupont Circle is far less imposing and more eclectic. *Save the Children Craft Shop* (1341 Connecticut Avenue) offers lovely arts and crafts from the organization's project areas around the world. *Kramerbooks & afterwords* (1517 Connecticut Avenue) reflects the cosmopolitan atmosphere of the neighborhood in its bookstore/café—a delightful combination of fiction and fettuccine. Numerous other shops invite extensive browsing.

Friendship Heights

Friendship Heights marks the District-Maryland border at Wisconsin Avenue, NW, and it's easily reached by Metrobus and Metrorail. You can find lots of department stores and fine specialty shops in a spacious setting, with the diversity and selection of city shopping but the convenience offered by suburbia. The area features the *Chevy Chase Shopping Center* and *Mazza Gallerie,* a dazzling collection of fine stores. Offering cream-of-the-crop merchandise, Mazza Gallerie shops include *Neiman Marcus,* the famous, extravagant Texas specialty store; *Kron Chocolatier; Pierre Deux,* featuring its own hand-blocked French provincial fabrics and accessories; and *F. A. O. Schwarz,* a fantasy land for kids and grown-ups, too. *Woodward & Lothrop* is next door on Wisconsin Avenue, and *Lord & Taylor* is genteelly tucked behind Mazza Gallerie on Western Avenue. *Gucci, Rive Gauche* and *Saks-Jandel* reside in elegance a bit further up Wisconsin Avenue, with *Saks Fifth Avenue* across the street.

Old Town, Alexandria

Just across the Potomac in Alexandria, Virginia, there's a charming enclave of historic sites, restaurants, galleries and small shops selling clothing, antiques, housewares, crafts and gifts for the discriminating shopper. *Hello World,* at 213 King Street, has an unparalleled selection of gifts, cards and other sundries. In fact, many witty and clever greeting cards by Sandra Boynton of Recycled Paper Products are stocked here before national introduction. *Gilpin House Book Shop,* at 208 King Street, is good for a browse, too, particularly in the children's room. *John Davy Toys,* a block behind King Street at 301 Cameron Street, is filled with classic and unusual playthings; it's the stuff of sweet nostalgia, as well. *Frankie Welch,* at 305 Cameron Street, designs her own sportswear and accessories for women.

Other Shopping Prospects

Other outstanding shops are scattered throughout the area. One of our favorites is *Jackie Chalkley Fine Contemporary Crafts,* which has beautifully designed clothing, jewelry and ceramics. One shop is located in the Willard Intercontinental Hotel Collection at 14th Street and Pennsylvania Avenue, NW; the other is in Fox Hall Mall at 3301 New Mexico Avenue, NW. Fox Hall Mall also has a choice maternity-clothing store, *New Conceptions,* and *Just So,* a children's boutique. Next door is *Sutton Place Gourmet,* a sumptuous, high-priced, elegant grocery store.

Tower Records, 2000 Pennsylvania Avenue, NW, has an astonishing array of records, tapes and compact discs in every musical style, from every corner of the globe; it's open 9 A.M. to midnight, 365 days a year.

The primary shop of interest in Chevy Chase is the *Cheshire Cat Children's Book Store,* a well-stocked and fun haven for kids, which offers mini-concerts and author get-togethers.

Bethesda, Maryland, along Wisconsin Avenue promises to be a shopper's treat. The arrival of the Metro has sharply altered the avenue here from a sleepy commuter route to a rather glitzy high-rise corridor; dusty neighborhood hardware stores have given way to office buildings, hotels, restaurants and upscale retail space. The transformation is still underway; one sure bet on what's complete is *Lowen's,* an immense, dazzling toy store stocked with hard-to-find high-quality imports, garden-variety toys, art and stationery supplies, kids' shoes and a soda fountain. A mesmerizing experience.

Shopping Malls

Washington is ringed by suburban shopping centers and malls, and there are several particularly outstanding ones. *White Flint,* a spectacular complex of about 115 stores, including *Bloomingdale's, I. Magnin* and *Lord & Taylor,* is in Rockville, Maryland, about a half-hour drive from Downtown. It's not far from the Capital Beltway (I-495); take Exit 34 north (Rockville Pike) and you'll see White Flint in about 1.5 miles. *Tyson's Corner,* in McLean, Virginia, features *Bloomingdale's, Nordstrom, Woodward & Lothrop, Hecht's* and about 140 other shops, restaurants and movie theaters. The Galleria at *Tyson's II* has just opened to rival its neighbor across the street with *Macy's, Saks Fifth Avenue,* and over 100 other elegant entries. This is about a 10-mile drive from Washington; take either the George Washington Parkway or the Capital Beltway to Route 123, Old Chain Bridge Road. The shopping center is at the intersection of Routes 495, 123 and 7. *Springfield Mall,* in Springfield, Virginia, has some more moderately priced stores among its 180 stores. The large department stores here are *Montgomery Ward, JC Penney* and *Garfinckel's.* To get to the Springfield Mall, take the Capital Beltway (I-495) to I-95 south and follow signs to Franconia. *Fair Oaks,* a shopping center in Fairfax, Virginia, has six major department stores—*Garfinckel's, Sears, JC Penney, Hecht's, Woodward & Lothrop* and *Lord & Taylor*—as well as 175 shops and restaurants. The best way to get there is to take the Capital Beltway (I-495) to Interstate 66 west and exit at Route 50 west.

For truly dedicated bargain hunters, a foray to *Potomac Mills Mall* is in order. The mall boasts 126 stores and restaurants; ultimately, there will be over 170. All the retail outlets are discount stores, offering clothing (from designer to casual) for all the family, shoes, furs, furniture, records, cosmetics and dinnerware. The banner store is *IKEA,* an immense Scandinavian furniture and housewares retailer selling assemble-it-yourself furniture at astonishingly low prices. Take I-95 south for 20 miles to Exit 52 (Dale City). Bear right to Potomac Mills Road; take a right to Gideon Road and another right into the mall.

While Metrobus and Metrorail serve suburban areas, an excursion to a shopping mall is much easier and quicker with a car. Most mall stores are open 10 A.M. to 9:30 P.M., Monday to Saturday, and some stores are open Sunday, noon to 5 or 6 P.M.

15

OUTDOOR

WASHINGTON/

SPORTS

———

Ever since Pierre L'Enfant first designed the federal city in 1791, green parks, open spaces and natural woodlands have been an integral part of the essence of Washington. To this day, Washington has one of the highest ratios of parks to residents among urban areas in the U.S.

The city is literally riven with large, natural, open spaces on which still stand virgin timber, native wildflowers and hundreds of varieties of trees and shrubs. While many areas, such as Rock Creek Park and Great Falls Park, are best appreciated by repeat visits, they are also accessible to the casual visitor for the simple pleasures of walking and looking, or more active enjoyment, such as jogging, biking and horseback riding.

In this chapter we shall list, and in some cases briefly describe, a full range of outdoor activities—from gardens to golf, from active participant sports to spectator sports. These lists are by no means complete; entire books have been devoted to Washington's parks alone. Rather, we have tried to concentrate on those activities and attractions that are most accessible and appealing to the visitor. The various park authorities listed at the end of this chapter can provide much additional information.

As a guide to appropriate clothing for outdoor Washington, here are average high and low temperatures for each month of the year in the D.C. area.

Month	High	Low
January	43°F	27°F
February	46	28
March	55	35
April	67	45
May	76	55
June	84	64
July	88	69
August	86	67
September	80	61
October	69	49
November	57	38
December	45	29

Other sporting opportunities are within a day's drive of Washington, including ocean beaches, downhill and cross-country skiing and white-water rafting. For details, contact the information offices (all in D.C.) of the following states: Delaware, Maryland, Virginia, West Virginia and Pennsylvania.

PICNICKING

Washingtonians are, by nature, a sedentary species; it is not unusual, therefore, that picnicking is far and away the most popular outdoor activity in the capital city. Not only is it popular, but it is extremely simple in Washington: much of the downtown area is one big picnic site. Some of the more popular areas are:

The Mall
Constitution Gardens
Pershing Park
Lafayette Park
Farragut Square
Dupont Circle
The banks of the Potomac—from Thompson's Boat Center to
    Memorial Bridge and in East and West Potomac parks

A bit farther out:

Rock Creek Park—Military Road area, Beach Drive, Glover Road. Phone 426-6829 for reservations for large picnic areas.

Great Falls Park—both Maryland and Virginia sides.

The banks of the Anacostia River.

Wolf Trap Farm Park—before show (see the "Entertainment" chapter).

Any of the county regional parks, such as Wheaton, Cabin John, Burke Lake.

Carry-outs, delicatessens, street food vendors and small grocery stores are found throughout the city, so handy picnic food is nearby. Check our recommendations in Chapters 3 through 10 for the best of the takeouts.

GARDENS

As you explore Washington's monuments and museums, you'll undoubtedly walk through or around many of the gardens listed below. Some of these parks are sufficiently interesting to warrant their own reports, and more extensive descriptions are elsewhere in the *Guide*, as noted.

Brookside Gardens. See Wheaton Regional Park site report in the "Nearby Maryland" chapter. Fifty acres of flowers, shrubs and trees with particularly fine displays of azaleas, roses and flowering bulbs. Other attractions include a Japanese pavilion, a large greenhouse of exotic flora and a Braille garden.

Circles and Squares. A few of the nicest of these parks in Northwest are:

Dupont Circle—Connecticut Avenue at P Street

Farragut Square—K Street between Connecticut Avenue and 17th Street

Lafayette Square—16th and H Streets, opposite the White House

MacPherson Square—15th and K Streets

Rawlins Park—E Street between 18th and 20th Streets

Washington's circles and squares, while the bane of the driver unfamiliar with their traffic flow, are an unending delight to the stroller. Administered both by the National Park Service and the District government, the various "vest-pocket" parks show an array of seasonal flowers, bulbs and flowering shrubs through the entire year. Washingtonians have come to watch carefully for the change of displays, because most of the bulbs are discarded after one season and given away to passersby on request!

These areas are a good place to examine the locals, who come out of their office burrows at lunch to bask in the noonday sun.

The D.C. Highway Department is in the process of creating curb cuts for wheelchairs and bikes in most downtown areas. At present, most circles and squares are wheelchair-accessible.

Constitution Gardens. Dedicated in May 1976, these Mall gardens are some 50 acres of rolling, tree-shaded lawns with a six-acre lake as a focal point. A footbridge leads to a one-acre island in the shallow lake. Designed principally for walking, jogging and picnicking, the gently contoured hills have paved pathways and are planted with over 5,000 trees, including oak, maple, dogwood, elm, crabapple and nearly 100,-000 other plants. Constitution Avenue between 17th and 23rd Streets, NW. Open all year. Wheelchair-accessible.

Dumbarton Oaks. See site report in "Georgetown/Foggy Bottom/The West End" chapter. Grand formal gardens—beds, fountains, pools, paths, stairways, nooks and crannies—on the Dumbarton Oaks estate.

Floral Library. A small wedge of blossoms between the Tidal Basin and the Washington Monument, the Floral Library presents a myriad of tulips in spring and annuals in summer and fall. Independence Avenue at the Tidal Basin. In bloom from spring to fall. Wheelchair-accessible.

Franciscan Monastery Grounds. See site report in the "Other D.C. Areas" chapter. Lovingly tended grounds, with reproductions of Holy Land shrines.

Gunston Hall. See site report in the "Suburban Virginia" chapter. Formal gardens of plants and flowers grown in colonial days, complete with ancient boxwood hedges.

Hillwood Museum Gardens. See site report in the "Northwest" chapter. Japanese and formal European gardens, rhododendron-lined paths, greenhouse with 5,000 orchids on the former estate of Marjorie Merriweather Post.

Kenilworth Aquatic Gardens. See site report in the "Other D.C. Areas" chapter. Spectacular displays of waterlilies, lotus and other water-loving plants, and riverside wildlife as well.

Kensington Orchids. Not a public garden, but a commercial concern. Still, if you are an orchid fancier, you will not have a better opportunity to examine so many varieties of orchids in one place: 3301 Plyers Mill Road, Kensington, MD 20895, (301) 933-0036. Capital Beltway (Route 495); take Connecticut Avenue north exit. Turn right on Plyers Mill Road to 3301. Open daily, 8 A.M. to noon, 1 to 5 P.M. Free admission. Wheelchair-accessible.

Kenwood, Maryland, Cherry Trees. A strictly seasonal but spectacular drive-through attraction. Cuttings and grafts from the Tidal Basin cherry trees have been added to native wild cherries for over 50 years. The results are stunning. When in flower, the trees turn Kenwood, an exclusive (and, of course, expensive) community, into a fairyland; gaudy but unforgettable: 5500 block of River Road, Bethesda, Maryland. Turn into Kenwood at Dorset Avenue.

Lady Bird Johnson Park—Lyndon Baines Johnson Memorial Grove. Imagine one million daffodils in bloom, followed by 2,700 pink-and-white dogwoods. Breathtaking! Lady Bird Park, dedicated in 1968 as thanks for her efforts to beautify the country, is located on what used to be called Columbia Island, the Virginia end of the Memorial Bridge. A handsome, 15-acre grove of white pine, dogwoods, azaleas and rhododendron form the natural background for the large Texas granite memorial to LBJ at the south end of the park. When visiting the LBJ Memorial and Lady Bird Park, be sure to note the handsome and graceful "gulls and waves" monument between the parkway and the Potomac. It is a memorial to Navy and Merchant Marine personnel, sculpted by Ernesto Begni del Piatta, and dedicated in 1934. George Washington Memorial Parkway at Arlington Memorial Bridge. Open all year. Wheelchair-accessible.

Meridian Hill Park. Meridian Hill overlooks downtown Washington with vistas to the Potomac and Anacostia rivers and the hills of Virginia. It's in close architectural harmony with the ornate marble "palaces" of 16th Street just north of the park. Meridian Hill Park shows both French and Italian influences—French, in the long promenades and a mall with heavy borders of plants that occupy the flat upper part; and Italian, in the opulent use of water, in falls, in jets and in the handsome cascade of 13 falls of graduated size leading down the slope of the park. Located at 16th and Euclid Streets, NW, two miles north of the White House. Open all year. Limited wheelchair accessibility due to hilly terrain and many steps.

Mount Vernon Grounds. See site report in the "Suburban Virginia" chapter. Grounds of the beloved estate of our first President, complete with colonial flower and vegetable gardens.

National Arboretum. See site report in the "Other D.C. Areas" chapter; 415 acres of gardens, trees, shrubs, overlooks and ponds, and a spectacular collection of bonsai in the Japanese pavilion.

United States Botanic Gardens. See site report in the "Capitol Hill" chapter. A lush conservatory with an incredible array of plants.

Washington Cathedral Grounds. See site report in the "Northwest" chapter. Rose and medieval herb gardens, perennial and yew walks, and wildflowers along a woodland path.

Washington Temple of the Church of Latter-Day Saints Grounds. See site report in the "Nearby Maryland" chapter. Award-winning gardens of annuals, perennials, trees and shrubs give year-round displays.

White House Grounds. See site report in the "Downtown" chapter. These spectacular, well-manicured plantings are open to the public on very limited occasions.

Woodlawn Plantation. See site report in the "Suburban Virginia" chapter. Old-fashioned roses, boxwood and assorted colonial plants in a classic garden painstakingly restored by the Garden Club of Virginia. Wooded nature trails.

HIKING—WOODLAND TRAILS

Serene woodland trails can crop up in the most unlikely places in Washington. You can be in snarling, rush-hour, downtown traffic one minute, and the next find a quiet byway where cars and noise and time don't exist. Some of the nicest trails can be found right in the middle of the city.

Many of the trails will be found cheek by jowl with the garden parks, so this section will overlap with the preceding list of gardens.

Hiking

Rock Creek Nature Center, 5200 Glover Road, NW, 426-6829, is the focal point of a variety of outdoor activities and educational programs for children and adults. The center is open 9 A.M. to 5 P.M. Tuesday to Sunday; closed Monday. Groups are welcome, by reservation. The center is ramped, and bathrooms are accessible. Some brochures are available in Braille, and the nature trail has special design features for those with visual impairments. The same basic activities are offered on a regular schedule, mostly on weekends—check when you get there.

1 P.M.—Children's Planetarium presentation. Ages four and up. Film and show, 35 minutes.

3 P.M.—Nature walk, a 45-minute guided walk. (Many self-guided walks of greater length start in the area of the center.)

4 P.M.—Adult Planetarium show. Ages seven and up. A longer, more comprehensive version of the 1 P.M. show, designed for older children and adults. Presentation lasts 45 minutes to an hour.

Other special programs are announced in the National Park Service publication, *Kiosk* (see the "Planning Ahead" chapter).

C&O Canal Historic Park. From Georgetown to Cumberland, Maryland: 184.5 miles. For a history and description of the canal, see site report in the "Nearby Maryland" chapter.

Georgetown. Pleasant walking anywhere. This segment of the canal tends to be crowded with bikers, joggers and strollers from its terminus in Georgetown for several miles upstream. The National Historic Park that contains the canal abounds in wildlife: beaver, fox, squirrel, raccoon, woodchuck, muskrat, great blue heron, waterfowl and woodpeckers—hairy, yellow-bellied sapsucker, red-bellied and pileated. The list could go on and on. Many old stands of trees remain—majestic beech, oak, maple, willow, sycamore. In the spring the redbud are a handsome sight—splotches of purple among the white and pink dogwood.

Barge Trips along the C&O Canal. A fun and unusual outdoor activity is to tour the historic C&O Canal aboard a barge, in 1876 style. The 90-minute tour is narrated by guides dressed in period costume. Tours are offered mid-April to mid-October, on Wednesdays, Thursdays and Fridays at 1 and 3 P.M., and on Saturdays and Sundays at 10:30 A.M., 1 and 3 P.M. Call 472-4376 or 472-6685 for further information. We advise you to call well in advance to make arrangements, especially if touring as a large group.

Billy Goat Trail. This four-mile trail can be accessed from the parking lot across from Old Angler's Inn on MacArthur Boulevard. The trail, which is steep and rocky, offers a remarkable variety of terrain, vistas, flora and fauna.

Great Falls. Great Falls, Maryland, is the site of the Great Falls Tavern, now a museum describing life on the old canal. Since Hurricane Agnes in 1977, the scenic overlooks on the Maryland side have been seriously diminished. Better views of the falls can be obtained from the Virginia side. Good walking trails on both sides of the Potomac.

Woodland Trails

Rock Creek Park. The park has 15 miles of hiking trails. Bridle paths may also be used for hiking. Maps can be found at the Visitor Information Center on Beach Drive near Military Road, or at the Park Headquarters at the Nature Center. Nice hikes can be combined with visits to the Nature Center, Planetarium and the stables within the park.

Montrose Park. Next to Dumbarton Oaks and Rock Creek Cemetery, Montrose Park is a genteel place. A clay tennis court with a gazebo, a playground and a field make up the upper portion of the park facing

R Street, and a lovely woodland path comprises the lower portion. The path goes through to Massachusetts Avenue, near the Naval Observatory.

National Arboretum. This is not exactly rough woodlands, but handsomely constructed paths show off many varieties of trees, shrubs and wildflowers, in season.

Woodend Nature Trail. Located at the headquarters of the Audubon Naturalist Society of the Central Atlantic States, 8940 Jones Mill Road, Chevy Chase, MD 20815, (301) 652-9188, the trail is part of a 40-acre estate bequeathed to the society. The mansion, by the way, was designed in the 1920s by John Russell Pope, architect of the National Gallery of Art and the Jefferson Memorial, and is a fine example of Georgian-revival domestic architecture. The estate is a haven for wildlife in the middle of suburban development, and counts among its residents some 29 species of birds, many small mammals and a family of red foxes. The society is extremely active in educational programs for schoolchildren, and organizes numerous outings in and around the Washington area. The society operates two bookshops, one at Woodend, and another at 1621 Wisconsin Avenue, NW, in Georgetown. The house and grounds (except the trail) at Woodend are accessible.

Regional Parks. All of the surrounding counties in Maryland and Virginia maintain parks with good hiking trails. For information, contact the various park authorities; addresses are listed at the end of this chapter.

For information and activities, serious hikers and backpackers should contact: The Potomac Appalachian Trail Club (638-5306) and the Sierra Club (547-2326).

JOGGING

Washington is well designed for the casual or serious runner; the wealth of the city parks gives joggers a wide choice of nice runs. Most of the better jogging areas are relatively flat, but with considerable visual interest. Many of the paths are centrally located, close to major hotels and other attractions, so a morning or evening run will not interfere with other events of the day.

The center of Washington jogging is the heart of the city—the Mall (packed-dirt paths), Ellipse and Tidal Basin (paved pathways). You can start virtually anywhere in this area, and jog in comfort, with only moderate traffic to impede you, and with relatively little need for a specific route in advance. *The Ellipse,* the park south of the White House, is just about a half mile around. An *Ellipse–Washington Monument* route is approximately 1.5 miles around from the White House, down 17th Street, around the edge of the monument grounds, and back up the other side of the Ellipse to your starting point. You can arrange longer runs by adding the Lincoln Memorial or some part of the Mall itself—from 14th Street all the way down to the steps of the Capitol (approximately 1.25 miles each way).

Rock Creek Park is a natural jogging area. Tree-shaded and usually 10 degrees cooler than the rest of the city, it is an oasis in the worst of the Washington summer heat and humidity. A nice run of about four miles would start where Rock Creek Parkway crosses under Connecticut Avenue. Head north in the park to Peirce Mill and retrace your steps. Along Rock Creek Parkway, starting at Cathedral Avenue, by the Shoreham Hotel, you will find a *Parcourse trail.* It has 18 stations, and is about 1.5 miles long.

Starting in Georgetown, the *C&O Canal Towpath* is perhaps the best single running surface in downtown Washington. A wide, packed-dirt trail, the towpath is home to runners, bikers and walkers, all of whom enjoy the serenity and beauty of this historic waterway. The National Park Service has erected mile posts all along the route up to Great Falls, so pace yourself as you run to your heart's content.

Hook up with the *Mount Vernon Bike Path* starting from the Lincoln Memorial, by taking the bridge across the Potomac (using the left sidewalk) and bearing left in Virginia. The paved path goes all the way to Mount Vernon, 15 miles or so downriver, but the best running is to the airport and back, a run of about 7.5 miles.

A run along the *Tidal Basin* and through *East Potomac Park* is another option. Starting from the Jefferson Memorial, head down either side of Ohio Drive, make the loop at the end of the park; continue past the Jefferson Memorial on the way back to take in the Tidal Basin loop, running under the beautiful cherry trees. This route is a must if you happen to hit D.C. when the trees are in bloom, but the crowds will cut down your speed.

BICYCLING

While in theory—and law—the bicycle has the same claim to the roadway as a motorized vehicle, urban cycling is still dangerous. We do not recommend bikes as a general means of transportation around Washington, although many residents bike regularly. The area abounds in good bike trails, however, many of which are the same as the jogging trails in the preceding section.

For the serious biker, the Potomac Area Council of American Youth Hostels and the Washington Area Bicyclist Association have coauthored the *Bicycle Atlas to the Greater Washington Area,* sold at bookstores or obtained direct from WABA, 1015 31st Street, NW, Washington, D.C. 20007, 944-8567. AYH is at the same address. Price at the present time is $9.95.

Bike rentals are reasonable. Try:

Thompson's Boat Center, Virginia Avenue at Rock Creek Parkway, D.C., 333-4861. Standard bikes only, some equipped with child-carrier seats. $2/hour, $7/day. Hours: 7 A.M. to 8 P.M.

Fletcher's Boat House, Canal and Reservoir Roads, D.C., 244-0461. Single-speed and kids' (20-inch) bikes. $1.75/hour, $6/day, two-hour minimum. Hours: 7:30 A.M. to 7:30 P.M.

Swain's Lock Boat House, 10700 Swains Lock Road, Potomac, MD, (301) 299-9006. Standard, 3-speed, kids', tandem bikes; some standards are equipped with child-carrier seats. $2 for first hour, $1 each hour thereafter, $6/day. Hours: weekdays 8 A.M. to dusk; weekends 7:30 A.M. to dusk.

Big Wheel Bikes, M Street, Georgetown, 337-0254. 3-speed, 10-speed, kids' bikes. $20/day. Hours: 10 A.M. to 6 P.M. Big Wheel store at 1004 Vermont Avenue, 638-3301, rents 3-speed bikes only.

Some of the best bikepaths are:

Arlington Cemetery–Lincoln Memorial–Rock Creek Parkway. A five-mile stretch, most easily accessed at Thompson's Boat Center along Rock Creek Parkway. You can bike either uptown toward the zoo, or downtown to Lincoln Memorial and across

Memorial Bridge to Arlington Cemetery (where you can connect to the Mount Vernon bikepath).

Upper Rock Creek Park. An 11-mile run from Beach Drive at
Tilden Street to East-West Highway in Chevy Chase, Maryland.
Several additional paths lead off of Beach Drive—explore
Glover Road, Oregon Avenue and Bingham Drive. Follow
signs. Level throughout. Bikes-only on the roadway Sundays, 9
A.M. to 5 P.M.

Mount Vernon Bikepath. Previously described.

C&O Canal Towpath. Previously described.

BOATING

Canoes, Rowboats and Paddle Boats

Canoes and rowboats are available for rental on the C&O Canal and
the Potomac River. The river can be very tricky; heed the advice of
the boatmen carefully.

Rentals at: *Thompson's Boat Center; Fletcher's Boat House; Swain's
Lock Boat House* (see "Bicycling" for addresses and phone numbers);
Jack's Boats, 35th and K Streets, NW (under the Whitehurst Freeway), 337-9642. At all locations rowboats will run around $10 a day.
Rowing shells and sailboards are available at Thompson's Boat Center for $10/hour (certification required for sailboards). Sailboats—14-
foot Phantoms—are also available at Thompson's for $8/hour.
Paddle boats are available for rent at the Tidal Basin; it's a fun way
to see the area; call 484-0845.

Boat Rides

C&O Canal—The mule-drawn barges, *Canal Clipper* and *George-
town,* offer 1½ hour excursions back to the nineteenth-century
canal life. The *Georgetown* leaves from The Foundry at 30th and
Thomas Jefferson streets, one-half block below M Street. The
Canal Clipper begins its voyage at Great Falls Park (see "C&O
Canal" in the "Nearby Maryland" chapter). The barges run from

mid-April to mid-October, and schedules, while variable, will undoubtedly include 10:30 A.M., 1 P.M., and 3 P.M. trips on the weekends. Additional trips on weekdays and a 5 P.M. excursion Sundays are often available. The cost on either boat is $4 for adults, $3 for seniors, and $2.50 for children 12 and under. Both boats are available for evening charter at a cost of approximately $400. For further details, call (202) 472-4376 (*Georgetown*) or (301) 299-2026 (*Canal Clipper*).

Potomac River—See the "Entertainment" chapter for a description of Potomac River rides.

Sailboats

The Potomac is not a premier sailing river, but rentals are available at:

Buzzard Point Marina—Half and V Streets, SW, 488-8400. Hobie Cats, Albacores, 20- to 26-foot Ensenadas.

Washington Sailing Marina—George Washington Memorial Parkway south of National Airport, 548-0001. Oday Widgeons.

If you want a first-rate sailing experience, spend a day on the Chesapeake Bay out of Annapolis. A good place for information, lessons and charters is the Annapolis Sailing School, (301) 267-7205. The Chesapeake Bay Yacht Racing Association, P.O. Box 1989, Annapolis, MD 21404, has a complete list of yacht clubs.

TENNIS

If you read the columns of Art Buchwald, you are aware of how important a role tennis plays in the lives of the ruling class. The surrounding jurisdictions have responded to this need with alacrity, building scores of courts throughout the area. Complete lists with addresses available at the phone numbers listed.

Alexandria, Parks Division, (703) 838-4343. 28 courts at 15 locations; six lighted. Open all year.

Arlington, (703) 558-2426. 98 courts at 29 locations; reserved courts for fee at Bluemont and Bancroft parks.

District of Columbia, 673-7646. 144 outdoor, 60 lighted at 45 locations; open all year, permit required; charges at three locations:

Hains Point, 554-5962; Peirce Mill, 723-2669 and 16th and
Kennedy Streets, NW, 723-2669. Pay courts are both hard and
soft; fees range from $8 to $16/hour depending on season and time
of day. Indoor courts under bubbles at Hains Point during winter.

Fairfax County, (703) 941-5008. 110 courts, 60 lighted; fee charges
at four sites; reservations required at fee courts.

Montgomery County, 235 free outdoor courts; courts turn over on the
hour. Indoor pay courts at Wheaton Regional Park, (301) 495-
2525, and Cabin John Park, (301) 469-7300; spot time usually
available.

Prince George's County, (301) 699-2415. 210 free courts at 90 locations, 45 with lights. Fees charged at two locations; call for information.

City of Rockville, (301) 424-8000. 34 courts, 15 lighted.

GOLF

District of Columbia. Two nine-hole courses and one 18-hole course
at Hains Point, 554-7660. Two nine-hole courses at Rock Creek
Park, 723-9832.

Maryland. 27-hole course, championship level at Northwest Park,
(301) 598-6100; 18-hole course at Needwood, (301) 948-1075.

Virginia. Burke Lake Park, Fairfax, (703) 323-6600; Greendale, Alexandria, (703) 971-6170.

Surrounding counties run other public links. Call the parks department in the area you are interested in for further information. Reservations a few days in advance are usually recommended. Club rentals
almost always available.

ICE SKATING

For the past several winters, Washington has been treated to the
unusual sight of a completely frozen Potomac River. Naturally, this
has occasioned several attempts to make use of the river as an ice-

skating rink or winter stock-car track. The local authorities have not been amused. But they have provided several legitimate outlets for winter sports fever.

District of Columbia. Besides the C&O Canal, on which skating is rarely allowed due to the uncertain nature of the ice, the Reflecting Pool, in front of the Lincoln Memorial, and the lake in Constitution Gardens are likely spots for good skating. An artificial rink—the *Sculpture Garden Outdoor Rink*—has been constructed between 7th and 9th Streets, NW, 289-7560, and will appear at the right time of year. The *Federal Home Loan Bank Board* Building (on 17th Street, just below Pennsylvania Avenue, NW) has a small rink favored by a downtown lunch crowd, like Rockefeller Center. *Pershing Park,* carved out of what used to be Pennsylvania Avenue from 13th to 15th Streets, NW, has a shallow pond used as a rink. *Fort Dupont Park* at 37th Street and Ely Place, SE, 581-0199, has a superior facility that is underutilized. Skate rentals are available at all facilities.

Maryland. *Wheaton Regional Park,* (301) 649-2250, and *Cabin John Regional Park,* (301) 365-0585, both have good artificial rinks. Skate rentals available.

Virginia. *Mount Vernon District Park,* (703) 768-3222, has an artificial rink. Skate rentals available.

HORSEBACK RIDING

District of Columbia:
Rock Creek Park Horse Center
Military Road and Glover Road, NW
362-0117
Open all year. Call for rates and availability.
The center does a lot of work with handicapped children; call if special services are desired.

Maryland:
Meadowbrook Stables
Meadowbrook Lane, Chevy Chase
(301) 588-6935
Open all year. Call for rates and availability.

Wheaton Park Stables (in Wheaton Regional Park)
  1101 Glenallen Avenue, Wheaton
  (301) 622-3311
  Open all year. Trails, ring.

Polo fans, take note: On Sunday afternoons in spring, summer and fall, polo matches are held on the Lincoln Memorial Polo Field located on Ohio Drive, between the Lincoln Memorial and the Tidal Basin. Local teams play one another and visiting teams from other parts of the United States and overseas. Call the National Park Service, 426-6700, for information.

PLAYING FIELDS

Here, as in every part of the country, find a school and you have found a playing field, usually more than one. Amateur, but reasonably serious, ballplayers—baseball, soccer, volleyball—find their way to the playing fields around the Lincoln Memorial and West Potomac Park. Established league games may prevent you from just fooling around when you want to, but early evenings and weekends, pickup games usually can be found when a league game is not scheduled.

SWIMMING

Local waters: not highly recommended. All local rivers and streams are polluted to a greater or lesser degree. Stick to the pools.

  If your hotel or motel does not have a pool, seek out the various free, public pools.

District of Columbia. Nineteen outdoor pools. Call 576-6436 for information.

Capitol East Natatorium. Indoor pool, 635 North Carolina Avenue, NE, 724-4495.

Montgomery County. Six pools with differing restrictions. Call Aquatics Division, (301) 468-4183, for details.

Prince George's County. Eight pools, indoor and outdoor. The major center is Allentown Road Aquatic Center, Camp Springs, (301) 449-5567, with a complex of three outdoor and two indoor pools.

Alexandria. Seven pools. Admission charged. Call (703) 931-6334 for details.

Arlington. Three indoor/outdoor pools. Call (703) 284-8076 for details.

Fairfax. Five pools. Call (703) 941-5000 for details.

Good beaches are within an hour's drive of the area; the closest is Sandy Point State Park, located off Route 50, just west of the Bay Bridge. Ocean beaches are at least a three-hour drive, and often involve heavy traffic. Local radio stations broadcast beach weather and traffic reports.

SPECTATOR SPORTS

Baseball. Washington has lost two major-league baseball teams in the past 20 years—to Minneapolis and to Texas. Now some cynics say neither team was a major loss, but, then, those folks probably don't care for apple pie either.

Baseball is still available, though.

The Baltimore Orioles, which in previous editions we called "perennial contenders" for the American League East crown, play out of Memorial Stadium, 1000 block of East 33rd Street, Baltimore, Maryland, one hour from downtown D.C. Tickets are available through Ticketron, 659-2601; the Orioles ticket office at 914 17th Street, NW, 296-2473; or from the Orioles box office, (301) 338-1300.

Basketball. The Washington Bullets, former NBA champs, play out of the Capital Centre. Tickets, available through Ticketron or the Capital Centre box office, (301) 350-3400, run from around $5 to $10. The Capital Centre is located off the Beltway (Route 495), accessible from either Exit 32 or 33. Good signs will lead you to the Centre.

University of Maryland, a member of the Atlantic Coast Conference, offers a top-flight brand of college basketball at Cole Field House. Call (301) 454-2123 for information, (301) 454-2121 for tickets. Perennial Big East Powerhouse, Georgetown, plays its home games at the Capital Center. Call (301) 350-3400 for ticket and schedule information.

Horse Racing. One or another of the area tracks is usually in season. Check local papers for details. Buses are usually available from various locations in the Washington area to the tracks in season. Ask for details if you call. Local sports pages will normally carry ads for bus services, as well.

Harness:
Rosecroft Raceway—Oxon Hill, Maryland, (301) 567-4000
Del Marva Downs—Berlin, Maryland, (301) 641-0600
Laurel Raceway—Laurel, Maryland, (301) 725-1800

Thoroughbred:
Bowie Race Course—Bowie, Maryland, (301) 262-8111
Laurel Race Course—Laurel, Maryland, (301) 725-0400
Pimlico Race Course—Baltimore, Maryland, (301) 542-9400
Shenandoah Downs—Charleston, West Virginia, (304) 725-2021

Steeplechase:
Steeplechase is a seasonal happening in both Virginia and Maryland. Four major events occur in the spring: the Fair Hill meeting, the Maryland Hunt Cup, the Virginia Gold Cup and the Middleburg Hunt Cup. In autumn, Middleburg, Montpelier and Fairfax hold major meets. Check the papers for details.

Football. The Washington Redskins have sold out RFK Stadium for the past decade. The waiting list for season tickets is years, so tickets are just not available.

Tickets are usually available, however, for local college teams. The Maryland Terrapins play at the College Park campus; call for ticket information at (301) 454-2121. The Naval Academy in Annapolis and Howard University in Washington also field competent teams. Check the paper for details of home games.

Hockey. Washington Capitals at the Capital Centre, (301) 350-3400, and Ticketron. Tickets from around $5 to $10.

16

ADVICE

TO GROUPS

The key to all successful group visits to Washington is careful advance planning. In this chapter, we have included some tips to help in this process. Be sure to read the "Planning Ahead" chapter for additional considerations when making your plans.

For groups, it is especially important to cover *every* phase of the trip in the preplanning process. A group is a cumbersome thing: it moves slowly and reacts badly to adverse situations. The more careful and complete the pretrip planning, the less likely that your visit can be ruined by misadventures.

It is never too early to begin the planning process. The group's ability to undertake certain tours, see a special site or meet with the particular person of most importance to the group depends on the availability of the specific resource at the precise time of the trip. Many thousands of groups come to Washington each year, bringing literally millions of visitors. Your group is just a droplet in the downpour. Many groups are repeatedly disappointed by the failure of their plans to materialize because of someone's "prior commitments." Proper advance planning can make *your* request the "prior commitment."

The second major concern of a group is the careful allocation of available funds. Too many times, a group will try to save money in ways that could result in unpleasant experiences for the group. In a group tour small matters—timing, locations, meal arrangements—take on exaggerated significance. For example, even though a group may come to the city with its own bus and driver, it may make sense to hire *another* bus and driver, or a step-on guide, who is thoroughly familiar with the city streets. Unfamiliarity with the geography, parking regulations and traffic patterns may mean missed appointments and destroyed mealtimes.

Metrobus runs an extremely efficient charter bus service, with drivers trained as sightseeing guides. A standard bus, seating 47 and standing 19, costs $200 for the minimum time of three hours. Additional hours thereafter cost $50 each. Kneeling buses to facilitate boarding people in wheelchairs are not currently available for charter service. Reservations should be made in advance—well in advance for the prime season, April to June. Call 637-1315 for information and reservations.

Guide Service of Washington, 733 15th Street, Suite 1040, NW, Washington, D.C. 20005, 628-2842, provides step-on guide service, in a variety of languages, from English to Mandarin Chinese (all major languages are available—French, Spanish, German, Italian, Chinese, Japanese, Arabic). Step-on service runs $67 for a four-bus tour with English-speaking guides, and $70 for foreign-language guides. The Guide Service guide will meet a group at its hotel; guides are thoroughly familiar with the area, and can direct bus drivers.

Washington has several competent firms that will organize your group's visit from top to bottom, if need be.

Washington, Inc., 1990 M Street, NW, Suite 310, Washington, D.C. 20036, 828-7000, is run by a knowledgeable group of women who themselves are close to the heartbeat of Washington; one of the owners is the wife of a senator, another the wife of a powerful lobbyist, another the former social secretary of the Carter White House and the fourth partner is a member of a family with long business ties to the city. The company organizes not only group tours, but social extravaganzas and special events for the political, social and corporate communities. Their programs are imaginative, thoroughly planned and of the highest quality.

Washington, Inc., will arrange a press conference for your group—and the audience asks the questions of a panel of well-known and well-informed people.

A flexible, three-day program called Seminar in Civics is offered for high school students. It covers the major institutions of government, tourist sites, museums, Goddard Space Flight Center, the Naval Observatory and evening entertainment.

The company boasts a long list of corporate clients and trade associations that have used their services during corporate meetings and conventions. The fees are not inconsiderable, but the growing list seems to indicate value received.

National Fine Arts Associates, 4801 Massachusetts Avenue, Suite 400, NW, Washington, D.C. 20016, 966-3800, offers a broad array of complete tour packages, and many unique tours as well. The principal business of the firm, as their name suggests, is art-related. Their clients include conventions, historical societies, museum groups from all over the country, college students and alumni associations. All the Fine Arts guides are art professionals, with advanced degrees in art history. Many, in fact, are teachers and professors.

The Fine Arts catalog of tours contains many unique programs, including special "country" tours—tours concentrating on the art, architecture, culture and food of a particular nation or region. French, Italian, Greek, Spanish, Chinese, Japanese and African tours are listed. Art tours may visit museums, galleries, houses and even artists' studios.

A variety of historic house tours are offered in Washington and the surrounding counties of Maryland and Virginia. Such tours may include private homes not ordinarily opened to tourists. Personalized limousine tours, while quite expensive, can provide an intimate and luxurious means by which to see the city. National Fine Arts asks that you write or call as far in advance of your visit as possible.

Every year, thousands of buses with school groups aboard parade through the city. One of the largest organizers of junior and senior high school trips to Washington is *Lakeland Tours,* 1290 Seminole Trail, Charlottesville, VA 22901, (804) 973-4321. Lakeland, a group travel agency, specializes in tours of Washington. One recent year it brought 700 groups, with over 30,000 students, to town. The company will provide a tailored program for any size group, with each tour priced according to the specific program. Lakeland's tours are accompanied by a company escort, as well as its own sightseeing guides.

In addition to student tours, Lakeland has had experience with every kind of group, including senior citizens and handicapped visitors.

A major wholesaler of Washington tours is *Washington Group Tours,* 1110 Vermont Avenue, NW, Washington, D.C. 20036, 955-5667. Working almost exclusively through airlines and travel agents (but accessible directly, too), Washington Group Tours handles all nature of groups—students, affinity organizations, seniors, handicapped. An affiliate company specializes in smaller conventions, up to 250, making all necessary arrangements—from the technical requirements of the convention itself to sightseeing tours and entertainment.

Commercial tour companies have several distinct advantages: by booking a large volume of business, with hotels, theaters, etc., they can sometimes deliver services at a lower price than might otherwise be available, or offer considerably expanded services at the same price you would ordinarily expect to pay. Second, familiarity with the city prevents disasters. Experience eliminates bad hotels, restaurants and entertainments. A reputable firm can offer some peace of mind and the assurance of a smooth visit.

If your group chooses not to use a local company to plan some part or all of the itinerary, consult your local travel agent, but take into account the various components of a successful trip: transportation, lodging, sightseeing, eating and entertainment.

TRANSPORTATION

Several alternatives have been mentioned previously: hiring a local bus company or a step-on guide, or the use of existing facilities, such as Tourmobile or Old Town Trolley Tour. It bears repeating that local drivers will get the group around the city faster and more safely than drivers unfamiliar with the streets. In the "Getting to and Around Town" chapter we have listed a few of the local companies offering bus or trolley tours. They will all be pleased to provide a vehicle for a group, so call or write ahead for charter information.

LODGING

Finding a suitable hotel for a large group can be a problem. Use the hotel appendix in this book for basic information as to size, rates and services. Be aware that many hotels will not accept groups, especially those with children. A pattern seems to have developed in the area. Downtown hotels, for the most part, do not need or want large groups, especially students, while the suburban Maryland and Virginia hotels welcome them. Route 1, or Jefferson Davis Highway, at Crystal City just across the Potomac and next to National Airport has several hotels that welcome groups. They include the Hospitality

House, Crystal City Marriott, Stouffer's National Center and the Quality Inn. Motels along the New York Avenue corridor (Route 50) also cater to groups, including such hotels as the Holiday Inn. The Alexandria Tourist Council, 221 King Street, (703) 838-4200, will assist groups with many aspects of their plans.

Among in-town hotels, the Washington Hilton, a very large hotel, has proved itself accommodating to groups of all kinds; it is so constructed as to be accessible to large numbers of buses for easy loading and unloading. Surprisingly, few hotels, even the new ones, are well designed for this purpose.

If any members of your group are handicapped, be sure to read the "Tips to Visitors with Disabilities" chapter. In addition, the hotel guide in the appendix highlights accessibility in hotels.

A final word about lodging: when making reservations, do so as far in advance as possible, and reconfirm two weeks before departure. Be sure to ask, when making reservations, whether the hotel has "quads"—that is, rooms that can accommodate four beds. Where applicable, four to a room can be a real dollar savings—the $80 room becomes, effectively, the $20 room, a real bargain in Washington.

SIGHTSEEING

In planning a schedule of sites, refer to the "One-, Two- and Three-Day Tours" chapter, which outlines a schedule that is feasible, whether for an individual or a group. When your itinerary is established, read the site reports and take note of any possible problems for your group. For example, you might not think to consider that the congressional galleries are not open to children under six, or that the Capitol subway cars are off-limits to kids under 12, unless accompanied by an adult.

Large groups may find it easier to break into small groups, visiting the same sites on different schedules, or different places according to differing interests. The smaller the group, the easier problems are to overcome, and fewer problems arise.

Take advantage of the special services accorded groups in both the Capitol and the Smithsonian, as well as other sites.

At the Capitol, your congressman or senator can help set up your group visit. Groups using the Capitol cafeterias must have written permission for the time and size of the group. Your congressional office can arrange it. Special rooms can be reserved through your congressmen and luncheon lectures arranged. Musical groups are permitted to perform on the Capitol steps, with written permission, also acquired through your congressional office. Requests for musical performances should be made well in advance.

The Smithsonian offers an orientation program for groups, designed for groups of 10 or more, ages 16 and older. A basic introduction to the Institution's 12 museums and galleries, and the National Zoo, is given in a 30-minute lecture and slide show. If your group has special interests, make note of them when applying for the orientation lecture. The program is offered, free of charge, seven days a week, but *by appointment only*. Call 357-2700, or write, at least one month in advance, to: Visitor Information Center, Group Orientation Program, Smithsonian Institution, Washington, D.C. 20560.

EATING

Washington has literally thousands of options for satisfying hunger pangs during the sightseeing day, but unless a group plans carefully, it may find itself a long way from *any* kind of food.

Breakfast is best taken care of in or around the hotel. Once your touring day is underway the possibilities expand. Many area restaurants and carry-outs will prepare box or bag lunches, plain or fancy, at an agreeable price. Downtown, try the *Upstairs/Downstairs*, 1720 H Street, NW, 298-8338, for good sandwiches, and *The Dutch Treat*, 1710 L Street, NW, 296-3219, for gourmet fare. On Capitol Hill, try *The American Café*, 227 Massachusetts Avenue, NE, 546-7690. If you are housed in one of the major hotel areas, other carry-outs can be found in the neighborhood. Arrangements for lunches can usually be made with 24-hour notice.

Cafeterias are almost invariably quick and inexpensive. Government cafeterias are one of the great food bargains in town. Try the Madison Building at the Library of Congress; it's big, with good food and a fabulous view; the National Gallery of Art, also quite handsome, and the assorted Smithsonian cafeterias (see site reports for addresses and hours) are also good bets. On the Hill, you can arrange to eat at the House Office Building cafeterias, or the Senate Office Building, or the Capitol itself.

Commercial cafeterias vary markedly in quality. The following are centrally located facilities, large enough to handle groups, and serve respectable food:

The White House
    Connection   1725 F Street, NW   842-1777
Sholl's Colonial   1990 K Street, NW   296-3065

The Pavilion at the Old Post Office, 1100 Pennsylvania Avenue, NW, 289-4224, has a "meal-deal" for groups—$4.75 will buy a meal, soda and dessert at any of the Pavilion's food stands. Write ahead or go to the management office, balcony level.

Outside of downtown, the shopping malls offer a variety of eating possibilities. See the "Shopping" chapter for addresses of the area malls. Some nearby malls that have decent cafeterias include the Crystal City Mall, Tyson's Corner, Springfield, and White Flint.

It is important to call ahead to restaurants, even the cafeterias listed above, and let them know when you want to arrive, how many are in your group and how you intend to pay, as individuals or on a single check.

Visitors in groups can descend en masse to several festival food halls; choices within are virtually unlimited and fast, whether you want to carry food out or eat there. Most of the seats may be packed at lunch, so avoid the crunch by lunching either early or late. Best bets are: *The Pavilion at the Old Post Office,* 1100 Pennsylvania Avenue, NW, 289-4224; *International Square,* 1825 I Street, NW, 223-1850; *The Shops at National Place,* 1300 Pennsylvania Avenue, NW; *Connecticut Connection,* Farragut North Metro stop, red line, underground at Connecticut Avenue and L Street, NW; and *Union Station,* 50 Massachusetts Avenue, NE.

Another possibility is fast food. The major fast-food chains operate in large numbers of in-town locations, so you can expect to find several additional restaurants beyond the ones listed here. Look in the white pages for chains other than those listed below.

K Street Eatery Lunch Box
  1411 K Street, NW
  825 20th Street, NW
  1622 I Street, NW
  1721 G Street, NW

McDonald's
75 New York Avenue, NE
911 E Street, NW
625 Pennsylvania Avenue, SE
1619 17th Street, NW
1909 K Street, NW
1401 K Street, NW
Burger King
1606 K Street, NW
1114 New York Avenue, NW
Roy Rogers
2023 I Street, NW
1341 G Street, NW
317 Pennsylvania Avenue, SE
401 M Street, SW
1235 New York Avenue, NW
1226 Wisconsin Avenue, NW
4130 Wisconsin Avenue, NW
Arthur Treacher's Fish'n Chips
14th and K Streets, NW
1518 Connecticut Avenue, NW

ENTERTAINMENT

Almost without exception, whatever an individual can do at night, so can a group. The possibilities are limited only by imagination and budgets. Obviously, groups must plan well in advance for limited-seating facilities, such as theaters and concert halls. At the Kennedy Center, group reservations may have to be made up to a year in advance to assure block seating. Most theaters, even movie theaters, offer group discounts, and we have noted such discounts in the "Entertainment" chapter. If in doubt, call and ask.

The Washington area has numerous excellent dinner theaters; many groups have found them to be ideal for evenings out. Other popular group activities include evening cruises of the Washington Boat Lines (see the "Outdoor Washington/Sports" chapter) and nighttime bus tours of the monuments, offered by most city bus tour companies.

USEFUL PHONE NUMBERS

Washington Area Convention & Visitor's Association	789-7000
1575 I Street, NW	
Hotel Association of Washington	833-3350
1219 Connecticut Avenue	
Better Business Bureau	393-8000
1012 14th Street, NW	Complaints: 393-8020
U.S. Capitol; House of Representatives;	224-3121
U.S. Senate	
Alexandria Tourist Council	(703) 549-0205

17

TIPS

FOR VISITORS

WITH DISABILITIES

WASHINGTON'S ACCESS RATING

In facilities, design and provision of services, Washington rates about average in consideration of the needs of disabled people. In some regards, however, the capital city ranks well above many other urban centers; the Metrorail system, the public-service sector, the Smithsonian Institution and the National Park Service are most notable in the plans and provisions for the treatment of visitors who have handicaps.

Since the Metro is so new, it was designed in compliance with recent federal laws prescribing accessibility standards. In general, stations and trains are well designed, and careful thought has been given to the best ways of providing optimal services to the extremely varied population of users. A more detailed discussion of services keyed to specific disabilities will follow.

For several reasons, the service sectors dealing with the general public—bus drivers, waiters, ticket sellers, retail clerks, cab drivers and so forth—are somewhat more enlightened than their counterparts in other cities in their dealings with people who have disabilities. Washington has been a good job market for folks with disabilities; the federal government dominates and its influence is so enormous that many employers have hired with equal employment opportunities firmly in mind. People with disabilities, therefore, have been better integrated into the work force than in most places in the U.S., and so are quite visible and mobile. One result has been the education through experience of service-sector employees in meeting the needs of people with impairments to their mobility, vision and hearing, as well as other disabilities. In addition, a multitude of consumer-oriented organizations founded by and for people with disabilities have their national headquarters in Washington and have developed programs for training people who deal directly with the public in how they can best provide services to the organizations' constituencies.

The Smithsonian and Park Service are exemplary in the facilities, exhibits, programs and tours they have developed to make the national treasures in their domain accessible to and enjoyable for people with disabilities. Guards and guides have been trained to deal with the problems faced by people with specific disabilities. With advance notice, both organizations will conduct special tours with oral or sign interpreters or tours designed for the visually impaired for practically every site under their jurisdiction. To make arrangements for these tours, call the Smithsonian at 357-2700 or TDD 357-1729 between 9 A.M. and 5 P.M. daily; call NPS on the Mall at 426-6841. The Smithsonian also publishes *A Guide for Disabled Visitors,* which details museum services and facilities designed for those with disabilities. This is available at the Smithsonian Institution Building or from the Visitor Information Associates Reception Center, Smithsonian Institution Building, Smithsonian Institution, Washington, D.C. 20560.

The most important piece of advice for a Washington visitor with handicaps is to ask: ask at information desks, ask museum guards, docents or anyone else connected with a site what specifically has been designed or can be experienced thoroughly by someone with your disability. We also recommend that you call ahead to recheck details that you will depend on for your visit; it would be a sad waste of energy to set off to see a particular exhibit or gallery only to discover that it has been phased out.

Beyond these points, Washington will probably present no greater challenges than you face in your daily life. If you do need assistance in some realm, Washington is home to any number of national and local consumer-oriented organizations of people with disabilities that may be able to offer advice and assistance. We've listed these organizations, addresses and phone numbers at the end of this chapter.

METROBUS AND METRORAIL

The Metrobus and Metrorail systems offer substantial (50–60 percent) fare discounts and priority-seating arrangements to people with

disabilities. For fare discounts you must obtain a Handicapped Identification Card. Since it's a rather complex process to get such an
identification card, your visit should be of some length to justify the
effort. Pick up an application at a Metro sales outlet, or call 962-1245
and they will send you one. The application must be completed by a
licensed physician; you then take the application to the Handicapped
Services Office on the lobby level of Metro Headquarters, 660 5th
Street, NW, from 8 A.M. to 4:30 P.M. on weekdays. An identification
card with a photograph will be issued to you. If this is an inconvenient
location, ID's are periodically issued in other locations throughout
the Metropolitan area; call 962-1245 for places and schedules.

To ride Metrorail, a special farecard is needed; it is available with
a Handicapped Identification Card at Metro outlets and many area
banks (call 637-7000 for specific locations). The farecard can then be
used in the automatic fare-collection equipment at every Metro station, charging you half the rush-hour fare to your destination, not to
exceed 60¢.

THEATER TICKETS

The Kennedy Center theaters and the National Theater offer a limited
number of half-price seats for people with disabilities at most performances. Ford's Theatre offers two tickets for the price of one at all
performances except Friday and Saturday nights. The Warner Theater offers discounts for some of its shows. At the Kennedy Center,
someone interested in obtaining discounted tickets must go to the
Friends of the Kennedy Center Office in the Hall of States and present
an ID to receive a discount voucher. This voucher is then presented
at the appropriate box office where the patron is offered a choice of
available seating. At the National, Ford's and Warner, a disability ID
must be presented at the box office when tickets are purchased.

FOR THOSE WITH LIMITED MOBILITY

Getting Around Town

The Metrorail system has been designed to be accessible to wheelchair
users, and it works well toward that purpose. Each station is serviced
by an elevator; it must be noted, however, that the elevators are not
always operating. Elevator locations are noted below:

Red Line

Glenmont	East side of Georgia Avenue by Kiss and Ride
Wheaton	SE corner of Georgia Avenue and Reedie Drive
Forest Glen	Main entrance
Silver Spring	South of Colesville Road at East-West Highway
Takoma	Carroll Street and Cedar Street, NW
Fort Totten	Galloway Street, Extended, south of Riggs Road, NE
Brookland/CUA	Bunker Hill Road, south of Michigan Avenue, NE
Rhode Island Avenue	Rhode Island Avenue and 8th Street, NE
Union Station/ Visitor Center	1st and G Streets, NE
Judiciary Square	F Street between 4th and 5th Streets, NW
Gallery Place	SE corner of 7th and G Streets, NW
Metro Center	NE corner of 12th and G Streets, NW
Farragut North	NE corner of Connecticut Avenue and K Street, NW
Dupont Circle	SW corner of Connecticut Avenue and K Street, NW
Woodley Park/ Zoo	SW corner of Woodley Street and Connecticut Avenue
Cleveland Park	NW corner Connecticut Avenue and Ordway Street
Van Ness/UDC	Middle of block west side of Connecticut Avenue between Van Ness and Veazey Streets
Tenleytown	NE corner Albemarle Street and Wisconsin Avenue
Friendship Heights	East Side of Wisconsin Avenue between Western Avenue and Jennifer Street
Bethesda	Main entrance
Medical Center	SW corner of Rockville Pike and South Drive
Grosvenor	Main entrance

White Flint	Main entrance
Twinbrook	Between the Kiss and Rides
Rockville	Across from Kiss and Ride and Bus Bays
Shady Grove	Between the Kiss and Rides

Blue Line

National Airport	Opposite North Terminal (Courtesy van service is available from station to airport terminal building)
Crystal City	Crystal City, north of 18th Street, east of Clark Street
Pentagon City	East side of Hayes Street between Army-Navy and 15th Street
Pentagon	East end of bus island
Arlington Cemetery	North side of Memorial Drive, west of Jefferson Davis Highway
Rosslyn	East side of N. Moore between 19th and Wilson
Foggy Bottom/ GWU	North side of I Street between 23rd and 24th Streets, NW
Farragut West	NW corner of 18th and I Streets, NW
McPherson Square	SW corner of 14th and I Streets, NW
Metro Center (Transfer Station)	East side of 12th Street north of G Street, NW
Federal Triangle	West side of 12th Street between Pennsylvania and Constitution Avenues, NW
Smithsonian	North of Independence Avenue, west of 12th Street, SW
L'Enfant Plaza	West of 7th Street between railroad crossing and C Street, SW
Federal Center, SW	SW corner of D and 3rd Streets, SW
Capitol South	West of 1st Street between C and D Streets, SW
Eastern Market	East of 7th Street and South of Pennsylvania Avenue, SE
Potomac Avenue	East side of 14th Street, SE between Potomac Avenue and G Street, SE
Stadium/Armory	19th and C Streets, SE
Benning Road	Benning Road and Central Avenue, NE

Capitol Heights	East Capitol Street and Southern Avenue
Addison Road	Central Avenue and Addison Road

Orange Line

Vienna	Center platform
Dunn Loring	Main entrance
West Falls Church	North end of pedestrian bridge
East Falls Church	Main entrance
Ballston	Fairfax Drive and Stuart Street, Arlington, VA
Virginia Square	Fairfax Drive and Monroe Street, Arlington, VA
Clarendon	Wilson Boulevard and North Highland Street, Arlington, VA
Court House	Wilson Boulevard and North Uhle Street, Arlington, VA
Rosslyn	See Blue Line
Foggy Bottom/ GWU	See Blue Line
Farragut West	See Blue Line
McPherson Square	See Blue Line
Metro Center (Transfer Station)	See Blue Line
Federal Triangle	See Blue Line
Smithsonian	See Blue Line
L'Enfant Plaza	See Blue Line
Federal Center, SW	See Blue Line
Capitol South	See Blue Line
Eastern Market	See Blue Line
Potomac Avenue	See Blue Line
Stadium/Armory	See Blue Line
Minnesota Avenue	Minnesota Avenue and Grant Street, NE
Deanwood Station	Minnesota Avenue and Quarles Street, NE
Cheverly	Route 50 and Columbia Park Road
Landover	Landover Road and Pennsylvania Drive
New Carrollton	Route 50 and Capital Beltway

Yellow Line

Huntington	Parking garage at south end of station
Eisenhower Avenue	Main entrance
King Street	Main entrance
Braddock Road	Main entrance
National Airport	See Blue Line
Crystal City	See Blue Line
Pentagon City	See Blue Line
Pentagon	See Blue Line
L'Enfant Plaza	See Blue Line
Archives	Main entrance
Gallery Place	See Red Line

The Metrobus fleet has more than 200 buses that are equipped with wheelchair lifts. A platform lowers to the curb, the person in a wheelchair rolls onto it and the platform rises to bus level where the wheelchair can be locked into a special slot. Unfortunately, this specialized service has not been absolutely reliable. Often users have waited from one to three hours for the special buses, and have been stranded when the lifts have failed to work (the lifts are checked each day before the buses leave on their routes). To schedule a lift-equipped bus, call 962-1825 before 1 P.M. the day before you need a ride.

To complement its regular service, Tourmobile operates a van equipped with wheelchair lift for the same cost as a regular ticket. The van makes all the Mall stops and waits for its passengers to return. Reservations must be made at least a day in advance by calling 554-7020.

Taxis around town are very good about transporting people with wheelchairs, as long as the chairs are collapsible. Expensive van service is available for people with motorized and noncollapsing wheelchairs; a one-way trip in town may cost more than $30.

Around the Mall and Downtown, most street corners have curb cuts, but other areas of the city (notably Georgetown) are woefully lacking. The Mall paths have hard-packed dirt surfaces which may be tiring for a wheelchair user to negotiate for any distance.

Office Buildings

Most federal buildings and new private office buildings are accessible to people in wheelchairs, but many structures in the city are still inaccessible. If you don't have specific information about your destination's entrance and facilities, definitely call ahead to ascertain their status. The Hubert H. Humphrey Building, a Department of Health and Human Services facility, is a model in design for people with disabilities (complete with talking elevator) but unfortunately most of the city lags far behind.

Hotels

Hotels in Washington have been termed marginally accessible by several wheelchair users. Even the newer hotels may not have bathrooms with wide enough doors to permit access. We've noted in the hotel list in the appendix which facilities term themselves accessible; when you make your reservations, be sure to double-check—ask for actual door widths and availability of grab bars to be certain you'll be comfortable. For some with physical disabilities, shower stalls are a necessity. Try the older hotels; the Mayflower has 20 rooms equipped with stalls.

Some other considerations when choosing your hotel: distance from the center of town, ease of catching cabs at that location, accessibility to eating facilities in or near the hotel.

Shopping

The Shops at National Place, The Pavilion at the Old Post Office and Georgetown Park are all equipped with ramps or at-grade entries and internal elevators. See the "Shopping" chapter.

Restaurants

Often restaurants seem to offer a trade-off between accessibility and quality; the best eating establishments seem to be above or below street level. If you do find a good restaurant that you can get into, almost certainly there will be no accessible bathroom. Georgetown has a good number of street-level restaurants and carry-outs; unfortunately, as we have mentioned, the lack of curb cuts may require someone in a wheelchair to travel a half a block to get to an alley entrance—and then he or she will be faced with heavy traffic when crossing the street. In warm weather, outdoor cafés abound and are quite accessible, since they are at street level. Other good bets are hotel restaurants, although some have been designed on differing levels to satisfy the architect's artistic sensibilities. The rule of thumb: call ahead.

Theaters and Movies

We note in the "Entertainment" chapter which theaters are accessible to people in wheelchairs. Always call ahead to reserve a space and to alert the theater staff of your arrival. Local movie theaters are usually accommodating as well, but call ahead to check on the specific house since many are quite small.

FOR THOSE WITH VISUAL IMPAIRMENTS

Getting Around Town

The Metrorail system represents a major hurdle for those who are blind or visually impaired: the farecard machines are entirely visual. Each station, however, has an information kiosk and attendant who will assist you in paying your fare and entering the system. A special handrail stretches from the mezzanine to escalator entrance. The platform edge is of a differing rough texture from the smooth platform, although the contrast is not dramatic enough to be truly helpful, and several tragic accidents have occurred involving people who were visually impaired. Trains and stops are announced on loudspeakers (although the speakers have been known to fail).

For those with visual disabilities, Washington's street system can be baffling. While the streets are laid out on a square grid, avenues are on the diagonal, creating numerous circles and squares at street/avenue intersections.

On the Mall, we strongly recommend the Tourmobile to provide an excellent narrated circuit tour of Washington's major points of interest.

Restaurants

Some restaurants in Washington have menus prepared in Braille; call the particular restaurant you are interested in to see if they offer this service. Since restaurant prices and offerings change so frequently, these special menus may often be out-of-date.

Communications

If you have one, bring a small radio with you to tune in on local news and events.

Many sites have recorded messages of activities; check the "Planning Ahead" chapter for a short listing.

Martin Luther King, Jr., Library in D.C., 727-2142, records on cassette tapes the *Washingtonian* magazine, an excellent local periodical that lists current entertainment and museum shows. These tapes, which lag about one month behind the current issue, are offered free of charge.

Entertainment

Ticketron, 659-2601, records a current listing of many cultural and sports events in the Washington area. The Kennedy Center also has a recorded listing of their current offerings as well as what's coming up. Listening to both will give you a good survey of Washington entertainment possibilities for which you need to purchase tickets. Descriptive recordings of National Theater programs are available at the Martin Luther King, Jr., Library. Arena Stage and the National Theater offer an exciting new "Phonic Ear" service for those with visual impairments; they provide earphones which, in addition to the dialogue, broadcast a description of the play's action. Call each theater for details.

The central YMCA, at 17th Street and Rhode Island Avenue, has originated "Project Venture," a Saturday morning program of physical activities for the visually and/or physically handicapped. Volunteers participate in one-on-one activities, which can include jogging, calisthenics, weightlifting and swimming in the Y's spanking new facility, as well as bike trips and picnics. You do not need to be a Y member to participate.

The Sites

Recall that many of Washington's points of interest offer special tours for people with visual disabilities; refer to the site descriptions for specific instructions on how to arrange for these tours.

FOR THOSE WITH HEARING IMPAIRMENTS

Communications

A number of Washington organizations and services have special numbers to call for use with telecommunication devices for the deaf (TDD). We note these numbers at the end of this section. In addition, many public places (airports, train stations, bus stations and some hotels and museums) are equipped with special well-marked amplifying telephones.

Entertainment

Several theaters in Washington are equipped with headphones for use by people with hearing impairments: they include the Kennedy Center, National Theater and Arena Stage. Arena also offers sign interpreters for some plays. Check the "Entertainment" chapter for phone numbers.

Many Washington movie theaters show topflight foreign films with subtitles. In addition, the array of Washington entertainment often includes mime, ballet and other dance, and gymnastics.

The Sites

Many of Washington's points of interest give special tours with sign language or oral interpretation for people with hearing impairments. Refer to the site reports for specific instructions on how to arrange for these tours. If special tours aren't available, but tours for the general public are given, notify the tour guide of your disability so that he or she can place you at the front of the group for easier hearing or lipreading.

Gallaudet College

Gallaudet is the world's only accredited liberal arts college for deaf persons; current enrollment is 1,500 students. Tours of the campus and visits to "The Look of Sound," a multimedia exhibit on deafness, can be arranged by calling 651-5100 or TDD 651-5030, or by writing Visitor's Coordinator, Alumni/Public Relations Office, Gallaudet College, Kendall Green, Washington, D.C. 20002.

HEARING-IMPAIRED PERSON'S QUICK GUIDE TO WASHINGTON

The D.C. Public Library publishes a small guide to Washington that can be obtained free of charge at the Martin Luther King, Jr., Memorial Library, 901 G Street, NW, Room 410, or by calling 727-2255 (TDD) or 727-1186 (voice).

Special Numbers for the Hearing-Impaired   (V-Voice T-TDD)

Emergency Numbers

D.C. Police & Fire Emergency	911 T
Montgomery County Police, Fire and Rescue	911 or (301) 762-7619 T
Alexandria Police Emergency	911 T
D.C. Office of Emergency Preparedness	727-6161 V/T
Virginia Hotline for the Deaf	759-2122 V/T
Virginia Relay & Crisis Center	(804) 924-5656 V/T

Transportation

Dulles International Airport	471-9776 T
Baltimore-Washington International Airport	(301) 859-7227 T
Washington National Airport (Traveler's Aid Society)	684-7886 T
Metrobus/Metrorail Information	638-3780 T

Tourist Sites

Arlington House & Arlington National Cemetery	285-2620 T
Bureau of Printing & Engraving	566-2673 V/T
U.S. Capitol	
House	225-1904 T
Senate	224-4049 T
Kennedy Center	254-3906 T
Smithsonian Institution	
Coordinator of Special Education	357-1696 T
Museum of American History	357-1563 T
Air & Space Museum	357-1696 T
Visitor Information	357-1729 T
National Park Service	285-2620 T
Information on Ford's Theatre, Frederick Douglass House, Kennedy Center, Lincoln Memorial, Old Stone House, Washington Monument	285-2599 V
Dial-A-Park	426-5256 T
	426-6770 V

Other Numbers

D.C. Department of Recreation	767-7464 T
D.C. Public Library—Librarian for the Deaf	727-2255 T
Montgomery County Department of Recreation	468-4562 T

NATIONAL ORGANIZATIONS

Disabilities in General

National Organization on Disability
910 16th Street, NW
Suite 600
Washington, D.C. 20006
(202) 293-5960 voice
(202) 293-5968 TDD

Information Protection and Advocacy Center for Handicapped
    Individuals, Inc.
300 I Street
Suite 204
Washington, D.C. 20002
(202) 547-8081

Access for the Handicapped, Inc.
5014 42nd Street, NW
Washington, D.C. 20016
(202) 966-5500

Society for Advancement of Travel for the Handicapped
5014 42nd Street, NW
Washington, D.C. 20016
(202) 966-3900

D.C. Center for Independent Living
1400 Florida Avenue, NW
Washington, D.C. 20002
(202) 388-0033

Mobility Impairments

National Easter Seal Society
1350 New York Avenue, NW
Washington, D.C. 20005
(202) 347-3066

National Rehabilitation Association
633 S. Washington Street
Alexandria, VA 22314
(703) 836-0850

Paralyzed Veterans of America
801 18th Street, NW
Washington, D.C. 20006
(202) 872-1300

National Spinal Cord Injury Association
National Capital Area Chapter
Spinal Cord Hot Line and Information Referral Service
Kensington, MD
(301) 460-3200

Disabled American Veterans Association
807 Maine Avenue, SW
Washington, D.C. 20024
(202) 554-3501

Blind and Visual Impairments

Columbia Lighthouse for the Blind
1421 P Street, NW
Washington, D.C. 20005
(202) 462-2900

National Federation for the Blind of D.C.
5014 42nd Street, NW
Washington, D.C. 20016
(202) 362-4141

American Council of the Blind
1100 Vermont Avenue, NW
Suite 1100
Washington, D.C. 20005
(202) 393-3666 or 1-800-424-8666

Blinded Veterans Association
1735 De Sales Street, NW
Washington, D.C. 20036
(202) 347-4010

Hearing Impairments

Gallaudet College
Kendall Green
Washington, D.C. 20002
(202) 651-5000 voice and TDD

Many services and facilities for deaf and hearing-impaired people are located at Gallaudet; they include:

National Information Center of Deafness
(202) 651-5109 voice
(202) 651-5585 TDD

National Center for Law and the Deaf
(202) 651-5373 voice and TDD

Kendall Demonstration Elementary School
(202) 651-5031 voice and TDD

Model Secondary School for the Deaf
(202) 651-5466 voice and TDD

A number of organizations serving deaf and hearing-impaired people are located at 814 Thayer Avenue, Silver Spring, MD 20910. They include:

National Association for the Deaf
(301) 587-1788 voice
(301) 587-1791 TDD

Telecommunications for the Deaf, Inc.
(301) 589-3786 voice
(301) 589-3006 TDD

Registry of Interpreters for the Deaf
51 Monroe Street
Suite 1107
Rockville, MD 20850
(301) 279-0555 voice and TDD

American Society for Deaf Children
(301) 585-5400 voice and TDD

Other organizations based in the Washington area include:

Alexander Graham Bell Association for the Deaf, Inc.
3417 Volta Place, NW
Washington, D.C. 20007
(202) 337-5220 voice and TDD

Deaf Pride, Inc.; Capital City Association of the Deaf
1350 Potomac Avenue, SE
Washington, D.C. 20003
(202) 675-6700

Otis House–National Health Care Foundations for the Deaf
1203 Otis Street, NE
Washington, D.C. 20017
(202) 832-2660 TDD

Interpreter Referral Services
651-5634 voice and TDD

Sign Language Associates
1725 K Street
Suite 802
Washington, D.C. 20006
(202) 861-0593 voice
(202) 861-0594 TDD

18

A WELCOME

TO INTERNATIONAL

VISITORS

For all its importance, sophistication and popularity as a tourist attraction for the international visitor, Washington is not very well equipped to deal with foreign guests. Americans have a well-deserved reputation for their lack of linguistic ability—or even interest. Relatively few people that the foreign tourist will come into contact with will be able to speak a foreign language. Consequently, the foreign visitor is well advised to plan as completely as feasible in advance, and come prepared to use, however haltingly, the English language. Washingtonians are, for the most part, extremely tolerant of those who have difficulty with English, and will usually be patient and helpful.

PLANNING THE TRIP

Foreign visitors to the United States are eligible for a variety of special-fare packages on airplanes, buses and trains. For the most part, these special fares can only be purchased overseas, so be sure to check with travel agencies before you leave home. The prices and restrictions that apply to special fares will change frequently, but at this writing, here are the programs:

Air

Many international carriers offer unlimited air-travel packages to the U.S., with widely varying fares, depending on your point of departure, the time of year, your age and the relationship of the participating travelers. Given the ordinary cost of air travel today, the fare is a great bargain. Check with various airlines to see if they offer anything that might be relevant to your travel plans.

Bus

The major bus companies have special discounted programs for international visitors. Again, we advise you to look into them before you start your trip, as you may have to purchase them before arriving. Greyhound's Ameripass program costs $99 for seven days of travel, $150 for 15 days and $225 for 30 days. Greyhound also has Spanish-language information at 800-531-5332.

Rail

Amtrak provides extensive train service, particularly in the Washington–New York–Boston corridor. After a number of years of poor service, the trains are experiencing a comeback. Equipment, service and roadbeds have all been improved. America is a big land; coast-to-coast travel by train is a several-day affair, so many visitors cannot afford the time to travel in so leisurely a fashion.

The International USA Railpass can be used anywhere on the Amtrak system in the U.S., and is good for 45 days after the first day of travel. Amtrak also offers 45-day regional passes; Washington falls in the East Coast Region, which includes every place east of the Mississippi River. The fares for these passes are (as of October 1988):

	USA Railpass	East Coast Region
Adult	$299	$159
Children 2–11	150	80
Children under 2	free	free

If you have not purchased your International Railpass overseas, contact one of Amtrak's Washington offices at Union Station and at 1721 K Street, NW, or write Amtrak International, 400 N Street, NW, Washington, D.C. 20001.

ARRIVAL

Traveler's Aid, with desks at all area airports—Dulles International, Washington National and Baltimore-Washington International—may be your first stop, especially if you have a problem: lost money, searching for the person who was to pick you up and other similar difficulties. Traveler's Aid also maintains a desk at Union Station. The organization, which is found throughout the country, has its main D.C. office at 1015 12th Street, NW, 347-0101. Help is available 24 hours a day, seven days a week.

The International Visitors Information Service (IVIS) devotes itself to foreign travelers, maintaining a 24-hour, seven-day Language Bank, 783-6540, which provides assistance in over 50 languages.

IVIS provides an information desk at Dulles International Airport and maintains an office at 733 15th Street, NW, Suite 300, 783-6540. The office is open Monday to Friday, from 9 A.M. to 5 P.M. Brochures are available in several languages. Foreign visitors should also check in at the Washington Area Convention and Visitors Association (1575 I Street, NW, 789-7000) for tourist information and assistance.

WHEN IN TOWN

Currency Exchange

Dulles and BWI both have exchange facilities, but they are not open long hours. In town, larger, downtown branches of most banks have international departments. Banking hours in the U.S. are usually 9 A.M. to 3 P.M. weekdays. Some banks are open Friday afternoons from 4 or 4:30 P.M. until 6 P.M. Very few banks have Saturday morning hours. Deak-Perrera, 1800 K Street, NW, 872-1233, in the heart of Downtown, provides multiple international financial services, including currency exchange, and is open 9 A.M. to 5 P.M. weekdays, 10 A.M. to 2 P.M. Saturday. Reusch International Monetary Services, 1140 19th Street, NW, 887-0990, is open 9 A.M. to 5:30 P.M. weekdays, and 10 A.M. to 2 P.M. Saturday. American Express, 1150 Connecticut Avenue, NW, 457-1300, provides international financial services and travel services from 9 A.M. to 6 P.M. weekdays.

Books and Newspapers

A few bookshops in town stock foreign-language materials. Near Dupont Circle, one of the major international centers in town, there are several such shops. The News Room (1753 Connecticut Avenue, NW, 332-1489) and the International Learning Center (1715 Connecticut Avenue, NW, 232-4111) carry foreign magazines, periodicals and newspapers. B and B Newsstand (2621 Connecticut Avenue, NW, 234-0494) also stocks a wide selection of foreign periodicals. Downtown, Waldenbooks (17th and G Streets, NW, 393-1490) and Sidney Kramer Books (1825 I Street, NW, 293-2685) both have a good selection of foreign-language dictionaries, English-language texts and periodicals.

Multilingual Tours

Multilingual tours are offered by Guide Service of Washington, 733 15th Street, NW, Suite 1040, 628-2842; Berlitz School of Languages, 1050 Connecticut Avenue, NW, 331-1160; and IVIS, 783-6540, as noted previously. In all cases, advance planning is strongly recommended.

Museum Tours in Foreign Languages

All Smithsonian museums have foreign-language brochures for self-guiding tours. In addition, the Hirschhorn provides taped tours, and the National Gallery of Art has guided tours, all in a variety of languages. See the "Mall" chapter for phone numbers, as advance notice will usually be required for guided tours. While many museums do not indicate whether foreign-language tours are available, it never hurts to call in advance to see if a special tour can be arranged. Don't hesitate to ask; where available, the service will be provided with enthusiasm.

Post Offices

U.S. post offices, unlike their European counterparts, do not house telephone and telegraph facilities. They are strictly for mail. Stamps purchased at post offices cost face value, but will cost more than face value if purchased at vending machines, drugstores or hotels.

Some American Customs

Tipping. Gratuities are not ordinarily added automatically to restaurant bills. A gratuity of 15 to 20 percent, depending on the quality of service, is expected. A bartender will expect the same gratuity as a waiter, for bar service. Tipping a maître d'hôtel is optional, but not ordinarily expected. Airport, train station and hotel porters will expect a tip of 50¢ to $1 per bag. Hotel maids should receive a $2 per day gratuity. Taxi drivers are not always tipped in Washington, but a gratuity of 10 to 15 percent for polite service and careful driving ought to be forthcoming. Theater and movie-house ushers, unlike European custom, are not tipped, nor are hotel-desk clerks (except for unusual services provided), or gas-station attendants, or store clerks. Hotel doormen are tipped, usually 50¢ to $1, for hailing a taxi. In parking lots, a 50¢ tip for retrieving a car is considered acceptable; for valet parking, $1 is appropriate.

Dress Codes. Americans are by nature an informal people. In recent years, many restaurants have relaxed dress requirements, but more expensive restaurants may require jacket and tie for men. Shorts are not appropriate attire in many expensive to moderate establishments. For foreign guests, native attire is always appropriate.

19

WASHINGTON
ON THE RUN:
ONE-, TWO- AND THREE-DAY
TOURS AND SPECIALIZED TOURS

Anyone with limited time and unlimited energy can still "see" Washington, though it will be a panoramic view rather than a closeup study. Whether you are a part of a group tour or in town for a business convention, there's enough variety in the nation's capital to satisfy any sightseeing appetite.

Limited time means, however, that you must plan your sightseeing carefully in advance, taking in the attractions you want to see in one area of town before heading off to another. Keep in mind that some sites, such as the White House, are open only during limited periods, and may require tickets.

In the following short tour suggestions, we have tried to highlight the major attractions. Your own interests may lead you to take out some of the sites we suggest, or add others more suited to your own inclinations. So we have summarized many of the tourist sites listed by *interest area;* this book will give you all the information you need to put together your individualized tour of the city and its environs.

DAY ONE

White House: VIP tours, which must be arranged well in advance through your senator or representative, begin at 8 A.M. For regular tours in summer, the White House ticket booths on the Ellipse are open from 8 A.M. till noon; the tours throughout the year begin at 10 A.M.

Tourmobile circuit of **Mall**: stay on for the 90-minute ride.

Lunch at **National Gallery of Art**: exit through East Building and reboard Tourmobile.

U.S. Capitol: take guided tour, unless you have antsy children with you—in that case, give yourself a brief tour, reboard Tourmobile and devote more time to National Air and Space Museum. If you're here for two or more days, save the Capitol till Day Two or Three.

Smithsonian Museum(s) of your choice: most popular are National Air and Space Museum and National Museum of Natural History.

Vietnam Veterans Memorial.

National Archives: if time permits.

Georgetown dinner and stroll: the extent of your walk will be a true test of your strength.

Washington Monument: short lines and romantic view at night—April to Labor Day.

DAY TWO

U.S. Capitol: take tour.

Supreme Court.

Library of Congress.

Lunch in **Capitol,** Capitol Hill restaurant, or picnic in front of **Library of Congress.**

FBI or **Bureau of Engraving and Printing**: take tour.

National Zoo; or if you're not a zoo fan,

National Cathedral: drive or take bus via Embassy Row on Massachusetts Avenue.

Dinner in Northwest or Downtown.

Dupont Circle—19th Street stroll; or

Nighttime entertainment (see the "Entertainment" chapter): theater, music, dance, etc. In summer, many entertainment options are free.

DAY THREE

Smithsonian Museums or **National Memorials** or **National Archives**: take the morning to fill in the Mall attractions you may have missed. Picnic lunch on the Mall.

Arlington National Cemetery, Arlington House (Custis-Lee Mansion): on your own or via Tourmobile.

Mount Vernon: if there's time, relax on the short boat trip from Mount Vernon's wharf.

Old Town, Alexandria: as time and energy permit, visit sites of interest and stroll about.

Dinner in Old Town.

MAJOR ATTRACTIONS ARRANGED BY INTEREST AREA

The American History Tour

Mall . . . Arts and Industries Building . . . National Museum of American History

Capitol Hill . . . Capitol building . . . Library of Congress . . . Supreme Court

Downtown and Northwest . . . Anderson House . . . DAR Continental Hall . . . Ford's Theater/House Where Lincoln Died . . . National Archives . . . National Portrait Gallery . . . Octagon House

Suburbs . . . Alexandria . . . Civil War battlefields . . . colonial farms: Oxon Hill, Claude Moore Colonial Farm, National Colonial Farm . . . Fort Washington . . . Mount Vernon . . . Sully Historic House . . . Woodlawn Plantation

The Art Tour

Mall . . . Freer . . . Hirschhorn . . . National Gallery of Art . . . *National Museum of American History . . . National Museum of African Art . . . Arthur M. Sackler Gallery

Downtown . . . Corcoran . . . *Interior Department Museum . . . National Museum of American Art . . . National Portrait Gallery . . . Phillips Collection . . . *Renwick . . . *Textile Museum

Commercial Art Galleries . . . Georgetown . . . P Street between 20th and 23rd Streets, NW . . . R Street from Connecticut Avenue to Florida Avenue . . . 7th Street between D and E Streets, NW

* Indicates museum with special emphasis on arts and crafts.

The Garden Tour

See the "Outdoor Washington/Sports" chapter for a complete, alphabetical guide to Washington's gardens and woodlands.

Washington . . . Botanic Gardens . . . Dumbarton Oaks . . . Hillwood . . . Kenilworth Aquatic Gardens . . . Meridian Hill Park . . . National Arboretum . . . Old Stone House

Suburbs . . . Brookside Gardens . . . The Historic Houses and Plantations

Remember: if you are visiting the city in April, you may catch the White House Garden Tour or the Georgetown Garden Tours. In September the White House Gardens open once again.

The Historic Home Tour

Washington . . . Anderson House . . . Frederick Douglass House . . . Hillwood . . . Octagon House . . . Old Stone House . . . Sewall-Belmont House . . . Woodrow Wilson House . . . Walk through Georgetown

Suburbs . . . Arlington House (Custis-Lee Mansion) . . . Carlyle House . . . Clara Barton House . . . Colonial Farms . . . Gunston Hall . . . Lee's Boyhood Home . . . Lee-Fendall House . . . Mount Vernon . . . Ramsay House . . . Sully Historic House . . . Woodlawn Plantation

The Military History Tour

Washington . . . Air and Space Museum . . . National Archives . . . National Guard Memorial (no site report): One Massachusetts Avenue, NW, 789-0031; 9 A.M. to 4 P.M. daily except weekends and holidays; exhibits of the American Militia and National Guard through 200 years of service. . . . National Museum of American History . . . Navy Yard . . . Walter Reed Medical Museum

Virginia . . . Arlington National Cemetery . . . Civil War battlefields . . . Fort Washington Park . . . Marine Corps Memorial . . . Old Guard Museum at Fort Myer (no site report): Building 249, Fort Myer, 692-9721; 10 A.M. to 4 P.M. Tuesday to Saturday; weapons and infantry items dating back to the Revolutionary War.

Maryland . . . Baltimore . . . Fort McHenry . . . Lightship *Chesapeake* . . . S.S. *Torsk* . . . U.S.S. *Constellation*

The Natural History Tour
Washington . . . C&O Canal . . . Museum of Natural History . . . National Aquarium—Department of Commerce . . . National Geographic Society . . . National Zoo . . . Theodore Roosevelt Island . . . Rock Creek Nature Center

Suburbs . . . Great Falls Parks . . . National Aquarium—Baltimore Inner Harbor . . . Regional Parks—Cabin John and Wheaton . . . Woodend—Audubon Naturalist Society

The Religious Tour
Catholic . . . Franciscan Monastery . . . National Shrine of the Immaculate Conception . . . St. Matthew's Cathedral (no site report), Rhode Island Avenue at Connecticut Avenue, NW

Protestant . . . Christ Church . . . Pohick Church . . . St. John's Church . . . Washington Cathedral

Jewish . . . B'nai B'rith . . . Lillian and Albert Small Jewish Museum . . . U.S. Holocaust Memorial Museum (1988)

Other . . . Islamic Center . . . Mormon Temple

The Science Tour
Washington . . . Air and Space Museum . . . Arts and Industries Building . . . INTELSAT . . . National Geographic Society . . . National Museum of American History . . . Naval Observatory . . . Walter Reed Medical Museum

Suburbs . . . National Aquarium in Baltimore . . . Beltsville Agricultural Research Center . . . Maryland Science Center—Baltimore Inner Harbor . . . NASA—National Aeronautics and Space Administration

HOTELS

Washington has, at last count, some 45,000 rooms in hundreds of hotels and motels, and new places keep opening all the time. Bear in mind, however, that many often change or close altogether. We do our best to provide you with enough information to bed you down safely.

You might also consult a travel agent or seek information and assistance from the following:

Washington Convention and Visitor's Association, 1575 I Street, NW, 789-7000. Call or write or stop in for a free copy of "A Guide to Lodging in the Nation's Capital," which lists many hotels and their services.

Hotel Association of Washington, P.O. Box 33578, Washington, D.C. 20033, 833-3350, publishes a free brochure representing their 70 member hotels. It's called "Just Waiting to Be Discovered."

Capital Reservations is an agency that arranges accommodations for families, groups and individuals at some 70 hotels. They can often book rooms at a discount comparable to corporate or government rates. For instance, a room that would normally cost $130 might be had for $90 instead. As with travel agents, there is no extra charge for this service. Call (800) VISIT-DC.

A few words about how we put this appendix together and some tips on hotel accommodations. Hotels are divided according to price: *budget accommodations* are under $45 a night, double occupancy (and some are well under $45—quite a bargain in today's economy); *moderate accommodations* will cost from $45 to $90 a night, of which there are many around town; *expensive* range from $90 to $135; *luxury accommodations* are $135 to $170; and *super luxury accommodations* are $170 and up. The selection is representative, not comprehensive. By and large, hotels listed are convenient to the major attractions of the city. We have purposely excluded inconvenient accommodations. All hotels listed meet, at the time of our research, the requirements of cleanliness that any traveler has the right to expect.

Descriptions are brief. Included are number of rooms, whether the hotel offers group rates (and therefore is willing to accept groups at all), the availability of weekend rates or packages, family rates offered, parking facilities, whether the hotel has a pool or restaurants and whether rooms are air-conditioned. Wheelchair accessibility is mentioned; and finally, convenient public transportation is noted. Special services, such as an airport shuttle bus, or special features, such as kitchen facilities in the room, are noted where appropriate. Convenience to particular areas of town and the character of the specific street on which the hotel is located may also be pointed out.

A special word about rates: rates quoted are those available for double occupancy at press time. No doubt, prices will go up. It seems likely that the rates for all hotels in a given category, whether budget or luxury, will go up about the same time, in about the same degree. Bear in mind that the classifications are for the purpose of defining the general characteristics of the hotel.

Because of the problem of keeping up with rate changes, new promotions and special deals, we have not given specific information about group rates, weekend rates or, in some cases, family rates. A few general comments are in order, however.

Group rates: Hotels will require a minimum number of rooms occupied to qualify for group rates. In most cases, the minimum is five rooms; in some cases, it's 10 rooms. Group reservations must be made as far in advance as possible. Many hotels require at least one month's notice, and some need up to six months. (The converse may also be true—reservations may not be able to be made more than, say, a year in advance.)

Weekend rates: As will be evident, most hotels in the moderate-to-luxury range will offer some kind of special weekend rate or package. This discount can be substantial! Our research has turned up cases in which $100 rooms go for less than half price. If a visit can be timed over a weekend, chances are that major savings will be realized—at least on hotel rooms. Luxury hotels, in particular, tend to offer weekend packages, rather than outright rate reductions. A package might include some meals (dinner, champagne breakfast or brunch), free parking instead of pay parking, extra little touches, such as fancy chocolates on your turned-down bed at nighttime, or a basket of fresh fruit to greet you.

Family rates: In our experience, you must ask directly whether children, of any age, will be charged for. Most hotels do have the ability to put additional beds in a room to accommodate children. Charges, if any, for extra beds will vary.

BED AND BREAKFASTS

For an alternative to the Washington hotel scene, there are a variety of bed and breakfasts, as well as furnished apartments in private homes. We list some here; consult the yellow pages for additional listings.

Bed 'n' Breakfast, Ltd., is a referral service to bed and breakfast accommodations in private homes in the metropolitan area. Rooms range from budget to luxury, depending on your preference, and stays can be arranged for one night or longer. For further information, write to Bed 'n' Breakfast, Ltd., P.O. Box 12011, Washington, D.C. 20005, or call (202) 328-3510. To help make your choice, they will provide you with information on numerous places to stay, including details on your host, the house, the accommodations, location, and rates.

The **Bed & Breakfast League, Ltd.,** represents bed and breakfast homes, apartments and small inns in the area. Rates for a room with a shared bath are generally $30 to $50 for a single and $40 to $65 for a double; rooms with a private bath are usually $45 to $55 for a single and $55 to $65 for a double. Children usually cost an additional $10 to $25. A two-night minimum stay is required, and a $25 nonrefundable deposit is required. To arrange plans through the League, call or write the office well in advance of your visit so that they can send you an application and a description of sample homes. Bear in mind that the office is closed weekends and on federal holidays; it is also closed for vacation the last two weeks of July and during Christmas. The League is located at 3639 Van Ness Street, NW, Washington, D.C., 20008, (202) 363-7767.

Bed & Breakfast Accommodations of Washington, Inc., offers rooms in Northwest Washington for $45 (single) and $55 (double). Call or write for details: 3222 Davenport Street, NW, Washington, D.C. 20008, (202) 363-9533 or 363-8909.

BUDGET ACCOMMODATIONS—UNDER $50

Allan Lee Hotel   2224 F Street, NW   **331-1224**
110 rooms. No group rates. No weekend rates. No family rates. Street or lot parking. No pool. Not wheelchair-accessible. AC. No restaurant. M—Foggy Bottom/GWU 1 block.
Older facility, close to Downtown attractions.

Braxton Hotel   1440 Rhode Island Avenue, NW   **232-7800**
79 rooms. No group rates. No weekend rates. No family rates. Street or lot parking. No pool. No restaurant. Doubles AC, singles no. Not wheelchair-accessible. M—McPherson Square 6 blocks.

Connecticut-Woodley   2647 Woodley Road, NW   **667-0218**
13 rooms. No group rates. No weekend rates. Street parking. No pool. No restaurant. AC. Not wheelchair-accessible. M—Woodley Park 1 block.
A nice guest house, close to major hotels, zoo, Downtown.

International Guest House   1441 Kennedy Street, NW   **726-5808**
Accommodates 15. No group rates. No weekend rates. No family rates. Street parking. No pool. Breakfast included. AC. One bath each floor. Not wheel-chair-accessible. M—none.
   Owned and operated by the Mennonite Church, and staffed by volunteers. Extremely reasonable rates. Favors overseas visitors. All rooms shared; doors locked at 11 P.M.

International Youth Hostel   1009 11th Street, NW   **737-2333**
No weekend rates. No family rates. Lot parking. No pool. No restaurant. Wheelchair-accessible (bathrooms not equipped). AC. M—Metro Center 3 blocks.

Murdock's Guest House   328 Massachusetts Avenue, NE   **547-7270**
6 rooms. No group rates. No weekend rates. Family rate. Some free parking. AC. Not wheelchair-accessible. M—Union Station 3 blocks.
   Guest house ambiance, right on Capitol Hill.

MODERATE ACCOMMODATIONS—$55–$95

The Carlyle Suites   1731 New Hampshire Avenue, NW   **234-3200**
176 suites. Group rates. Weekend rates. Family rates. Free parking. No pool. No restaurant. AC. Limited accessibility—steps in lobby, bathrooms not handicapped-equipped. M—Dupont Circle 2 blocks.
   Priced close to budget; convenient to Downtown.

Channel Inn   Maine Avenue and 6th Street, SW   **554-2400, (800) 368-5668**
100 rooms. Weekend rates. Family rates—children under 12 free in same room. Group rates. Free parking. Outdoor pool. Restaurant. AC. Not wheel-chair-accessible. M—L'Enfant Plaza 5 blocks.

Connecticut Avenue Days Inn   4400 Connecticut Avenue, NW   **244-5600**
155 rooms. Group rates. Weekend rates. Family rates—18 and under free in same room. Free parking. No restaurant. No swimming pool. Wheelchair-accessible, and four rooms with specially equipped bathrooms. AC. M—Van Ness 2 blocks.

Farragut West Hotel   1808 I Street, NW   **393-2400**
75 rooms. Group rates seasonal. Weekend rates seasonal. Family rate—under 16 free. No pool. No restaurant. AC. Wheelchair-accessible (bathrooms not specially outfitted). M—Farragut West across street.
   In the heart of Downtown, 2 blocks from White House, World Bank. Similar to many European city hotels—small, simple.

Holiday Inn of Silver Spring   8777 Georgia Avenue, Silver Spring, MD   **(301) 589-0800, (800) HOLIDAY**

230 rooms. Group rates. Weekend rates. Family rates—children under 18 free in same room. Free parking. Outdoor pool. Restaurants. AC. Wheelchair-accessible, some bathrooms handicapped-equipped. M—Silver Spring 3 blocks.

Days Inn Crystal City Hotel 2000 Jefferson Davis Highway, Arlington, VA **(703) 920-8600, (800) 325-2525**
434 rooms (in 1989). Group rates. Weekend rates. Family rates. Free parking. Outdoor pool. Restaurant. AC. Wheelchair-accessible—portable handicapped equipment for 10 rooms. M—Crystal City 1 block.
Mentioned frequently as excellent with groups and meetings up to 500. Courtesy bus to National Airport.

Days Inn Silver Spring 8040 13th Street, Silver Spring, MD **(301) 588-4400**
143 rooms. Group rates. No weekend rates. Family rates—under 16 free in same room. Free parking. Outdoor pool. Restaurant. AC. Not wheelchair-accessible. M—Silver Spring 15-minute walk.

Hotel Harrington 11th and E Streets, NW **628-8140**
300 rooms. Group rates. No weekend rates. Family rates—children under 11 free in room. Free parking. No pool. Cafeteria, snack bar. AC. Not wheelchair-accessible, bathrooms not handicapped-equipped. M—Metro Center 1 block.
An older hotel, but clean and well maintained. Popular with families.

Howard Johnson's Motor Lodge 2601 Virginia Avenue, NW **965-2700, (800) 654-2000**
192 rooms. Group rates. Weekend rates. Family rates—children 12 and under free in same room. Free parking. Outdoor pool. Restaurant. AC. Not wheelchair-accessible. M—Foggy Bottom 2 blocks.

Inn at Foggy Bottom Hotel 824 New Hampshire Avenue, NW **337-6620**
95 rooms. Group rates. Weekend rates. Family rates—under 12 free in same room. No pool. Pay parking. Restaurant. Not wheelchair-accessible. M—Foggy Bottom 1 block.
Half of the rooms have kitchenettes.

Days Inn Downtown 1201 K Street, NW **842-1020**
218 rooms. Group rates. Weekend rates. Family rates—children under 18 free in same room. Pay parking. Outdoor pool. Restaurant. AC. Wheelchair-accessible, but bathrooms not handicapped-equipped. M—McPherson Square 3 blocks, Metro Center 4 blocks.

Normandy Inn 2118 Wyoming Avenue, NW **483-1350**
74 rooms. Group rates. Weekend rates. No family rates. Pay parking. No

pool. Tearoom, breakfast only. AC. Some rooms wheelchair-accessible. M—Dupont Circle 5 blocks. Complimentary afternoon tea.

Ramada Inn Central   1430 Rhode Island Avenue, NW   **462-7777**
186 rooms. Group rates. Weekend rates. Family rates—under 18 free in same room. Outdoor pool. Restaurant. Pay parking. AC. Not wheelchair-accessible. M—McPherson Square 3 blocks.

Sheraton Inn Washington Northwest   8727 Colesville Road, Silver Spring, MD   **(301) 589-5200, (800) 325-3535**
287 rooms. Group rates. Weekend rates. Family rates—children under 18 free in same room. Limited free parking. Indoor pool, gym. Restaurants. AC. Limited wheelchair accessibility—bathroom doors must be removed. M—Silver Spring 10-minute walk.

Skyline Inn Best Western   South Capitol and I Streets, SW   **488-7500**
203 rooms. Group rates. Weekend rates. Family rates—under 18 free in same room. Free parking. Outdoor pool. Restaurants. AC. Limited wheelchair accessibility—4 rooms with handgrips. M—Capitol South 5 blocks.

Tabard Inn   1739 N Street, NW   **785-1277**
42 rooms. No group rates. Seasonal weekend rates. No family rates. No parking—pay lots in area. No pool. Restaurant. AC. Not wheelchair-accessible. M—Dupont Circle 2 blocks.
   An intimate inn on a handsome street close to Dupont Circle.

Windsor Park Hotel   2116 Kalorama Road, NW   **483-7700**
43 rooms. Group rates. No weekend rates. Family rate. Street parking. No pool. No restaurant. AC. Not wheelchair-accessible.
   Convenient to Embassy Row.

THE NEW YORK AVENUE STRIP

New York Avenue is a primary route into the city for cars, buses and trucks. Surroundings are functional and industrial—railroad tracks, car dealers, gas stations. There is acceptable public bus transportation (approximately 15 minutes to Downtown). Motels here tend to be large, able to handle buses and other groups. Many of the motels are associated with national chains. Since there are so many motels clustered in the area, some rooms are almost always available. Rates will be in the budget to moderate range.

Best Western Regency   600 New York Avenue, NE   (800) 528-1234
                                                          546-9200

Days Inn of Washington   2700 New York Avenue, NE   832-5800

EconoLodge   1600 New York Avenue, NE   (800) 446-6900

Envoy Best Western   501 New York Avenue, NE   543-7400

EXPENSIVE ACCOMMODATIONS—$95–$140

Anthony Hotel   1823 L Street, NW   **223-4320**
99 suites. Group rates. Weekend rates. No family rates. Limited parking—pay lots in area. No pool. Restaurant. AC. Not wheelchair-accessible. M—Farragut North 2 blocks.
   A functional Downtown hotel; rooms come with kitchenettes. Rates for families and groups are moderate and a good buy.

Bellevue Hotel   15 E Street, NW   **638-0900**
140 rooms. Group rates. Weekend rates. Family rates—children 17 and under free in same room. Free overnight parking. No pool. Restaurant. AC. M—Union Station 2 blocks.
   A pleasant hotel popular with Europeans. Close to the Capitol.

Georgetown Dutch Inn   1075 Thomas Jefferson Street, NW   **337-0900**
47 suites. 9 penthouses. Group rates. Weekend rates. Family rates—under 14 free in same room. Free parking. Outdoor pool. Restaurant. Wheelchair-accessible through garage. AC. B—30, 32, 34.

National Clarion   300 Army-Navy Drive, Arlington, VA
   (703) 892-4100, (800) 848-7000
650 rooms. Group rates. Weekend rates. Family rates—under 16 free in same room. Pay parking. Indoor pool, gym. Restaurants. AC. Wheelchair-accessible—12 rooms with handicapped-equipped bathrooms. M—Crystal City, Pentagon City, Pentagon.

Park Terrace Hotel   1515 Rhode Island Avenue, NW
   232-7000, (800) 228-9822
189 rooms, 33 apartment units. Group rates. Weekend rates. Family rates—under 16 free, over 16 additional $10 each in same room. Free parking. Free passes to YMCA. Restaurants. AC. Wheelchair-accessible. M—Dupont Circle 4 blocks.

Quality Embassy Square Suites   2000 N Street, NW   **659-9000**
180 rooms. Group rates. Weekend rates. Family rates—under 15 free in same room. Pay parking. Outdoor pool. Restaurant. AC. Not wheelchair-accessible. M—Dupont Circle 2 blocks.

Embassy Suites-Quality Inn   1750 22nd Street, NW
   857-3388, (800) EMBASSY
215 suites. Weekend rates. Group rates. Restaurant. Parking. 2 handicapped-equipped rooms on main floor.

Highland Hotel   1914 Connecticut Avenue, NW   **797-2000**
140 suites. Group rates. Weekend rates. Family rates—children under 14 free in same room. Pay parking. No pool. Restaurant. AC. Not wheelchair-accessible. M—Dupont Circle 4 blocks.

Converted apartment house, with European touches—concierge, 24-hour telex service, turn-down service.

Quality Hotel Central   1900 Connecticut Avenue, NW
   332-9300, (800) 228-5151
149 rooms. Group rates. Family rates—under 14 free in same room. Free parking. Outdoor pool. Restaurant. AC. No wheelchair accessibility. M—Dupont Circle 4 blocks.

Holiday Inn Georgetown   2101 Wisconsin Avenue, NW
   338-4600, (800) HOLIDAY
296 rooms. Group rates. Weekend rates. Family rates—under 18 free in same room. Free parking. Outdoor pool. Restaurant. AC. Wheelchair-accessible—3 rooms fully equipped. B—30, 32, 34.

Hotel Washington   15th Street and Pennsylvania Avenue, NW   **638-5900, (800) 424-9540**
366 rooms. Group rates. Weekend rates. Family rates—under 14 free in same room. No parking—lots in area. No pool. Restaurants. AC. Wheelchair-accessible—30 rooms equipped. M—Federal Triangle 2 blocks.

Just across the street from the Treasury Department, close to Downtown shopping.

Lombardy Hotel   2019 I Street, NW   **828-2600**
125 rooms. Group rates. Weekend rates. Family rates—children under 16 free in same room. No parking—pay lots in area. No pool. Restaurant. AC. Not wheelchair-accessible. M—Farragut West 3 blocks.

Morison-Clark Inn   Massachusetts Avenue and 11th Street, NW   **898-1200**
54 rooms. Group rates. Weekend rates. Family rates. Pay parking lots in area. No pool. Restaurant. AC. Some rooms in new wing. Wheelchair accessible. M—Metro Center 5 blocks.

This beautifully restored inn bills itself as Washington's only "historic inn," as its structures date back to the mid-19th century. The restaurant has already received rave reviews.

Quality Inn-Downtown   1315 16th Street, NW   **232-8000, (800) 368-5689**
135 rooms. Group rates. Weekend rates. Family rates—under 16 free in same room. Pay parking. Pool one block. Restaurant. AC. Public areas wheelchair-accessible. No equipped rooms. M—Dupont Circle and Farragut North 4 blocks.

Ramada Renaissance Hotel   1143 New Hampshire Avenue, NW   **775-0800**
355 rooms. Group rates. Weekend rates. Family rates—under 18 free in same room. Pay parking. No pool. Health club. Restaurants. AC. Fully wheelchair-accessible. 7 equipped guest rooms. M—Foggy Bottom 1 block.

The River Inn   924 25th Street, NW   **337-7600**
128 suites. Group rates. Weekend rates. Family rates—under 12 free in same room. Pay Parking. No pool. Restaurant. AC. Wheelchair-accessible. M—Foggy Bottom 1 block.
   All rooms are suites; a sophisticated quiet environment. Close to Kennedy Center.

Washington Hilton and Towers   1919 Connecticut Avenue, NW   **483-3000 (800) HILTONS**
1154 rooms. Group rates. Weekend rates. Family rates—all children free in same room. Pay parking. Outdoor pool and tennis. Health club. Restaurants. AC. Wheelchair-accessible—45 rooms fully equipped. M—Dupont Circle 3 blocks.
   Major convention and meeting site.

LUXURY ACCOMMODATIONS—OVER $140

The Canterbury Hotel   1733 N Street, NW   **393-3000**
99 suites. Group rates. Weekend rates. Family rates—children under 16 free in same room. Pay parking. No pool on premises—passes issued to nearby hotel pool. Restaurant. AC. Wheelchair-accessible. 1 guest room fully equipped. M—Dupont Circle 2 blocks.
   This hotel recently underwent a major renovation. Every room is equipped with a kitchenette. All rooms are suites.

The Capital Hilton   16th and K Streets, NW   **393-1000**
549 rooms. Group rates. Weekend rates. Family rates—children free in same room. Pay parking. No pool. Health club. Restaurants (Twigs, Trader Vic's). AC. Wheelchair-accessible—12 rooms fully equipped. M—McPherson Square and Farragut North 3 blocks each.

Dupont Plaza Hotel   Dupont Circle and New Hampshire Avenue, NW   **483-6000, (800) 421-6664**
310 rooms. Group rates. Weekend rates. Family rates—under 14 free in same room. Pay parking. No pool. Restaurant. AC. Not wheelchair-accessible. M—Dupont Circle 1 block.

Embassy Row Hotel   2015 Massachusetts Avenue, NW   **265-1600**
196 rooms. Group rates. Weekend rates. Family rates—under 18 free in same

room. Pay parking. Rooftop pool. Restaurant. AC. Limited wheelchair accessibility. M—Dupont Circle 2 blocks.
A relatively new hotel, elegant and gracious.

The Georgetown Inn   1310 Wisconsin Avenue, NW   **333-8900**
95 rooms. Group rates. Weekend rates. Family rates—children under 14 free in same room. Pay parking. No pool. Restaurant. AC. Not wheelchair-accessible.
Located in the heart of Georgetown.

Guest Quarters   801 New Hampshire Avenue, NW   **785-2000**
101 suites. Group rates. Weekend rates. Family rates—$5 each added. Pay parking. Outdoor pool. No restaurant. AC. Limited wheelchair accessibility—bathrooms not handicapped-equipped. M—Foggy Bottom 1 block.
All rooms are suites. Located close to Kennedy Center.

Henley Park Hotel   926 Massachusetts Avenue, NW   **638-5200,
(800) 227-8474**
96 rooms. Weekend rates. Group rates. Restaurant. Pay parking. AC. Not wheelchair accessible.
One and a half blocks from the Convention Center.

Loew's L'Enfant Plaza Hotel   480 L'Enfant Plaza East, SW   **484-1000,
(800) 223-0888**
372 rooms. Group rates. Weekend rates. Family rates—children under 14 free in same room. Pay parking. Outdoor pool. Restaurants. AC. Wheelchair-accessible—some rooms equipped. M—L'Enfant Plaza, in complex.

Marriott Crystal City   1999 Jefferson Davis Highway, Arlington, VA
(703) 521-5500, (800) 228-9290
340 rooms. Group rates. Weekend rates. Family rates. Free parking. Indoor pool. Restaurants. AC. Wheelchair-accessible—a few fully equipped rooms. M—Crystal City 1 block.
A good hotel for groups. Shuttle to National Airport.

Marriott Hotel   1221 22nd Street, NW   **872-1500, (800) 228-9290**
349 rooms. Group rates. Weekend rates. Family rates. Pay parking. Indoor pool. Restaurants. AC. Wheelchair-accessible—six rooms fully equipped. M—Foggy Bottom 4 blocks.
Convenient to Dupont Circle, Downtown and Georgetown. Built atop a Washington restaurant landmark—Blackie's House of Beef.

Mayflower Stouffer Hotel   1127 Connecticut Avenue, NW   **347-3000,
(800) 468-3571**
724 rooms. Group rates. Weekend rates. Family rates—under 18 free in same room. Pay parking adjacent. No pool. Restaurants. AC. Wheelchair-

accessible—equipped bathrooms. 8 guest rooms fully equipped. M—Farragut North 1 block.

A Washington landmark that recently underwent a major renovation, in the heart of Downtown.

Omni Georgetown Hotel 2121 P Street, NW **293-3100, (800) THE-OMNI**
300 rooms. Group rates. Weekend rates. Under 17 free in room. Pay parking. Outdoor pool. Restaurant. AC. Wheelchair accessible. M—Dupont Circle 3 blocks.

Most rooms kitchenette-equipped.

One Washington Circle One Washington Circle, NW **872-1680**
154 rooms. Group rates. Weekend rates. Family rates. Pay parking. Outdoor pool. Restaurants. AC. Limited wheelchair accessibility—bathrooms not equipped. M—Foggy Bottom 2 blocks.

Both an apartment house and hotel, convenient to all areas of city—close to George Washington University and Kennedy Center.

Phoenix Park Hotel 520 North Capitol Street, NW **638-6900, (800) 824-5419**
87 rooms. Weekend rates. Group rates. Family rate—children under 12 free in same room. Restaurant. Pay parking.

Three blocks from the Capitol. One block from Union Station.

Stouffer's Concourse Hotel 2399 Jefferson Davis Highway, Arlington, VA **(703) 979-6800, (800) HOTELS-1**
388 rooms. Group rates. Weekend rates. Family rates—special rate and under 18 free in same room. Pay parking. Indoor pool. Restaurants. AC. Wheelchair-accessible—15 rooms fully equipped. M—Crystal City 2 blocks.

Often recommended for small meetings and conventions. Close to Pentagon and National Airport.

Vista International Hotel 1400 M Street, NW **429-1700**
398 rooms. Weekend rates. Group rates. Restaurant. Pay parking. Family rate—limit of one child free in same room. Twelve guest rooms fully accessible to the handicapped.

Washington Court on Capitol Hill 525 New Jersey Avenue, NW **628-2100**
272 rooms. Weekend rates. Group rates. Restaurant. Pay parking. Twelve rooms fully accessible for handicapped guests.

Near Capitol Hill.

Watergate Hotel 2560 Virginia Avenue, NW **965-2300**
237 rooms. Group rates. Weekend rates. Family rates—under 16 free in same room. Pay parking. Indoor pool. Restaurants. AC. Wheelchair-accessible. M—Foggy Bottom 2 blocks.

Located in the famous Watergate complex of apartments, offices and shops. The complex has many features open to hotel guests—gym, massage. Rooms have kitchenettes. Jean-Louis, one of the best and most expensive of restaurants, is here. Next door to Kennedy Center.

Wyndham Bristol   2430 Pennsylvania Avenue, NW   **955-6400, (800) 822-4200**
240 suites. Weekend rates. Group rates. Family rates—children 18 and under free in same room. Restaurant. Pay parking.
New West End spot. Highly regarded grill.

SUPER LUXURY ACCOMMODATIONS—$175 AND UP

The Four Seasons Hotel   2800 Pennsylvania Avenue, NW   **342-0444**
197 rooms. Group rates. Weekend rates. Family rates—under 18 free in same room. Pay parking. No pool. Restaurants. AC. Wheelchair-accessible—5 rooms fully equipped for the handicapped. M—Foggy Bottom 5 blocks.
One of the area's most elegant hotels. Gracious, full of the small details that make a hotel a pleasure. Afternoon tea and champagne breakfast becoming extremely popular. Very expensive.

The Grand Hotel   2350 M Street, NW   **429-0100, (800) 848-0016**
260 suites. Group rates. Weekend rates. Children under 16 free in room. Restaurants. Parking. Wheelchair-accessible—rooms/bathrooms equipped and special elevators and ramps.

Grand Hyatt   100 H Street, NW   **582-1234**
891 rooms. Group rates. Weekend rates. Family rates—children under 18 free in parents' room. Pay parking. AC. Handicapped—2 rooms per floor fully accessible; public restrooms accessible and equipped. M—Metro Center (direct access mid-1989).

Guest Quarters   2500 Pennsylvania Avenue, NW   **333-8060**
125 suites. Group rates. Weekend rates. Family rates—children under 18 free. Pay parking. AC. Limited wheelchair accessibility—bathrooms not handicapped-equipped. M—Foggy Bottom 3 blocks.

Hay-Adams Hotel   800 16th Street, NW   **638-2260**
143 rooms. No group rates. Weekend rates. No family rates. Pay parking. No pool. Restaurants. AC. Wheelchair-accessible—some rooms equipped for the handicapped. M—Farragut West 2 blocks.
The Hay-Adams is housed in one of the city's most handsome buildings, facing Lafayette Square and the White House.

Hyatt Regency Washington on Capitol Hill   400 New Jersey Avenue, NW   **737-1234, (800) 228-9000**

834 rooms. Group rates. Weekend rates. Family rates—children under 12 free in same room. Pay parking. Indoor pool. Health club. Restaurants. AC. Wheelchair-accessible—6 rooms fully equipped. M—Union Station 2 blocks.

Despite the city's height limitation, the Hyatt manages to incorporate the Hyatt trademark—a multistory, dramatic lobby.

Jefferson Hotel   16th and M Streets, NW   **347-2200, (800) 368-5966**
105 rooms. Weekend rates. Group rates. Restaurant on premises. Parking.

Madison Hotel   15th and M Streets, NW   **862-1600, (800) 424-8577**
369 rooms. Group rates. Weekend rates. No family rates. Pay parking. No pool. Restaurants. AC. Limited wheelchair accessibility—bathrooms not equipped for the handicapped. M—McPherson Square 2 blocks.

Long the standard of excellence for Washington's luxury hotels. Careful, considerate and gracious service are its hallmarks.

J.W. Marriott   1331 Pennsylvania Avenue, NW   **393-2000,**
(800) 228-9290
900 rooms. Weekend rates. Group rates. Restaurant. Parking. Accessible—9 rooms are handicapped-equipped. Adjacent to National Theater and 2 blocks from the White House.

Omni Shoreham   2500 Calvert Street, NW   **234-0700, (800) THE-OMNI**
770 rooms. Weekend rates. Group rates. Restaurant. Parking on premises.

The Ritz-Carlton Hotel   2100 Massachusetts Avenue, NW   **293-2100,**
(800) 424-8008
247 rooms. Group rates. Weekend rates. Family rates—kids 12 and under free. Pay parking. No pool. Restaurants. AC. Limited wheelchair accessibility—bathrooms not handicapped-equipped. M—Dupont Circle 2 blocks.

Authentic antiques grace the public areas; rooms are elegant. Located right on Embassy Row; the multilingual staff is accustomed to dealing with foreign guests.

Sheraton-Carlton Hotel   16th and K Streets, NW   **638-2626,**
(800) 325-3535
200 rooms; 15 suites. Group rates. Weekend rates. Family rates—under 18 free in same room. Pay parking. Restaurant. AC. Wheelchair accessible—one fully equipped guest room per floor. M—Farragut West or North 3 blocks.

A lovely building newly restored, elegant and reminiscent of an earlier, more stately age. Close to all Downtown sights, one block off Lafayette Square.

Sheraton Washington Hotel   2660 Woodley Road, NW   **328-2000,**
(800) 325-3535
1500 rooms. Group rates. Weekend rates. Family rates—under 18 free in

same room. Pay parking. Outdoor pools. Restaurants. AC. Wheelchair-accessible—50 rooms fully equipped. M—Woodley Road 1 block.

One of the major convention hotels, recently renovated.

Shoreham Hotel   2500 Calvert Street, NW   **234-0700**
770 rooms. Group rates. Weekend rates. Family rates—under 17 free in same room. Pay parking. Outdoor pool. Restaurants. AC. Limited wheelchair accessibility—16 rooms fully equipped. M—Woodley Road 2 blocks.

Westin Hotel   2401 M Street, NW   **429-2000, (800) 228-3000**
416 rooms. Weekend rates. Group rates. Restaurant. Parking. Nine guest rooms for the handicapped.

The heart of the West End.

Willard Intercontinental Hotel   1401 Pennsylvania Avenue, NW
   628-9100, (800) 327-0200
365 rooms. Weekend rates. Group rates. Restaurant. Parking. Some rooms equipped for handicapped guests.

A dazzling restoration of a historically important meeting place. It is here in Peacock Alley that the term "lobbyists" originated.

CALENDAR OF
ANNUAL EVENTS

JANUARY
- Opening of Congress
- Inauguration and festivities (every four years)
- Washington Antique Show
- Birthday celebrations of Light-Horse Harry Lee and Robert E. Lee at Lee's Boyhood Home (548-1789)
- Ice Capades, Capital Centre (350-3400)

FEBRUARY
- Lincoln's Birthday celebration at Lincoln Memorial, February 12 (485-9666)
- Washington's Birthday celebration at Washington Monument, February 22 (838-5005)
- Washington's Birthday parade, Alexandria; nation's largest (838-4200)
- George Washington Birthright Ball and Buffet, Gadsby's Tavern (838-4200)
- Old Home Tour of eighteenth- and nineteenth-century homes, including Mount Vernon (838-4200)
- Revolutionary War Encampment, Ft. Ward, VA (838-4848)
- Washington International Boat Show (547-9077)
- Chinese New Year, Chinatown
- Torpedo Factory Annual Mardi Gras Costume Ball, Alexandria (683-4768)

MARCH
- Cherry Blossom Festival, Mall—date varies depending on trees; may be in April (485-9666)
- St. Patrick's Day parade, Constitution Avenue
- Smithsonian Kite Carnival, Mall (357-3030)

- Tour of the Defenses of Washington, Ft. Ward bus tour of Washington's Civil War forts (838-4848)
- Kite Festival, Gunston Hall (550-9220)
- Living History Weekend, Lee's Boyhood Home and Lee-Fendall House (838-4200)
- Needlework exhibit, Woodlawn Plantation (780-4000)
- Easter sunrise services, Arlington National Cemetery—can be in April (692-0931)
- Easter egg roll, White House—can be in April (456-2323)
- Chirping Easter egg hunt for visually impaired children, Mall (485-9666)

APRIL

- Annual Spring Quilt Show, Torpedo Factory (671-6481)
- Georgetown House and Garden Tours (333-4953)
- Seminary Hill Tour of Homes and Gardens; part of Historic Garden Week of Virginia (550-9220)
- Jefferson's Birthday celebration, Jefferson Memorial, April 13 (485-9666)
- Annual White House News Photographers Association Exhibit, Library of Congress (287-5223)
- Annual Azalea Festival of Arts and Crafts, Ft. Ward, VA (838-4843)
- Washington Antique Show (547-9077)
- Ringling Brothers/Barnum and Bailey Circus (364-5000)
- Smithsonian Institution Crafts Fair
- Old Town House Tour, Alexandria (751-4409)

MAY

- White House Garden Tour (456-2323)
- Annual Fair, Washington Cathedral (537-6200)
- Capitol Hill House Tour
- A Day in Old Virginia; lunch, fashion show, craft sale—Ft. Ward, VA (838-4344)
- Memorial Day—National Symphony free concert, Capitol grounds; Jazz Festival, Alexandria (838-4843); services at Tomb of Unknown Soldier
- Middle East Festival, Alexandria (838-4843)

JUNE

- Civil War reenactment, Alexandria (838-4843)
- Smithsonian Institution's Boomerang Tournament
- Potomac River Fest
- Irish Festival, Alexandria (838-4843)

JULY

- Fourth of July—Fireworks and celebration, the Mall; National Symphony free concert, Capitol grounds; Alexandria Independence Day celebration
- Black American Festival, Alexandria (838-4843)
- Folk Life Festival, Smithsonian Institution, Mall (357-2700)
- Annual National Folk Festival, Wolf Trap Park (941-6066)

- Grand Prix Tennis, Rock Creek Park
- Virginia Scottish Games and Gathering of Clans, Alexandria (838-5005)
- Colonial Crafts Day, Gunston Hall (550-9220)
- Evenings of music, champagne, dancing on the green, Woodlawn Plantation (780-4000)
- Bastille Day Waiters Race, Dominique's Restaurant (452-1132)

AUGUST
- 1812 Overture, U.S. Army Band, Washington Monument grounds (696-3643)
- Civil War reenactment, Ft. Ward, VA (838-4344)
- Tavern Days, Gadsby's Tavern Museum (838-4242)
- Hispanic Festival, Adams-Morgan/Columbia Road
- Lollipop Concert, U.S. Navy Band, Jefferson Memorial (433-2394)
- Frisbee Festival, National Air and Space Museum (366-1581)

SEPTEMBER
- Mexican and Central American Independence Day Festival (232-6965)
- Labor Day, National Symphony free concert, Capitol grounds
- White House Garden Tour (456-7041)
- Alexandria House Tour and Tea (751-4572)
- Militia Muster Day, Carlyle House (549-2997)
- International Children's Festival, Wolf Trap Farm Park (941-6066)
- Greek Festival, Saint Sophia Greek Orthodox Cathedral; food, dancing, band (333-4730)
- Adams-Morgan Day (462-5113)
- Star-Spangled Banner, Georgetown Anniversary; street celebrations
- Washington International Art Fair
- Fall Harvest Festival, Oxon Hill Farm (839-1177)
- Caribbean Arts Festival, Fondo del Sol Visual Arts Center (483-2777)
- Washington Cathedral Open House (537-6200)

OCTOBER
- White House Garden Tour (472-3669)
- Celebration of Lafayette's visit, Lee's Boyhood Home
- Octoberfest: Gadsby's Tavern (838-4200)
- Washington International Horse Show, Capital Centre (350-3900)
- Opening Ceremony of Supreme Court (first Monday)
- Jousting on the Mall (426-6700)
- Colonial Crafts Fair, Decatur House (673-4030)
- U.S. Sailboat and Power Boat Show, Annapolis
- War Between the States Chili Cookoff, Alexandria (836-7449)
- Eighteenth-Century Ball, Gadsby's Tavern (838-4242)

NOVEMBER
- Washington's Review of Troops, Gadsby's Tavern (549-0205)
- Washington International Horse Race, Laurel (725-0400)

- Marine Corps Marathon (640-2121)
- Armistice Day Celebration, Woodrow Wilson House (673-4034)
- Veteran's Day ceremony, Arlington National Cemetery
- Many, many Christmas craft fairs, continuing through December

DECEMBER

- Candlelight tours and caroling: Lee's Boyhood Home, Gadsby's Tavern, Arlington House, Carlyle House, Lee-Fendall House, Woodlawn Plantation (838-4200)
- Evening candlelight tour, White House (456-7041)
- Caroling at Kennedy Center, "Twelve Days of Christmas" concerts, *Nutcracker*
- Scottish Christmas Walk, Alexandria (838-4200)
- Scottish New Year's Celebration, "Hogmanay," Gadsby's Tavern (838-4200)
- Historic Caroling, Gunston Hall (550-9220)
- Christmas Pageant of Peace, Lighting of the National Christmas Tree (485-9666)
- Annual Christmas Program, Wolf Trap Farm Park (944-6066)
- Pearl Harbor Day ceremonies, Marine Corps Memorial, December 7 (285-2601)
- Open House, Corcoran Gallery of Art (638-3211)
- Tree of Lights, Mormon Temple (587-0144)
- Numerous Christmas activities, Annapolis (301-268-TOUR)

For information on the changing calendar of events, the following numbers may be helpful:

Smithsonian Special Events Office	357-2627
National Park Service Public Affairs	485-9666
Alexandria Tourist Council	838-4200
Washington Area Convention and Visitors Association	789-7000

Check *Where* magazine and *The Washington Post* weekend section for scheduled events.

INDEX

ABOUT THE AUTHORS

JUDY DUFFIELD has been a devoted fan of Washington since her arrival in the area more than fifteen years ago. In past years she has been a teacher and an editor for a variety of concerns—a national consulting firm, the D.C. government, and a federally funded project. With two sons now in public school, Judy Duffield is putting her MBA to work at Sidney Kramer Books.

BILL KRAMER is a native Washingtonian. He is the owner of several bookstores in Washington: Kramerbooks & afterwords, the bookstore/café mentioned in the *Guide,* and Sidney Kramer Books, a professional and technical bookstore. He is married to Judy Duffield.

CYNTHIA SHEPPARD, originally from the Boston area, contracted Potomac fever at a tender age. She has worked in government, publishing and business in Washington. Although she now lives in Massachusetts, she often returns to her adopted second home.